MONETARY POLICY

Monetary Policy

GOALS, INSTITUTIONS, STRATEGIES, AND INSTRUMENTS

Peter Bofinger

in collaboration with
Julian Reischle
and
Andrea Schächter

OXFORD

UNIVERSITY PRESS

OXFORD

UNIVERSITY PRESS

Great Clarendon Street, Oxford OX2 6DP

Oxford University Press is a department of the University of Oxford.
It furthers the University's objective of excellence in research, scholarship,
and education by publishing worldwide in

Oxford New York

Athens Auckland Bangkok Bogotá Buenos Aires Cape Town
Chennai Dar es Salaam Delhi Florence Hong Kong Istanbul Karachi
Kolkata Kuala Lumpur Madrid Melbourne Mexico City Mumbai Nairobi
Paris São Paulo Shanghai Singapore Taipei Tokyo Toronto Warsaw

with associated companies in Berlin Ibadan

Oxford is a registered trade mark of Oxford University Press
in the UK and in certain other countries

Published in the United States
by Oxford University Press Inc., New York

British Library Cataloguing in Publication Data

Data available

Library of Congress Cataloging in Publication Data
Bofinger, Peter.
Monetary policy : goals, institutions, strategies, and instruments / Peter Bofinger.
p. cm.
Includes bibliographical references and index.
1. Monetary policy.   2. Monetary policy—Europe.   3. Monetary policy—United States.
4. European Central Bank.   I. Title.
HG230.3 .B64 2001   332.4'6–dc21   2001034045

ISBN 0-19-924057-4
ISBN 0-19-924856-7 (pbk.)

1 3 5 7 9 10 8 6 4 2

Typeset by Charon Tec Pvt. Ltd, Chennai, India
Printed in Great Britain
on acid-free paper by
T.J. International Ltd., Padstow, Cornwall

Preface

When I had to hold my first classes on monetary policy many years ago, I was amazed by the fact that there are almost no textbooks or comprehensive treatises on monetary policy. As a result I wrote such a book, together with Julian Reischle and Andrea Schächter, which appeared in German in 1996. The positive assessment of this book by the academic community (Fase 1998) has encouraged me to consider an English version. The last four years having been an extremely active and exciting time for monetary theory and policy, the outcome now differs in many respects from the original German text. Nevertheless, it is still shaped by the same guiding principles. While the focus is on policy-relevant issues, the book always tries to provide the necessary theoretical background. In contrast to textbooks on 'Money, Banking, and Financial Markets', which normally describe and analyse only the domestic monetary policy, this book adopts a comparative approach which always includes the practices in the most important currency areas of the world. With the high degree of international financial market integration, a student of monetary policy has to know more than what is going on in his or her own country.

As this book is the outcome of a long process of work, it is difficult to thank all those who have made it possible. There is no doubt that I have greatly benefited from working as an economist at the Deutsche Bundesbank in the years 1985–90. In the last nine years, my students at Würzburg University inspired me with their critical questions on the available paradigms of monetary economics and gave me important feedback on draft material. It was always very important to be able to discuss my ideas with my colleagues and assistants. I am especially grateful to Christoph Harff, Oliver Hülsewig, Kai Pfleger, Julian Reischle, Andrea Schächter, Nicolas Schlotthauer, and Timo Wollmershäuser. Annemarie Reussner, Andre Geis, Heiko Müller, and Christiane Klemp provided valuable technical assistance. I would also like to thank Hans-Joachim Jarchow, Dieter Nautz, Lars Svensson, and the members of the Ausschuss für Geldtheorie and Geldpolitik of the Verein für Socialpolitik for insightful and useful comments on different parts of this book. A very special note of thanks is due to many central banks, above all the Deutsche Bundesbank, the European Central Bank, and the Bank of Japan, which supported this book by providing data and other important information.

Würzburg   P.B.

Author's note: All figures and tables (including the data used for their calculation) are available on the internet at www.monetary-policy.net.

All comments on the book should be mailed to Peter Bofinger at bofinger@t-online.de.

Contents

Part I. Theoretical Fundaments of Monetary Policy

Contents

Part II. Domestic Aspects of Monetary Policy

Part III. Monetary Policy in an Open Economy

Figures

Tables

Boxes

Abbreviations

AD	Aggregate demand
AS	Aggregate supply
BCAM	Bank Charter Act model
BGM	Barron–Gordon model
BIS	Bank for International Settlements
BoC	Bank of Canada
BoE	Bank of England
BoJ	Bank of Japan
CIP	Covered interest rate parity
CIS	Commonwealth of Independent States
CPI	Consumer price index
CPIX	All groups consumer price index excluding credit services
EC	European Community
ECB	European Central Bank
ECM	Error correction mechanism
ECU	European Currency Unit
EMS	European Monetary System
EMU	European Monetary Union
EONIA	Euro overnight index average of interbank overnight rates
ER	Excess Reserves
ERM	Exchange Rate Mechanism
ESCB	European System of Central Banks
EU	European Union
Fed	U.S. Federal Reserve System
FOMC	Federal Open Market Committee
FRB	Federal Reserve Bank
G7	Group of the seven leading industrial countries (United States, Japan, Germany, France, Canada, United Kingdom, Italy)
GDP	Gross domestic product
GNP	Gross national product
HICP	Harmonised index of consumer prices
IMF	International Monetary Fund
IS	Curve describing equilibrium of investment and saving
JGB	Japanese government bonds
MCI	Monetary conditions index
MFI	Monetary financial institutions
MPC	Monetary Policy Committee
NAIRU	Non-inflation accelerating rate of unemployment
LM	Curve describing equilibrium on the money market
M1, M2, M3, M4	Money stock aggregates
MR	Minimum reserve
NDA	Net domestic assets

OECD	Organization for Economic Cooperation and Development
PPP	Purchasing power parity
PSL	Private sector liquidity
PTA	Policy Target Agreements
RBNZ	Reserve Bank of New Zealand
REER	Real effective exchange rate
RPIX	Index for retail price inflation excluding mortgage interest payments
RPIY	RPIX minus the first round effects of indirect taxes
SPF	Survey of Professional Forecasters
SR	Sveriges Riksbank (Swedish Central Bank)
UIP	Uncovered interest rate parity

Introduction

In 1981, Karl Brunner (1916–1989), one of the twentieth century's leading scholars in the field of monetary theory and policy, wrote:

Central banking [has been] traditionally surrounded by a peculiar and protective political mystique. . . . The mystique thrives on a pervasive impression that central banking is an esoteric art. Access to this art and its proper execution is confined to the initiated elite. The esoteric nature of the art is moreover revealed by the inherent impossibility to articulate its insights in explicit and intelligible words and sentences. Communication with the uninitiated breaks down. The proper attitude to be cultivated by the latter is trust and confidence in the initiated group's comprehension of the esoteric knowledge. (Brunner 1981: 5)[1]

Two decades later, after Alan Greenspan's impressive performance as chairman of Federal Reserve System since August 1987, most observers would totally agree with Brunner's dictum. Nevertheless, this view is not universally accepted. Alan Blinder, after serving as a vice-chairman of the Federal Reserve Board and as a member of the Council of Economic Advisers, came to the following assessment:

Having looked at monetary policy from both sides now, I can testify that central banking in practice is as much art as science. Nonetheless, while practising this dark art, I have always found the science quite useful. (Blinder 1997: 17)

I hope this book will show that there is indeed a solid core of a science of monetary policy which is able to provide a set of techniques that are indispensable for successful central banking.[2] Of course, mystique plays a role too, but I will leave this sphere of monetary policy to other writers.

The book is structured in three main parts. Parts I and II discuss the theory and the implementation of monetary policy from the perspective of a relatively large central bank such as the European Central Bank, the Federal Reserve, and the Bank of Japan. Thus, the focus is on the domestic issues of monetary policy. In Part III an open-economy perspective is adopted. This procedure gives the reader a comprehensive overview of the

---

[1] A similar statement can be found at the end of a treatise by the Swiss economist Jürg Niehans (1988: 336): 'However, economics must not fall victim to the illusion that central banking will ever become a science. . . . Whatever progress is made in monetary theory, central banking will probably remain an art.'

[2] See Alfred North Whitehead (1978: 338): 'The condition for excellence is a thorough training of technique.'

aspects that are relevant from a closed-economy perspective before she is confronted with the complexities that arise in an open economy.

Part I presents the theoretical building blocks that are needed for an understanding of monetary policy, but it does not serve as a complete survey on all issues of present-day monetary theory. Chapter 1 starts with alternative definitions of money and the microeconomic functions of money. Theoretical approaches to the demand for money and their empirical evidence are discussed in Chapter 2. Chapter 3 presents traditional theories to the money supply process and a price-theoretic model that is required for an analysis of the operating procedures of all major central banks. From this starting point, Chapter 4 deals with the most important channels for the transmission of monetary policy impulses: the quantity theory, the interest rate channel, and the expectations channel.

Part II discusses monetary policy from a domestic perspective. Chapter 5 starts with the ultimate goals of central banking. It shows above all that an obligation to pursue price stability as the main target of monetary policy is sufficiently flexible to cope with demand and supply shocks in the short and medium term. Chapter 6 deals with the debate on 'rules versus discretion' in monetary policy. It comes to the conclusion that the arguments of the traditional debate are not strong enough to justify the imposition of rigid rules. The same applies to the more recent debate which is based on the time inconsistency of a central banks' plans. Chapter 7 is focused on the triad of independence, accountability, and sanctions. While most central banks now enjoy a high degree of independence, a systematic process of accountability is still lacking and direct sanctions are almost always absent.

In Chapter 8 and the subsequent chapters I switch from the institutional framework (the hardware of central banking) to strategic aspects (the software of central banking). First, I discuss some of the 'simple rules' that have been developed in the last decades and ask in what way they could be used as a 'heuristic', facilitating the difficult decision processes of central bankers and their dialogue with the public. Chapter 9 assesses the performance of the Bundesbank, the European Central Bank, the Federal Reserve System, the Bank of England, and the Bank of Japan, above all the aspect of whether the policy decisions have been guided by some specific rule. Chapter 10 deals with the instruments of monetary policy. After a general discussion which leads to a minimalist approach, Chapter 11 provides a short discussion of different concepts of 'seigniorage' and the role of seigniorage financing in processes of hyperinflation.

Part III is devoted to the international context in which all central banks are operating. In Chapter 12 the most important building blocks of open-economy macroeconomics are presented: the mechanics of foreign exchange market intervention, the covered and uncovered interest rate parity theory, and the purchasing power parity theory. Chapter 13 discusses the policy options for central banks in both large and small currency areas. For central banks in smaller countries, it is important to observe that the combination of interest rate and exchange rate target has to be compatible with uncovered interest parity *and* with domestic macroeconomic conditions. I show under which conditions a fixed nominal exchange rate target can serve as a rule for monetary policy. In addition, more flexible solutions (crawling pegs) are discussed.

For a very busy reader, the main lessons of this book can be summarized in ten 'dos and don'ts':

1. Create the central bank constitution so that decision-makers have a long-term time horizon. This requires a high degree of monetary policy independence from the political sphere.
2. Define a price stability target over the medium term which is flexible enough to accommodate supply shocks and leaves it up to the discretion of the central bank whether it is suitable to react to short-term demand shocks.
3. Use a short-term interest rate as the operating target of monetary policy.
4. In order to keep the management of short-term rates simple, use standing facilities for the provision of liquidity.
5. Use all information on private inflation expectations as an important indicator of future price developments.
6. Rely on the self-stabilizing mechanism of private inflation expectations if the inflation rate is low. Follow a policy of 'interest rate smoothing'; or, in a free variation of Milton Friedman's (1968: 12) lesson no.1, 'Prevent interest rate changes from being a major source of economic disturbance'.[3]
7. Avoid negative real short-term interest rates under all circumstances.
8. If the knowledge about the outgap is good, follow an interest rate policy that is determined by the Taylor rule; otherwise, a Taylor rule on the basis of the inflation rate provides good guidance only in situations involving demand shocks.
9. Avoid exchange rate targets that are incompatible with uncovered interest parity.
10. Avoid a major real appreciation by a policy of sterilized interventions that is compatible with the tenet no. 9.

---

[3] Friedman (1968: 12) said: 'The first and most important lesson that history teaches about what monetary policy can do—and it is a lesson of the most profound importance—is that monetary policy can prevent money itself from being a major source of economic disturbance.'

We will see that in the last decades a negative performance of monetary policy was almost always related to a violation of one these basic principles. Thus, what matters in the first instance is a good technology of central banking. The art of monetary policy comes into play if a very good or an excellent performance is to be achieved.

PART I

THEORETICAL FUNDAMENTS OF MONETARY POLICY

The scientific basis of monetary policy is provided by monetary theory. Its models are the road maps which policy-makers should use for their daily work as well as for the design of new institutional solutions. Fortunately or unfortunately, the academic profession has produced a vast quantity of such maps in the last century. Some of these maps depict very remote areas, some concentrate on issues that are of little interest for policy-makers, some use a scale that is either too large or too small, which can make orientation difficult. In order to keep this book to a compact size, I have tried to provide a selection of models and approaches that I think are useful for practical monetary policy. Of course, any attempt to define what is 'relevant' is highly arbitrary, and therefore I do not pretend that this part of the book gives a comprehensive presentation of the state of the art of monetary theory; for this purpose the reader is referred to the book of Walsh (1998).

1

What is Money?

What this chapter is about

- The definition of money raises a difficult classification and aggregation problem.
- A simple microeconomic solution to this problem can be found if currency in circulation is used as a 'crystallization point' for the definition. Adding perfect substitutes to this item leads to the concepts of the monetary base and the money stock M1.
- The standard approach in the literature uses the functions of money as a point of departure. However, this approach is prone to a circularity. In addition, only the means of payment function provides a useful criterion for the definition of money. It leads again to the monetary base and M1.
- The broader concepts of money (M2 and M3), which are simply derived by econometric tests, lack a sound theoretical basis.

1.1. INTRODUCTION

The definition of 'money' is a natural starting point for any comprehensive monograph or textbook on monetary theory and monetary policy. Unfortunately, although a myriad of books and articles have been written on these issues, the definition of money can still be regarded as an almost unresolved issue:

If a principal purpose of definition is to bring 'peace at mind' ... monetary economics has failed us. The definition of its central concept has been unsettled for many decades and is more controversial than ever. (Osborne 1992: 602)

In fact, the variety of instruments used on today's financial markets makes it extremely difficult to resolve the two main problems in establishing a satisfactory definition of money. The first concerns how a borderline can be drawn between those financial assets that are regarded as money and those that are simply 'other financial assets'. This problem is referred to as the 'classification problem' of the definition of money. Second, if such a borderline has been drawn, what are the weights that are used for aggregating the different 'monetary assets' into a single asset called 'money'? This problem is referred to as the 'aggregation problem' of the definition of money. The most common approach to the solution of these problems is to define 'money' by the *functions* of 'money': this goes back to John Hicks, who wrote:

Money is what money does. Money is defined by its functions. (Hicks 1967: 1)

It is obvious that this approach is prone to a circularity that is one of the main reasons for the unsatisfactory state of the 'definition of money'. If it is not clear what 'money' is, it is also not possible to describe the functions of 'money'. Therefore, in addition to this approach, I present two other ways of defining money:

1. a *microeconomic* approach, which uses currency in circulation as a 'crystallization point' for the definition of more comprehensive concepts of money;
2. an *econometric* approach, which defines 'money' according to the statistical properties of alternative monetary aggregates.

1.2. A MICROECONOMIC APPROACH TO THE DEFINITION OF MONEY

A relatively simple approach to the definition of money starts with the obvious. It assumes that currency in circulation must be a component of any definition of money. In other words, no one would accept a definition of money that excludes this asset. With this crystallization point, simple microeconomic logic can be used to derive two important concepts of money. If currency in circulation is regarded as money, then all assets that are perfect substitutes can also be regarded as money.

1.2.1. *Defining the monetary base and M1*

From the perspective of *commercial banks*, a perfect substitute for currency in circulation are reserves that these banks hold with the central bank. If a bank is in need of currency, it can always convert its reserves with the central bank (R) into currency (C) at negligible transaction costs. And if a bank's cash balances are too high, it can always exchange them for reserves. Deposits with other banks are another perfect substitute but in aggregation over all banks they add up to zero. This perfect substitutability between reserves and currency leads to a first important concept of 'money': the *monetary base* (B). This is defined as follows:

$$B = C + R.$$

$$(1.1)$$

There are many prominent economists who consider the monetary base the most relevant concept of money.[1] As a more detailed analysis of the process of money supply will show (Chapter 3), the monetary base differs from all other concepts of money in that it is a completely exogenous variable. Many economists regard *exogeneity* as a decisive quality of 'money'.[2]

From the perspective of *private non-banks*, an almost perfect substitute to currency in circulation are sight deposits. Today, especially with cash-dispensers, it is almost always possible to transfer an overnight deposit (D) into currency at very low transaction costs. This leads to a second important concept of money, the *money stock M1*. This is defined as:

$$M1 = C + D. \tag{1.2}$$

Thus, for the money stock M1 and for the monetary base, the classification problem can be solved rather easily by the criterion of perfect substitutability. This also gives an answer to the aggregation problem. If the assets included in each of two definitions of money can be regarded as perfect substitutes, their weights should be a factor of one.

1.2.2. *Broader monetary aggregates (simple-sum aggregates)*

In monetary policy the money stock M1 is regarded as an important indicator, but most central banks look also at more broadly defined monetary aggregates, which are labelled M2, M3, or even M4. The European Central Bank (ECB) uses a 'reference value' for the money stock M3 as a 'pillar' of its stability-oriented monetary policy strategy (Chapter 9). The ECB defines these broader aggregates as follows:

M2 = M1 + Deposits with agreed maturity up to 2 years[3]
     + Deposits redeemable at notice up to three months;[4]   (1.3)

M3 = M2 + Repurchase agreements + Money market
     fund shares/units and money market paper
     + Debt securities issued with maturity up to 2 years.   (1.4)

---

[1] See e.g. Tobin (1980: 320): 'If there is a quantity that is the monetary anchor of the economy, this is it.' Or Osborne (1992: 606): 'The money of the monetary theory is the monetary base.'

[2] See James Tobin (1980: 319): '[T]he nominal supply of money is something to which the economy must adapt, not a variable that adapts itself to the economy—unless the policy authorities want it to.' And Milton Friedman (1971: 2): 'Suppose that the ... quantity [of money] that people hold at a particular moment of time happens to exceed the quantity they wish to hold. Individuals will then seek to dispose of ... their excess money balances .... However, they cannot as a group succeed. ... One man can reduce ... his money balances only by persuading someone else to increase his.'

[3] Other central banks call such (or similar) assets 'time deposits'.

[4] Other central banks call such (or similar) assets 'savings deposits'.

All these assets have been held with monetary financial institutions (MFIs) in the euro area. This definition includes the *Eurosystem* (i.e. the European Central Bank and the national central banks that participate in the European Monetary Union), credit institutions, and money market funds that are located in the euro area.

From a microeconomic perspective, the usage of these broader monetary aggregates is not so easy to justify. It is obvious that not all assets that are included in M3 and M2 can be regarded as perfect or close substitutes to currency in circulation. This becomes evident also from the fact that currency and overnight deposits are normally non-interest-bearing, while all the other assets included in M2 and M3 bear positive interest rates which can sometimes deviate considerably from zero. For such broader monetary aggregates, therefore, it becomes difficult to solve the classification and aggregation problem.

- If some of the components of a specific monetary aggregate are no longer perfect substitutes for currency, it is difficult to explain why these assets are regarded as 'money' while other assets are excluded. The borderline between 'money' and 'other financial assets' becomes arbitrary.
- With an imperfect substitutability of assets, it is also not clear which weights should be used in order to calculate a monetary aggregate. The widespread practice of most central banks simply to sum up components that are not perfect substitutes ('*simple-sum aggregates*' like M2 or M3) is difficult to reconcile with elementary microeconomic principles.

Thus, all broader simple-sum monetary aggregates raise a serious classification and aggregation problem.

1.2.3. *The Divisia index*

An interesting solution for the aggregation problem of more broadly defined aggregates are the so-called Divisia monetary aggregates based on the Divisia index.[5] The main idea behind this index is a weighting scheme for the components of the broader monetary aggregate that reflects the differences in their moneyness. It is assumed that these differences can be measured by the 'user costs' of financial assets.[6] *User costs* are defined as the costs of using a more liquid asset with a low yield instead of a less

---

[5] Francois Divisia (1889–1964) was a French statistician. The Divisia approach was proposed mainly by William Barnett (1980, 1982). A survey on the use of Divisia indices in monetary theory and policy is provided by Barnett *et al.* (1992). For a comprehensive theoretical analysis, see Reischle (2000).

[6] A model-based reasoning for the following concept of the so-called 'user costs' is provided by Barnett (1978).

liquid asset with a higher yield. For this purpose, a reference asset—which should not be liquid, at least in principle—has to be defined. Its yield (R) serves as a benchmark. In practice, the benchmark is normally the yield of long-term bonds, which are regarded as the most 'illiquid' asset. The user costs (π_i) of all other assets can be calculated as the discounted difference between the yield of an asset (i_i) and the reference yield:

$$\pi_i = \frac{(R - i_i)}{1 + R}. \tag{1.5}$$

Taking the user costs as the 'price' of holding a monetary asset, it is straightforward to apply index theory to solve the aggregation problem. The big advantage of the Divisia index over other statistical index formulas—for example Laspeyres', Paasche's, or Irving Fisher's 'Ideal Index'—is the easy interpretation of its general principle: the growth rate of the (Divisia) monetary aggregate (D) corresponds to the weighted sum of the growth rates of the different assets. Using logs, for i different monetary assets m_i, one obtains

$$\ln D_t - \ln D_{t-1} = \sum_{i=1}^{n} s_{i,t}^* (\ln m_{i,t} - \ln m_{i,t-1}), \tag{1.6}$$

with the weighting scheme $s_{i,t}^*$ defined as

$$s_{i,t}^* = \frac{s_{i,t} + s_{i,t-1}}{2} \quad \text{and} \quad s_{i,\tau} = \frac{\pi_{i,\tau} m_{i,\tau}}{\sum_{j=1}^{n} \pi_{j,\tau} m_{j,\tau}} \quad \tau = t - 1, t. \tag{1.7}$$

It is important to note that it is not the user costs that serve as the weights for the different assets, but their shares at the sum of the 'expenditures for holding monetary assets'. Because statistical indices have to be calculated for two different points in time, the weight in the 'time discretionary' Divisia index formula (1.6) consists of the (simple) average of the weights for the two moments, $t - 1$ and t.

While the Divisia index offers a convincing answer to the aggregation problem, it can contribute little to the solution of the classification problem. This is due to the fact that the concrete reference asset (long-term bonds with 10 or 30 years' maturity?; government bonds or corporate bonds?) has to be chosen in an arbitrary way. Therefore the dividing line between 'money' and 'other financial assets' still remains somewhat blurred. In practice, this problem becomes even more obvious since Divisia indices are normally calculated for the components of the traditional simple-sum aggregates, i.e. M1 and M3.

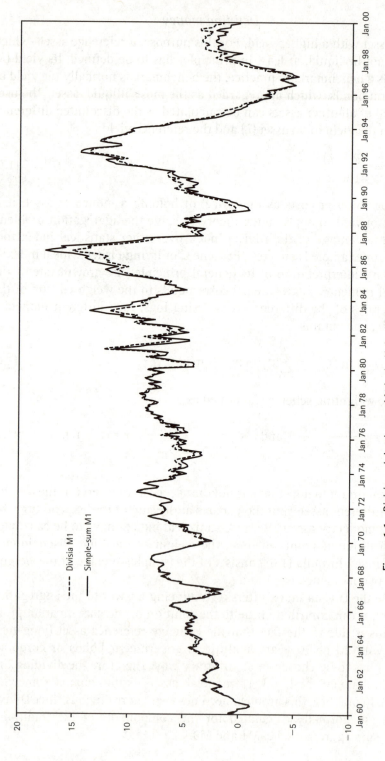

Figure 1.1. *Divisia and simple-sum M1 in the United States, 1960–2000 (by month)*
Source: Federal Reserve Bank of St Louis.

Legend:
- - - - Divisia M1
——— Simple-sum M1

A main problem of this definition of money is that it defines the money-ness of different assets by interest differentials. As these differentials vary considerably over time, the index would imply that the moneyness of, say, a non-interest-bearing sight deposit is higher in times of high long-term interest rates than in times of low interest rates. Whereas one cannot fully exclude the fact that the liquidity of a monetary asset varies over time, one gets inconclusive results in times of an inverse yield curve. According to the user-cost concept, this would mean that the liquidity (or moneyness) of long-term bonds is higher than that of short-term time deposits. In practice, to solve the difficult conceptual problem of the definition of the 'illiquid' reference asset, one uses a long-term bond interest rate and takes an additional charge, high enough to avoid negative user costs. In addition to the problem of the correct measure for liquidity, it is unsatisfactory to have no information about the value of the money stock but only about its change. Although the change in monetary aggregates (or, better, their growth rates) is of special importance in the discussion of monetary policy, knowledge about the money stock is helpful in assessing the liquidity situation of an economy. Cumulating the growth rates starting at a fixed point in time can help to overcome this problem, but the obtained stock value depends crucially on the (arbitrarily) chosen starting value and the calculation procedure of the growth rates because the Divisia index normally is path-dependent.

In practical monetary policy, Divisia indices have played no major role. Neither the ECB nor the Bank of Japan publishes regular data for Divisia monetary aggregates. The lack of interest in this concept is due partly to the fact that monetary targeting in general is not a very attractive solution for most central banks. In addition, in its communications with the general public, a central bank has to take into account that the rationale of such aggregates is very difficult to understand. Nevertheless, the Bank of England calculates and publishes data for Divisia monetary aggregates as one of many indicators in its *Inflation Report*. Figures 1.1 and 1.2 show that in the United States the difference between the simple-sum M1 aggregate and a Divisia M1 aggregate is very limited. However, for M3 in periods with high interest rates (e.g. 1979–82) the Divisia index behaves differently from the simple-sum index. Thus, for a consequent monetary targeting of a broader monetary aggregate, the differences between the two aggregates are not trivial.

1.2.4. *Conclusion*

In sum, only the monetary base and the money stock M1 have a sound microeconomic foundation. For the broader monetary aggregates M2 and

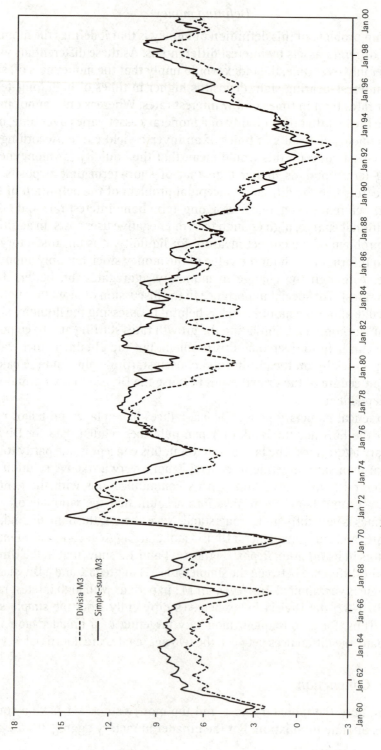

Figure 1.2. *Divisia M3 and simple-sum M3 in the United States, 1960–2000 (by month)*

Source: Federal Reserve Bank of St Louis.

M3, no convincing solution to the classification problem has yet been found. The Divisia index at least provides an answer to the aggregation problem, but it has not been very attractive for policy-makers. Thus, the current practice of the ECB, which attaches a 'prominent role' to the (simple-sum) money stock M3, relies on a rather arbitrary solution to the classification and aggregation problem of the definition of money.

1.3. DEFINING MONEY BY ITS FUNCTIONS

Without a definition of 'money', it does not seem very promising to speak of the functions of 'money'. Nevertheless, the definition of 'money' by its functions is very popular in the literature. Most authors avoid the problem of circularity by the implicit assumption that the functions of 'money' are so obvious that they need no theoretical derivation. Traditionally, the functions of money are presented in the form of the so-called *triad* of the money functions, which comprises:

1. the function of the means of payment,
2. the function of the store of value, and
3. the function of the unit of account.

1.3.1. *Money as a means of payment*

The function of money as a means of payment is certainly its most important function. An economy in which an asset is generally accepted as a means of payment is much more efficient than an economy where this is not the case. Without 'money', all economic transactions have to be carried out as an exchange of goods against goods. This would require a *double coincidence of wants*: 'The shivering baker needs to find a hungry taylor.' Whenever a bilateral exchange is impossible, economic agents have to incur search and information costs to build up indirect chains of exchange.[7]

A theoretical alternative to the instrument of money is an economy with a perfect capital market. In this case, each agent can always bridge the gap between the goods he can sell today (loaves of bread) to one agent and the

---

[7] See Jevons (1882: 1): 'Some years since, Mademoiselle Zélie, a singer of the Théatre Lyrique at Paris, made a professional tour round the world, and gave a concert at the Society Islands. In exchange for an air from *Norma* and few other songs, she was to receive a third part of the receipts. When counted, her share was found to consist of three pigs, twenty-three turkeys, forty-four chickens, five thousand cocoa-nuts, besides considerable quantities of bananas, lemons, and oranges. At the Halle in Paris, as the prima donna remarks in her lively letter, printed by Mr Wolowski, this amount of live stock and vegetables might have brought four thousand francs which would have been good remuneration for five songs. In the Society Islands, however, pieces of money were very scarce; and as Mademoiselle could not consume any considerable portion of the receipts herself, it became necessary in the mean time to feed the pigs and the poultry with the fruit.'

goods he needs today (a coat) from another agent, by borrowing on the capital market. Thus, the use of money can be explained only for situations with imperfect information and with transaction costs. Of course, this is the real world.

Defining money by the function of the means of payment leads to a similar result as that derived by the microeconomic approach in Section 1.2. For transactions among *banks*, the means of payment is the monetary base, i.e. deposits with the central bank. Again deposits with other banks can also be used but they cancel in aggregation. For transactions among *non-banks* (and among banks and non-banks), only the components of the money stock M1 can be used as a means of payment: with all other components of the money stock, M2 and M3, direct payments either among banks or among non-banks are not possible. Thus, this function would clearly exclude broader monetary aggregates from a definition of money.

1.3.2. *Money as a store of value*

If money is used as a means of payment, it necessarily also serves to some extent as a store of value. Friedman and Schwartz (1970) describe money as a 'temporary abode of purchasing power'. As a person who receives an asset for payment cannot spend it simultaneously, he or she always has to hold it for a certain period of time. Thus, all assets that are used as a means of payment should be qualified at least to some extent as a store of value. In periods of hyperinflation, all agents will try to keep the time period during which they hold money as short as possible, which aggravates the inflationary process. But this also reduces the willingness to accept a certain asset as a means of payment. Thus, in many high-inflation countries, instead of the national currency, the US dollar has been used as a means of payment and as a store of value ('dollarization'). In other words, an asset has to provide some quality as a store of value in order to function as a widely accepted means of payment.

The function of store of value is of little help if it is used as the sole criterion for the moneyness of a financial asset, since almost any financial asset (and even many non-financial assets) can be used as a store of value. The result would be an extremely broad definition of 'money'.[8] The statistical concept for such a broad definition is the concept of *monetary wealth*, i.e. the sum of all financial assets that are held in an economy (see Appendix 1.2). While such a solution would overcome the classification

---

[8] See Brunner and Meltzer (1971: 803): 'Defining money as a temporary abode of purchasing power does not distinguish between properties of assets or between a monetary and a barter economy in a manner independent of the exchange function.'

problem, it would still be confronted with a difficult aggregation problem. However, in the academic literature, and also in practical monetary policy, such a broad aggregate plays no decisive role.

1.3.3. *Money as a unit of account*

The third function of money is somewhat different from the first and the second function. The functions of the means of payment and the store of value refer to concrete *assets* (currency, time deposits, savings deposits). The function of the unit of account is provided by an abstract currency *unit* that is the legal currency for a certain area. For the member countries of the European Monetary Union (EMU) the euro became the legal currency on 1 January 1999. The former national currency units are still in use until the end of the year 2001, but legally they are non-decimal subunits of the euro.

It is obvious that this function of 'money' cannot be used to solve the classification problem of money, since all financial assets have to be denominated in some currency unit. Nevertheless, it is useful to present this function of money in some more detail.

As a *numeraire* for the exchange of goods and services, money (or, more precisely, a common monetary unit) helps to reduce transaction and information costs. Without money, the prices of all goods would have to be expressed in terms of the prices of other goods. Thus, with n goods, an economy would have $(n/2)(n-1)$ relative prices. Such a situation would be associated with high transaction costs, because it would be very difficult to make price comparisons: is a shirt that costs 36 apples in one shop cheaper than the same shirt that costs 12 bottles of beer in another? If an economy has a common unit of account or numeraire, it is possible to express the prices of all goods in the terms of the nth good which serves as a numeraire. Thus, the $(n/2)(n-1)$ *relative* prices are reduced to $n-1$ *absolute* prices. Like the function of the means of payment, the function of the numeraire leads to an enormous reduction of transaction costs.

As a *standard of deferred payments*, money helps to organize the intertemporal exchange of goods. If a worker wants to consume less than she earns in the present and consume more than she earns in the future, she can organize such a transfer by using financial markets or banks. In a debt contract which is used for that purpose, a standard of deferred payments has to be specified. It defines the value of the debt at the time of repayment and can be different from the means of payment that has to be used for the discharge of that debt. For instance, if A today lends 100 euro to B for one year, A and B could agree to use the US dollar as the standard of deferred payments, which means that the debt (including the interest payment of, say, 5%) would be defined in the actual euro exchange rate of the dollar. At a rate of 1.00 dollar per euro, the debt would be 105 dollars. For the discharge of the debt, they could agree to use the euro. Thus, in one year B would have to pay the amount of 105 dollars times the actual euro exchange rate of the dollar. If it is 1.10 dollars, the repayment would be 95.45 euros.

As a *standard for measuring increases in wealth*, money helps to aggregate the different assets in a balance sheet (which can be denominated in different currency units). This function is of special importance in the context of taxation and enterprise accounting. An interesting aspect of that function is that the measured increase in wealth can be different if the balance sheets for two different years are made up, for instance, in dollars or in euros.

1.4. DEFINING MONEY BY ITS STATISTICAL PROPERTIES

A 'pragmatic' approach to definition of 'money', and thus to the solution of the classification and aggregation problem, is adopted by many academics and central banks. Instead of trying to define the 'relevant' money stock from theoretical considerations and testing hypotheses based on it empirically, the opposite procedure is applied: the relevant money stock is defined by its statistical properties. For instance, the European Central Bank prefers the money stock M3 to the money stock M1 mainly for the following reason:

The available empirical evidence suggests that broad monetary aggregates (i.e. measures of money that include a wide spectrum of deposits, embracing time and savings deposits, as well as close substitutes for them, such as marketable short-term bank liabilities) exhibit the properties required for the announcement of a reference value. In the past, the demand for euro area broad money has been stable over the long run. Broad aggregates have been leading indicators of developments in the price level. This contrasts with the empirical properties of euro area narrow money, which, although controllable using short-term nominal interest rates, exhibited neither stability with nor significant indicator properties for the price level.[9] (ECB 1999a: 48)

The problems of this approach for the definition of money are very clearly described by D. K. Osborne:

Belief in this proposition [the stability of the demand for money] has led some monetarists to *define* money as that (set of liquid assets) which has a stable demand function. This definition is rarely stated in so many words, but it is implicit in some of the best works on money demand .... Whether implicit or explicit, the definition

---

[9] With the same arguments, the Deutsche Bundesbank (1995) also favoured M3 over M1.

puts the cart before the horse. We have to define and identify money *before* we can test the stability of its demand. This stability (if it exists) is to be demonstrated empirically, not deemed true axiomatically. ... The theory says that money does *a,b,c*, ... If we then define money as that which comes closest to doing *a,b,c*, ..., we have accepted the theory as true (or true enough for our purpose) and forgone all opportunities to test it. (Osborne 1992: 603)

Thus, instead of deriving hypotheses from a theory and confronting them with the challenge of falsification, which according to the research principles laid down by Karl Popper (1959) is a fundamental requirement for any scientific progress, this approach fosters an immunization of theories against reality. Nevertheless, it explains why broad monetary aggregates are more popular than the money stock M1 in monetary policy, although the narrow aggregate relies on a much more solid theoretical basis.

1.5. THE IMPORTANCE OF A 'CORRECT' DEFINITION OF MONEY

In spite of the considerable theoretical and statistical difficulties that are involved in arriving at a 'correct' definition of money, many central banks have been able to pursue efficient and successful monetary policies. This implies that a 'correct' definition of money is not always necessary for the conduct of an efficient monetary policy. As we shall see in the discussion of different transmission processes of monetary policy (Chapter 4), this process can be analysed either in terms of quantities of money or in terms of relative prices, above all the structure of interest rates. The first approach rests on the Quantity Theory of Money and the monetarist paradigm, while the second is based mainly on Keynesian approaches.

It is clear that the correct definition of money is of crucial importance to a monetary policy strategy that strictly follows a monetarist philosophy. However, we shall see that no central bank has ever followed a monetarist approach for a prolonged period of time (Chapter 9). Thus, the profound problems of a theoretically correct definition of money that have plagued, and will continue to plague, academics at universities can be taken somewhat more lightly by policy-makers at the central banks.

Appendix 1.1. Definitions of money in the euro area, the United States, Japan, and the UK

A comparison of the definitions of money in the euro area, Japan, the United Kingdom, and the United States is provided by Table A1.1. This

Table A1.1. *Definitions of money*

	M1	M2	M3	M4
Euro area (ECB)	Currency in circulation + Overnight deposits	M1 + Deposits with agreed maturity up to 2 years + Deposits redeemable at notice up to 3 months	M2 + Repurchase agreements + Money market fund shares/units and Money market paper + Debt securities up to 2 years	–
Japan	Currency in circulation + Deposit money	M1 + Quasi-money	Not reported, but: M2 + Certificates of deposit (CDs)	
United Kingdom	According to ECB	According to ECB	According to ECB	Notes + Coin + Bank deposits + Building society deposits (including CDs, Sterling, commercial paper, and other short-term paper)
United States	Currency + checkable deposits	M1 + Household holdings of savings deposits, time deposits, and retail money market funds	M2 + Institutional money funds + Managed liabilities of depositories, namely large time deposits, repurchase agreements, and Eurodollars	

Sources: European Central Bank (www.ecb.int); Bank of Japan (www.boj.co.jp); Bank of England (www.bankofengland.co.uk); Federal Reserve Board (www.bog.frb.fed.us).

shows that M1 is defined in rather similar ways by all four central banks; for the broader aggregates, however, the definitions are more different reflecting the varying degrees of importance of alternative financial assets in these economies.

Appendix 1.2. **The concept of (net) financial assets (flow of funds analysis)**

The broadest 'monetary aggregate' is an aggregate that includes all financial assets in an economy. While this approach would solve the classification problem of defining money, it would be rather difficult to find a convincing solution to the aggregation problem, since such an aggregate would include cash as well as government bonds with a maturity of thirty years. Here I present the concept of (net) financial assets, since it provides important insights into fundamental macroeconomic accounting identities.

As a simple-sum measure, many countries publish data on financial assets and liabilities of their economy (flow of funds accounts). For a better understanding of these relationships, we start with a very simplified balance sheet of a private agent:

Assets	Liabilities
Real assets (RA)	Liabilities (L)
Financial assets (FA)	Equity (E)

Assets include only two categories: real assets and financial assets. On the liabilities side, the balance sheet includes liabilities and the equity (or total wealth) of the private agent. An additional concept can be derived by calculating net financial assets (NFA) as the difference between financial assets and liabilities:

$$NFA = FA - L. \tag{A1.1}$$

Equity (or total wealth) is then the sum of net financial assets and real assets:

$$E = RA + NFA. \tag{A1.2}$$

For a *closed economy*, aggregate total wealth can be calculated as the sum of the total wealth of its inhabitants:

$$\sum E_i = \sum RA_i + \sum NFA_i. \tag{A1.3}$$

In a closed economy, each individual financial liability is matched by an individual financial asset so that

$$\sum FA_i = \sum L_i \quad \text{and} \quad \sum NFA_i = 0. \tag{A1.4}$$

As a result, we get for the closed economy

$$\sum E_i = \sum RA_i. \tag{A1.5}$$

In other words, the wealth of a closed economy is always identical with its real assets. For changes in wealth, we can formulate (A1.3) as

$$\Delta \sum E_i = \Delta \sum RA_i + \Delta \sum NFA_i. \tag{A1.6}$$

Again, as $\Delta \sum NFA_i = 0$, we get

$$\Delta \sum E_i = \Delta \sum RA_i. \tag{A1.7}$$

This leads to the well-known identity,

$$S \equiv I, \tag{A1.8}$$

since on the right-hand side of (A1.7) $\Delta \sum RA_i$, the sum of individual increases of real wealth, is identical with investment, and on the left-hand side $\Delta \sum E_i$, the sum of individual increases in total wealth, is identical with saving.

In an *open economy*, domestic agents can build up a positive or negative balance of net financial assets *vis-à-vis* the rest of the world so that $\sum NFA_i > 0$ or < 0. As changes in the net financial assets *vis-à-vis* the rest of the world are identical with the current account (*CA*), so that

$$\Delta \sum NFA_i = CA, \tag{A1.9}$$

equation (A1.8) can be written as

$$S \equiv I + CA. \tag{A1.10}$$

Table A1.2. *Financial assets and liabilities in Germany, 1998 (DM billion)*

Sector	Financial assets	Liabilities	Net financial assets
Households	5,682.2	417.4	5,264.8
Producing enterprises	3,162.9	5,173.1	−2,010.2
Housing	23.7	1,925.2	−1,901.5
Financial institutions	11,754.6	11,269.0	485.6
Government	630.2	2,393.9	−1,763.7
Rest of the world	3,644.5	3,720.1	765.6

Source: Deutsche Bundesbank (1999*b*).

The identity of the current account with the sum of individual savings in the form of financial assets is often overlooked in political debates. It implies that countries with a high savings ratio of the household sector, which is traditionally the sector with high financial assets, will end up with a current account surplus as long as other sectors in the economy do not incur high net financial liabilities. From this perspective, it is not surprising that Japan, with a very wealthy and at the same time rapidly ageing population, had a high current account surplus during the 1990s.

Disaggregating financial assets and liabilities according to the main sectors of an economy gives a good picture of the financial structure of that economy. As data for the euro area are not yet available, we present such data for Germany (Table A1.2). For the United States, flow of funds accounts are available under www.federalreserve.gov/releases/Z1/Current/Data.htm.

2

The Demand for Money

What this chapter is about

- It explains the most important theories on the demand for money and presents the empirical evidence for the different approaches.
- The quantity theory shows that the demand for money is a demand for real balances and depends proportionately on real GDP. Its main assumption is a stable velocity of money.
- Keynesian approaches explain the role of the interest rate as a determinant of money demand.
- Milton Friedman adds wealth as another important determinant.
- For the euro area, one can show that the demand for the money stock M3 depends on all these factors. As far as interest rates are concerned, the relevant variable is the spread between long-term and short-term interest rates.

2.1. INTRODUCTION

The demand for money is closely related to functions and to the definition of money. As we have seen, 'money' can be defined in quite different ways. Thus, the demand for 'money' will be different depending on the combination of assets that are included in a specific monetary aggregate. The standard approaches to the demand for money focus on a narrow concept of money as it is defined by the money stock M1. Thus, in the basic models it is assumed that money is a non-interest-bearing asset. However, with some modifications, a theory of the demand for broader monetary aggregates can also be developed.

The demand for money is an important building block in macroeconomic theory. It constitutes a main link between the monetary sphere and the real sector of an economy. Chapters 3 and 4 will cover these transmission processes in detail. Above all, Chapter 3 will show that the demand for the money stock M1 is closely related to the demand for bank credits. In fact, if an individual goes to a bank and asks for an instalment credit, what he really tries to obtain is not a credit but a certain amount of money that is available on his bank account.

2.2. THE QUANTITY THEORY OF MONEY AND THE CAMBRIDGE APPROACH

The quantity theory of money can be regarded as the earliest explanation of the demand for money. Today it still plays an important role as a building block for more complex approaches (see Chapter 4). Its starting point is the so-called *equation of exchange*, which was developed by Irving Fisher (1911):

$$MV_T \equiv PT, \tag{2.1}$$

where M is the quantity of money, V_T is the velocity of circulation, P is the price level, and T is the volume of transactions. As V_T cannot be measured empirically, the equation of exchange is in this form a mere identity. In addition, there is also no reliable statistical information on the volume of transactions, nor does this variable play an important role in macroeconomic analysis. Therefore, proponents of the quantity theory assume that volume of transactions moves more or less in parallel with the real GDP (Y). This leads to the standard form of the quantity theory:

$$MV \equiv PY, \tag{2.2}$$

where V is the velocity for this specific formulation of this equation. It is often related to as the 'income velocity of money'. Equation (2.2) is still an identity and not yet a theory of money demand. This requires some assumption about the velocity of circulation. The early proponents of the quantity theory assumed that V would be a rather stable variable that is determined mainly by the institutional features of a country's payments system and by the payments habits of its inhabitants. If the velocity is regarded as a constant ($\overline{V}$), the quantity theory can be formulated as a theory of the demand for money:[1]

$$M^D = \frac{1}{\overline{V}} PY. \tag{2.3}$$

This is the so-called cash balance approach, which was developed by Cambridge economists in the beginning of the twentieth century,[2] above

---

[1] It is important to note that the early contributions to the quantity theory of money (Mill 1848, Fisher 1911) were not interested in a theory of the demand for money *per se* but rather in a model that allows one to explain the effect of changes in the money stock on the price level (see Chapter 4).

[2] See Keynes (1930: 205): 'The "real balances" equation ... is descended from a method of approach long familiar to those who have heard Professors Marshall and Pigou in the lecture rooms of Cambridge. ... But it has a much longer descent, being derived from Petty, Locke, Cantillon and Adam Smith.'

all by Alfred Marshall (1923) and Arthur C. Pigou (1917). It is often formulated with the inverse of the velocity, the so-called Cambridge k:

$$M^D = \bar{k}PY. \tag{2.4}$$

This rather simple theory contains two important elements for any theory of money demand. It shows that the demand for money

1. is proportional to the amount of real transactions, represented by the real GDP; and
2. is proportional to the price level. This postulates a one-to-one relation. It can also be interpreted in a way that the demand for money is actually a demand for a real quantity of money:

$$\frac{M^D}{P} = \bar{k}Y. \tag{2.5}$$

An important difference between the cash balance approach and subsequent theories of the demand for money is the lack of an interest rate variable. This implies that the demand for money does not depend on the level of interest rates. It is obvious that such a theory can deal with the function of money only as a means of payment.

As Figures 2.1 and 2.2 show, empirically the main assumption of the quantity theory—a stable velocity of money—cannot be confirmed. In Germany it has followed a more or less stable falling trend which became steeper towards the end of the 1990s. This result is surprising at first sight,

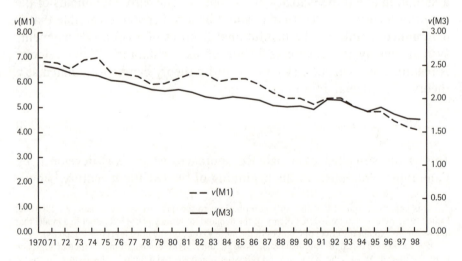

Figure 2.1. *Velocity for Germany, 1970–1998*

Source: Own calculations based on data from IMF, *International Financial Statistics.*

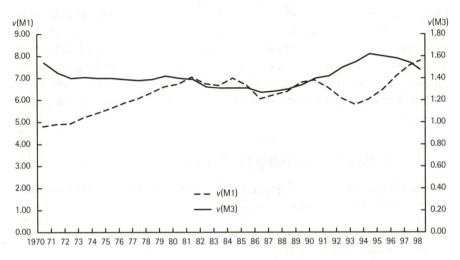

Figure 2.2. *Velocity for the United States, 1970–1998*
Source: Own calculations based on data from IMF, *International Financial Statistics.*

since it indicates that in recent decades more money per unit of nominal GDP has been required, in spite of massive innovation in financial technology. We will see that this anomaly is due mainly to the fact that money holdings also depend on the wealth of the population. In the United States, the velocity of M1 (which is traditionally the preferred monetary aggregate in the United States) followed an upward trend during the 1970s, but because of widespread financial innovation this changed completely in the 1980s. This break was a main reason why the United States abandoned monetary targeting in 1982 (see Section 9.4).

2.3. THE INTEREST RATE AS A DETERMINANT OF THE MONEY DEMAND

The need to incorporate the interest rate as a key determinant of the money demand was recognized above all by Irving Fisher (1930). Whether money is defined in the sense of M1, consisting of non-interest-bearing assets, or in the sense of M2 or M3, including interest-bearing assets, the opportunity costs of holding money are always determined by the interest rate(s) of alternative assets. Thus, a main aim of the theory of money was to explain why people are willing to hold either non-interest-bearing cash and demand deposits or savings and time deposits that offer a lower yield than other assets.

The literature provides two different answers to these questions. In his theory of 'liquidity preference', John Maynard Keynes (1936) assumes that there is a 'speculative motive' that might induce investors to hold non-interest-bearing money as an alternative to interest-bearing bonds. This explanation explicitly refers to the *store-of-value* function of money. In an inventory approach to the demand of money which focuses on the *means-of-payment* function, William J. Baumol (1952) and James Tobin (1956) introduce transaction costs for the exchange of money into other assets.

2.3.1. *The theory of liquidity preference*

In his theory of liquidity preference, Keynes (1936) introduces three motives for holding money:

1. a transaction motive (which Keynes 1936: 195 calls an 'income motive' and a 'business motive');
2. a precautionary motive;
3. a speculative motive.

The first two of these motives are more or less identical with the quantity theory. The transaction motive explicitly recognizes the role of transactions in the demand for money. The precautionary motive can be regarded as a cash balance approach under uncertainty, as economic agents do not always know with which transactions they will be confronted. In Keynes' theory this leads to an additional demand for money. However, it is determined by the same arguments as in equation (2.3). Thus, both motives 'are mainly a resultant of the general activity of the economic system and the level of money-income' (Keynes 1936: 196).

The more difficult part is the speculative motive. Applied to the money stock M1, it assumes that people are willing to hold (non-interest-bearing) money exclusively as a store of value. It is obvious that quite restrictive assumptions are needed in order to generate such a demand for money. In the theory of liquidity preference it is assumed that, in addition to money, only one other financial asset is available: an interest-bearing non-redeemable bond (a *consol*). Another implicit assumption is that the time horizon for the decision process is finite.

Under these conditions, an investor will prefer to hold her financial wealth in money only if the investment in bonds is associated with a financial loss during the holding period. For a period of, say, one year the return (R) from an investment in bonds is

$$R = i_B B + \left(\frac{i_B}{i_{t+1}} - \frac{i_B}{i_t} \right) B, \tag{2.6}$$

where i_B is the exogenous interest rate of the bond and B its nominal value; the second part of the right-hand side of the equation is defined by the difference between the market value of the bond at the beginning and end of the period. The market value of a perpetual bond can be calculated using the formula for a perpetual annual payment (*annuity*). For a market long-term interest rate i and for $q = 1 + i$, the present value (*PV*) of an annuity x is

$$PV = x\left(\frac{(q^n - 1)}{[q^n(q - 1)]}\right).$$ (2.7)

For $n \to \infty$, the present value becomes x/i. Thus, a bond that pays a permanent annual interest income of i_B has a market value of i_B/i.

An investor will prefer the non-interest-bearing money if the bond holdings generate a negative return. Thus, she will hold money because of the speculative motive if

$$0 > i_B B + \left(\frac{i_B}{i_{t+1}} - \frac{i_B}{i_t}\right)B.$$ (2.8)

This can be rearranged to

$$0 > 1 + \left(\frac{1}{i_{t+1}} - \frac{1}{i_t}\right).$$ (2.9)

Thus, the return of the bond holding becomes negative if

$$i_{t+1} > \frac{i_t}{(1 - i_t)}.$$ (2.10)

In other words, this inequality describes the maximum increase of the market interest rate from t to $t + 1$ for which the holding of bonds is still superior to holding non-interest-bearing money. For a return of zero, the critical future interest (i_{t+1}^*) is

$$i_{t+1}^* = \frac{i_t}{(1 - i_t)}.$$ (2.11)

This means that an investor will refrain from investing in bonds if she expects an increase in the interest rate that exceeds this critical rate. Thus, the speculative demand for money depends on the expectations of investors about changes in interest rates. As the rate that is used for discounting future interest payments must be a long-term rate, it follows that the speculative demand for M1 depends on expectations about long-term interest rates. With a given expected interest rate for $t + 1$, an individual

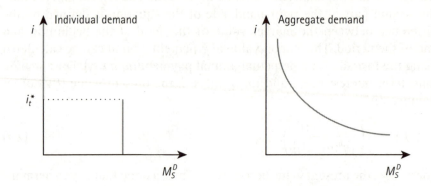

Figure 2.3. *The speculative demand for money*

investor will hold her wealth either completely in bonds or completely in money.[3] Under the assumption that this expected interest rate (i_{t+1}^e) is exogenous, an individual demand curve can be drawn where the demand for money depends on the interest rate in t only. For the actual interest rate, the critical value (i_t^*) is

$$i_t^* = \frac{i_{t+1}^e}{(1 - i_{t+1}^e)}. \tag{2.12}$$

The individual speculative demand curve for money based on this critical rate is shown in Figure 2.3. As different investors have different expected interest rates, the aggregation of the individual demand curves leads to a downward-sloping curve. It implies that the speculative demand for money M_S^D depends negatively on the long-term interest rate:

$$M_S^D = f(i_t), \qquad \text{with } \partial M_S^D / \partial i_t < 0. \tag{2.13}$$

Together with a transaction demand for money, $M_T^D = f(Y)$, and a precautionary demand for money, $M_P^D = f(Y)$, the total demand for money becomes

$$M^D = M_S^D + M_T^D + M_P^D = f(i, Y). \tag{2.14}$$

The practical relevance of the speculative demand for money has not been discussed too intensively. Under present institutional arrangements,

---

[3] Under the assumption of uncertainty about the future interest rates, the portfolio model of James Tobin (1958) arrives at the result that individual investors will normally hold a portfolio that consists of both money and bonds. In all other important respects, the money demand derived with the Tobin model comes to conclusions that are identical with those of the speculative motive under certainty. Above all, an increase in interest rates leads to a reduction of the money demand.

it is obvious that no investor would hold non-interest-bearing money even if she expected a strong increase in long-term rates. She could always hold time deposits or saving deposits, which are interest-bearing assets and which at the same time provide a perfect protection against changes in long-term interest rates. Thus, for the narrow monetary aggregate M1 a speculative demand can be ruled out completely. This is different for the broader monetary aggregates M2 and M3. To an investor that has to decide how to allocate her financial wealth in M3 and bonds, the expected long-term rate is an important factor. When long-term rates are very high, many market participants will expect a decline and will hold a large part of their portfolio in bonds and a smaller share in the money stock M3. When long-term interest rates are very low, the demand for M3 will be relatively high. Many empirical studies of the demand for money show a clear impact of long-term interest rates on the demand for the money stock M3. For this finding, the speculative motive for holding 'money' provides an important explanation.

If money is bearing a positive interest rate (i_M), it will be preferred to bonds if

$$i_M B > i_B B + \left(\frac{i_B}{i_{t+1}} - \frac{i_B}{i_t} \right) B, \qquad (2.15)$$

which can be rearranged into

$$\frac{i_M - i_B}{i_B} > \frac{i_t - i_{t+1}}{i_{t+1} i_t}. \qquad (2.16)$$

This shows that the speculative demand for an interest-bearing monetary aggregate like M3 depends on

1. actual bond yields (i_t) and expectations on future bond yields (i_{t+1}), and
2. the interest rate (i_M) for the interest-bearing components of such an aggregate.

We will see that the difference between bond yields and the short-term interest rate (i.e. the interest rate for time deposits) is an important explanatory variable for the demand for M3 in the euro area.

2.3.2. *The inventory model of Baumol and Tobin*

A completely different approach is chosen by Baumol and Tobin. In their inventory model, only the transaction motive is taken into account: people hold money because they want to use it for payments. Thus, this model applies mainly to the money stock M1. Again, the choice of assets is restricted to non-interest-bearing money and interest-bearing bonds. It is assumed that the transfer from money into bonds is associated with fixed transaction costs (c).

The model derives the optimal money holdings for a household that receives a monthly income which is completely spent for the purchase of goods and services (PY). It assumes that the purchases are spread evenly over the month. According to the practice in the United States, the household receives the income in the form of a cheque with which the head of household has to go to the bank in order to credit it to his account. Thus, at the beginning of the month the money stock (M) of the household is

$$M = PY. \tag{2.17}$$

The householder is now confronted with the following decision problem. He can convert parts of his money stock into bonds. This will generate an interest income but there are the transaction costs for buying bonds. The inventory approach allows us to identify the optimum number of such exchange transactions. It also determines the optimum average money holdings.

The *average* money holdings during the month are determined by the monthly income (PY) and by the number of transactions (n) including as the first transaction, the exchange of the cheque into a sight deposit:

$$M = PY/2n. \tag{2.18}$$

This relationship is shown in Figure 2.4. The opportunity costs (OC) of holding money are the average money holdings multiplied with the interest rate of the bonds (i):[4]

$$OC = Mi. \tag{2.19}$$

The monthly transaction costs (TC) for converting money into bonds are

$$TC = (n - 1)c. \tag{2.20}$$

This assumes that the transaction costs are independent of the amount that is transferred and that they are required only for the exchange of money into bonds. The reverse transaction and the crediting of the cheque is free of charges.

The total monthly costs for the payments services (PS) are:

$$PS = TC + OC = Mi + (n - 1)c. \tag{2.21}$$

[4] As the optimization is made for the period of one month, the interest rate is an interest rate per month.

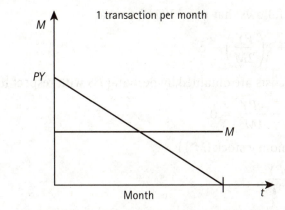

Average money stock: $M = PY/2$

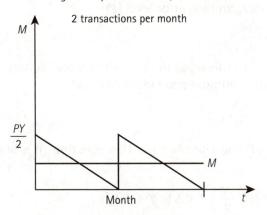

Average money stock: $M = PY/(2 \times 2)$

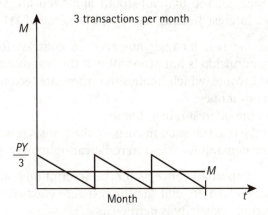

Average money stock: $M = PY/(2 \times 3)$

Figure 2.4. *The Baumol–Tobin model*

From (2.18), it follows that $n = PY/2M$, so that

$$PS = Mi + c\left(\frac{PY}{2M}\right) - c. \tag{2.22}$$

The minimum costs are obtained by deriving PS with respect to M:

$$\frac{dPS}{dM} = i - \frac{cPY}{2M^2} = 0. \tag{2.23}$$

The optimum money stock (M^*) is

$$M^* = \sqrt{\frac{cPY}{2i}}. \tag{2.24}$$

The nominal transaction costs can be regarded as the product of the real transaction costs c_R and the price level (P):

$$c = c_R P. \tag{2.25}$$

Inserted into (2.24), this leads to the optimum real money stock, which is identical with the optimum real money demand:

$$\left(\frac{M}{P}\right)^* = \sqrt{\frac{c_R Y}{2i}}. \tag{2.26}$$

Using m for M/P and transforming this equation in a logarithmic form gives

$$\ln m = 0.5 \ln\left(\frac{c_R}{2}\right) + 0.5 \ln Y - 0.5 \ln i. \tag{2.27}$$

The main results of the Baumol–Tobin approach are as follows. The demand for non-interest-bearing money in the sense of M1 depends

- positively on the real income; however, in contrast to the quantity theory, the relationship is not proportional: the real money stock grows less than real income, which implies that there are 'economies of scale' in the holding of money;
- negatively on the interest rate of bonds;
- positively on the real transaction costs—if the transactions costs become very small, the demand for non-interest-bearing money goes to zero.

This leads to two important concepts for the description of money demand functions: *income elasticity* and the *interest rate elasticity* of the money demand. The income elasticity is defined as

$$\varepsilon_{m,Y} = \frac{dm/m}{dY/Y} = \frac{d\ln m}{d\ln Y}. \tag{2.28}$$

The interest rate elasticity is defined as

$$\varepsilon_{m,i} = \frac{\mathrm{d}m/m}{\mathrm{d}i/i} = \frac{\mathrm{d}\ln m}{\mathrm{d}\ln i}. \tag{2.29}$$

In the Baumol–Tobin model both elasticities are equal to 0.5. The cash balance approach can also be analysed in this way. In logarithmic form, (2.5) becomes

$$\ln m = \ln \overline{k} + \ln Y. \tag{2.30}$$

Thus, the income elasticity is equal to 1, while the interest rate elasticity is 0.

The Baumol–Tobin model provides a relatively plausible explanation for the demand for non-interest-bearing money. Let us assume that an average household obtains a monthly income of €2,000, that the bond yield is 6% per annum, and the real transaction costs for buying bonds are €10. Inserting these data in (2.26) leads to an optimum money demand of €1,414 or 0.7 transaction per month. As the number of transactions is an integer, the optimum number of transactions is 1; i.e., the household does not exchange its money holdings into bonds at all.

While the Baumol–Tobin model has the advantage of incorporating the interest rate as a determinant for the demand of a narrowly defined monetary aggregate (M1), it suffers from several limitations.

1. For an 'average' income, the costs of exchanging parts of the income into bonds are prohibitively high. For the example described above, an annual interest rate of 60% is required in order to make it profitable to exchange the money stock once every month into bonds (i.e. $n = 2$).

2. In most countries bank fees are not a constant price per transaction. Instead, they are proportional to the value of the bonds acquired. At a standard fee of 0.5%, an annual interest rate of 6% is required to make an exchange into bonds profitable at least once in a month.

3. As the approach focuses on the period of one month, it is unable to deal with alternative assets, especially time and savings deposits which have a minimum holding period of at least one month. It is obvious that a comprehensive theory of money would have to analyse the payment programmes for longer periods, for instance a year. With such a focus, it would be also possible to analyse optimum money holdings for payments that are made at larger intervals (e.g. payments for holidays or Christmas).

Because of these flaws, the Baumol–Tobin model is unable to explain the empirical fact that the demand for M1 depends normally on short-term interest rates rather than long-term rates.

2.4. THE MONEY DEMAND FUNCTION OF CAGAN

For periods of hyperinflation Phillip Cagan (1956) developed a money demand function where the real demand for money depends only on the expected inflation rate:

$$\frac{M^D}{P} = f(\pi^e). \tag{2.31}$$

Compared with the Baumol–Tobin model, this function completely neglects the real income and the real interest rate as determinants of the demand for money. The real interest rate is omitted because this function uses the expected inflation rate instead of the nominal interest rate. According to the so-called Fisher relation (see Appendix A8 to Chapter 8), the real interest rate r is

$$r = i - \pi^e. \tag{2.32}$$

The approach of Cagan can be justified for periods of hyperinflation where the inflation rate reaches such high numbers that impact of the real income and the real interest rate becomes very low.

The concrete money demand function used by Cagan is:

$$\frac{M^D}{P} = e^{-\alpha \pi^e}. \tag{2.33}$$

In logarithmic form, this function becomes

$$\ln m = -\alpha \pi^e. \tag{2.34}$$

As the inflation term is not in logarithms, the term α is the *semi-interest elasticity* of the demand for money. Cagan's demand function plays an important role for the analysis of hyperinflations (see Chapter 11).

2.5. WEALTH AS A DETERMINANT OF THE DEMAND FOR MONEY

Especially for the broad monetary aggregates, it seems obvious that the wealth of an individual is another important determinant of the demand for money. This has been emphasized above all by Milton Friedman (1956), who argued that the demand for money should be treated in the same way as the demand for goods or services:

as in the usual theory of consumer choice, the demand for money ... depends on three major sets of factors: (*a*) the total wealth to be held in various forms—the analogue of the budget restraint; (*b*) the price of and return of wealth and alternative forms; (*c*) the tastes and preferences of the wealth owning units. (Friedman 1956: 4)

According to Friedman, the total wealth of an individual is the sum of five components: money, bonds, shares, real assets, and human capital. Thus, a theory of the demand for money would need information on these five components of total wealth and on the returns of money, bonds, shares, real assets, and human capital. For 'ultimate wealth holders',[5] Friedman (1987) formulates such a demand function for money as follows:

$$\frac{M^D}{P} = f(Y, w, i^e_M, i^e_B, i^e_E, u), \tag{2.35}$$

where w is the fraction of wealth in non-human form; i^e_M and i^e_B, i^e_E are the expected nominal rates of return on money, bonds, and physical assets (including changes in their prices); and u is a 'portmanteau symbol standing for other variables attached to the services of money' (Friedman 1987: 9). As it would be extremely difficult to quantify all real assets, all human capital, and the respective returns, the empirical relevance of Friedman's approach is very limited. Nevertheless, it shows that it is important to pay attention to wealth variables as determinants of the demand for money. For Germany, the share of M1 and M3 in the total financial assets of private households has remained remarkably stable since 1980 (Figure 2.5).

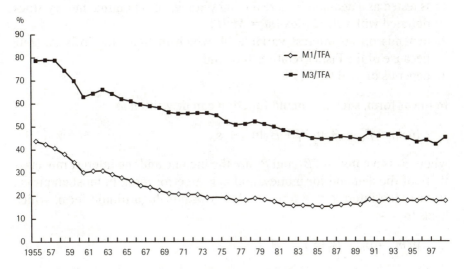

Figure 2.5. *M1 and M3 as percentages of total financial assets (TFA) of private households in Germany, 1955–1998*
Source: Own calculations based on data from Deutsche Bundesbank.

[5] For business enterprises, above all, the variable w has to be excluded; see Friedman (1987: 9).

Empirical demand functions show that it is important to include total wealth–at least indirectly–as a determinant of the demand for money: as total financial assets grow at a faster rate than real GDP, a constant share of money in total financial assets implies that the income elasticity of money is greater than 1.

As far as Friedman is concerned, in his practical recommendations for monetary policy, he mainly relied on the simple quantity theory of money.

2.6. EMPIRICAL DEMAND FUNCTIONS FOR MONEY

Most empirical demand functions are built on a relatively simple structure which incorporates the main findings of the standard theories of the demand for money. For the non-interest-bearing money stock M1, the basic specification is

$$\frac{M^D}{P} = f(Y, i). \tag{2.36}$$

According to this formulation, the demand for money

1. is tested as a demand for a real money stock, i.e. a nominal money stock deflated with price index ($m = M^D/P$);
2. depends on an interest variable (i), which includes the inflation rate because of the Fisher relationship; and
3. depends on real GDP (Y).

In linear form, such a demand function can be written as

$$\ln m_t = \beta_0 + \beta_1 \ln Y_t + \beta_2 \ln i_t + \varepsilon_t, \tag{2.37}$$

where β_0 is a constant, β_1 and β_2 are the income and the interest rate elasticity of the demand for money, and ε_t is an error term. In most empirical studies, the interest rate term is used in a non-logarithmic form, which leads to

$$\ln m_t = \beta_0 + \beta_1 \ln Y_t + \beta_2 i_t + \varepsilon_t. \tag{2.38}$$

In this formulation, β_2 is the *semi-interest elasticity* of the money demand. It shows the percentage by which the real demand for money changes if the interest rate changes by one percentage *point*:

$$\beta_2 = \frac{d \ln m_t}{d i_t}. \tag{2.39}$$

If the money demand is estimated for an interest-bearing monetary aggregate such as M2 or M3, the basic specification becomes[6]

$$\frac{M^D}{P} = f(Y, i^{own}, i^{out}, \pi), \tag{2.40}$$

where i^{own} and i^{out} stand, respectively, for the nominal rates of return on assets included in and excluded from the definition of the monetary aggregate. In applied work this equation is often approximated by a (semi-)log-linear form:

$$\ln m_t = \beta_0 + \beta_1 \ln Y_t + \beta_2 i_t^{own} + \beta_3 i_t^{out} + \beta_4 \pi_t + \varepsilon_t. \tag{2.41}$$

In this equation β_1 measures the income elasticity of money, while β_2, β_3, and β_4 are, in turn, the semi-elasticities with respect to the own and alternative interest rates of money and with respect to the inflation rate. The own rate of money is normally proxied by the short-term money market rate (i_M), the alternative rate by the long-term bond yield (i_B). According to the basic theory of money demand, the expected sign for the parameters are $\beta_1 > 0$, $\beta_2 > 0$, $\beta_3 < 0$, $\beta_4 < 0$, and possibly $\beta_2 = -\beta_3$. A surprising feature of this specification is the inclusion of the inflation rate as a determinant of the demand for money. It was argued above that the impact of the inflation rate on the demand for money can be neglected because it is already included in the nominal interest rate (the Fisher relation). However, if the difference between the short-term and the long-term nominal rate is included in a specification of the money demand, the impact of the inflation rate gets lost. As $i_B = \pi + r_B$ and $i_M = \pi + r_M$, with r_M and r_B representing the real interest rates, the difference between both rates becomes[7]

$$i_B - i_M = r_B - r_M. \tag{2.42}$$

Therefore it becomes necessary to include the inflation term explicitly. The elasticity of the inflation is negative, since a higher inflation rate implies higher opportunity costs of holding money compared with real assets.

A specific problem of empirical estimations of the demand for money is the *non-stationarity* of the real money stock, the real income, and sometimes also the interest rate variables. In ordinary least-squares (OLS) estimations this can lead to spurious regressions. However, this is not the case if non-stationary variables are *cointegrated*.[8] The degree of *integration* of a

---

[6] See Ericsson (1999) and Coenen and Vega (1999).

[7] This calculation assumes that the inflation terms in the long-term and short-term rates are identical.

[8] For a more detailed discussion, see the Appendix of this chapter.

non-stationary variable is defined as d, if it is necessary to calculate d times the first differences of this variable until it becomes stationary. Cointegration means

1. that the residuals of a static regression of integrated variables are stationary (measured by the test for a unit root based on the augmented Dickey–Fuller (1981) statistics, which is identical with the fact
2. that a linear combination of variables that are integrated of the degree d results in a variable that is integrated at a lower degree.

Therefore, tests for the cointegration of the relevant data are an important element of estimates of the demand for money. If the variables are cointegrated, it is possible to differentiate between a long-term and a short-term relationship. The long-term relationship is based on the non-stationary variables of a money demand function like (2.41). The residuals of such an estimation are used for the estimation of a short-term relation ('error correction model'), which can be specified as follows:

$$\Delta \ln m_t = \alpha_0 + \sum_{i=1}^{n} \beta_i \Delta \ln m_{t-i} + \sum_{i=1}^{m} \gamma_i \Delta \ln Y_{t-i} + \sum_{i=1}^{s} \delta_i \Delta i_{t-i}$$

$$- \lambda \ln \hat{\varepsilon}_{t-2} + v_t. \tag{2.43}$$

The short-term relation describes the adjustment of the real money stock to the long-term equilibrium relation. The speed of adjustment is represented by the parameter λ.

For the euro area, Coenen and Vega (1999) have presented the following long-run money demand function for the money stock M3:

$$\ln m_t = 1.140 \ln Y_t - 0.820 \, (i_{Bt} - i_{Mt}) - 1.462 \pi_t + u_t.$$

This result is in line with many other empirical tests for Europe (Fase and Winder 1999) and for Germany (see the survey by Schächter 1999). It shows that the *income elasticity* is significantly higher than 1 (1.14). As already mentioned, this outcome can be explained by the influence of wealth on the demand for money. For instance, in Germany, monetary wealth of private households has been growing more strongly than nominal GDP. If households try to maintain a constant share of money in their total wealth, this implies a growth rate of money that exceeds the growth rate of real income.

The influence of the *interest rate* is measured by the spread between the long-term and the short-term rate; the semi-elasticity is negative (-0.82). The same applies to the semi-elasticity of the inflation rate, which is -1.46. Coenen and Vega (1999) show that these results can provide a plausible explanation for the decline in the velocity of money in the euro area in the last two decades of the twentieth century. This can be attributed to an income elasticity of greater than 1 and to the fact that inflation has fallen considerably since the early 1980s. An important result of the study by Coenen and Vega (1999: 12) is that the parameters of their equation 'turn out to be pretty stable in recent times, both within and out of the estimation period'.

Econometric tests for '*Europe*'[9] which were made in the 1990s come to the conclusion that a 'European' money demand is stable and above all more stable than the national money demands. For the broader monetary aggregates, most of these studies use the bond yield or the differential between the bond yield and a short-term interest rate as explanatory variables. For estimates of the demand for the narrow aggregate M1, normally a short-term interest rate is used. Most studies come to the conclusion that the interest elasticity of M1 is negative.

For monetary policy, almost all studies of the money demand imply that broad monetary aggregates are not influenced by short-term interest rates; and if such an influence is identified the elasticity is positive, as a higher short-term rate makes it more attractive to hold time deposits instead of bonds. This finding has important implications for the strategy of monetary targeting (see Chapter 8).

Econometric tests for the money demand in the *United States* turned out to be a somewhat difficult matter. The reason for this is related primarily to a substantial change in the behaviour of the velocity of money. As already mentioned, up to the early 1980s velocity followed a relatively stable upward trend. Money grew somewhat less quickly than income. Thus, the income elasticity of money demand was less than 1. Since then, as a result of financial innovations, velocity has become rather unstable. In the beginning of the 1990s, therefore, numerous empirical studies investigating the long-run money demand no longer came to conclusive results.

However, a recent study by Ball (1998) has led to fairly precise estimates by simply extending the data-set to 1996. The underlying estimation equation is similar to (2.38), which implies that the money stock is defined as non-interest-bearing M1. The interest rate used in the study is a short-term commercial paper rate. Even by using different estimation techniques, Ball came to quite consistent results, with values for the income elasticity β_1 near 0.5 and for the interest elasticity β_2 near -0.05.

---

[9] The countries included in these studies are not always identical with the present EMU members; for a survey, see Schächter (1999).

Appendix 2.1. Cointegration

Regressing non-stationary variables against each other can lead to spurious results, in the sense that conventional significance tests will tend to indicate a relationship between the variables when in fact there is none. Therefore, Engle and Granger (1987) have developed a method of cointegration. In general, a variable is said to be stationary if its mean and variance are constant over time and the value of covariance between two time periods depends only on the distance or lag between the two time periods, and not on the actual time at which the covariance is computed (Gujarati 1995). A time series y_t is said to be integrated of order 1, I(1), or non-stationary if the first difference Δy_t is a stationary time series. A stationary time series is said to be I(0).

Suppose that there are two time series y_t and x_t, both integrated of order I(1). Then y_t and x_t are said to be cointegrated if there exists a β such that $y_t - \beta x_t$ is stationary, i.e. if I(0). If there exists a linear combination between the two variables which is stationary, the regression equation,

$$y_t = \beta x_t + \mu_t, \tag{A2.1}$$

makes sense, because y_t and x_t do not drift too far apart from each other over time. In other words, a stable long-run equilibrium relationship between the two variables exists (Engle and Granger 1987).

If y_t and x_t are not cointegrated, which means that the linear combination is integrated, e.g. of order I(1), both time series do drift away from each other as time goes on. In this case the relationship between variables y_t and x_t that is obtained by regressing y_t on x_t is 'spurious' (see Maddala 1992).

A further step in investigating two cointegrated time series is to analyse their short-run relationship. Even if a long-term equilibrium relationship between y_t and x_t exists, there is still the possibility of a disequilibrium in the short run. One way to investigate the short-term dynamics of two cointegrated time series is by the error correction mechanism (ECM), which is known as the Granger representation theorem. A simple example of an ECM equation is

$$\Delta y_t = \alpha_0 + \alpha_1 \Delta x_t + \alpha_2 \mu_{t-1} + \varepsilon_t, \tag{A2.2}$$

where Δ as usual denotes the first difference, μ_{t-1} is the one-period-lagged value of the residual from the cointegration regression equation, i.e. the empirical estimate of the long-term equilibrium error term, and ε_t is the error term with the usual properties (white-noise). The ECM regression relates the change in y_t to the change in x_t and the 'equilibrating' error in the previous period. In this regression Δx_t describes the short-term disturbances in x_t, whereas the error correction term μ_{t-1} captures the adjustment towards the long-run equilibrium. If the coefficient of the residual α_2 is statistically significant, it shows which proportion of the disequilibrium in y_t in one period is corrected in the next period (Gujarati 1995).

3

The Money Supply Process: Starting Point of the Transmission Process

What this chapter is about

- It explains how a central bank can control the lending business of commercial banks, which in most cases is synonymous with supplying money to bank customers.
- It first presents the traditional multiplier model, which is very simple but lacks a price-theoretic framework.
- In order to explain the impact of changes in central bank interest rates on bank lending, it presents a price-theoretic model of the money supply process which is especially suitable for large economies such as the euro area and the United States.
- An appendix considers the impact of different shocks to the money supply process.

3.1. INTRODUCTION

The money supply process deals with the interface between the central bank and the commercial banks. At this point the indirect and complex processes of monetary policy transmission always start independently of the theories on the subsequent stages of this process, which are discussed in Chapter 4. It is, therefore, of crucial importance that the right starting point is chosen.

According to the two main definitions of money in Chapter 2, the process of money supply is related to

1. the creation of the *monetary base*, which is dominated by the central bank, and
2. the creation of the *money stock* in definitions of M1, M2, or M3, which is determined by the interplay between the central bank, commercial banks, and the non-bank sector.

This chapter shows that in somewhat simplified terms the monetary base can be regarded as an 'input factor'—controlled by the central bank—for the process by which the money stock M1, M2, or M3 is created as 'output' by the commercial banks.

3.2. CREATION AND CONTROL OF THE MONETARY BASE BY THE CENTRAL BANK

The fact that a central bank can exercise control over the economy derives from its unique position as a *monopolistic supplier* of the monetary base. In all modern countries, this is guaranteed by its monopoly over the supply of banknotes and coin.[1] That a central bank can control the 'raw material' is necessary for the money creation process and its way of doing this can best be explained by taking a look at a typical central bank balance sheet (Table 3.1).

Table 3.1. *Consolidated financial statement of the European System of Central Banks, 2 June 2000 (in €million)*

Assets	Balance	Liabilities	Balance
1. Gold and gold receivables	115,667	1. Banknotes in circulation	355,498
2. Claims on non-euro area residents denominated in foreign currency	265,353	2. Liabilities to euro area financial sector counterparties denominated in euro	114,669
3. Claims on euro area residents denominated in foreign currency	19,344	3. Debt certificates issued	6,265
4. Claims on non-euro area residents denominated in euro	4,850	4. Liabilities to other euro area residents denominated in euro	40,153
5. Lending to financial sector counterparties in the euro area denominated in euro	201,975	5. Liabilities to non-euro area residents denominated in euro	7,242
6. Securities of euro area residents denominated in euro	25,030	6. Liabilities to non-euro area residents denominated in foreign currency	14,362
7. General government debt denominated in euro	59,026	7. Other liabilities	63,717
8. Other assets	83,675	8. Revaluation accounts	118,007
		9. Capital and reserves	54,981
Total assets	774,894	Total liabilities	774,894

Source: www.ecb.int.

---

[1] For the euro area, Article 106 of the EU Treaty stipulates: '(1) The ECB shall have the exclusive right to authorise the issue of banknotes within the Community. The ECB and the national central banks may issue such notes. The banknotes issued by the ECB and the national central banks shall be the only such notes to have the status of legal tender within the Community. (2) Member States may issue coins subject to approval by the ECB of the volume of the issue. The Council may, acting in accordance with the procedure referred to in Article 252 and after consulting the ECB, adopt measures to harmonise the denominations and technical specifications of all coins intended for circulation to the extent necessary to permit their smooth circulation within the Community.'

In the case of the euro area, the 'central bank' balance sheet is a consolidated statement of the ECB's balance sheet and of those twelve national central banks that participate in the European Monetary Union. The technically correct term for the ECB plus these twelve central banks is 'European System of Central Banks' (ESCB) or 'Eurosystem' (see Chapter 6). The main items on the *asset* side of the ESCB are gold holdings, foreign exchange reserves, lending to banks in the euro area, and holdings of government debt. The *liabilities* side is dominated by banknotes in circulation, reserves of banks in the euro area, and government deposits, which are included in the position 'Liabilities to other euro area residents denominated in euros'.

For analytical purposes, we can in fact simplify this central bank balance sheet by taking the balance of the central bank's claims and liabilities *vis-à-vis* foreign counterparties and *vis-à-vis* the government sector in order to arrive at a net position in each case:

- $NP_{CB/F}$ comprises the central bank's net position *vis-à-vis* the foreign sector (including the central bank's gold holdings);
- $NP_{CB/G}$ comprises the central bank's net position *vis-à-vis* the government sector.

In addition,

- $Cr_{CB/B}$ includes all credits that the central bank provides to the domestic banking sector;
- C is defined as the amount of currency in circulation; thus, we remove the distinction between the note circulation and the combined note and coin circulation;[2]
- R is defined as all deposits that are held by euro area banks with the ESCB;
- $BAL_{CB/OAL}$ includes all other assets and liabilities of the central bank.

A simplified balance sheet is presented as Table 3.2. It is now possible to write down the monetary base (B) in terms of its source (assets side):

$$B = NP_{CB/F} + NP_{CB/G} + Cr_{CB/B} - BAL_{CB/OAL}, \tag{3.1}$$

or, in terms of its application (liabilities side),

$$B = C + R. \tag{3.2}$$

Both formulations illustrate important aspects of the money creation process.

---

[2] This distinction is due to the fact that, according to Article 106 (2) of the EU Treaty, the right of coinage belongs to the national governments. Accordingly, the ESCB statement shows only the amount of banknotes in circulation, although in other statistics it always records the amount of the combined notes and coins in circulation as well.

Table 3.2. *Simplified balance sheet of the Eurosystem, 2 June 2000 (€million)*

Assets	Balance	Liabilities	Balance
1. Net position *vis-à-vis* the foreign sector (including gold holdings)	370,676	1. Currency in circulation	371,400
2. Net position *vis-à-vis* the domestic government sector	47,734	2. Deposits of the domestic banking sector	114,669
3. Credits to the domestic banking sector	201,957	3. Balance of other assets and liabilities	134,298
Total net assets	620,367	Total liabilities	620,367

Source: Own calculations based on data from www.ecb.int.

3.2.1. *The use of the monetary base*

Equation (3.2) helps to clarify the two main reasons why monetary base is needed in an economy. First, as we have seen from Chapter 1, money is needed as a transaction medium in any economy. This situation has not basically changed even in those countries where a significant volume of payments can also be carried out without using cash; for instance, in Germany from the mid-1970s onwards the note and coin circulation has risen substantially faster than nominal GDP. Among the reasons suggested for this, alongside moonlighting, tax evasion on investment income, rising bank charges, and drug trafficking,[3] is the increasing use of the Deutschmark as a parallel currency in eastern Europe and the CIS states.[4] It remains to be seen whether the euro will play a similar role after the issuance of euro banknotes in 2002.

Second, central bank balances are held exclusively by banks. In most countries the demand for central bank balances originates primarily in the statutory minimum reserve requirements (Chapter 10). Any balances held above these requirements are regarded as excess reserves (ER). Central bank balances are often non-interest-bearing. So the banks try to keep such balances as low as possible. In the euro area, the minimum reserves of the banks are remunerated with the interest rate of the main refinancing instrument (Chapter 10). As excess reserves are non-interest-bearing, the banks try to keep such balances as low as possible. When measured against

---

[3] Evidence for the extensive use of cash in illegal transactions is provided by the fact that DM500 and DM1,000 denominations make up about 44.3% the total value of the Deutschmark banknote circulation at the end of 1999; see Deutsche Bundesbank (2000*b*: 118).

[4] Seitz (1995) has carried out a detailed study of this subject.

the reserve requirement, i.e. the amount of reserves that the banks are obliged to hold, they correspond to about 0.5% in the case of the euro area. Accordingly, equation (3.2) can also be formulated as

$$B = C + MR + ER. \tag{3.3}$$

In countries without minimum reserve requirements (Switzerland, United Kingdom) the banks' central bank balances are extremely small. Such voluntary holdings are referred to as *working balances*. They are needed by the banks for settling their liabilities to other banks in the clearing process. The level of demand for working balances in a system without minimum reserves is so low because, in a system in which the central bank uses the interest rate as its operating target (Chapter 10), the banks can assume that the central bank will supply them with enough central bank money at all times; the examples of the United Kingdom, Japan, and the United States show that the central bank is active at the money market several times per day (Sections 10.5–10.7).

Thus, on the application side we can see that the demand for monetary base is determined mainly by cash holdings and to a certain extent also, in countries with statutory minimum reserve requirements, by the need to hold minimum reserves. This need for monetary base is the main lever whereby a central bank can influence the money creation process.

3.2.2. *The sources of the monetary base*

In order for the central bank to be able to control the money creation process, it must be able to exercise adequate control at all times over the supply of monetary base. If we look at the source side of the monetary base (expressed in terms of change), we can identify the channels whereby central bank money can be created and see what influence the central bank exercises over them.

$$\Delta B = \Delta NP_{CB/F} + \Delta NP_{CB/G} + \Delta Cr_{CB/B} - \Delta BAL_{CB/OAL}. \tag{3.4}$$

Three sources of the monetary base need to be distinguished: (1) intervention on the foreign exchange market, (2) lending to the State, and (3) lending to domestic commercial banks.

1. The central bank's net external position rises ($\Delta NP_{CB/F} > 0$) if it purchases foreign currency from a domestic credit institution and credits the latter with the countervalue on its account at the central bank. Such transactions usually take place in the context of *foreign exchange market interventions*, when, in order to support a foreign currency, a central bank

makes foreign currency purchases in that currency. The central bank's net position declines when it tries to avoid a depreciation of its currency by offering foreign currency on the foreign exchange market.

2. The central bank's net position *vis-à-vis* the government increases ($\Delta NP_{CB/G} > 0$) if a central bank grants a *loan to the State*: As long as the State holds the countervalue of the loan on deposit at the central bank, the position $NP_{CB/G}$ remains unchanged. The monetary base increases as soon as the State spends these funds in payments to private-sector economic agents which are credited to an account at a commercial bank. The monetary base can also be increased via this source if the central bank purchases government securities in the conduct of its open-market policy (see Chapter 10).

3. A central bank grants a *loan to a domestic commercial bank* ($\Delta Cr_{CB/B} > 0$). It may do this under a *credit facility* (e.g. the marginal refinancing facility of the ECB), or it can lend to commercial banks under an auction procedure (*securities repurchase agreements*) (see also Chapter 10).

Only when the central bank can determine all such transactions largely at its own discretion is it able to manage the monetary base in line with its targets. This requires above all the following institutional arrangements.

1. The central bank must not be forced to bring about an excessive expansion in the central bank money supply through foreign exchange market intervention. This principle can be threatened if a central bank participates in an exchange rate system with fixed exchange rates. However, control of the monetary base can still be possible, even in the event of sizeable foreign exchange market intervention, provided that a central bank is able to offset the expansion in the monetary base caused by $\Delta NP_{CB/F}$ by reducing its lending to the banks ($\Delta Cr_{CB/B}$) so that $\Delta NP_{CB/F} = -\Delta Cr_{CB/B}$. This procedure, which is known as *sterilization*, will be discussed in more detail in Chapter 12. A particularly impressive example of this was provided at the time of the EMS crisis of September 1992, when the Bundesbank managed in a short space of time to sterilize the whole of the DM92 billion involved in the intervention operations (Deutsche Bundesbank 1993).

2. A central bank must not be induced to provide unlimited finance to cover state deficits. Nearly all cases of high inflation are attributable to this form of financing via the 'banknote printing press' (see Chapter 4). For this reason, Article 101 of the EC Treaty prohibits any direct state financing by a central bank in all EU countries.

3. A central bank must be able to control its lending to the commercial banks. In the majority of countries, this condition does not present a major problem.

Theory

3.3. CONSOLIDATED BALANCE SHEET OF THE BANKING SYSTEM AND THE SUPPLY OF THE MONEY STOCK

While the 'input factor' in money creation is to be found exclusively in the central bank balance sheet, the money supply 'output' can be deduced from the consolidated balance sheet of the banking system as a whole. In such a calculation, the balance sheet of the central bank and the balance sheets of all the commercial banks are aggregated into a single balance sheet. For this purpose, all claims and liabilities between individual banks and between banks and the central bank are netted out (i.e. consolidated). Thus, the consolidated balance sheet of the banking system shows only claims and liabilities with respect to non-banks. Table 3.3 presents the consolidated balance sheet of the euro area's monetary financial institutions (MFIs). This term includes the Eurosystem and commercial banks in the euro area. Again, some simplifications have been made. Assets and liabilities of the banking system *vis-à-vis* foreigners are netted out and presented in the form of a net position ($NP_{BS/F}$). Credits to the public sector and to the private sector are aggregated to $Cr_{BS/G}$ and $Cr_{BS/Pr}$, respectively. The liabilities side shows the components of M3: currency in circulation (C), overnight deposits (OD), time deposits with a maturity of up to two years (TD),

Table 3.3. *Consolidated financial balance sheet of the euro area MFIs, including the Eurosystem, end-May 2000 (€billion)*

Assets	Balance	Liabilities	Balance
1. Net external assets (including gold holdings)	189.3	1. Currency in circulation	337.2
2. Credits to the domestic government sector	2,008.5	2. Sight deposits	1,656.8
3. Credits to the domestic private non-bank sector	6,474.5	3. Time deposits with agreed maturity up to 2 years and deposits redeemable at notice up to 3 months	2,156.3
		4. Other liabilities included in M3	781.1
		5. Longer-term liabilities of MFI	2,768.6
		6. Balance of other assets and liabilities	966.9
Total net assets	8,666.9	Total net liabilities	8,666.9

Source: www.ecb.int.

savings deposits (SD),[5] and other short-term liabilities of the banking system (OSL); LL are the long-term liabilities of the banking system, i.e. bank deposits and bank bonds that are not included in M3; and $BAL_{BS/OAL}$ are all other assets and liabilities of the banking system.

From this simplified balance sheet, the money stock M3 (and all the other monetary aggregates) can be defined via the application side, which shows the forms in which M3 is held:

$$M3 = C + OD + TD + SD + OSL. \tag{3.5}$$

The money stock M3 can also be deduced via the source side:

$$M3 = NP_{BS/F} + Cr_{BS/G} + Cr_{BS/Pr} - LL_{BS} - BAL_{BS/OAL}. \tag{3.6}$$

This equation can also be written in first differences:

$$\Delta M3 = \Delta NP_{BS/F} + \Delta Cr_{BS/G} + \Delta Cr_{BS/Pr} - \Delta LL_{BS} - \Delta BAL_{BS/OAL}. \tag{3.7}$$

It allows us to analyse by which transactions the money stock M3 is increased. Four basic types of transaction will be briefly described here with the help of examples:

1. A resident private individual sells a claim *vis-à-vis* a foreigner (e.g. a foreign cheque) to a bank, which credits him with the countervalue on his current account. M3 expands and there is an increase in $NP_{BS/F}$.
2. A domestic authority (central, regional or local) borrows from a domestic bank, which credits the authority with the countervalue on its current account. Again, there is a rise in M3 and a simultaneous increase in the position $Cr_{BS/G}$.
3. A domestic company borrows from its bank. The countervalue is credited to the company's current account. Increases are registered in M3 and in the position $Cr_{BS/Pr}$.
4. A resident private individual terminates a savings deposit with a notice period of more than three months on maturity. The amount is credited to her current account. M3 increases, while there is a reduction in the position LL_{BS}.

Thus, the money stock M3 can be created as a result of very different operations, in which money creation is not necessarily associated with credit creation, as the first and last examples demonstrate. However, the broader the definition of the money supply (e.g. M3 instead of M1), the closer the correspondence between money and credit. In very general terms, we can think of money creation as a process whereby money is created whenever

---

[5] In the euro area, 'deposits redeemable at notice up to three months'.

a bank purchases from a non-bank an instrument that represents a claim, i.e.

1. a claim against a foreign counterparty ($NP_{BS/F}$);
2. a claim against the State ($Cr_{BS/G}$);
3. a claim against private domestic non-banks ($Cr_{BS/Pr}$);
4. a 'claim against itself' (LL_{BS}); this term goes back to Keynes (1930: 21).

At the general level, the money supply generation process is very similar to the process whereby the monetary base is created. In the latter case the central bank purchases such claims mainly from commercial banks, while in the former they are exclusively purchased from non-banks.

3.4. THE MECHANISTIC MULTIPLIER PROCESS

So far we have deduced the creation of the monetary base and the money stock solely through balance sheet analysis. While it is quite obvious that the central bank can control the creation of the monetary base very directly, we have to find how it can influence the creation of the money stock. The literature offers two different approaches to this question:

1. the mechanistic model of the money multiplier, and,
2. more complex, price-theoretic models.

After a presentation and critical discussion of the traditional money multiplier, this section presents a price-theoretic model which allows us to analyse the effect of central bank actions on the money stock and commercial bank interest rates.

3.4.1. *Money creation ≡ credit creation*

As has already been explained, the 'input factor' of the money creation process can be determined from the central bank balance sheet. For the purposes of the analysis of the money supply, we shall take an even more simplified version of the central bank balance sheet than that already given in Table 3.2 (see Table 3.4). The assets side consists solely of the loans that

Table 3.4. *A very simplified central bank balance sheet*

Assets	Liabilities
Credits to domestic banks	Currency in circulation
	Reserves of domestic banks

the central bank grants to the banks for funding purposes. The liabilities side is made up of notes and coins in circulation (C) and the banks' central bank balances (R). The monetary base is thus defined as

$$B = Cr_{CB/B} = C + R. \tag{3.8}$$

This implies above all that we no longer take into account foreign assets as a means for creating monetary base. Thus, the model provides a rather good description of the situation in large economies with flexible exchange rates like the United States or the euro area. In addition, we assume that the central bank grants no credits to the government, which also corresponds to the situation in many countries (Chapter 6). The balance of other assets and liabilities is assumed to be zero.

In a similar way, we simplify the consolidated balance sheet of the banking system. Again, we neglect the net foreign position. For the credits of the banking system, we do not differentiate between credits to the government and credits to the private sector: the position $Cr_{B/NB}$ includes both components. The balance of other liabilities and assets is also assumed to be zero. No distinction is made, in the case of deposits (D), between, say, different maturities or interest rates or between private or official depositors. Long-term liabilities of the bank system are also neglected (Table 3.5). Expressed in the form of an equation, the money supply and total lending can then be written as follows:

$$M = C + D = Cr_{B/NB}. \tag{3.9}$$

Equation (3.9) shows that in this pared-down model the money supply is equal to total lending. The non-banks' demand for bank credit is identical with a demand for cash or deposits (= demand for money) which are used for transactions. Therefore, each bank loan supplied implies that money is supplied in the form C or D. The simplification made here, namely that money creation is synonymous with credit creation, does not lead to any restriction to the general validity of the money supply model that will be derived below. The crucial point is what was already mentioned: banks create money by buying claims, in either a securitized form (bonds) or a non-securitized form (credits). Consequently, the credit market (or, more

Table 3.5. *A very simplified consolidated balance sheet of the banking system*

Assets	Liabilities
Credits to domestic non-banks	Currency in circulation Deposits of domestic non-banks

generally, the market for claims) and the 'macroeconomic' market for money are exact mirror images of each other.

3.4.2. *Deriving the multiplier*

In its simplest form, this multiplier is a coefficient which describes the relationship between the volume of money stock and the monetary base:

$$\text{Multiplier} = m = \frac{M}{B}. \tag{3.10}$$

This can be deduced as a simple tautology from the determining equations for the money stock M1 and the monetary base (B). As already mentioned, the money stock M is made up of cash (C) and deposits (D) only:

$$M = C + D. \tag{3.11}$$

The relationship of cash holdings to deposits (C/D) is referred to as the cash holding ratio (b). Equation (3.11) thus becomes

$$M = bD + D = D(b + 1). \tag{3.12}$$

As already stated in (3.2), the monetary base can be represented as the sum of cash holdings (C) and banks' balances at the central bank (R):

$$B = C + R. \tag{3.2}$$

The relation that the banks' central bank balances bear to deposits (R/D) is represented by the reserve ratio (r). This gives

$$B = bD + rD = D(b + r). \tag{3.13}$$

The multiplier can then be determined by dividing (3.12) by (3.13):

$$\frac{M}{B} = m = \frac{1 + b}{b + r}. \tag{3.14}$$

If we assume realistically that the reserve ratio has a value of less than unity, i.e. that no bank will hold a 100% reserve, the money creation multiplier will always be greater than 1.[6] For the euro area, the multiplier is calculated in Box 3.1.

The multiplier formula is also often derived for an alternative cash holding ratio (b'), which indicates the proportion of cash holdings to the

---

[6] The existence of cashless transactions is also postulated ($D > 0$), so that not all of the money supply is held in the form of cash ($b < \infty$).

Box 3.1. *The money multiplier of the euro area*

In the case of the euro area, we obtain the following values for the money stock M3 on 30 April 2000:

M3 = €4,901 billion
D = €4,564 billion (deposit components included in M3)
C = €338 billion
R = €101 billion
B = €439 billion

The values for b and r can then be determined as follows:
$b = C/D = 0.074$
$r = R/D = 0.022$
$$m = \frac{1 + 0.074}{0.074 + 0.022} = 11$$

The multiplier is thus 11, a value that can be obtained via either the multiplier formula or the ratio M/B.

total money supply and therefore can be described as the cash outflow ratio:

$$b' = \frac{C}{M}.$$

The multiplier can then be calculated by reformulating (3.13) as follows:

$$B = b'M + rD. \tag{3.13'}$$

Since $D = M - C$, the following equation holds true:

$$B = b'M + r(M - b'M) = M[b' + r(1 - b')]. \tag{3.13''}$$

From this, we can directly derive the multiplier as

$$\frac{M}{B} = \frac{1}{b' + r(1 - b')}. \tag{3.14'}$$

Here too it becomes clear that the money creation multiplier is always greater than 1, since the cash and reserve holdings respectively make up only a fraction of the total money supply or deposits ($b' < 1, r < 1$).

Since the multiplier relation was derived from pure accounting equations, we are not yet able to produce an economic model of the money supply process. However, this does not prevent many textbooks from attempting to explain the actual process of money creation in these terms. The main flaw of this approach is the complete neglect of interest rates and of behavioural relationships. In other words, the multiplier process is an adequate description of the reality only if interest rates do not matter for the behaviour of the central bank, commercial banks, and private lenders. This would be the case only in a *disequilibrium situation,* where at given interest rates commercial banks and private lenders have an unsatisfied demand for credits from the central bank and commercial banks, respectively.

On these very specific assumptions, the sequence of events leading to an expansion in the money supply would be as follows.

1. The process starts with the central bank's decision, e.g. to reduce the minimum reserve ratio. Thus, at the same level of reserves, the banks hold excess reserves as their minimum reserve holdings have declined (equation (3.3)).

2. The commercial banks now attempt to get rid of their excess reserves. The multiplier model assumes that commercial banks do not reduce their lending from the central bank. In this case, the expansionary effect would be lost immediately. Instead, it is assumed that the commercial banks will decide to increase their lending to non-banks by exactly the same amount as the increase in excess reserves.

3. Private individuals (or public institutions) are now willing to increase their loans from commercial banks, e.g. to buy consumer or investment goods. As a result, cash holdings in the economy increase in accordance with *b*, and at the same time there is an increase in deposits (*D*). The banks in turn must hold higher minimum reserves at the central bank on their additional deposits, in accordance with the reserve ratio (*r*).

After the first round the banks still have excess reserves. They use them again for more lending to private non-banks. This process comes only to an end when the excess reserves have been fully used up in cash holdings and in the additional minimum reserves that the banks hold as a consequence of the growth in deposits. The maximum possible lending to private individuals $(\Delta Cr_{B/Pr})$ can thus be easily determined, since in these models it is assumed that the change in the money supply (ΔM) is identical with the change in total lending $(\Delta M = \Delta Cr_{B/Pr})$.

A numeric example of the mechanistic process of multiple money creation is given in Table 3.6. Following 'seepage' of the full amount of the excess reserve in the form of cash and minimum reserves available for lending $(\Delta C + \Delta MR = 1500)$, a maximum credit and money creation of €3,000 is arrived at. This means that in this example the multiplier assumes

Table 3.6. *The mechanistic multiplier model*

Period	Excess reserves at beginning of period	Credits provided $(= \Delta M)$	Increase in currency in circulation $(= \Delta C)$ with $b' = \frac{1}{3}$	Increase in deposits $(= \Delta D)$	Increase in minimum reserves (ΔR) with $r = \frac{1}{4}$	Excess at the end of period
1	1,500	1,500	500	1,000	250	750
2	750	750	250	500	125	375
3	375	375	125	250	62.5	187.5
4	187.5	...	...	...	...	...
...	...	...	...	...	...	...
Sum over all periods	...	3,000	1,000	2,000	500	...

the value 2, which could also have been directly calculated by means of equation (3.14′) as

$$\frac{M}{B} = \frac{1}{\frac{1}{3} + \frac{1}{4}\left(1 - \frac{1}{3}\right)} = 2.$$

3.5. A PRICE-THEORETIC MODEL OF THE MONEY SUPPLY

It is obvious that, in spite of its popularity, the mechanistic multiplier model has some serious shortcomings. They are all related to the complete neglect of interest rates. Thus, this approach can say very little about how monetary policy is actually operated. It is well known that all central banks implement their policy by changing key interest rates and not by targeting the monetary base (Chapter 10).

Although the problems of the mechanistic multiplier model were mentioned early on by Tobin (1963), the literature has still failed to devise a simple money supply model that takes account of these aspects. A few textbooks on monetary theory do try expanded versions, but these usually tackle only one of the problems raised and continue to bear the marks of the mechanistic approach to the process of money creation.[7] A special problem of models that were developed for the institutional framework of the United States is that they are not easily applicable to the situation in the

---

[7] See Jarchow (1998) and McCallum (1989). Most models are largely based on the work on the money supply process carried out by Brunner and Meltzer (1964, 1966).

euro area. This is due to the fact that the Federal Reserve's techniques of controlling the money market (Chapter 10) are very different from the continental European approach which has been adopted by the ECB.

In order to present a rather complex topic in a relatively easily understandable way, the model presented below is based on the very simplified consolidated balance sheet that we already used for the mechanistic multiplier. A main feature of this simplification is that the credit market (or, more general by, the market for claims) and the 'macroeconomic' market, i.e. the market for the money stock M1, are exact mirror images of each other. Thus, if these two markets are identical, we can confine ourselves in the following to

1. the *demand for money function*, which—under the assumptions of this section—is the same as the credit demand function, and
2. the *credit supply function*, which is the same as the money supply function.

As in the traditional money creation model, we shall assume constant prices, so that no distinction needs to be made between real and nominal magnitudes.

3.5.1. *The money demand (≡ credit demand)*

From Chapter 2 we know that the demand for money is a positive function of income and a negative function of the interest rate, which represents the opportunity costs of holding money. This function is here assigned to the credit market (or loan) interest rate (i_c). This can be explained with the opportunity cost concept that underlies all modern theories of the demand for money. In the case of our very simplified economy, the only alternative to holding money is to repay bank credits. Thus, it is the credit interest rate that determines the demand for money. We also assume that money is not interest-bearing.

$$M^D = Cr^D = Cr^D\left(\overset{(-)}{i_C}, \overset{(+)}{Y}\right). \tag{3.15}$$

In order to solve our model formally, it is necessary to insert concrete values for the demand for money function. This will be done by means of a linear function, which applies equally to the demand for money and the demand for credit:

$$M^D = Cr^D = \mu + \gamma Y - \alpha i_C, \quad \text{since } M^D = Cr^D \geq 0, \ \gamma Y \geq \alpha i_C. \tag{3.16}$$

3.5.2. *The credit supply (≡ money supply)*[8]

In the following we assume that the money supply process is driven by the credit business of the banking system. This implies that the central bank uses the short-term interest rate as its operating target (Chapter 10) so that its supply of reserves is completely elastic at a given interest rate. Thus an individual bank (and the banking system as a whole) can always create money by granting loans since it can always obtain the required liquidity from the central bank. In contrast to the traditional money multiplier approach, which basically relies on quantitative constraints on bank lending, in our approach the central bank's control over the money supply depends on its power to control the short-term interest rate.

3.5.2.1. *Credit supply of an individual bank*

In our model of the money supply we assume a banking system with n identical banks which act as price takers. Each bank takes the loan rate (i_C) and the deposit rate (i_D) as given. The central bank as a monopolistic supplier of reserves sets the interest rate in the money market (i_R). For an individual bank j, the balance sheet identity is:

$$Cr_{B/NB}^{j} + R^{j} = D^{j} + Cr_{CB/B}^{j}, \tag{3.17}$$

with loans vis-a-vis non-banks $(Cr_{B/NB}^{j})$ and minimum reserves (R^{j}) on the asset side and deposits (D^{j}) and credits from the central bank $(Cr_{CB/B}^{j})$ on the liability side. For the sake of simplicity we do not take into account the possibility that an individual bank can also lend from another bank on the interbank market. Banks are supposed to hold no excess reserves and the level of minimum reserves (R^{j}) is determined through:

$$R^{j} = rD^{j}, \tag{3.18}$$

where (r) is the minimum reserve ratio $(0 < r < 1)$, which is set by the central bank. According to the practice of the ECB we assume that minimum reserves are interest bearing and yield a return of (i_R), the central bank's refinancing rate.

Following the traditional reserve management models suggested, for instance, by Orr and Mellon (1961), Klein (1971), Niehans (1978), or Baltensperger (1980), we assume that a single bank takes its level of deposits as given, depending on stochastic flows. However, since the central bank sets the money market rate (i_R), the supply of reserves becomes perfectly elastic, making a liquidity management in terms of excess reserves

---

[8] For this model Oliver Hülsewig has made very valuable suggestions.

superfluous. At any time each bank can refinance an unexpected drain of deposits at the prevailing money market rate from the central bank (or to other banks). In the case of an unexpected influx of deposits, we assume that each bank can always reduce its refinancing credits with the central bank.

The profit function of an individual bank is

$$\Pi^j = i_C Cr^j_{B/NB} - i_D D^j - i_R(Cr^j_{CB/B} - R^j) - 0 - V, \tag{3.19}$$

and depends on the difference between the interest revenue in the credit business with non-banks and its costs. The latter include the refinancing costs (either for deposits or credits from the central bank) as well as fixed operating costs (0) and the variable costs of the credit business (V). We assume that the variable costs are determined mainly by the default costs, which depend on the total amount of credits and the default probability (d):[9]

$$V = dCr^j_{B/NB}. \tag{3.20}$$

Further, we assume that the risk of default is a function of the amount of credits granted relative to the overall macroeconomic situation which we measure by real income (Y).

$$d = f(Cr^j_{B/NB}/Y). \tag{3.21}$$

For this function we use a simple linear approximation:

$$d = \beta Cr^j_{B/NB}/Y. \tag{3.22}$$

Thus, the variable costs of the credit business rise more than proportionately with the amount of credits granted:

$$V = \beta(Cr^j_{B/NB})^2/Y. \tag{3.23}$$

Bank j maximizes its profits by choosing its optimal volume of loans subject to its balance sheet identity (3.17). Solving the balance sheet constraint in consideration of the minimum reserve requirement (3.18) for the credits from the central bank and substituting into the bank's profit function (3.19) yields

$$\Pi^j = Cr^j_{B/NB}(i_C - i_R) - D^j(i_D - i_R) - 0 - \beta(Cr^j_{B/NB})^2/Y. \tag{3.24}$$

---

[9] Empirical evidence supports this hypothesis. See e.g. Stöß (1996), who finds a positive relation between macroeconomic performance and the creditworthiness of enterprises.

From this we get the following first-order condition for optimal loan supply:

$$\frac{\partial \Pi^j}{\partial Cr^j_{B/NB}} = i_C - i_R - 2\beta Cr^j_{B/NB}/Y = 0. \tag{3.25}$$

The characteristics of (V) ensure that the second-order condition for a profit maximum is fulfilled:

$$\frac{\partial^2 \Pi^j}{\partial (Cr^j_{B/NB})^2} = -2\beta/Y < 0$$

The optimal loan supply of an individual bank is characterized by the fact that marginal revenue (i_C) equals marginal costs $(i_R + 2\beta Cr^j_{B/NB}/Y)$. The latter comprise the central bank's refinancing rate and the marginal costs stemming from the possible default of bad loans. Solving equation (3.25) for $(Cr^j_{B/NB})$ we obtain the optimal supply of loans:

$$Cr^j_{B/NB} = \frac{i_C - i_R}{2\beta} Y, \tag{3.26}$$

which indicates that a single bank grants loans only if there is a positive interest rate margin. Loan supply is c.p. increasing in the loan interest rate (i_C) and real income (Y) and decreases with regard to the central bank's refinancing rate (i_R) and the risk of default (β). We can see that the volume of deposits (D^j) and the deposit rate (i_D) have no impact on the optimal supply of loans. This is due to the assumption that from the perspective of an individual bank both are exogenously given. Nevertheless, we expect that because of arbitrage between the deposit market and the money market the deposit rate will converge to the central bank's refinancing rate. (Freixas and Rochet, 1997: 53).

The derivation of a single bank's optimal supply of loans (3.26) rests on the assumption that deposits are interest bearing and reserves yield a positive return, the central bank refinancing rate. Note, however, that (3.26) also holds in the alternative cases, with no interest payments on deposits and/or on reserves.

3.5.2.2. Credit supply of the banking system
The analysis of the behaviour of an individual bank implies the assumption of a single homogenous macroeconomic loan market. Since all banks are identical, the behaviour of a single bank corresponds in an equilibrium for the reason of symmetry with the behaviour of all other banks. The banking sector's aggregate supply of loans is the sum of the supplies of the individual

banks, that is, for a fixed n, the banking sector's aggregate loan supply is:

$$Cr_{B/NB} = \frac{i_C - i_R}{2\beta} nY,$$ (3.27)

or implicitly:

$$Cr^S = Cr^S\left(\overset{(+)}{i_C}, \overset{(-)}{i_R}, \overset{(-)}{\beta}, \overset{(+)}{Y} \right),^{10}$$ (3.28)

whereby all variables that do not carry the subscript (j) refer to the banking system. The slope of the credit supply curve in the interest rate/quantity diagram (Figure 3.1) is positive and amounts to $di_C/dCr^S = 2\beta/nY$. The refinancing rate is a parameter of location of this curve.

An important difference between the individual and the aggregate credit supply concerns the impact of loans on deposits. For an individual bank one can assume that its lending activity does not affect its level of deposits; for the banking system any increase in credits is identical with an increase in deposits. Or, as already mentioned, the credit supply is identical with the money supply.

3.5.3. *The 'macroeconomic' market for money (= market for the money stock M1)*

The credit ($\equiv$ money) supply function and the money ($\equiv$ credit) demand function are shown in Figure 3.1. This can be regarded as a representation

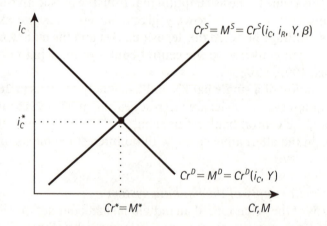

Figure 3.1. *The 'macroeconomic' money (= credit) market*

---

[10] Since we assume that the number of banks (n) is constant, it can dropped in the credit supply function.

of the macroeconomic money ($\equiv$ credit) market, as it depicts the amount of money ($\equiv$ credit) depending on the credit interest rate i_C. An equilibrium on this market is characterized by an intersection of the demand and supply curves.

$$Cr^D = Cr^S = Cr \qquad \text{or} \qquad M^D = M^S = M. \tag{3.29}$$

It is also important to remember that this is the market on which 'money', as defined by the money stock M1, is bought and sold. This is why we call it the 'macroeconomic' money market.

3.5.4. *The 'money market' (= market for the monetary base)*

The 'macroeconomic' market for money is completely different from the 'money market' which many people know from newspapers. The latter is a market for the monetary base that is traded among commercial banks or between the central bank and commercial banks. As we have seen in Section 3.2, the central bank is a monopolist supplier of the monetary base. Thus, while the commercial banks can trade the monetary base among themselves in order to redistribute a given amount of monetary base, an increase in the monetary base can be realized only by the central bank. This allows us to treat the commercial banks' aggregated demand curve for the monetary base as an inverse demand curve. Thus, the central bank can choose on that curve any combination of the i_R and B that it wishes (Figure 3.2). As an increase in the refinancing rate has a negative impact on

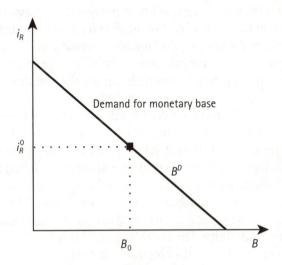

Figure 3.2. *The market for monetary base*

the credit supply, it is quite obvious that this demand curve is downward-sloping. A more rigorous explanation will be given in the next section.

If the central bank is targeting the refinancing rate (*interest rate targeting*), the monetary base is an endogenous variable that is determined by the behaviour of the commercial banks according to their demand function for the monetary base. On the other hand, if the central bank is targeting a certain level of the monetary base (*monetary base targeting*), the refinancing rate becomes endogenous. In a deterministic situation with a demand curve for central bank money, both targeting techniques lead to the same results as regards the quantity and price of the monetary base. The specific features of the two alternative approaches become evident only if we explicitly model the occurrence of shocks.

When in this model we describe the costs of making available central bank money as refinancing costs, we are thinking not only of the explicit funding rates that banks must pay the central bank for the use of standing facilities or repo instruments (Section 10.2.3), but also of the shadow price for central bank money, which banks have to pay when they sell interest-bearing state bonds or external claims to the central bank (in the context of outright open-market operations or foreign exchange market interventions), receiving in return non-interest-bearing central bank money (Section 10.3.1).

3.5.5. *The complete model*

From the separate descriptions given above of the markets for the money stock M1 and the monetary base, we can now put together a comprehensive money supply model, which explicitly combines the behaviour of the three agents involved in the money creation process (central bank, banks, and non-banks). The different stages of this process become clear if we incorporate Figure 3.1, Figure 3.2, and the multiplier relation in one graph (Figure 3.3).

The amount of total lending (which equals the volume of the money stock) together with the equilibrium credit interest rate are determined on the 'macroeconomic' money ($\equiv$ credit) market, represented in quadrant I. The supply of credit is directly influenced by the central bank, since the refinancing rate is a crucial cost factor in bank lending. Thus, the credit supply curve in Figure 3.3 applies only to a given refinancing rate (here: i_R^0). For the equilibrium money ($\equiv$ credit supply) (M_0), the banks require a quantity B_0 of the monetary base. This can be deduced by means of the *multiplier relation*, which is depicted in quadrant II. The slope of this curve must be smaller than unity. The combination i_R^0 and B_0 in quadrant III then represents a point on the banks' demand for central bank money. Thus, at a refinancing rate of i_R^0, the banks are willing to demand the amount B_0 of monetary base.

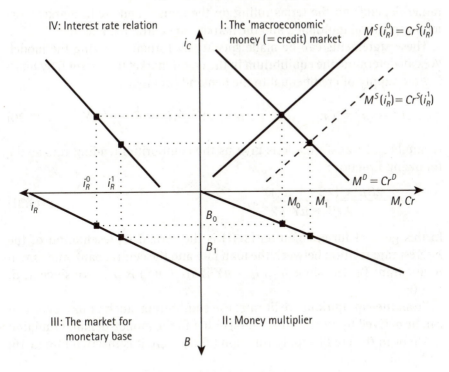

IV: Interest rate relation

I: The 'macroeconomic' money (= credit) market

$M^S(i_R^0) = Cr^S(i_R^0)$

$M^S(i_R^1) = Cr^S(i_R^1)$

$M^D = Cr^D$

III: The market for monetary base

II: Money multiplier

Figure 3.3. *The money supply process*

In order to determine the complete demand curve for the monetary base, it is necessary to analyse how the banks react to variations in the refinancing rate. A reduction in the rate for central bank money to i_R^1 enables the banks either to lend at lower rates of interest or to lend a greater amount at each respective interest rate, which is synonymous with a rightward shift in the credit supply curve. The refinancing rate operates, as shown in equation (3.25) as a 'shift parameter' of the credit supply curve. From the new equilibrium money supply (M_1), now located at a higher level, we can again use the multiplier to determine the required monetary base (B_1), which has increased because of the greater amount being lent. If we join up the two points in the third quadrant, we obtain a downward-sloping demand curve for central bank money, as was already assumed in Figure 3.2.

Joining up the two equilibrium points in quadrant IV gives a positive relationship between the refinancing and the lending rate. For each equilibrium interest rate on the credit market there is a precisely corresponding funding rate. Thus, the *interest rate relationship* can be interpreted similarly to the multiplier correlation between the money supply and the monetary base in the second quadrant, but the slope need not necessarily be greater than unity. As the system's 'residual', the slope of the interest rate relationship rather depends on the terms ruling on the money and credit markets, the money creation multiplier, and the market for central bank money.

These statements can be made specific by formally solving the model. We can determine the equilibrium in the credit market (quadrant I) by making the supply of credit equal to the demand for credit:

$$Cr^D = Cr^S = Cr, \quad \text{i.e.} \quad \mu + \gamma Y - \alpha i_c = \frac{i_C - i_R}{2\beta} nY. \tag{3.30}$$

A number of transformations give us the equilibrium lending rate as the following function:

$$i_c = \frac{2\beta\mu + (2\beta\gamma + ni_R)Y}{2\alpha\beta + nY}. \tag{3.31}$$

In this general form, equation (3.31) is the formal representation of the interest rate relation between the loan rate and the central bank rate drawn in quadrant IV. The slope $\partial i_c / \partial i_R = nY/(2\alpha\beta + nY)$ is positive since α, β, $n > 0$.

From the equilibrium credit rate, the equilibrium stock of money/credit can be derived by substituting (3.31) either in the money demand function (3.16) or in the credit supply function (3.27). Here it is inserted into (3.16) and yields:

$$M = Cr = \mu + \gamma Y - \alpha \frac{2\beta\mu + (2\beta\gamma + ni_R)Y}{2\alpha\beta + nY}$$

$$= \frac{nY}{2\alpha\beta + nY}(\mu + \gamma Y - \alpha i_R). \tag{3.32}$$

Together with the multiplier relation (equation (3.10)), this can finally be used to derive the *demand function for central bank money*:

$$B^D = \frac{1}{m}M = \frac{nY}{(2\alpha\beta + nY)m}(\mu + \gamma Y - \alpha i_R). \tag{3.33}$$

This shows a negative relationship between the costs of central bank credits and the quantity demanded. The slope of the curve is:

$$\frac{dB^D}{di_R} = -\frac{\alpha nY}{(2\alpha\beta + nY)m} \quad \text{with } \alpha, \beta, n, m, Y > 0. \tag{3.34}$$

The concrete values of the monetary base or the central bank rate depend on the operating procedure of the central bank. If it targets the monetary base (B^*), the refinancing rate is determined endogenously.

$$B = B^S = B^D = B^* \quad \text{(\textit{Monetary base targeting})} \tag{3.35}$$

If the central bank targets the refinancing rate (i_R^*) instead, the monetary base results from the demand function, which also depends on the conditions on the macroeconomic money and credit market.

$$B = B^S = B^D(i_R^*) = \frac{nY}{(2\alpha\beta + nY)m}(\mu + \gamma Y - \alpha i_R^*)$$

(Interest rate targeting) (3.36)

The results can be summarized as follows. The central bank can directly determine the conditions on the 'money market', i.e. the market for the monetary base or central bank money. The money stock is the result of an interdependent process of the operations of three agents: central bank, commercial banks, and non-banks. The decision of commercial banks to grant loans to non-banks and, simultaneously, to create money depends crucially on the refinancing rate for central bank credits. If all functions were stable and known to the central bank, it could perfectly control the money stock (or the credit interest rate i_C) with both operating procedures (monetary base or interest rate targeting).

Above all, through its refinancing rate the central bank can exert a very direct influence on the credit interest rate of commercial banks. A strong impact of the refinancing rate on the credit interest rate of commercial banks can be observed empirically for Germany (Figure 3.4), where the overnight rate (which is closely controlled by the refinancing rate; see Section 10.2.3.1) and the credit interest rate for large current account credits from banks to non-banks as well as the banks' rate for short-term time deposits move more or less in parallel. However, in periods of monetary restriction (with high nominal and real short-term rates) the lending rate is not immediately adjusted to the higher refinancing costs.

It is important to note that the model is based on a *short-term or medium-term* perspective. In the *very short run* the money stock has to be regarded as an almost exogenous variable, as commercial banks cannot reduce their credit portfolio overnight. Thus, their sensitivity to changes in the refinancing rate is relatively low, which means the demand curve for central bank money in the third quadrant becomes relatively steep (interest inelastic). Changes in the money stock in the very short-run would require extremely large changes in the central bank rate, which most central banks try to avoid. And even a huge increase in the refinancing rate would not guarantee that the money stock is sufficiently reduced. With a sluggish response from the non-bank sector in the very short-run, the banks could get into a situation where they are unable to fulfil their minimum reserve requirements.

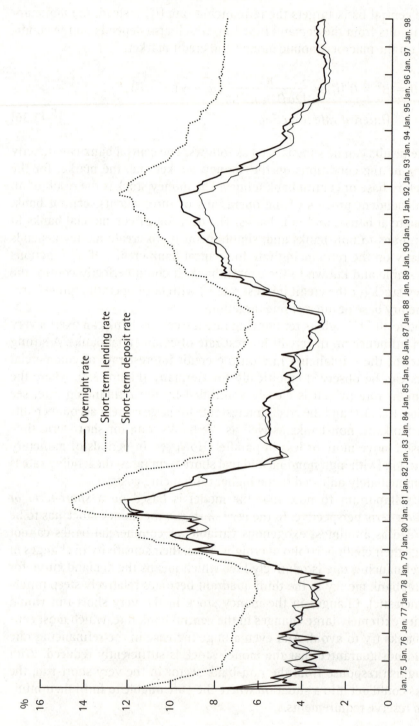

Figure 3.4. *Money market rates and short-term bank rates in Germany, 1970–1998 (monthly average)*

Source: German Bundesbank.

Appendix 3.1. A 'Poole analysis' for shocks

In a deterministic world, the model would imply that a central bank has complete control over the economy independently of the control procedure it uses. But in reality, all central banks show a clear preference for using a short-term interest rate as the operating target of monetary policy. This can be explained by introducing the more realistic case of stochastic shocks.

This kind of analysis goes back to Poole (1970), who evaluated the merits of interest rate targeting and monetary targeting at the level of the macroeconomic money market (see Appendix 4.1). Our model shows that the more relevant level for such an analysis is the market for central bank money, as this is the field that the central bank can directly control with its operating targets.[11] All stochastic shocks studied here are variations of additive error terms that have to be added to the money demand, credit supply, and money multiplier equation of the model. We abstract from shocks that affect the slopes of the curves on the macroeconomic money market.

Money demand shocks

In the case of an unstable money demand, the money demand curve shifts to M_1^D or M_2^D, as shown in Figure A3.1. In this analysis we assume that the currency ratio and the money multiplier remain unchanged, i.e. that changes in the two components (currency and deposits) work in the same direction. Shocks that affect the multiplier will be described later.

For a given money supply function, shifts of the money demand curve to M_1^D and M_2^D result in the new equilibrium money stocks M_1^* and M_2^* and the corresponding credit market rates i_C^1 and i_C^2. The variation in money demand also affects commercial banks' demand for the monetary base. If money demand increases to M_1^D, then, *ceteris paribus*, banks (at the initial central bank rate i_R^0) increase their demand for central bank credits to B_1. This is equivalent to an outward shift of the monetary base demand curve in quadrant III. Moreover, the 'interest rate curve' in quadrant IV is affected and shifts upwards.

The ultimate effects of money demand shocks depend crucially on the central bank's operating procedure. If it pursues a policy of *interest rate targeting*, i.e. fixes the level of the central bank rate (here, i_R^0), the money demand disturbances will be transformed into fluctuations of the monetary base. The central bank will offer exactly the amount of high-powered

---

[11] A similar analysis has been performed by McCallum (1989), with the difference that in his model the target interest rate is not the refinancing rate, but the lending rate on the macroeconomic money market.

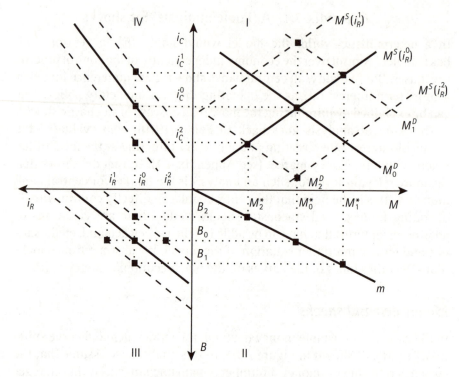

Figure A3.1. *Money demand shocks*

money that commercial banks need to realize the new equilibrium money stocks M_1^* and M_2^*. Thus, an unstable money demand results in money stock changes as well as in changes of the credit rate, although the central bank rate is kept constant.

If the central bank targets the *monetary base*, the monetary base (here, B_0) is always kept constant. In the case of money demand disturbances and resulting shifts in the commercial banks' base demand, the central bank rate has to be adjusted. For instance, if the demand for high-powered money increases, the refinancing rate must be raised to i_R^1, such that B_0 will be realized on the new base demand curve. The higher costs of refinancing reduce the credit supply and shift the banks' supply curve upwards just enough so that the equilibrium money stock is reached at the initial level M_0^*. Analogously, in the case of a reduction in the money demand, the central bank rate has to reduce interest rates to i_R^1 so that the credit supply increases.

Thus, if money demand shocks are prevalent in an economy, the policy implications are as follows.

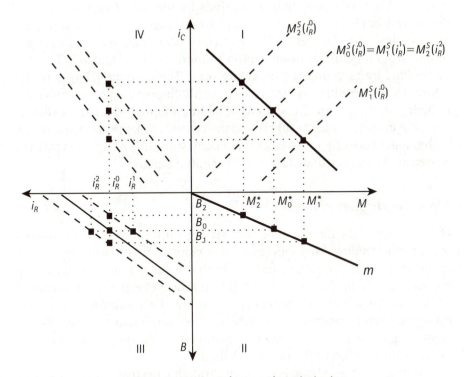

Figure A3.2. *Credit (= money) supply shocks*

1. If the central bank uses the money stock as its intermediate target, the monetary base must be its operating target, as the effects of the money demand shocks on the money stock can be completely compensated by fluctuations of the central bank rate.
2. If the central bank uses the commercial banks' lending rate (i_C) as its intermediate target, the central bank rate must be its operating target, as this policy leads to lower fluctuations of i_C.

However, a perfect control of i_C is not possible under either operating procedure.

Money (≡ credit) supply shocks

A second shock involves disturbances that shift the credit/money supply curve, as shown in Figure A3.2. Such shocks are related to the behaviour of commercial banks, concerning for example changes in technology. One can see that such disturbances lead to shifts of the demand for monetary base and the 'interest rate curve' for a given central bank rate.

Again, the final outcome is determined by the operating procedure of the central bank. In the case of interest rate targeting, the central bank has to allow for changes in the monetary base, and the credit/money supply instability fully transmits into variations of M (M_1^* and M_2^*). This can be avoided by targeting the monetary base. The ensuing changes in the central bank rate will cause shifts of the credit (money) supply curves back to their initial position. Thus, if credit/money supply shocks are predominant, the monetary base is superior to the central bank rate as an operating target, independently of whether the money stock (M) or the loan rate (i_c) is used as the intermediate target of the central bank.

Money multiplier shocks

Fluctuations of the money multiplier are the third source of disturbances in the present model. They can result from changes in the currency ratio or the reserve ratio. The latter can be excluded if the commercial banks are required to hold minimum reserves. The empirical evidence shows that the banks' working balances normally lie below the compulsory reserves. However, even in systems with extremely low minimum reserve requirements, e.g. in the United Kingdom, excess reserves do not play a major role in the determination of the money multiplier.

Assuming that the shock is initiated through a decrease in the currency ratio, the multiplier line in Figure A3.3 becomes flatter (m_1). The increase in the multiplier means that the banks need less base money for financing their loan supply. Accordingly, the shock in the multiplier has no direct effect on banks' supply of loans, but it affects the demand for the monetary base. The impact of this shock on the demand for central bank credits can be derived by partially differentiating (3.36) with respect to the multiplier:

$$\frac{dB^D}{dm} = - \frac{nY}{(2\alpha\beta + nY)m^2}(\mu + \gamma Y - \alpha i_R) < 0, \qquad (A3.1)$$

$$\text{if} \quad \mu + \gamma Y - \alpha i_R > 0, \qquad \text{or} \quad \mu + \gamma Y > \alpha i_R. \qquad (A3.2)$$

Condition (A3.1) indicates that an increase in the multiplier induces banks to reduce their demand for the monetary base. This condition always holds if the term in parentheses on the right side is positive (see (A3.2)), which should normally be the case since Y is rather large compared with the other variables.

More formally, the nonfinancial sector's demand for money (equation (3.16)) is positive if:

$$\mu + \gamma Y > \alpha i_c. \qquad (A3.3)$$

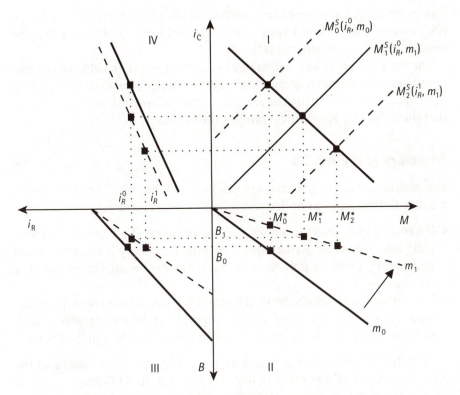

Figure A3.3. *Multiplier shocks*

Substituting the term on the right-hand side for the first term in (A3.2), we obtain:

$$\alpha i_C > \alpha i_R, \quad \text{or} \quad i_C > i_R. \tag{A3.4}$$

Thus, the demand for the monetary base is always decreasing with a rise in the money multiplier, if the loan interest rate exceeds the central bank's refinancing rate. Intuitively, this result is plausible, since banks grant loans to the nonfinancial private sector only in case of a positive interest rate margin. Otherwise, the banks' supply of loans and consequently the demand for the monetary base would be zero.

Again, the operating procedure of the central bank determines how the shock will be transmitted. If the central bank holds the interest rate constant, money multiplier shocks lead to fluctuations in the monetary base (B_1). However, there is no effect on the money stock (M_0^*) and the loan rate (i_C^0). In the case of base targeting there are disturbances on M and i_C. The stabilization of B_0 requires a reduction of the refinancing rate (i_R^1), which lowers the costs for central bank credits and therefore shifts the credit supply curve of commercial banks to the right, with the implication that the stock of money increases to (M_1^*).

The policy implications are straightforward. If multiplier shocks are predominant, the refinancing rate is always the superior operating target. In particular, with such disturbances, the control of interest rates guarantees that the monetary authorities stabilize the economy.

Summary of the results

The results of our analysis are summarized in Table A3.1. For both intermediate targets no clear policy recommendations can be given:

- If a central bank uses the *money stock* as its intermediate target, the monetary base should be used as operating target, but only if money demand and money/credit supply shocks are more important than multiplier shocks.
- If a central bank targets the *credit rate* (i_C), it should use the refinancing bank rate as its operating target, but only if multiplier and money demand shocks are more important than money/credit supply shocks.

In reality, a set of refinancing rates is used by all central banks as the operating target of monetary policy (Chapter 10). In addition, no central bank is targeting the money stock in a consequent way (Chapter 9). From the analysis in this Appendix, one can say that this approach is an optimum strategy if shocks of the money/credit supply are of secondary importance compared with shocks in the money demand and the multiplier.

Finally, our Poole-type analysis at the level of the market for central bank money shows that the shocks that have to be analysed are quite different from the shocks at the level of the macroeconomic money market (see the Appendix to Chapter 4).

Table A3.1. *Results of the shocks in the money supply process*[a]

| | Sources of shocks | | |
Intermediate target	Money demand	Credit (money) supply	Money multiplier
Credit rate of commercial banks (i_L)	IT > MT	BT > IT	IT > BT
Money stock (M)	BT > IT	BT > IT	IT > BT

[a] BT = monetary base targeting; IT = interest rate targeting.

4

Monetary Policy Transmission

What this chapter is about

- There is a broad consensus among economists that the uncertainty about the short-run effects of monetary policy is high, and above all that the lags of monetary impulses are long and variable. Thus, all attempts at fine-tuning the economy by means of monetary policy are problematic.
- The main lessons of the quantity theory are very clear: a direct access of the government to the central bank has been a main cause of high inflation. It also implies that monetary policy should adopt a medium-term orientation.
- The aggregate demand channel (or interest structure channel) shows how monetary policy affects the demand side of the economic process via changes in the structure of interest rates. As a Keynesian framework, it provides a theoretical basis for any activist monetary policy.
- The expectations channel (which is based on the Phillips curve) leads to two different implications. On the one hand, it shows that the inflation process is stabilized by price rigidities and adaptive expectations; it is, therefore, a theoretical framework for a medium-term oriented monetary policy that rests on the credibility and reputation of a central bank. On the other hand, this channel can be used for a policy of surprise inflation: monetary policy can create employment effects via the supply side, if actual inflation is higher than expected inflation.

4.1. INTRODUCTION

With the description of the money supply process, we have already made the first steps into the difficult area of monetary policy transmission. In this chapter the subsequent stages will be discussed. The main objective of all theories on monetary transmission is the analysis and description of the long, indirect, and complex relationship between monetary policy actions of a central bank (e.g. an increase in the repo rate) and their effect on the final targets of macroeconomic policy (e.g. the price level).

In addition, as each transmission theory is embedded in a more general theoretical framework, it also delineates the role that monetary policy can and should play in the macroeconomic process. It is obvious that such issues are the centrepiece of each monetary theory. They have been debated at length and quite controversially by all famous academics. For the purpose of this book, we can do no more than highlight the most important channels of transmission. Above all, we will not present a comprehensive introduction to macroeconomic theory: for this, readers should consult the standard macroeconomic textbooks.

It will become evident from what follows that among the vast number of theoretical studies there are comparatively few that really get to grips with the detailed structure of the transmission process. This is an illustration of the 'black box' approach (Mishkin 1995: 656), which pervades modern economics and which leads many economists to content themselves with a 'reduced-form evidence' of the direct relationship between the money supply and the ultimate targets. This approach was above all propagated by monetarists, and it replaced the more detailed 'structural models' that were preferred by Keynesian economists. For this reason it is not surprising that Otmar Issing, chief economist of the ECB, when contemplating the present state of knowledge regarding the transmission process, came to the following conclusion:

With regard to the operation of the single monetary policy, we can only safely say that we know, at best, the broad contours of the euro-area transmission mechanism right now. What we can say for sure, however, is that there is a considerable likelihood that the way monetary policy is transmitted may change making the task of the ECB even more difficult. (Issing 1999*d*: 2)[1]

The following analysis describes in some detail three key channels for the transmission of monetary impulses:

1. the channel of the *quantity theory*, which relies on a direct impact of the money supply on macroeconomic demand;
2. the *interest rate channel* (or aggregate demand channel), which relies on changes in the structure of interest rates and their impact on investment and other components of aggregate demand (the IS/LM model, Tobin's *q*, yield structure);
3. the *expectations channel*, which relies above all on the impact of inflation expectations in wage negotiations; this mechanism is usually presented in the form of a Phillips curve, which operates via the supply side of the economy.

We shall see that each of these three transmission mechanisms can be observed in practice. The predominant relationship at any given time will

---

[1] See also Mervyn King (1999: 12): 'in the short run, before policy has fully worked though, the effect of monetary policy on real variables is extremely uncertain because the transmission mechanism is neither sufficiently well understood nor sufficiently stable over time for policy easily to target real variables'.

depend on the specific institutional circumstances and the economic policy objectives of the central bank. For smaller open economies these three transmission channels have to be supplemented with an *exchange rate channel* that is based on the purchasing power parity theory. This channel will be examined in Chapter 12.

4.2. LIMITED KNOWLEDGE ABOUT THE TRANSMISSION PROCESS

The limited knowledge about the transmission process is due to several factors that are described in detail by Blinder (1998). First of all, there is *model uncertainty*; i.e., there is no consensus among economists about the 'right' model or on the 'right econometric' techniques. Second, the transmission of monetary impulses from the central bank to the real economy is associated with *long and variable lags*. A famous study on the monetary history of the United States in the period 1867–1960 produced by Milton Friedman and Anna Schwartz (1963) is particularly important in this connection. The authors' research focused on the question of whether it was possible to use monetary policy as a means of countercyclical economic management in the sense of Keynesian 'demand management'. They came to the conclusion that the main obstacles are the long and variable lags to which monetary policy is subject. They found that:

1. when the authorities are pursuing a restrictive monetary policy, there is an average lag of 12 months, with a fluctuation range of 6 to 29 months;
2. when they are pursuing an expansionary policy, there is an average lag of 18 months, with a fluctuation range of 4 to 22 months.

For the euro area, the European Central Bank (2000*b*: 56) states that 'an unexpected, temporary rise in the short-term interest rate of about 25 basis points tends to be followed by a temporary fall in output after two quarters. Prices are far more sluggish and only start to fall significantly below zero after six quarters. The confidence bands around these estimates are large, pointing to the considerable degree of uncertainty which surrounds estimates of the effects of monetary impulses.'

Because of the varying length of such lags (which are shown in greater detail in Box 4.1), there is a danger that monetary policy measures that were designed to be countercyclical end up being pro-cyclical in effect. It can happen, for example, that a monetary policy introduced during a recession in order to stimulate economic activity begins to take effect only when the economy is already in the recovery phase. A discretionary policy can therefore become an independent cause of macroeconomic instability.

> **Box 4.1.** *Lags in monetary policy*
>
> Disturbance (e.g. recession)
>
>
> **Inside lag (reaction of the central bank)**
>
> - *Information lag*   Availability of the data on the current cyclical situation is typically subject to a one to three month delay.
> - *Recognition lag*   A decline in GNP in one quarter, for example, does not necessarily indicate a recession: a longer observation period is needed.
> - *Decision lag*   In the case of monetary policy, this is very short. (In the euro area, the ECB Council meets every fortnight.)
>
>
> Monetary policy measure (change in the operating target)
>
>
> **Intermediate lag (reaction of the banks and financial markets)**
>
>
> Effect on bank lending, interest rates for enterprises and households, money supply
>
>
> **Outside lag (reaction of non–banks, investment decisions, savings decisions)**
>
>
> Effect on private expenditures, demand and supply for labour, and eventually on macro-economic targets
>
>
> Elimination of the disturbance

In sum, the uncertainty about the effects of monetary policy in the short run limits the ability to fine-tune economic processes by means of monetary policy. This caveat is of special importance in the context of very complex rules that have been developed for the strategy of inflation targeting (see Chapter 8). However, the good performance of many central banks, especially in the 1990s (see Chapter 9), and of the Federal Reserve in the 1950s and 1960s indicates that there must be some relatively simple and relatively robust rules of thumb. For instance, during the period 1952–67 the Federal Reserve achieved an average annual inflation rate of 1.4% with an average annual real GDP rate of 5.8%.

4.3. THE QUANTITY THEORY CHANNEL

Although quantity theory is usually used only as a framework for the above-mentioned black box approach, it is based on a simple but strictly defined conception of the transmission process. It is easy to identify what this is if we bear in mind that the quantity theory was developed in the period of metallic currency.[2] The characteristic feature of such a system is that money is available only in the form of gold and silver coins. This automatically dispenses with the whole problem of the money supply process in a two-tier banking system, as described in the previous chapter. Under such conditions an expansion in the money supply can come about only as a result of mining gold and silver, which is minted in the form of coins.

4.3.1. *Gold and silver currency*

Under a metallic standard, if rich new sources of gold and silver are found, as happened for example in the sixteenth century following the discovery of America, this has a direct effect on the money supply, as it has always been possible to mint gold and silver coins for a small fee (known as *seigniorage*—see Chapter 11). Since gold and silver coins are generally accepted as means of payment, the holders of coins can now directly increase demand. The essential macroeconomic relationship for a transmission process according to the principles of quantity theory is a functional relationship of the type

$$PY^D = f(M). \tag{4.1}$$

Under such conditions, nominal macroeconomic demand is determined exclusively by the money supply. On the basis of the quantity equation (see Section 2.2),

$$M\bar{V} = PY, \tag{4.2}$$

equation (4.1) can be formulated as

$$Y^D = \frac{M}{P}\bar{V}. \tag{4.3}$$

For a given money supply, i.e.

$$M^S = M_0 = M^D, \tag{4.4}$$

we can then represent equation (4.3) as the macroeconomic demand curve:

$$Y^D = \frac{M_0}{P}\bar{V}. \tag{4.5}$$

---

[2] Its discovery is assigned to the year 1568, when the relationship was first formulated by Jean Bodin (1530–96). For more details, see Schumpeter (1954: 311).

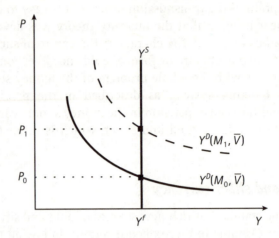

Figure 4.1. *Aggregate demand and supply under the gold standard*

The proportional relationship that, according to quantity theory, exists between changes in the money supply and the price level can be demonstrated if we combine this demand hyperbola with a classic macroeconomic supply curve (see Figure 4.1). Thus, for a given money supply M_0, there exists a price level P_0 at which macroeconomic demand corresponds to full employment output Y^f. An expansion in the money supply to M_1 will then result in an upward shift in the demand hyperbola and hence in a rise in the price level from P_0 to P_1.

Quantity theory is thus based on the very simple transmission relationship which asserts that an increase in the money supply will lead directly to an increase in macroeconomic demand. It becomes clear from this that quantity theory as a description of the transmission mechanism offers an adequate picture of reality only where macroeconomic demand is so markedly determined by changes in the money supply that other determinants, such as real income or the interest rate level, can be ignored. During periods when sizeable new deposits of gold were discovered, this is no doubt a very accurate description of reality.

4.3.2. *Central bank financed state expenditure*

Such a direct channel of transmission on the demand side can also exist under a formal paper currency system. This is to be found whenever the State is able to finance its expenditure mainly by borrowing from the central bank. From equation (3.1), we can see that in such circumstances an increase in the monetary base and hence in the money supply will be a

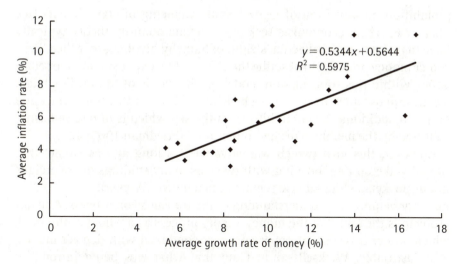

Figure 4.2. *Monetary growth and inflation in industrial countries, 1960–1999*
Source: Own calculations based on data from IMF, *International Financial Statistics.*

direct concomitant of additional state expenditure. This relationship has also been known about for a long time.[3]

All periods of major inflation can be attributed to central bank financed state expenditure, especially for the purposes of financing the conduct of a war. Since there is a very close relationship here between macroeconomic demand and the money supply, it is not surprising that we can find many empirical examples of the relationship between money supply growth and inflation postulated by quantity theory. None the less, Figure 4.2 and calculations by Gerlach (1995) show that the evidence for the quantity equation is less clear if we also consider countries with relatively low inflation rates.[4]

4.3.3. *'Helicopter money'*

The transmission channel of the quantity theory becomes problematical under the institutional conditions that prevail in most industrial countries today, i.e. a formal paper currency system in which there is also a statutory

---

[3] 'The issues of a Government paper, even when not permanent, will raise prices; because Governments usually issue their paper in purchases for consumption' (Mill 1844: 589).

[4] 'This paper has shown that cross-sectional regressions of long-run averages of inflation on money and real income growth typically display substantial parameter instability. In particular, the finding of a one-to-one relationship between money growth and inflation is sensitive to the inclusion of data from a few countries with very high inflation rates. While this lack of stability may not be surprising, it has apparently never been demonstrated in the literature before' (Gerlach 1995: 19).

prohibition on any form of central bank financing of state deficits (see Chapter 6). Then, economists seeking to defend quantity theory typically have to resort to an intellectual sleight of hand by invoking so-called 'helicopter money' in order to describe the effects of an expansionary monetary policy within this transmission model. In the words of Milton Friedman, 'Let us suppose now that one day a helicopter flies over this community and drops an additional $1000 in bills from the sky which is of course hastily collected by the members of this community' (Friedman 1969: 4).

However, this idea (which was advanced as long ago as Hume) that 'we all wake up one morning with twice as many shillings or sovereigns in our pockets, while all else remains unchanged' (Wicksell 1922: 182) is not very helpful to an understanding of the transmission process. A major problem is the fact that the money supply process as a whole is obscured, which, under a system of paper currency combined with deposit money, is unjustifiable. Wicksell pointed out that what was being introduced in order to explain reality was not a 'simplification of that reality' but 'a purely paradoxical relationship which in the nature of things can never and will never occur...' (1922: 182).

The concept of helicopter money also features in a number of more recent theoretical approaches. For example, 'overlapping-generations' models assume that each individual, when born, receives a transfer of money by the state (Blanchard and Fischer 1989: 169). Since such models completely ignore the money creation process,[5] they are hardly suitable for describing monetary transmission processes in highly developed industrial countries.[6]

Thus, the problem with using the quantity theory under present conditions is that its central tenets concerning transmission no longer correspond to the actual circumstances on the money and financial markets. It is not surprising, therefore, that its transmission processes can be presented only in the form of a black box.

4.3.4. *Implications for monetary policy*

In spite of its simplifications, the quantity theory plays an important role in macroeconomic policy. Its main fields of application are

---

[5] See also Hoover (1995: 30): 'The second reason that these models miss the causal efficacy of interest rates is that there is no mechanism for interest rates to be determined other than through the shadow prices associated with consumption, leisure and saving choices. The financial sectors in these models are simply not rich enough. Partly this is a result of the models assuming representative agents. Robinson Crusoe does not need a financial system.'

[6] In the words of Meltzer (1995: 101): 'Overlapping-generations models of money...have not proved fruitful. These models have not produced either an accepted foundation for macro theory or a verified theory of aggregate output, prices and interest rates.'

1. medium-term oriented monetary policy strategies, and
2. macroeconomic stabilization programmes in countries with high inflation.

Because of its neoclassical background, the quantity theory is not able to deal with macroeconomic demand and supply shocks. Thus, it can describe and prescribe only a medium-term oriented framework for a monetary policy that maintains a neutral policy stance. The most prominent strategy that is derived from the quantity theory is the strategy of monetary targeting (see Chapter 9). Also, as the quantity theory is based on the assumption of the *neutrality* of money, it cannot describe the costs that are associated with high inflation. We shall discuss these costs in Chapter 5.

As already mentioned, the quantity theory offers a very good explanation of inflation processes if a government finances its expenditures mainly with credits from the central bank. If such processes are stopped, the quantity theory can be used to develop a framework for macroeconomic stabilization by calculating the maximum amount of the deficit that is compatible with a return to price stability. For this purpose, the quantity theory has to be formulated in terms of growth rates:

$$\hat{M}^* = \hat{Y} + \pi^* - \hat{V}. \tag{4.6}$$

With the forecast values for $\hat{Y}$ and $\hat{V}$ and the targeted inflation rate, a target growth rate for the money stock $\hat{M}^*$ can be calculated.

With the money multiplier, the target growth rate of the money stock can be translated in a target growth rate for the monetary base:

$$\hat{M}^* = \hat{B}^* + \hat{m}. \tag{4.7}$$

For a constant multiplier, the growth rate of the money stock and the monetary base are identical. As

$$\hat{B}^* = \frac{\Delta B^*}{B}, \tag{4.8}$$

it is possible to calculate the absolute change of the monetary base (ΔB^*) that is compatible with a return to price stability. The balance sheet identity (equation (3.4)) shows that this absolute change is determined as follows:

$$\Delta B = \Delta NP_{CB/F} + \Delta NP_{CB/G} + \Delta Cr_{CB/B} - \Delta BAL_{CB/OAL}. \tag{4.9}$$

Thus, using estimates for $\Delta NP_{CB/F}$, $\Delta Cr_{CB/B}$, and $\Delta BAL_{CB/OAL}$, the maximum increase of the central bank financed government deficit ($\Delta NP_{CB/G}$) can be calculated.

This framework has been used as the basis for IMF stabilization programmes in many high-inflation countries. It is clear that many arbitrary assumptions have to be made, above all concerning the velocity of money and the net foreign assets of a central bank. Nevertheless, for a successful disinflation process, a strict limitation of the central bank financed deficit is unavoidable. Otherwise, the central bank is not able to control its operating targets.

The usefulness of the quantity theory of money in medium-term oriented monetary policy strategies will be discussed in detail in Chapters 9 and 10.

4.4. INTEREST RATE CHANNELS

Since the processes of the quantity theory apply only under very specific conditions, other models are required for a standard description of monetary policy. The workhorse for almost all textbooks, and also for many recent theoretical studies (Svensson and Woodford 2000; Walsh 1998), incorporates those theories that explain monetary transmission with changes in interest rates (nominal or real) or with changes in interest rate structures (Taylor 1995). In principle, this general approach is consistent with the conclusion of the influential Radcliffe Report, published in 1959, which recommended that those deciding monetary policy should regard 'the structure of interest rates rather than some notion of the "supply of money" as the centre-piece of monetary action'.[7] More than thirty-five years later, Smets, surveying models from twelve countries, came to the following conclusion:

In most of the central banks' macroeconometric models the transmission process of monetary policy is modelled as an interest rate transmission process. The central bank sets the short-term interest rate, which influences interest rates over whole maturity spectrum, other assets prices, and the exchange rate. These changes in financial variables then affect output and prices through the different spending components. The role of money is in most cases a passive one, in the sense that money is demand determined. (Smets 1995: 226)

The important role of the interest rate in transmission process can also be illustrated with Figure 4.3. This shows that in Germany all post-war recessions were preceded by a major increase in the real short-term interest rate.

---

[7] Radcliffe Report (1959: sect. 397). The Report was produced by a UK Committee of Experts appointed in 1957 and had an important influence on the monetary debate in the 1960s.

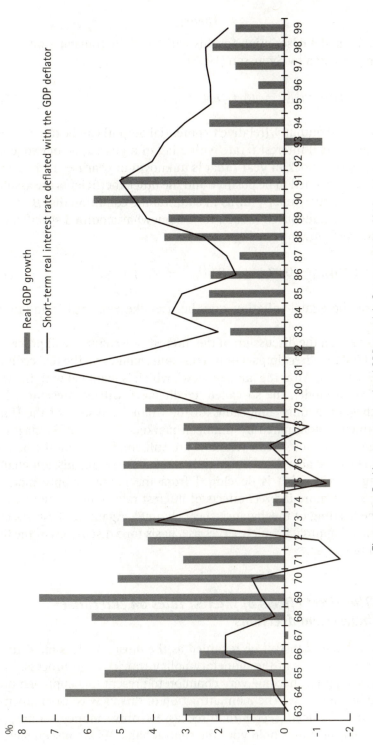

Figure 4.3. *Real interest rates and real GDP growth in Germany, 1963–1999*
Source: Own calculations based on data from IMF, *International Financial Statistics.*

A simple model description for this variant of the transmission process has been presented by Svensson (1997):

$$y_{t+1} = \beta_1 y_t - \beta_2(i_t - \pi_t) + \beta_3 x_t + \eta_{t+1}, \tag{4.10}$$

where real (log) output y_t (relative to potential output) can be targeted with a short-term (real) interest i_t rate with a lag of a year; x_t is an exogenous variable; η_t is a shock in year t that is unknown in year $t-1$; the coefficients β_2 are assumed to be positive and the other coefficients are assumed to be non-negative; and β_1 fulfils in addition the condition that $\beta_1 < 1$. In a recent paper Rudebusch (2000), for a somewhat modified specification, arrives at the following result:

$$y_t = 1.15 y_{t-1} - 0.27 y_{t-2} - 0.9(i_{t-1} - \pi_{t-1}^e) + \eta_t. \tag{4.11}$$

Instead of the actual inflation rate, he uses the expected inflation rate (π_{t-1}^e).

In this section the discussion of the interest rate channel will proceed as follows. First the *direct* impact of interest rate changes on the real economy will be discussed. After the 'money view', which is identical with the well-known IS/LM model, the so-called 'credit view' will be presented. Both approaches are mainly applicable for the financial system of the United States which is dominated by financial markets. This is different for the euro area where most credit relations are still conducted via the banking system. Thus, we also discuss a mainly bank-based transmission channel ('banking view') which is developed from the money supply model of Chapter 3. The more *indirect* effects of interest rate changes are discussed under the heading of the 'balance sheet channel'. Again, we first present a more general approach which serves as a basis for a discussion of the literature on this topic.

4.4.1. *The direct effects of interest rates on enterprise investment decisions*

The IS/LM model can still be regarded as the most widely-shared framework for an analysis of the monetary policy transmission process. In the last few years it has become very common to present this approach under the label 'money view'. The main attraction of this view is its simplicity. It reduces the *financial sector* to three assets only: money, bonds, and reserves that the banks hold with the central bank. As a consequence, the role of banks is extremely limited: 'On the asset side of their balance sheets, banks do nothing unique—like the household sector, they too invest in bonds' (Kashyap 1997: 43).

As money is regarded as non-interest bearing and the central bank's refinancing rate (together with a short-term money market rate) is neglected, the only financial interest rate is the rate for bonds. Normally whether these bonds are issued by the private or the government sector is not discussed. Because of the assumption of sticky prices, changes in nominal interest rates are identical with real interest rates.

The upward slope of the LM curve is derived under the assumption that the central bank can perfectly control the money base via the simple money multiplier (see Section 3.4). This also implies a perfect control over the money stock. If the money stock is given, an increase in real income, which requires a higher amount of transaction balances, is only possible if the bonds rate increases since this reduces the speculative demand for money or the opportunity costs of holding money (see Section 2.3).

This simplified financial sector is contrasted with the *real sector* of the economy where the demand for investments depends on the relation between:

- the real rate of return of these investments; Keynes (1936) refers to this as the 'marginal efficiency of capital'; Wicksell (1922) speaks of the 'natural rate of interest'; and
- the bonds rate which has to be regarded as a lending rate (if the bonds are issued by the private sector) or as rate reflecting the opportunity costs of investments (if the bonds are issued by the government); Wicksell (1922) refers to this as the 'money rate of interest'.

In the IS/LM model the relation between these two interest rates allows one to derive the IS curve. For a given marginal efficiency of capital, the lower the (real) lending rate, the greater the number of profitable investment projects. This results in a downward-sloping path of the IS curve. The logic of this interest rate relation also underlies the concept of Tobin's q (see Box 4.2).

The main message of the IS/LM model is very clear. If an economy is confronted with a negative demand shock, the interest rate mechanism is by itself not able to lead back to a full-employment equilibrium. Figure 4.4. shows that after a shift of the IS curve from IS to IS', the interest rate declines from i^* to i', which leads to an equilibrium output level of Y', which is below the full-employment level Y^*. This lack of a self-stabilizing macroeconomic mechanism constitutes the main difference between Keynesian economics and the neoclassical approach of the Quantity Theory.

Box 4.2. *Tobin's q*

The q relationship developed by James Tobin (1969) is still regarded as an important explanatory approach for the monetary transmission process. This magnitude is defined as follows:

$$q - Relation = \frac{Market\ value\ of\ an\ enterprise}{Replacement\ value\ of\ an\ enterprise}. \tag{B4.1}$$

It is now relatively easy to show that this is basically only a different formulation of the relationship between the natural and money rates of interest. It is to be assumed that the market value (MV) of the enterprise is calculated in accordance with the capitalized earnings value method:

$$MV = \sum_{t=1}^{n} (r_t - e_t) \frac{1}{(1 + i)^t}. \tag{B4.2}$$

We thus calculate the expected surpluses of receipts (r_t) over expenditure (e_t) and discount these with the market interest rate, which corresponds to the money rate of interest. The replacement costs constitute the denominator of the q relationship. These can now be interpreted as the initial expenditure (E_0) on an investment programme that produces the surpluses of receipts over expenditure in equation (B4.2).

This now enables us to calculate an internal rate of return (i_N):

$$0 = -E_0 + \sum_{t=1}^{n} (r_t - e_t) \frac{1}{(1 + i_N)^t}. \tag{B4.3}$$

If this is interpreted as the natural rate of interest, it will be seen that in the last analysis the q relationship represents the relationship between the money and natural rates of interest. Thus, for an infinite time horizon and constant surpluses of receipts over expenditure, the following holds true:

$$q = \frac{MV}{E_0} = \frac{\sum_{t=1}^{n} (r_t - e_t)[1/(1 + i)^t]}{\sum_{t=1}^{n} (r_t - e_t)[1/(1 + i_N)^t]}, \tag{B4.4}$$

or, for $n \rightarrow \infty$,

$$q = \frac{i_N}{i} \tag{B4.5}$$

The advantage of Tobin's formulation is that the market values of the enterprises can be empirically determined by the share prices.

Accordingly, the IS/LM model requires an activist role of monetary policy: only if the central bank increases the monetary base and hence the money stock which leads a downward shift in the LM curve from LM to LM' and a further reduction of the interest rate from i' to i'', a return to the full-employment equilibrium will be possible.

While the IS/LM model is very useful for an analysis of such basic issues, it is certainly not suitable for a more detailed analysis of the financial

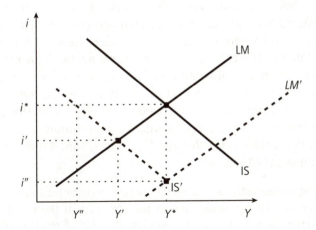

Figure 4.4. *Demand shocks in the IS/LM model*

dimensions of the money transmission process. As Dale and Haldane (1993) have shown, the IS/LM approach suffers from two black boxes. First, it simplifies the interaction between monetary authorities and the banking system by assuming that the central bank uses the monetary base as its operating target. Until today, this simplification has shaped the thinking about the transmission process: 'All theories of how interest rate changes affect the real economy share a common starting point. A monetary policy action begins with a change in the level of *bank reserves*.' (Cecchetti 2000: 174).

But in spite of its popularity in economic theory, monetary base targeting plays no role in actual monetary policy (Chapter 10). Thus, already the first step of most theoretical models leads in the wrong direction. In order to provide a more realistic approach, we have developed a price-theoretic money supply model in Chapter 3 which is able to analyse the effects of changes in the refinancing rates of central banks.

The second black box of the IS/LM model (or the money view) concerns the endogenous interaction between banks and the non-bank sector. This neglect of the credit business of the banking system is especially problematic in the case of the euro area where corporate bonds do not play a decisive role in enterprise finance. Presently the amount of bank credits to private customers is about fifteen times higher than the amount of bonds issued by the private sector. This is completely different in the United States where the outstanding amount of corporate bonds and commercial paper is 1.6 times higher than the amount of bank loans to enterprises. In other words, the ideal transmission model for the United States is a capital-market based model while for the euro area it must be a bank-based model.

Given these shortcomings of the 'money view' it is not surprising that in the late 1980s a so-called '*credit view*' or '*lending view*' was developed. It is important to note that the lending view does not hinge critically on whether or not there is quantity rationing on the loan market (Kashyap 1997: 43). The main contribution of this view is the incorporation of bank loans into the IS/LM model. Thus, it maintains the basic design of the money view which is characterized by a neglect of the central bank's refinancing rate and by a predominance of corporate bonds for enterprise finance. For instance, Gertler and Gilchrist (1995: 45) describe this transmission process as follows:

'According to the credit view, monetary policy works at least in part by altering the flow of credit. An important step in the argument is the contention that legal reserve requirements on deposits provide the Federal reserve with considerable direct leverage over the quantity of funds that banks may obtain. Assuming that prices are temporarily sticky, an open market sale reduces the real quantity of deposits banks can issue. This in turn induces banks to contract lending, which ultimately constrains the spending of borrowers who rely primarily on bank credit.'

Due to the ancillary role of bank loans in this approach most authors assume that the effect of monetary policy on banks' loan supply schedules 'is on top of any increase in the interest rate on open-market securities such as Treasury bills' (Kashyap and Stein 2000: 407). 'In a nutshell, the credit view asserts that in addition to affecting short-term interest rates, monetary policy affects aggregate demand by affecting the availability or terms of new bank loans.' (Bernanke 1993: 55-7). As empirical tests have found no clear evidence of this prediction (Oliner and Rudebusch 1996*a* and 1996*b*), many authors have come to the conclusion that a credit (or bank lending) channel should be dismissed altogether or that its importance has diminished over time (Bernanke and Gertler 1995: 42).

Compared with the IS/LM model the advantages of this approach are rather limited. Especially for the euro area it makes little sense to use a model which assumes that bonds are the main financing instrument of enterprises. A more general flaw is the lack of a price-theoretic underpinning of the money supply, i.e. the complete neglect of the central bank's refinancing rate in the transmission process.

Both problems can be solved if one uses the money supply model presented in Chapter 3 which can be used to derive a '*banking view*' for the discussion of the effects of interest rate changes on aggregate demand. For that purpose an LM-curve has to be derived from the model (Figure 4.5).

As the money demand depends on real income, an increase in real income shifts the money demand curve to the right. This leads to a new equilibrium

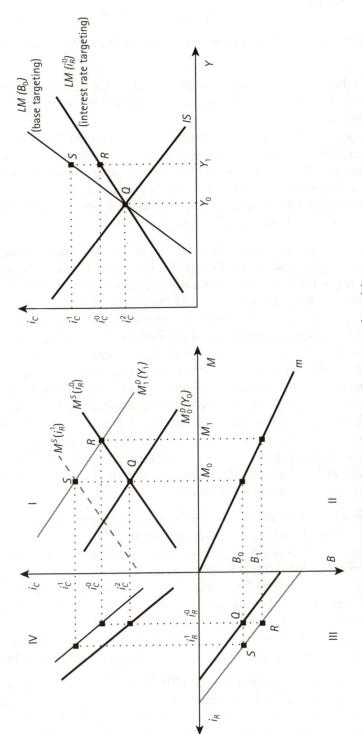

Figure 4.5. *The LM-curve in the price-theoretic money supply model*

Note: For ease of exposition the effects of real income on banks' aggregate loan supply are assumed to be zero.

on the credit market which depends on the operating target of the central bank.

- If central bank targets the *money market rate* (i_R), the new equilibrium is the intersection between the unchanged money/credit-supply curve and the shifted money demand curve in point R.
- If the central bank targets the *monetary base*, the equilibrium money stock must remain constant. This requires an increase in the refinancing rate from i_R^0 to i_R^1 which shifts the money/credit-supply curve to the left so that it intersects with the shifted money demand curve in point S. Under this targeting option the increase in the loan rate (i_c) is higher than under interest rate targeting.

For both cases the equilibrium combinations of Y and i_c can be shown in i_c/Y-diagram which leads an analogue to the LM-curve, i.e. the loci of combinations of i_c and Y where the macroeconomic money market is balanced. In the same way as in the traditional LM-curve the central bank can shift this curve with its operating targets. An increase in the refinancing rate (which is identical with a reduction of the monetary base) shifts the credit supply curve and the LM-curve to the right (Figure 4.6).

This LM-curve which has been derived from our price-theoretic model for the money supply can now be combined with a traditional IS-curve. The only modification is that the investment demand depends now on the interest rate for bank loans. This framework provides a simple description of the effects of a central bank's interest rate policy on the real sector of the economy. It is important to note that monetary policy always affects an interest rate and a money/credit aggregate simultaneously and that its effects take place on two different levels:

- At the level of the *market for the monetary base* (or reserves) monetary policy changes the level of reserves and the central bank's refinancing rate. The latter also has a very direct effect on the money market rates which are targeted with that rate (see Chapter 10).
- At the level of the *market for credit* (or the 'macroeconomic money market') the loan rate changes together with the equilibrium amount of loans which in our model is identical with the money stock. Thus, by increasing or lowering its refinancing rate, the central bank can shift the LM-curve which exerts a positive or a negative effect on aggregate demand.

From the logic of our model it makes no difference whether a bank provides a credit in a securitized form (corporate bond) or a non-securitized form (loan). What matters is the fact that in both cases the bank will incur a need for central bank reserves. This can be due to payments that the credit

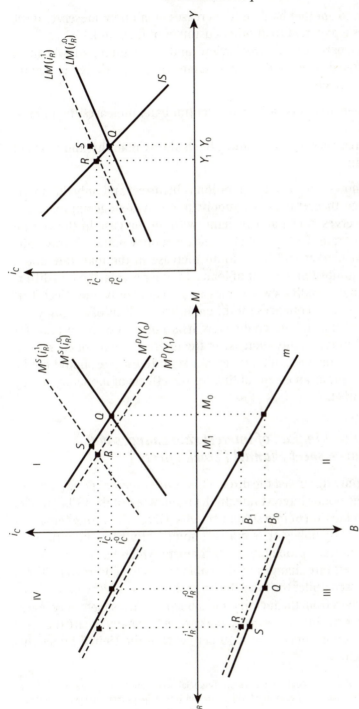

Figure 4.6. *Restrictive monetary policy in the 'banking view'*

Note: The central bank raises the short–term interest rate from i_R^0 to i_R^1. The leads from point Q to point S in the demand curve for monetary base (quadrant III). It shifts the credit supply curve (quadrant I) to the left. In the IS/LM–diagram the real income Y_0 now requires a higher interest rate which implies an upward shift of the LM–curve. This shifts the money demand curve (quadrant III) to the left so that the new equilibrium is in point R with a lower real income. It shows that the new equilibrium on the macroeconomic money market is also in R. Finally, the shift in the money demand has an effect on the demand for monetary base so that this curve (quadrant I) shifts upwards.

customer makes to another bank or to increases in minimum reserves if the customer makes a payment to another customer of that bank.

The difference between the 'credit view' and our 'banking view' can be easily demonstrated. The credit view assumes that a restrictive monetary has two distinct effects:

- With its open-market operations the central bank increases the interest rate for bonds.
- By reducing reserves it *additionally* affects the availability and terms of new bank loans.

Our approach shows that such a separation is incorrect and only due to the neglect of a price-theoretic money supply. In our two-stage approach the reduction of reserves goes hand-in-hand with an increase in the central bank refinancing rate. This initial effect at the money market is transmitted to the credit market and leads to an increase in the loan rate and a decline in the equilibrium amount of loans. In other words, the two different effects which the credit view assumes are in reality only one effect. This also has important consequences for the empirical analysis of a credit view. For our interpretation of the credit view it is not necessary to look for effects that are 'on top of any increase in the interest rate on open-market securities'. Such an increase of a money market interest rate should not be seen in isolation but as an essential link for the effects of monetary policy on the credit market.

4.4.2. *The indirect impact of interest rate changes via the balance sheet channel ('stock effects')*

So far we have only discussed the direct effects of monetary policy actions on the loan or the bonds interest rate. In the framework of the IS/LM model their effect is a reduction of investment activity. Given the strong impact of a restrictive monetary policy on overall economic activity the literature has identified an important propagation mechanism which basically rests on the effect of interest rate changes on the balance sheets of borrowers. These effects are discussed under the label 'balance sheet effect'.[8] The importance of this effect derives from the fact that most business firms have very leveraged balance sheets. This is especially the case in Germany where the ratio of own funds to total funds is only 19 per cent; in the United States this ratio is 50 per cent.

---

[8] Bernanke *et al.* (1994) describe this effect as the 'financial accelerator', since it means that relatively small interest rate changes are associated with marked effects on investment and macroeconomic activity.

The theoretical basis of the balance sheet effect is the widely-known leverage effect. Thus, with a given expected return on assets (r_A) and a given capital structure (debt to equity; D/E), the expected return on equity (r_E) depends on the expected return on debt (r_D). This relation can be derived as follows. The expected return on assets can be regarded as the weighted average of the expected return on equity and the return on debt:

$$r_A = r_D \frac{D}{(D + E)} + r_E \frac{E}{(D + E)}. \tag{4.12}$$

This can be rearranged to

$$r_E = r_A + (r_A - r_D)\frac{D}{E}. \tag{4.13}$$

Thus, monetary policy can influence the return on equity as long as it can influence the return on debt. As central bank interest rates affect above all short-term interest rates (see Chapter 10), the impact of central bank induced interest rate changes on r_E is higher,

1. the more short-term the financial structure of enterprises, and
2. the higher the leverage (D/E) of enterprises.

For the United States Bernanke and Gertler (1995: 36–37) have shown that increases in the federal funds rate which is controlled by the Federal Reserve (see Section 10.5) translate almost immediately into increases in the 'coverage ratio' (the ratio of interest payments by nonfinancial corporations to the sum of interest rates and profits) which ultimately leads to weaker balance sheet positions. In addition, they show that 'something over 40 per cent of the short-run decline in corporate profits is the result of higher interest payments.' (Bernanke and Gertler 1995: 38). The same applies to Germany. Figure 4.7 shows that the net interest payments (interest paid minus interest received) are very much determined by the money market rate that was directly controlled by the Bundesbank (see Section 10.2.3). And in Figure 4.8 one can see that changes in net interest payments have a direct impact on the profits of enterprises. This is confirmed by the series of 'profits plus net interest payments', which is much more stable than actual profits. In other words, the interest rate policy of a central bank can directly affect enterprise profitability.

Besides this direct impact a restrictive monetary policy has also some more indirect effects on firms' balance sheets. Above all, high interest rates can lead to a decline in asset prices which reduces a firm's collateral. In addition, they can affect a firm's downstream customers so that its expected return on assets declines which also reduces its return on equity.

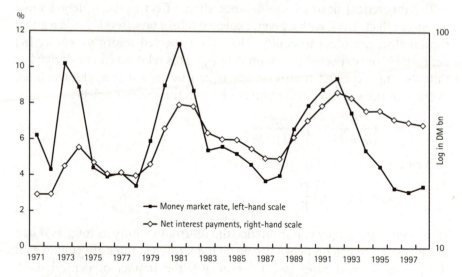

Figure 4.7. *Money market rates and net interest payments in Germany, 1971–1998*
Source: Own calculations based on data from Deutsche Bundesbank.

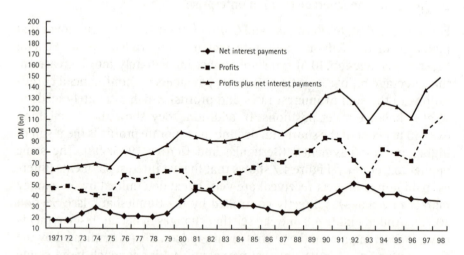

Figure 4.8. *Profits and net interest payments of German enterprises, 1971–1998*
Source: Own calculations based on data from Deutsche Bundesbank.

Due to information asymmetries, moral hazard problems, as well as bankruptcy laws the balance sheet plays an important role for a firm's ability to obtain external finance (Cecchetti 1995: 83–4). Thus, a restrictive monetary policy leads to an increase in the cost of external funds compared with the costs of internal funds. It can also lead to a complete credit rationing (Stiglitz and Weiss 1981).

As far as the empirical analysis of this effect is concerned it is important to note that it affects all enterprises as long as they rely on external funds with interest rates that can at least partially be adjusted according to short-term interest rates. In other words, the balance sheet channel effect is of a very general nature. In the literature it is often assumed that small enterprises are more affected by the balance sheet channel than large enterprises. This can be due to the fact that small enterprises are higher leveraged than large enterprises. Deutsche Bundesbank (1999c) shows that this is the case in the Germany but not in France. In addition, since large enterprises are normally obliged to publish very detailed information the problem of asymmetric information can also be higher for small enterprises. For the United States Oliner and Rudebusch (1996a and 1996b) show that a broad credit channel exists and that it operates through small firms.

4.4.4. *Monetary policy implications of the interest rate channel*

There is no doubt that the interest rate channel plays a key role in the transmission of monetary impulses to the real economy. For instance, in the period 1990–98 an average short-term real interest rate of 4.5% in the euro area and of 2.3% in the United States (see Table 8.3) can be regarded as an important macroeconomic explanation for the much better performance of GDP and employment in the United States. The importance of the interest rate channel is also supported by the widespread use and the robustness of the Taylor rule (see Section 8.5) as an important rule for monetary policy.

Thus, while it is virtually uncontested that the central bank of a major country is in principle able to trigger expansionary and restrictive effects in the real economy by varying its funding rates, it is difficult to explain how with this channel a central bank might target a relatively stable and low inflation rate over a longer time period.

In the first place, the channels of transmission represented in the money supply model in conjunction with the IS/LM–AS/AD model are extremely complex, since they cover all the relevant markets in the economy. Therefore, in order to be able to arrive at a precise inflation rate using the instruments at its disposal, a central bank would need to know the precise nature of all the behaviour functions and the relevant lag structures contained in these models. And even if this were possible, it would still have to take account of the possible occurrence of shocks that cannot be forecasted.

Second, the relationships described in these models are all comparative-static in nature.[9] Thus, while they can provide useful insights for a monetary policy that is confronted with demand or supply shocks, for an analysis of inflation, which is a dynamic process, their usefulness is rather limited.

Under these conditions, it is difficult to imagine that a central bank could rely on the interest rate channel only in order to achieve a low inflation rate year by year. It was no doubt this difficulty that Milton Friedman essentially had in mind when he referred to the 'long and variable lags' affecting monetary policy and concluded that any form of discretionary monetary policy is doomed to failure. However, against this background, Friedman's proposed alternative of targeting a constant growth rate in the money supply is no less problematic. If major shocks were to occur in the various functional relationships, this would, despite a 'k per cent rule', result in major fluctuations in the inflation rate. This point is also made by the critics of monetarism, who believe that such a rule is as unhelpful as instructing the helmsman of a ship to hold a fixed rudder in a storm.[10] Within the framework of the IS/LM model, the comparative advantages of a constant money stock versus a constant interest rate have been discussed by Poole (1970) for demand and supply shocks. This interesting analysis is presented in Appendix 4.1. But as it relies on the unrealistic assumption that shocks cannot be observed, and thus that a policy of interest rate targeting implies a constant interest rate, it is more of a didactic than of political use.

Despite the inadequacies of analysing the transmission channel in terms of interest rate theory, the actual results of monetary policy in many countries would suggest that this is not the whole truth. As already mentioned, many central banks have achieved a very successful monetary policy, so that Friedman's (1968) pessimistic views on discretionary monetary policy were not validated by the evidence.

Thus, it seems likely that, in addition to the channels of the quantity theory and the interest rate theory, there is a further way in which monetary impulses are transmitted. Considering that all the major independent

[9] McCallum (1989) provides a dynamic representation of the IS/LM model. However, he simplifies things considerably by assuming a 'steady state', i.e. that all variations in the magnitudes over time will be at constant rates of change. Thus, the model is of little use for purposes of actual monetary policy.

[10] See Blinder (1987: 402): 'One of the traditional arguments for rules is that we really do not understand the inner workings of the economy very well, and so are better off not tampering with the economic machinery. In reality, however, such ignorance severely undercuts the case for instrument-based rules. For if we do not understand how changes in the money supply affect inflation and unemployment, or if the linkages from money to ultimate economic variables are fragile and ephemeral, then it is unlikely that we can design a money supply rule that we would really want to live with. Such a rule would be like stubbornly holding a fixed rudder in a stormy and unpredictable sea. Under such conditions, most ships will do better with even a modestly competent helmsman.'

central banks that are seriously committed to a policy of price stability generally manage to achieve this objective, we would also deduce that the structure of such a transmission process must be both simple and robust.

4.5. EXPECTATIONS CHANNELS (THE 'PHILLIPS CURVE')

4.5.1. *Two different approaches*

This leads to the expectations channel of monetary policy transmission, which basically rests on inflation expectations. This channel, which is also often presented under the label of the 'Phillips curve', can be applied in two completely different ways.

1. Many studies concentrate on whether monetary policy measures can be used to stimulate output and employment. Some of these models take perfect control of inflation simply as given. This approach is characterized by a short-term oriented, activist monetary policy.
2. A completely different approach uses the expectations channel in order to explain the relatively good control of the inflation rate by central banks, which is by no means obvious. In this dynamic context, monetary policy is characterized by a stability-oriented, medium-term orientation.

A key ingredient of the expectations channel are *price rigidities*, above rigidities of nominal wages which are due to transaction costs. Thus, the crucial role of expectations arises out of the need to fix prices and wages in advance. In this section we will start with an exposition of price rigidities and of the process of wage formation. Then we will show how a central bank can make use of price rigidities for a stability-oriented monetary policy. The activist approach based on the Phillips curve will be discussed at the end of this section.

4.5.2. *Price and wage rigidities*

Price rigidities are due to the fact that price adjustments can be costly. Thus, unlike in Walras's neoclassical model, they are not continuously adjusted to the market situation (Meltzer 1995). In the literature these costs are summarized under the heading 'menu costs', referring to the cost of changing the menu in a restaurant. These include all costs that are associated with price adjustments: the printing of price lists, the costs of negotiating wage agreements and of adjusting vending machines, etc. (see Chapter 5).

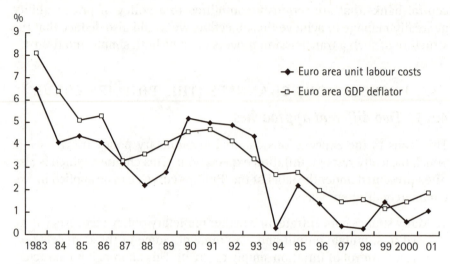

Figure 4.9. *Wages and inflation in the euro area, 1983–2001*
Source: OECD, *Economic Outlook.*

1. The most important example of such *intertemporal price-setting* (Stützel 1979) is to be found on the labour market, where nominal wages are usually fixed in collective pay agreements that run for a year or sometimes longer.[11] More frequent (e.g. monthly) wage adjustments would entail substantial negotiating costs. Wage rates are important for future price developments for two reasons: on the supply side they are the most important cost component, and on the demand side they determine the trend in wage income, which accounts for 56% of the total national income in the euro area. Figure 4.9 shows the degree to which the inflation rate in a relatively closed economy like the euro area is influenced by unit labour costs.

2. The fact that pay agreements tend to run for one year or longer is an important reason why many businesses do not continuously adjust their prices to the demand situation. Such price rigidities differ from intertemporal price-setting in that they are not contractually determined. A study by Blinder (1994) shows in the case of the United States that the median of the per annum price adjustments is 1.3. From a microeconomic point of view, these price rigidities may well be associated with 'menu costs', but they are also due to the fact that in the short term a business cannot automatically tell the difference between transitory and permanent shifts in demand.[12]

[11] In the United States they often run for two to three years (Gordon 1990).
[12] Meltzer (1995: 105): 'I do not challenge the existence of menu costs, but the emphasis here is on uncertainty and information costs—the cost of learning about current and prospective market conditions.'

3. A further instance of particularly marked intertemporal price-setting is to be found in the case of those contracts that are traditionally concluded for prolonged periods, such as tenancy and lease agreements. In view of the transaction costs associated with moving into and out of accommodation, it would be very risky for the tenant/lessee to agree to, say, monthly price adjustments. This effect is based on the *contract-specific investment*[13] undertaken by a tenant moving into new accommodation. This would enable the lessor to behave 'opportunistically' on the occasion of the first rent adjustment and to impose substantial rent increases on the tenant. With agreements of this type, the inflation expectations ruling at a given point of time result in predetermined prices (or price increases) for several years in advance. The quantitative significance of such effects is considerable. In the harmonized consumer price index (HICP) of the euro area, rent expenditure represents 9% of consumer expenditures.

4.5.3. *The process of wage and inflation determination on the basis of the Phillips curve*

Because of price and wage rigidities, the process of wage determination plays an essential role in the transmission process of monetary policy. In the literature this issue is traditionally discussed under the heading of the 'Phillips curve'. In the following different forms of this curve will be discussed.

4.5.3.1. *Original and modified Phillips curves*
The original Phillips curve goes back to the English economist Alban Phillips (1958), who had observed a strong impact of the labour market situation on nominal wages.[14] His theory can be formalized as follows:

$$\Delta w_t = f_1(U_{t-1}), \qquad \text{with } \partial f_1/\partial U_{t-1} < 0. \tag{4.14}$$

The rate of change in nominal wages (measured by the first difference of w, the logarithm of the nominal wage) between the observation period t and the previous period $t - 1$ is thus a negative function of the unemployment

---

[13] For details, see the numerous works on the new institutional economics, in particular Furobotn and Richter (1997).

[14] 'When the demand for labour is high and there are very few unemployed we should expect employers to bid wages up quite rapidly, each firm and each industry being continually tempted to offer a little bit above the prevailing rates to attract the most suitable labour from other firms and industries. On the other hand it appears that workers are reluctant to offer their services at less than the prevailing rates when the demand for labour is low and unemployment is high so that wage rates fall only very slowly. The relation between unemployment and the rate of change of wage rates is therefore likely to be highly non-linear' (Phillips 1958: 283).

rate for the previous period (U_{t-1}).[15] Phillips demonstrated that over the long term a stable negative relationship existed between the rate of change in nominal wages and the unemployment rate. This relationship was particularly marked in the periods 1861–1913 and 1948–57.

The key insight that nominal wages are determined by the labour market situation—or, more generally, the cyclical situation of the economy—constitutes an important element of all modern forms of the Phillips curve.

However, with its focus on nominal wages, the original Phillips curve did not yet allow an explanation of the inflation rate. This was provided by the *modified Phillips curve*, which was developed by Samuelson and Solow (1960). They showed that, with mark-up pricing, the rate of change in nominal wages is equal to the sum of the inflation rate and productivity increases (λ):

$$\Delta w_t = \lambda + \pi_t. \tag{4.15}$$

If the growth in productivity is constant over time, a stable relationship exists between the rate of increase in nominal wages and the inflation rate. If (4.15) is inserted in the original Phillips curve, the modified Phillips curve is derived as

$$\pi_t = f_1(U_{t-1}) - \lambda. \tag{4.16}$$

Here the productivity factor λ influences only the absolute level of the inflation rate: it has no effect on the slope of the modified curve. For example, a permanent increase in labour productivity would lead to a leftward shift in the modified Phillips curve.

Figure 4.10 shows a modified Phillips curve calculated for the United States by Samuelson and Solow (1960: 192). The shape of the curve seems to imply a choice between a situation of price stability and a 5.5% unemployment rate (point A) and a situation in which a somewhat lower unemployment rate (3%) accompanies a 4.4% inflation rate (point B). However, Samuelson and Solow (1960: 193) expressly pointed out that this curve was probably at best stable only in the short term, since it could shift at any time as a result of technical progress or changes in expectations.[16]

[15] The rate of increase in nominal wages is usually defined as follows: $\hat{W}_t \equiv (W_t - W_{t-1})/W_{t-1}$. Here an alternative definition is chosen, in which the rate of increase corresponds to the difference in the natural logarithms of two observation periods: $\hat{W}_t \equiv \Delta w = \ln W_t - \ln W_{t-1} = \ln(W_t/W_{t-1})$. The advantage of this latter definition is that it is easier to calculate with and, despite the use of discrete values, is similar to the constant definition of a rate of increase. The numerical difference between the two discrete concepts is small if the rate of increase according to the first definition is relatively small.

[16] Although Samuelson and Solow (1960: 185) mention the importance of expectations in the economic process, they are silent about their actual role.

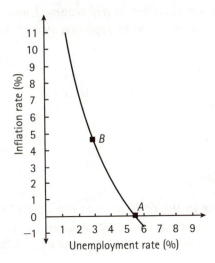

Figure 4.10. *A modified Phillips curve for the United States*
Source: Samuelson and Solow (1960: 192).

Above all, in the political discussions of the 1960s and 1970s, this evidence was regarded as a scientific proof that there is a trade-off between inflation and unemployment, i.e. that an inflationary policy can contribute to a permanent reduction of unemployment. In fact, attempts were made worldwide during this period to exploit the trade-off of the Phillips curve for economic policy purposes by consciously accepting a degree of inflation as the price for positive employment effects. These issues will be discussed in the following section.

4.5.3.2. *The expectations-augmented Phillips curve*
A major flaw of the original and the modified Phillips curves is the complete neglect of inflation expectations. This can be explained by the fact that in the late 1950s and early 1960s inflation rates were extremely low. Thus, as far as employees were concerned, there was no significant difference between the change in their nominal and real wages. In other words, 'money illusion' (i.e. the assumption that an increase in nominal wages is identical with an increase in real wages) was not a major problem.

In the course of the 1960s, inflation rates increased worldwide. As a result, inflation expectations began to play a major role in wage negotiations. The necessary revision of the Phillips curve was provided by Milton Friedman (1968) and Edmund Phelps (1967). It is based on the simple idea that what matters for workers in wage negotiations is not the increase in nominal wages, but the increase in real wages. Thus, in (4.14) the rate of change in nominal wages has to be replaced by the rate of change in real wages:

$$\Delta\left(\frac{w_t}{\ln P_t}\right) = f_2(U_{t-1}), \qquad \text{with } \partial f_2/\partial U_{t-1} < 0 \tag{4.17}$$

or

$$\Delta w_t - \pi_t = f_2(U_{t-1}). \tag{4.17}$$

As the actual change in the price level at the time of the collective wage agreements is not known, π_t has to be replaced by the expected inflation rate (π_t^e). Accordingly, (4.17') can be represented as follows:

$$\Delta w_t = f_2(U_{t-1}) + \pi_t^e. \tag{4.18}$$

The change in nominal wages now no longer reflects just the situation on the labour market, but also the inflation expectations of the two sides involved in the wage negotiations. If a constant growth in productivity over time is also assumed, by taking account of (4.15) in (4.18) we obtain the *expectations-augmented modified Phillips curve*:

$$\pi_t = f_2(U_{t-1}) - \lambda + \pi_t^e. \tag{4.19}$$

Thus, with a constant productivity growth, the inflation rate is determined by the unemployment rate and the expected inflation rate at the time when wage negotiations are made.

Again, the expectations-augmented Phillips has also been used to study the employment effects of monetary policy. Like the productivity factor λ, the expected inflation rate π_t^e determines only the position of the expectations-augmented Phillips curve. As Figure 4.11 shows, downward-sloping expectations-augmented Phillips curves are obtained for different inflation expectations, with a rising inflation expectation shifting the curve to the right. It is obvious that this relationship is valid only for the short term, since positive employment effects can be achieved only if the actual inflation rate is higher than the expected rate. In the longer term it can be assumed that the actual and expected inflation rate will be identical $(\pi = \pi^e)$. Thus,

$$\lambda = f_2(U). \tag{4.20}$$

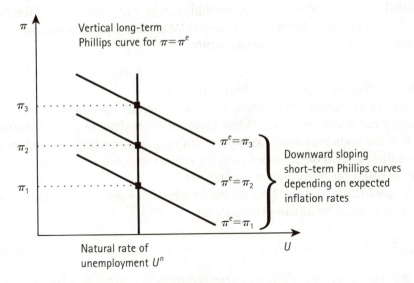

Figure 4.11. *Long-term and short-term Phillips curves*

If the inverse function is derived from this, it can be seen that the unemployment rate is determined exclusively by the growth in productivity, which is determined by the real economy and is assumed to be constant:

$$U = f_2^{-1}(\lambda). \tag{4.20'}$$

Thus, the *long-term Phillips curve* is vertical. Unemployment here no longer depends on nominal magnitudes and is therefore described as 'the natural rate of unemployment'. This term is derived from Milton Friedman (1968), for whom it means the level of unemployment that occurs in long-term overall equilibrium if market imperfections exist on the labour and commodity markets. Such a rate of unemployment includes structural and frictional unemployment.

A related concept is the non-accelerating inflation rate of unemployment, or *NAIRU*. The difference between the natural rate and the NAIRU is reflected in the methods used to generate empirical estimates of the two concepts (King 1998). The natural rate of unemployment describes a *long-term* relationship and can be estimated by reference to a structural model of the labour market that has explicit microeconomic underpinnings. In contrast, the NAIRU, which stresses a *short-term* relationship, is estimated using a system of time series equations relating inflation to past and present economic shocks. The sole criterion for judging the success of estimates of the NAIRU is their short-term correlation with inflation. Thus, the

NAIRU is simply the level of unemployment such that the difference between it and the current rate of unemployment is all that is necessary to describe short-run inflationary pressure.

4.5.3.3. *New versions of the Phillips curve*

In the more recent literature somewhat different specifications of the Phillips curve can be found. While their common element is the substitution of the unemployment rate by the output gap and a positive impact of the output gap on the inflation rate, they differ strongly as far as specification of inflation expectations is concerned.

A specification of the Phillips curve which is widely used today goes back to a model by Taylor (1979, 1980):

$$\pi_t = E_t \pi_{t+1} + \alpha_1 y_t + \varepsilon_t. \tag{4.21}$$

In this so-called *new Phillips curve* inflation is determined by expected inflation and by the output gap y_t, i.e. by the real (log) output relative to potential output. The starting point of Taylor's model is a *two-period* staggered wage-setting process in which x_t is the logarithm of the wage rate specified in contracts beginning in period t. Thus, in each period firms face average wage costs (w) of:

$$w_t = \frac{1}{2}(x_{t-1} + x_t). \tag{4.22}$$

If we assume a constant mark-up (q), the price level is:

$$p_t = w_t + q. \tag{4.23}$$

The same applies to the expected price level in the next period. If we assume that the mark-up is zero, the price level is identical with the firms' wage costs:

$$p_t = w_t. \tag{4.24}$$

The average wage that the workers demand for the whole contracting period is formed as follows: first-period wages equal the price level, second-period wages equal the expected price level. In addition Taylor assumes that the average real contract wage is increasing in the level of real economic activity represented by real output. Thus,

$$x_t = \frac{1}{2}(p_t + E_t p_{t+1}) + k y_t. \tag{4.25}$$

Accordingly, the wage contract for the previous period was

$$x_{t-1} = \frac{1}{2}(p_{t-1} + E_{t-1}p_t) + ky_{t-1}. \tag{4.26}$$

Walsh (1998) extends the Taylor model by inserting (4.25) and (4.26) into (4.23):

$$p_t = \frac{1}{2}(p_{t-1} + E_t p_{t+1}) + k(y_t + y_{t-1}) + \frac{1}{2}\varepsilon_t, \tag{4.27}$$

where $\varepsilon_t \equiv E_{t-1}p_t - p_t$ is an expectational error term. In order to get an expression in terms of the rate of inflation, Walsh introduces $\pi_t = p_t - p_{t-1}$ and $E_t\pi_{t+1} = E_t p_{t+1} - p_t$, which finally yields the somewhat counter-intuitional forward-looking Phillips curve specification:

$$\pi_t = E_t\pi_{t+1} + 2k(y_t + y_{t+1}) + \varepsilon_t. \tag{4.21'}$$

Although the Taylor model is widely used today, it seems odd that price rigidities have absolutely no impact on the determination, so that the actual inflation rate is determined by the expected inflation rate only. Therefore, it seems necessary to analyse the Taylor model in somewhat more detail. A crucial assumption is that wages are identical with the price index. In reality, this is certainly not the case. Wages in wage contracts are always determined by multiplying the wage in the previous wage period with the price index of the present period divided by the price index of the previous period. In other words, the new wage is calculated by multiplying the old wage by an inflation rate. Thus, the problem with Taylor's approach is that he uses a price index for t, which is by itself an empty concept, since an index must always be defined with respect to a base period. This neglect of the base period explains why no lagged inflation term shows up in the 'new Phillips curve'.

This can easily be shown if the Taylor model is reformulated in terms of changes in wages:

$$x_t = x_{t-1} + \frac{1}{2}(p_t - p_{t-1}) + \frac{1}{2}(E_t p_{t+1} - p_t) \tag{4.28}$$

or

$$\Delta x_t = \frac{1}{2}(\pi_t + E_t\pi_{t+1}). \tag{4.29}$$

As in the Taylor model, we assume that the nominal wage increase also depends on the level of economic activity in t:

$$\Delta x_t = \frac{1}{2}(\pi_t + E_t\pi_{t+1}) + ky_t. \tag{4.30}$$

If there is no mark-up, the inflation rate equals the wage rate. As the Taylor model assumes a staggered wage setting, where in each period 50% of the wages are set, the inflation rate in t is obtained as an average of the wage increases agreed at the beginning of period t and period $t + 1$:

$$\pi_t = \tfrac{1}{2}(\Delta x_t + \Delta x_{t-1}). \tag{4.31}$$

Inserting (4.30) into (4.31) yields

$$\pi_t = \frac{1}{2}\left[\frac{1}{2}(\pi_t + E_t\pi_{t+1}) + ky_t + \frac{1}{2}(\pi_{t-1} + E_{t-1}\pi_t) + ky_{t-1} \right]$$

$$= \frac{1}{4}(2\pi_t + E_t\pi_{t+1} + \pi_{t-1} + \varepsilon_t) + \frac{k}{2}(y_t + y_{t-1}), \tag{4.32}$$

with ε_t being defined as above. Rearranging, we finally come to the following Phillips curve:

$$\pi_t = \tfrac{1}{2}(\pi_{t-1} + E_t\pi_{t+1}) + k(y_t + y_{t-1}) + \tfrac{1}{2}\varepsilon_t. \tag{4.33}$$

This variant is almost identical with the so-called Fuhrer–Moore (1995) specification of the Phillips curve:

$$\pi_t = \tfrac{1}{2}(\pi_{t-1} + E_t\pi_{t+1}) + \alpha_1 y_t + \varepsilon_t. \tag{4.34}$$

Thus, the Fuhrer–Moore specification can be regarded as a correctly formulated Taylor specification. The main implication is that there is always inertia in inflation when there is inertia in wages. This is different from the mainstream view presented in Walsh (1998: 217): 'The key aspect of this specification is that while prices display inertia there is no inertia in the rate of inflation.'

A simple numerical example shows that the Taylor–Walsh specification and the specification presented here lead to the same wage development over time (Table 4.1). In contrast to Taylor and Walsh, it assumes that the first wage level (x_{t-1}) is given. For simplification, the output gap is assumed to be zero.'

If one additionally assumes that wages are set for only one period in advance, and that the inflation rate for that period is not known when wages are negotiated (because wage contracts do not overlap any longer), (4.29) becomes very simple:

$$\Delta x_t = E_t\pi_t. \tag{4.35}$$

Table 4.1. *A numerical example*

t	p_t	$x_t = \frac{1}{2}(p_t + E_t p_{t+1})$	$x_t = x_{t-1} + \frac{1}{2}(p_t - p_{t-1}) + \frac{1}{2}(E_t p_{t+1} - p_t)$
$t-1$	100	101	101
t	102	103,5	103,5
$t+1$	105	106	106
$t+2$	107	...	...

Accordingly, (4.30) can be written as

$$\Delta x_t = E_t \pi_t + k y_t. \tag{4.36}$$

As $\pi_t = \Delta x_t$, the inflation equation becomes

$$\pi_t = E_t \pi_t + k y_t. \tag{4.37}$$

Thus, we get back to the traditional expectations-augmented Phillips curve.

4.5.4. *How expectations are formed*

So far, we have left it open how the inflation expectations in the different Phillips curves are formed. The macroeconomic literature recognizes three basic mechanisms: extrapolative, adaptive, and rational expectation formation (Jarchow 1998). An additional variant is 'bounded rationality'.

4.5.4.1. *Extrapolative expectations*
The simplest example of this type of expectation formation is where economic agents assume that the actual inflation rate for the coming period (π_t) is equal to the inflation rate for the previous period (π_{t-1}). With such *static inflation expectations*, the expected inflation rate for period t (π_t^e) is

$$\pi_t^e = \pi_{t-1}. \tag{4.38}$$

In a more complex variant, the expected inflation rate can also be formed as a weighted average of past inflation rates:[17]

$$\pi_t^e = \alpha_1 \pi_{t-1} + \alpha_2 \pi_{t-2} + \cdots + \alpha_n \pi_{t-n}$$

$$\text{where } 0 < \alpha_i < 1 \text{ and } \sum_{i=1}^{n} \alpha_i = 1. \tag{4.39}$$

---

[17] This variant of the extrapolative expectations hypothesis originates with Irving Fisher (1930).

4.5.4.2. *Adaptive expectations*

In the case of adaptive expectations, the expected inflation rate also depends on past inflation expectations, but here economic agents take account of the expectation errors that have occurred in earlier years:

$$\pi_t^e = \pi_{t-1}^e + \beta(\pi_{t-1} - \pi_{t-1}^e) \qquad \text{where } 0 < \beta < 1, \tag{4.40}$$

or

$$\pi_t^e = \beta\pi_{t-1} + (1 - \beta)\pi_{t-1}^e. \tag{4.40'}$$

Thus, for example, if in period $t - 1$ the actual inflation rate turned out to be higher than the expected rate, when expectations are formed for t an appropriate add-on will be applied to the inflation expectation for $t - 1$. The factor β describes the speed of adjustment. Since the same process of expectation formation is followed for π_{t-1}^e as for π_t^e, (4.40') can also be written as

$$\pi_{t-1}^e = \beta\pi_{t-2} + (1 - \beta)\pi_{t-2}^e. \tag{4.41}$$

If this is inserted into (4.40'), we obtain

$$\pi_t^e = \beta\pi_{t-1} + (1 - \beta)[\beta\pi_{t-2} + (1 - \beta)\pi_{t-2}^e]. \tag{4.42}$$

The value for all other and all past inflation expectations can also be substituted as appropriate, producing the following series:

$$\pi_t^e = \beta\pi_{t-1} + \beta(1 - \beta)\pi_{t-2} + \beta(1 - \beta)^2\pi_{t-3} + \cdots \qquad \text{or}$$

$$\pi_t^e = \beta\sum_{n=0}^{\infty} (1 - \beta)^n\pi_{t-n-1}. \tag{4.43}$$

This is also a weighted average of all past values, since the sum of the weighting factors again comes to unity. This is because, by the rules for geometric series (with $0 < \beta < 1$),

$$\sum_{n=0}^{\infty} (1 - \beta)^n = \frac{1}{\beta}. \tag{4.44}$$

And so the sum of the weighting factors is

$$\beta\sum_{n=0}^{\infty} (1 - \beta)^n = \beta\frac{1}{\beta} = 1. \tag{4.45}$$

Adaptive expectation formation is thus in principle similar to extrapolative expectation, as represented in (4.39), in so far as both procedures go back as far as possible into the past.

4.5.4.3. *Rational expectations*
The hypothesis of rational expectations, which is based on research carried out by Muth (1961) and Lucas (1976), operates on the assumption that economic agents no longer take as their reference point the past values of a given variable. Instead, they form their expectations with the help of an economic model using all the information available at the time of forecasting (I_{t-1}). Thus,

$$\pi_t^e = E[\pi_t | I_{t-1}].$$ (4.46)

This procedure, which is based on future-oriented data, can be illustrated by means of a simple example. Let us suppose a massive increase in state expenditure in period t, which is financed via the banknote printing press. The public is informed of this measure at the beginning of period t. Assuming that supply in the economy remains constant, the inflation rate will also rise during period t. In the case of adaptive or extrapolative expectations, such a measure will have no effect on inflation expectations for period t, since expectations are based exclusively on the inflation rates for the preceding periods. However, if expectations are formed 'rationally', economic agents will at the beginning of period t process the available information using a macroeconomic model. The most simple method would be to process the announcement of the additional expenditure financed by the central bank with the help of the quantity theory model (Section 4.3). Thus, an increase in the money supply in period t would imply a higher inflation rate in that period. Inflation expectations would be revised upwards right at the start of period t, i.e. even before any change was observable in the current inflation rate.

At a general level, the hypothesis of rational expectations makes the key assertion that new information (shocks) can directly affect the formation of expectations and in that case may be even more important than information derived from the past performance of the variable to be forecast. However, to claim that there is an optimal macroeconomic model for forecasting the inflation rate that should result in all economic agents sharing the same inflation expectations is to overstate the case.

4.5.4.4. *'Bounded rationality'*
The problems of forecasting that are associated with the rational expectations model lead us to the concept of 'bounded rationality' (Simon 1992),

which hitherto has featured mainly in microeconomic analyses. The under-lying idea of this approach can be described in the following terms:

The term 'bounded rationality' is used to designate rational choice that takes into account the cognitive limitations of the decision-maker—limitations of both knowledge and computational capacity. (Simon 1992: 266)

In the context of the relationships that concern us here, this means that economic agents are aware of the fact that an optimal inflation fore-cast should always be based on a comprehensive macroeconomic model using all available information; but they also realize the limits of such models:

The cognitive limits are not simply limits on specific information. They are almost always also limits on the adequacy of the scientific theories that can be used to predict the relevant phenomena. ..., the accuracy of predictions of the economy by computer models is severely limited by lack of knowledge about fundamental economic mechanisms represented in the models' equations. (Simon 1992: 267)

In the field of macroeconomic theory, these ideas were already put forward by Keynes:

It would be foolish, in forming our expectations, to attach a great weight to mat-ters which are very uncertain. It is reasonable, therefore, to be guided to a consid-erable degree by the facts about which we feel somewhat confident, even though they may be less decisively relevant to the issue than other facts about which our knowledge is vague and scanty. For this reason the facts of the existing situation enter, in a sense disproportionately, into formation of our long-term expectations; our usual practice being to take the existing situation and to project it into the future, modified only to the extent that we have more or less definite reasons for expecting a change. (Keynes 1936: 148)

Thus, the concept of 'bounded rationality' clearly favours adaptive expect-ations over rational expectations. However, it does not rule out that in periods with major shocks expectations are formed in a forward-looking way.

4.5.5. *Determination of the inflation rate: empirical evidence*

The empirical evidence for the three Phillips curves in equations (4.21), (4.34), and (4.37) is rather different. It is widely agreed that the inflation rate follows a strong autoregressive process.[18] For instance, Haldane

---

[18] As a byproduct of these results, it makes little difference whether actual or forecasted values of the inflation rate are used in econometric analysis (Levin *et al.* 1999).

Table 4.2. *Autoregression of the inflation rates, 1976–1998*[a]

Country	Coefficient	R^2	S.E. of regression
Canada	0.90	0.75	1.73
France	0.93	0.91	1.31
Germany	0.89	0.56	1.12
Italy	0.93	0.84	2.37
Japan	0.78	0.71	1.42
United Kingdom	0.81	0.63	2.99
USA	0.91	0.65	1.82
Austria	0.87	0.56	1.21
Netherlands	0.85	0.75	1.18
Switzerland	0.80	0.21	1.67

[a] Calculation of inflation rates is based on the consumer price index.
Source: Own calculations based on data from IMF, *International Financial Statistics.*

summarized the results of a conference on these issues as follows:

More than one representative noted that, in practice, projections do little better than a random walk—a 'no-change' forecast—in predicting inflation over the short run.[19] (Haldane 1995: 253)

This is also confirmed by Table 4.2, which shows the autoregression of the inflation rate, for selected countries. As a result, many models use the following inflation equation that goes back to Svensson (1997):

$$\pi_{t+1} = \alpha_1 \pi_t + \alpha_2 y_t + \varepsilon_{t+1}. \tag{4.47}$$

Rudebusch (2000) comes to values of 0.71 for α_1 and 0.13 for α_2.

This evidence speaks for the simple expectations-augmented Phillips curve on the basis of *extrapolative expectations*. If we replace the unemployment rate in (4.19) with the output gap, add an error term, and neglect the productivity term, we get

$$\pi_{t+1} = \alpha_1 \pi_{t+1}^e + \alpha_2 y_t + \varepsilon_{t+1}. \tag{4.48}$$

For extrapolative expectations, the inflation expectation is simply the inflation rate of the previous period:

$$\pi_{t+1}^e = \pi_t. \tag{4.49}$$

If we insert this into (4.33), we can derive the Svensson equation from the traditional expectations-augmented Phillips curve.

---

[19] For Germany, Döpke and Langfeldt (1995) come to a similar result.

For the Fuhrer–Moore specification, Fuhrer (1997: 349) shows 'that expectations of future prices are empirically unimportant in explaining price and inflation behaviour'; a similar result can be found in Deutsche Bundesbank (2001). This also applies to the 'new Phillips curve', which is based on the Taylor model. This specification is confronted with the major problem that inflation depends positively on the lagged output rather than negatively. This is demonstrated by Gali and Gertler (1999). If (4.48) is lagged by one period, and if α_1 assumed to be about 1, we obtain

$$\pi_t = \pi_{t-1} - \alpha_1 y_{t-1} - \varepsilon_{t-1} + \eta_t, \tag{4.50}$$

where $\eta_t \equiv \pi_t - \pi_t^e$. But, as Gali and Gertler show with US data, using (quadratically) detrended log GDP as a measure of the output gap, the empirical equation is

$$\pi_t = \pi_{t-1} + 0.081 y_{t-1} + \eta_t. \tag{4.51}$$

A reasonable description of inflation in the euro area with the traditional Phillips curve is also provided by Gali *et al.* (2000). Thus, the empirical evidence speaks in favour of the old-fashioned expectations-augmented Phillips with strongly adaptive expectations. A major problem of many empirical tests of the 'new Phillips curve' is that the values for expected inflation are estimated with actual inflation data for the forecast period. This approach is adequate only if private agents use rational expectations.

4.5.6. *The Phillips curve as a device for explaining the output effects of monetary policy*

So far we have discussed the Phillips curve mainly as a theoretical device for the explanation of the process of wage and price formation. While this was Phillips's central aim, it was already mentioned that the curve has also been used for a reverse causality. Instead of explaining inflation with the situation on the labour market, the inflation rate is regarded as a main determinant of the employment situation. A vulgar interpretation of the late 1960s and early 1970s was that a higher inflation rate could permanently lead to a lower unemployment rate. While the economics profession never adopted this naive version, the view that monetary policy can reduce unemployment with a higher inflation rate in the short term still plays an important role in the macroeconomic debate. In Chapter 6 we will see that theoretical discussion of the 1980s and 1990s was shaped largely by the belief in the exploitation of a short-term Phillips curve for employment purposes. In addition, the standard textbook version of the AS/AD model rests on this curve for the derivation of the 'Keynesian' version of the aggregate supply curve.

The theoretical basis of this interpretation of the Phillips curve is provided by the neoclassical labour market, where the real wage determines the demand and the supply of labour. Monetary policy can affect this market only under specific conditions, such as the following.

- There is unemployment because of too high real wages. This can be due to nominal wages that are set by trade unions. By generating a price level that is higher than the price level anticipated by trade unions, the real wage can be reduced temporarily so that employment can be increased.
- In a situation without unemployment, an increase in employment by means of monetary policy is possible only if the increase in the price level is realized by the employers but not by the employees. This rather unrealistic scenario was developed by Robert Lucas (1972, 1973).

It is obvious that such employment effects of monetary policy are of a very short-term nature. In the first case, the involuntary reduction in real wages can be corrected at the next wage round. In the second case, a different perception of inflation by employees and employers can also be regarded as only a very temporary phenomenon.

An exploitation of such a short-term trade-off is especially difficult because of the long lags with which monetary policy affects the price level. With lag of six quarters in the euro area, trade unions would be able to forecast the inflationary effects of the ECB's monetary policy and ask for higher nominal wages before the effects of inflation materialize.

Empirically, it is rather difficult to detect the true causality between inflation and unemployment as far as it is based on the supply-side effects of a Phillips curve relation. The Phillips curve for Germany (Figure 4.12) shows several periods with a negative correlation between unemployment and inflation (1965–70 and 1982–92). This can be interpreted as a proof of either

- the impact of the labour market situation on the inflation rate, or
- the employment effects of an expansionary or restrictive monetary policy via the interest rate channel.

In the first period the low inflation rate and the very high demand for labour clearly support the first interpretation. In the second period the trade-off is certainly related to monetary policy, but it can be explained mainly by the restrictive—and in the second half of this period

Theory

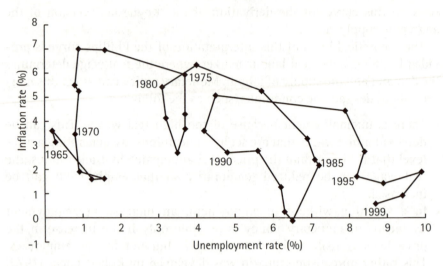

Figure 4.12. *The Phillips curve for Germany, 1965–1999*
Source: OECD, *Economic Outlook.*

expansionary–effects of the Bundesbank's interest rate policy (see Figure 4.3). Thus, it is not proof of the supply-side effects of a Phillips curve relation. Figure 4.12 also shows that the natural rate of unemployment increased considerably from 1965 to 1999. In the period 1968–73, one can identify a vertical Phillips curve at an unemployment rate of 1%, a second vertical curve at about 3.5% (1975–81), a third at about 6.5% (1983–9), and a fourth at 8.5% (1993–9).

The Phillips curve for the United States is less clear-cut (Figure 4.13). It also shows periods with a temporary trade-off (1965–9 and 1976–83). In contrast to Germany, there is an almost horizontal Phillips curve in the period 1992–9. Although unemployment has been rather high between 1974 and 1990, it is rather difficult to identify a permanent outward shift of a vertical Phillips curve.

For the euro area the long-term Phillips curve is astonishingly vertical (Figure 4.14). For the period 1983–2000 (earlier data are not available) the natural rate is at 10%. In addition, from 1987 to 1997 a slightly negatively sloped Phillips curve can be detected.

4.5.7. *Implications for monetary policy*

As already mentioned, the expectations channel, which is based on the expectations-augmented Phillips curve, leads to two completely different approaches to monetary policy.

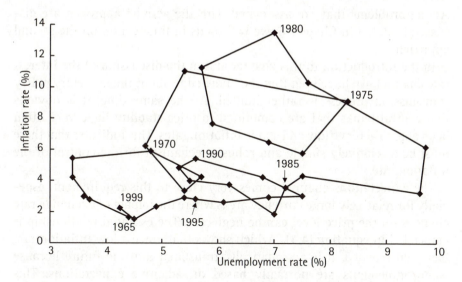

Figure 4.13. *The Phillips curve for the United States, 1965–1999*
Source: OECD, *Economic Outlook.*

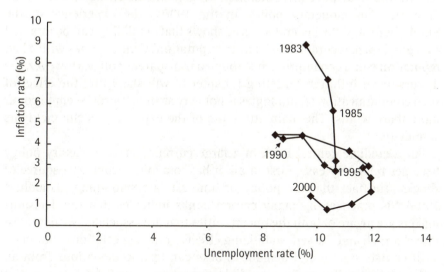

Figure 4.14. *The Phillips curve for the euro area, 1983–2000*
Source: OECD, *Economic Outlook.*

1. An *activist central bank* can try to exploit the short-term trade-off and pursue a policy of 'surprise inflation' with the aim of generating short-term employment effects.
2. For a *stability-oriented central bank*, the expectations channel provides an important mechanism for maintaining inflation at a low level.

As the problems that are associated with the activist approach are discussed in detail in Chapter 6, we will focus in this section on the second approach.

In the introduction to this chapter and in the discussion of the interest rate channel, we have seen that the knowledge about the monetary policy transmission process is rather limited. At the same time, it is obvious that central banks that are committed to price stability have very often been able to achieve low and stable inflation rates. This indicates that there must be a relatively simple and robust mechanism for the control of the inflation rate.

The expectations channel comes very close to this requirement, especially for relatively large currency areas where the impact of exchange rate changes on the price level can be neglected. The essential relationship is embedded in equation (4.31), which shows that, once a low inflation rate has been reached, it is automatically translated into the future because wage agreements are normally based on adaptive expectations. This explains why 'credibility', i.e. the public's belief that a central bank is able and willing to achieve price stability, became one of the key words in the discussion on monetary policy in the 1990s. The experience of the Bundesbank and the Federal Reserve shows that credibility can be attained by a good track record which leads to 'reputation'. Central banks with a bad reputation can try to improve it through a transparent policy. However, the discussion of inflation targeting (Chapter 8) will show that the effect of such communication technologies is not very strong. 'Deeds' seem to count more than 'words'. The main attraction of the expectations channel is its simplicity.

For a credible central bank in a large currency area, monetary policy becomes relatively easy. First of all, it has to avoid becoming a source of shocks. The fact that the policy of 'interest rate smoothing' (Goodhart 1995)[20] is practised by many central banks indicates that the decision-makers are aware of both the uncertainties that are associated with interest rate channel, and the self-stabilizing effects of the expectations channel.

Of course, supply and demand shocks can lead to deviations from an inflation target. But again, a credible central bank can take advantage of the expectations channel since the private sector will continue to expect a low inflation rate which facilitates a return to price stability. In situations

[20] See e.g. Issing (1993*a*: 2): 'This policy is sometimes known as a policy of "tiny steps" [*Trippelschritte* in German]. This description, which is apparently meant to be pejorative, overlooks the fact that the direction was always downwards and that prudence was the correct policy in a difficult situation. It is sensible, when operating in today's confusing and difficult national and international economic environment, not to move in giant leaps.'

with severe shocks (the oil crises of 1973–4 and 1980–1; German unification), where the private sector revises inflation expectations upwards, a
central bank has to make use of the interest rate channel and engineer a
major recession. As equation (4.32) shows, this creates a downward pressure on the inflation rate which has to be maintained until inflation expectations come down to a level that is compatible with price stability.

By assigning a high priority to price stability in the central banking
legislation (see Chapter 5) and adopting a transparent approach to monetary policy decision-making (see Chapter 8), the authorities can help to further stabilize private individuals' expectations so that any temporary
disturbances in, say, the demand for money are not interpreted as an
attempt at surprise inflation.

4.6. SUMMARY

This chapter has presented the most important transmission channels of
monetary policy. Depending on concrete circumstances, each of them can
be relevant for monetary policy. The *quantity theory channel* is most important in situations of highly indebted governments that use central bank
credit as their main source of financing. This channel provides a good
description of such an inflation process as well as a clear framework for a
stabilization programme. The quantity channel can also be used as an
important benchmark for a medium-term oriented monetary policy. The
interest rate channel is the workhorse for a monetary policy that tries to
cope with supply and demand shocks. It shows that changes in interest rates
have a direct effect on interest-sensitive expenditures, above all investment
expenditures. Probably even more important are the effects of interest rate
changes on enterprise balance sheets ('balance sheet channel'). By reducing
or increasing enterprise profits, a central bank can exert strong indirect
effects on investment decisions and on the firms' demand for labour. The
expectations channel, which is based on the Phillips curve, has two completely different policy implications. On the one hand, it provides a simple
and robust framework for a monetary policy that tries to keep the inflation
rate low; thus, it adds a dynamic component to the comparative-static
framework of the interest rate channel. Alternatively, it can be used to
describe an activist monetary policy that aims at stimulating employment
via the supply side. As this approach rests on 'inflation surprises', it can only
be used for an explanation of very short-term effects of monetary policy.

Our analysis of the transmission mechanisms has fairly obvious implications for the macroeconomic role assigned to monetary policy. First of
all, it shows that a countercyclical fine-tuning of macroeconomic processes

is a very difficult task. The mechanics of the interest rate channel are complex and indirect. A further difficulty lies in the fact that any attempt at active management of the economy can have repercussions on the expectations channel. All this seems to vindicate the critical stance adopted by Milton Friedman *vis-à-vis* a discretionary monetary policy. However, contrary to Friedman's views, it is relatively easy to keep the inflation rate at a low level without creating undue instability in the real sphere of the economy.

Our analysis in Part II of monetary policy proceeds in a reverse order. It starts in Chapter 5 with a discussion of the final targets of monetary policy. Chapters 6 and 7 describe the institutional framework that is required to guarantee that monetary policy will realize the final target(s) as far as possible. Chapter 8 deals with the 'simple rules' and with more sophisticated strategies that have been proposed by academics and practised by central banks in the last quarter-century. The instruments of monetary policy are presented in Chapter 10. The interplay between the government revenues from central banks and monetary policy is analysed in Chapter 11 under the heading of 'seigniorage'.

As even the central banks of large currency areas are confronted with sometimes massive exchange rate changes, the international aspects of monetary policy need a special analysis. These issues are presented in Part III.

Appendix 4.1. The original Poole model

In an appendix to Chapter 3 a modified version of the Poole model was presented. In this chapter the same approach is used to compare the advantages of a policy of a constant money stock with a policy of a constant interest rate (loan rate) in situations with macroeconomic shocks. Thus, this analysis focuses on the macroeconomic market for money (or loans), which describes a more advanced stage of the transmission process than the modified Poole model in Chapter 3. While the literature discusses only the original Poole model, we think that the modified model provides a better description of a central bank's control options, since it focuses on the monetary base and a short-term interest rate both of which can be directly controlled by monetary policy.

The original model goes back to a piece of research by William Poole (1970). This was developed at a time when the issue of intermediate targets and indicators was in the forefront of the monetary debate. The theoretical framework for Poole's research is the IS/LM model, which he uses in order to examine, graphically and algebraically, those circumstances in which interest rate targeting is preferable to monetary targeting. In the following discussion we shall consider only the graphic representations.

Poole assumes that the central bank can perfectly control either the money stock $(M = M^*)$ or the interest rate $(i = i^*)$.[21] In order to identify which strategy is superior, he analyses how shocks in the IS and LM curves affect real output. As Poole's analysis neglects the impact of the two shocks on the price level, we extend his approach to a simple aggregated supply–demand model with flexible prices, and we also examine the effects of supply shocks.

It has already been mentioned that the results of the model depend crucially on the assumption that the shocks are not observable by the decision-makers in a central bank. As soon as the precise nature of a shock can be identified, monetary policy could adjust the interest rate (or the money stock) in order to provide an optimum policy response.

A4.1.1. *Shocks in the IS curve*

We start with fluctuations of the IS curve, e.g. between IS_1 and IS_2. Such shocks can be due to shifts in the demand for goods (e.g. changes in investment or consumer demand,.

As a first strategy, we analyse *monetary targeting*, which means a constant money supply M^*. In this case, the fluctuations of the IS curve affect the aggregate demand curve, which shifts between Y_1^D and Y_2^D. The intersections of these aggregate demand curves with the aggregate supply curve determine real output, which fluctuates between Y_1 and Y_2. At the same time, the price level varies between P_1 and P_2. This has repercussions on the real money supply and hence on the LM curve. As a result, the LM curves intersect with the IS curves at points Y_1 and Y_2.

If a central bank follows the strategy of *interest rate targeting*, the central bank will adjust the money supply in such a way that the LM curve cuts the IS curve at the desired interest rate i^*. Figure A4.1 shows that, if IS shocks occur, the fluctuations in the price level and real output will then be even greater than with monetary targeting. The reason for this is that the interest rate can no longer serve as an adjustment mechanism. In order to meet its interest rate target, the central bank must, in the event of an expansionary IS shock (IS_1), expand the nominal money supply (M_1). This reinforces the expansionary effect (shift to Y_1^D) and increases the pressure

---

[21] In the following discussion controllability will be understood to mean that the central bank is able to realize a desired value for its targeting variable. For the sake of simplicity, and because of the static formulation of the model structure, it aims at the constancy of a value regarded as optimal. In other words, the central bank tries to minimize the variance of the target variable.

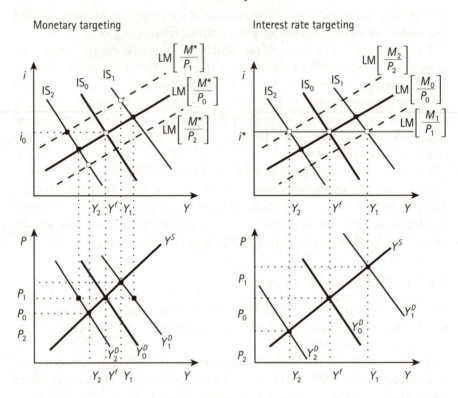

Figure A4.1. *IS shocks*

on the price level.[22] If a restrictive IS shock occurs (IS_2), the monetary policy measures operating in the same direction (M_2) will have a similarly reinforcing effect, and this too will lead to larger deviations from the ultimate goal than in the case of a constant money supply.

Thus, in the event of IS shocks, monetary targeting is clearly superior to interest rate targeting, independently of whether a central bank targets the price level or real output.

A4.1.2. *Money demand shocks*

Shocks in the demand for money lead to stochastic shifts in the LM curve (from LM_1 to LM_2) (Figure A4.2). A policy of *interest rate targeting* keeps the

---

[22] In principle, the sequence of events described here should be represented as an iterative process. The rise in the price level triggered by the shift in the IS curve also, of course, has negative effects on the LM curve in this case. However, the central bank will not allow the resulting further increase in interest rates, and the nominal money supply will immediately increase. This will continue until it reaches a new equilibrium at an unchanged interest rate.

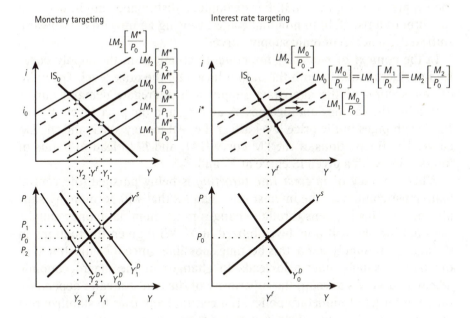

Figure A4.2. *LM shocks*

interest rate at the target level *i**. Thus, the monetary disturbance is from the outset offset by an adjustment in the money supply. As a result, the LM curve does not change its position despite the change in the demand for money. Thus, real output (Y^f) and the price level (P_0) also remain unchanged.

However, when the central bank pursues a policy of *monetary targeting* (*M**), the disturbances in the LM curve are transferred to the real economy. The aggregate demand curve fluctuates between Y_1^D and Y_2^D leading to fluctuations in output between Y_1 and Y_2 and in the price level between P_1 and P_2. Because of the changes in the price level and their effect on the real money stock, the fluctuations of the LM curve are somewhatmitigated.

As a result, interest rate targeting is superior to monetary targeting if an economy is confronted with shocks in the money demand. This confirms the general observation that a stable money demand is a basic condition for monetary targeting (Chapter 8). Again, the result applies to a central bank that targets the price level as well as to a central bank that targets real output.

A4.1.3. *Supply shocks*

In addition to the shocks in the IS and LM curves, which were the only ones considered by Poole, the AS/AD model also enables us to analyse shocks on the supply side (Figure A4.3). For example, a disturbance might occur in the form of a rise (fall) in nominal wages, causing an upward (downward) shift in the macroeconomic supply curve.

In the context of *monetary targeting*, fluctuations in the supply curve lead to fluctuations in both the output level and the price level. The point of intersection of the aggregate supply and aggregate demand curves determine the equilibrium incomes Y_1 and Y_2, and the price levels P_1 and P_2. The changes in the price level affect the real money stock and the LM curve. The fluctuations of the LM curve (LM_1 and LM_2) lead to points of intersection with a given IS curve at Y_1 and Y_2.

When a policy of *interest rate targeting* is being pursued, the central bank must counteract the interest rate changes that will accompany supply shocks. This happens through changes in the nominal money supply. National income will now be stabilized at Y^f. With given fluctuations in the aggregate supply curve this becomes possible, since the adjustment in the money supply now also leads to changes in the macroeconomic demand curve. As a result, the superiority of the two strategies depend on the final target of monetary policy. If a central bank tries to stabilize real output, interest rate targeting is superior to monetary targeting; if it tries to stabilize the price level, monetary targeting is superior to interest rate targeting.

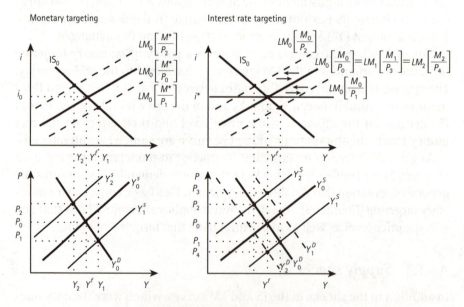

Figure A4.3. *Supply shocks*

In conclusion, it can be stated that, in the context of the (modified) Poole model, interest rate targeting is the more suitable monetary policy approach if money demand shocks predominate or if a central bank targets real output in a situation with a supply shock. On the other hand, monetary targeting is preferable in the event of real shocks—either on the demand side (IS curve) or on the supply side—if a central bank targets the price level.

Of course, these theoretical conclusions cannot be applied directly to economic policy issues, since the model structure is beset with a multitude of problems. Above all, the assumption that the shocks are completely unobservable is rather questionable under present-day conditions, which are characterized by large private and public economic research departments which have all relevant data available without major delays.

Appendix 4.2. The concept of the 'price gap'

The theoretical concept of the 'price gap' (also referred to as the 'P-star' or P^* model) is closely associated with writings on quantity theory. This approach was developed at the end of the 1980s by members of the Federal Reserve Board, in order to model the relationship between the money supply and the price level in such a way that it could be empirically examined (Hallman *et al.* 1989, 1991).[23]

Prima facie, the concept is relatively simple, which is why it is used for quantitative analyses, especially inflation forecasts. In particular, it describes the short- and medium-term adjustment processes that take place in the event of monetary shocks.

The main idea of this concept is that the current price level approximates its long-term equilibrium value only after a time lag. In other words, the adjustment process for the current price level has a different dynamic from that for the long-term price level.

In its original form, the concept of the price gap[24] consists of a short-term and a long-term quantity equation. In the long-term perspective, the long-term price level (P^*) is dependent on the actual money supply (M), the long-term velocity of circulation (V^*), and the long-term or potential real output (Y^*):

$$P^* = \frac{MV^*}{Y^*}, \tag{A4.1}$$

---

[23] The Chairman of the Federal Reserve System, Alan Greenspan, had asked the authors to investigate the suitability of money supply M2 as an indicator for long-term price trends. Greenspan had proposed using the 'output gap' model (OECD 1994). By expanding the output gap by a 'velocity of circulation gap', the authors arrived at the 'price gap'.

[24] Strictly speaking, the concept of the price gap is a concept of the price level gaps.

or, in logarithms:

$$\ln P^* = (\ln M + \ln V^*) - \ln Y^*. \tag{A4.1'}$$

Therefore, a rise in the money supply will, when output and velocity of circulation have reached their medium-term equilibrium values, be reflected in a higher price level. By analogy with (A4.1), the following holds true for the short-term perspective:

$$\ln P = (\ln M + \ln V) - \ln Y. \tag{A4.2}$$

The short-term price level is thus determined by current values of the parameters of the quantity equation. Divergences can occur between the long-term price level and the current price level. If we take the difference between (A4.1') and (A4.2), we obtain

$$(\ln P - \ln P^*) = (\ln Y^* - \ln Y) + (\ln V - \ln V^*). \tag{A4.3}$$

The price relationship $(\ln P - \ln P^*)$ in (A4.3) designates the price gap. The right-hand term describes the possible causes of deviations in the current price level from the equilibrium value. Thus, for example, a negative price gap $(\ln P < \ln P^*)$ occurs when a high level of productive capacity utilization causes real output Y to rise above its equilibrium value Y^* or if the current velocity of circulation V falls below the level of the long-term velocity of circulation V^*. Both situations can be triggered by excessive money supply growth, which can lead to increased productive capacity utilization if monetary holdings affect demand. It can also cause excess liquidity if the additional monetary holdings are hoarded, resulting in a decline in V. In the long-term quantity equation, Y^* and V^* are unaffected by the growth in the money supply. The long-term price level P^* must therefore react fully to the rise in M.

The crucial factor now is the dynamic of the short-term adjustment process. It is assumed that, owing to price rigidities (see Section 4.5.2), the price level will reach its new equilibrium value only after a time lag. This relationship is illustrated in Figure A4.4. At point of time t_0 there is a one-off expansion in the money supply from M_0 to M_1. As a consequence, the long-term price level increases from P_0^* to P_1^*. The current price level, on the other hand, moves from gradually P_0 to P_1 (broken line). The adjustment process is completed in t_1 when the current price level has reached the new equilibrium value P_1^*. The essential factor now is the influence on the inflation rate of the price gap that exists between t_0 and t_1. In the comparative-static analysis undertaken here, the information we obtain on the inflation rate relates only to the period of the short-term adjustment. Before the disturbance, i.e. up to point of time t_0, the inflation rate is zero. The same

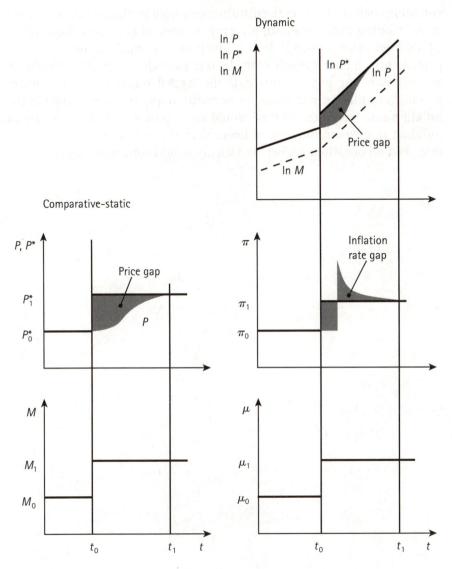

Figure A4.4. *Price gaps*

applies to the period following completion of the adjustment process, i.e. after point of time t_1. Between these two points of time comes a period with a positive inflation rate. In concrete terms, therefore, the existence of a price gap implies the presence of a temporary inflationary impulse.

We might also try using the price gap concept in connection with a dynamic analysis. If we assume a steady-state situation, the equilibrium conditions before and after the disturbance would be characterized by constant inflation and money supply growth rates. A monetary disturbance would then entail a change from a given money supply growth rate to a permanently higher growth path. In this case the 'price gap' would be an 'inflation rate gap'. In this case the lagged transition from a lower to a higher inflation rate would of necessity imply that the change in the inflation rate from time to time would show positive values: the current inflation rate would initially be lower than the new permanent inflation rate, then on occasions higher, and finally would converge with it.

PART II

DOMESTIC ASPECTS OF MONETARY POLICY

The decision-makers in a central bank are confronted with rather difficult task. With their *instruments*, they can very directly control a short-term interest rate (e.g. the one-month money market rate) which serves as the *operating target* of monetary policy. But the main aim of monetary policy is a control of the *final targets* of the economic process (price stability, real growth, full employment), which have been set in such a way as to maximize the ultimate goal of social welfare.

The analysis of the monetary policy transmission process has shown that the relationship between operating targets and final targets of monetary policy is rather complex, indirect, and in some important aspects still not fully understood. Therefore, academics and central bankers have always tried to design 'simple rules' in order to facilitate the day-to-day management of monetary policy. The indicators that are used by such systems are often described as *intermediate targets* of monetary policy (e.g. the money stock or the exchange rate). Thus, the structure of the transmission process can be described as follows:

$$\text{Instruments} \Rightarrow \text{operating targets} \Rightarrow \text{intermediate targets}$$
$$\Rightarrow \text{final targets} \Rightarrow \text{ultimate goal.}$$

Our analysis in Part II of monetary policy proceeds in a reverse order. It starts in Chapter 5 with a discussion of the final targets of monetary. Chapters 6 and 7 describe the institutional framework that is required to guarantee that monetary policy will realize the final target(s) as far as possible. Chapter 8 deals with the 'simple rules' and with more sophisticated strategies that have been proposed by academics and practiced by central banks in the last quarter-century. The instruments of monetary policy are presented in Chapter 10. The interplay between the government revenues from central banks and monetary policy is analysed in Chapter 11 under the heading of 'seigniorage'.

As even the central banks of large currency areas are confronted with sometimes massive exchange rate changes, the international aspects of monetary policy need a special analysis. These issues are presented in Part III.

5

The Ultimate Goal and
the Final Targets of Monetary Policy

What this chapter is about

- The ultimate goal of monetary policy is social welfare. This chapter discusses how the final goals of monetary policy should be set in order to maximize social welfare. Above all, it considers whether a central bank should be more concerned about a stable price level or a stable nominal income.
- In the long run, price stability is clearly the main goal of monetary policy. By safeguarding an efficient use of money in its main functions, monetary policy contributes to an efficient spatial and intertemporal allocation of resources and thus to real growth.
- In the short and medium run, monetary policy should focus its efforts on stabilizing nominal income. In situations with demand shocks, this is identical with stabilizing the price level. In situations with supply shocks, a preference for a stable nominal GDP has the advantage of avoiding unnecessary fluctuations of real income. Because of the long and variable lags of monetary policy, all forms of an activist monetary policy should be applied with great care.
- Combining the short, medium, and long run, it becomes clear that monetary policy maximizes social welfare by contributing to real growth in the long run (which requires a low inflation rate) and to a stable real income path in the short and medium run (by compensating demand shocks and by accommodating supply shocks).
- A clearly defined policy assignment is possible only if monetary policy is formally obliged to pursue price stability. At the same time, some room for manoeuvre is required to cope with supply shocks. This is in line with many central bank laws and is the practice of central banks in many countries, which combine a general goal for price stability with adequate escape clauses (medium-term orientation, focus on core inflation, inflation targets instead of price level targets).

5.1. INTRODUCTION

The central bank is one of the most powerful actors in the macroeconomic arena. As there are different goals of macroeconomic policy (high employment, economic growth, price stability, equilibrium in the balance of payments) and other weighty players (national government, trade unions, employers' associations, European and supranational institutions), a clear policy assignment is extremely important.

5.1.1. *The loss function of central banks*

The ultimate goal of monetary policy is always the welfare of the population. Therefore, the literature describes the decision problem of a central bank, as far as the final macroeconomic goals are concerned, as a 'social welfare function'. This is usually represented as a simple loss function (Svensson 1999*b*), which has to be minimized by the central bank:

$$L_t = \frac{1}{2}\left[(\pi_t - \pi^*)^2 + \lambda\left(\frac{Y_t - Y^*}{Y^*}\right)^2\right]. \tag{5.1}$$

Its arguments are deviations of the inflation rate (π) from a target rate (π^*) and the output gap, i.e. the deviation of the actual output (Y) from potential output (Y^*) divided by potential output. The squaring of the deviations in the social welfare function implies that positive and negative deviations are similarly negative for the society and that large deviations are more heavily weighted than small ones.

The factor λ determines the weight of output and inflation in the loss function. For $\lambda = 0$ a central bank is concerned only with inflation ('inflation nutter'). This approach is called *strict inflation targeting*. For $\lambda > 0$ the term *flexible inflation targeting* is used. For $\lambda = 1$ the output and the inflation target are given the same weight in the central bank's policy decisions. This variant is similar to a *nominal income target* of monetary policy, which can be formulated as follows:

$$L_t = \frac{1}{2}[(\pi_t + y_t - y_{t-1}) - (\pi + \Delta y)^*]^2. \tag{5.2}$$

Under a nominal income target, a central bank tries to minimize the difference between the actual growth rate of nominal GDP (the sum of the inflation rate and the growth rate of real GDP, which is the difference between the logs of real output) and the target growth rate of nominal GDP. The main difference between the two approaches concerns the impact of differences between real output in the previous period and that in the present period, which are recorded in the nominal income target but not in the flexible inflation target as long as no output gap exists.[1]

Given the wide spectrum for λ and the choice between inflation targeting and nominal income targeting, monetary policy can opt for quite

---

[1] For the difference between nominal GDP-growth targeting and flexible inflation targeting see Svensson (1999*b*: 642).

different approaches. Monetary history has seen central banks that were trying mainly to stabilize output (especially in the 1970s and 1980s) and others that were concerned mainly with price stability. The latter was the case in the 1950s and 1960s, with the international exchange rate system of Bretton Woods, where the monetary policy in almost all countries was dominated by the stability-oriented approach of the US Federal Reserve System.

The present discussion is dominated by two different approaches. As early as 1923, Keynes had argued in favour of price stability as the main target of monetary policy:

it would promote confidence and furnish an objective standard of value, if, an official index number having been complied ... to register the price of a standard composite commodity, the authorities were to adopt this composite commodity as their standard of value ... prevent[ing] a movement of its price by more than a certain percentage in any direction away from the normal. (Keynes 1923: 148)

Today, it is above all central bankers who regard price stability as the main target of monetary policy. In contrast to this view, many academics argue in favour of defining the final goal of monetary policy in terms of both inflation and real GDP:

It is widely agreed that the goals of monetary policy are a low rate of inflation ('price stability') *and* a small gap between actual real GDP and potential GDP. (Feldstein and Stock 1994: 8; emphasis added)

Thus, it is often argued that monetary policy should target the nominal GDP: 'But it seems fair to say that the consensus today favors nominal income as the most suitable objective of monetary policy' (Hall and Mankiw 1994: 74). Among the main proponents of this approach are Meade (1978), von Weizsäcker (1978), Tobin (1980, 1983), R. E. Hall (1983), Taylor (1985), and McCallum (1984, 1987).

5.1.2. *Preference for price stability in actual monetary policy*

During the 1990s, almost all central banks in the world explicitly adopted price stability as their main final target. A somewhat misleading label for this new orientation is 'inflation targeting'. In most countries price stability as the *dominant* target of monetary policy is now prescribed in the central bank constitution. The most notable exception is the United States. Section 2A of the Federal Reserve Act states:

The Board of Governors of the Federal Reserve System and the Federal Open Market Committee shall maintain long run growth of the monetary and credit aggregates commensurate with the economy's long run growth potential to increase production, so as to promote effectively the goals of maximum employment, stable prices, and moderate long-term interest rates.

The final target of the European Central Bank is defined in Article 105(1) of the EC Treaty:

The primary objective of the ESCB shall be to maintain price stability. Without prejudice to the objective of price stability, the ESCB shall support the general economic policies in the Community with a view to contributing to the objectives of the Community as laid down in Article 2.

In its stability-oriented monetary policy strategy,[2] the ECB has given the following definition of its inflation target:

Price stability shall be defined as a year-on-year increase in the Harmonised Index of Consumer Prices (HICP) for the euro area of below 2%. .... Price stability is to be maintained over the medium-term. (European Central Bank 1999*a*: 46)[3]

In many other countries, too, the general target of 'stable prices' has been defined in a more precise way, including the relevant price index and escape clauses (see Section 5.4.3). In contrast to the ECB, this definition is often made by the government or in co-operation between central bank and government. Concrete values are shown in Table 5.1.

Table 5.1. *Numerical inflation targets of central banks*

Central bank	Target
Bank of Canada	1%–3%
Bank of England (BoE)	2.5% ($\pm$1%)
Deutsche Bundesbank (implicit target; see Chapter 9)	1985–96: 2%; 1997–8: 1.5%–2.0%
European Central Bank (since 1999)	$0 < \pi^* < 2\%$ (no precise definition of a band)
Reserve Bank of Australia	2%–3%
Reserve Bank of New Zealand	0%–3%
Sveriges Riksbank	2% ($\pm$1%)
Swiss National Bank	Less than 2%

Source: Central bank reports.

---

[2] The strategy was published in ECB Press Releases of 13 October 1998 and 1 December 1998 (www.ecb.int). It is discussed in detail in European Central Bank (1999*a*).

[3] The European Central Bank (1999*a*: 46) has also clarified that 'the use of the word "increase" in the definition clearly signals that deflation, i.e. prolonged declines in the level of the HICP index, would not be deemed consistent with price stability'.

Table 5.2. *Output gaps of more than 1% in the G7 countries, 1982–2000*

Duration of output gap	Positive output gap	Negative output gap
2 years		USA (1982–3), UK (1992–3) Japan (1994–5)
3 years	Japan (1990–2), Germany (1990–2), Italy (1988–90), Euro area (1990–2), USA (1998–2000)	USA (1991–3), Japan (1998–2000), Italy (1983–5), Italy (1992–4), UK (1982–4), Canada (1982–4)
4 years	UK (1987–90), Canada (1987–90)	Germany (1996–9), Euro area (1982–6)
5 years and more		Japan (1983–7), Germany (1982–7), France (1983–7), France (1993–8), Italy (1996–2000), Canada (1991–8), Euro area (1993–9)

Source: Own calculations based on data from OECD, *Economic Outlook.*

5.1.3. *Two different time horizons for monetary policy*

In the following sections the merits of these two different approaches to monetary policy will be discussed in more detail. As a guiding principle, a distinction between a long-term and short-term perspective is made. We assume that the long-term perspective is characterized by the fact that the economy is affected by neither demand nor supply shocks. The experience shows that demand and supply shocks can lead to quite persistent output gaps (Table 5.2). Therefore, the 'short-term' perspective can include periods of up to four years. It is then mainly a semantic question whether the medium run is related to the short run or the long run. In the following we will not explicitly refer to the medium run, so the short run and the long run each include part of the medium run.

5.2. THE LONG-TERM VIEW: ONLY PRICE STABILITY MATTERS

An important starting point for a definition of the targets of monetary policy in the long run concerns the results of our discussion about the transmission process. From this macroeconomic point of view, it has become very clear that in the long run, monetary policy is not able to affect real magnitudes. Thus, its contribution in the long run is a neutral policy stance which contributes to an efficient use of money in its main functions. From this neutrality hypothesis it would make little sense to define the nominal income as a long-run target of monetary policy. As the nominal income is very much determined by real factors, monetary policy could not be made responsible for a long-term decline of its growth rate. It would also make little sense to compensate a decline in real growth with a higher inflation rate. Thus, as a long-term goal, nominal income is certainly much less suitable than the target of price stability.

5.2.1. *Costs of inflation*

The macroeconomic discussion in Chapter 4 has left it open why price stability is a goal *per se*: Keynesian approaches have nothing to say about the long run, and the quantity theory together with the natural rate hypothesis come to the result the monetary effects are neutral in the long run. A problem of the neutrality hypothesis is that it suggests that an economy could live with 1000% inflation per annum as well as with price stability. This is also supported by a look at a typical microeconomic utility function, where the utility of a household depends on its consumption of goods (c) and its leisure (l). In an intertemporal setting, the household seeks to maximize a multiperiod utility function (McCallum 1989):

$$u(c_t, l_t) + \beta u(c_{t+1}, l_{t+1}) + \beta^2 u(c_{t+2}, l_{t+2}) + \ldots \tag{5.3}$$

The parameter β is a discount factor that is positive but smaller than unity. As neither money nor the inflation rate is explicitly included in this utility function, the impact of inflation on the well-being of the population is not obvious. In the following we will see how inflation can affect either the availability of goods or the amount of time that households can devote to leisure. In the literature these microeconomic issues are discussed under the label of the 'costs of inflation'.

As inflation erodes the value of money, the costs of inflation are closely related to the three functions of money (Chapter 1). Thus, inflation has the effect that money is not fully, or perhaps not at all, used as a means of payment, as a store of value, or as a unit of account. We will see that it is useful to distinguish between a hypothetical situation in which the inflation rate is correctly anticipated by households and firms, and one in which this is not the case (Laidler and Parkin 1975).

5.2.1.1. *Correctly anticipated inflation*

If inflation is correctly anticipated, all economic agents will be able at all times accurately to predict the future inflation rate (Fischer and Modigliani 1978: 10).[4] In a neoclassical world it is difficult to imagine that this would lead to allocative distortions. In fact, all costs of inflation are related to the

---

[4] Strictly speaking, the case of a correctly anticipated inflation rate can itself be regarded as a very theoretical reference scenario, since it requires that all economic agents have identical inflation expectations.

deviations from neoclassical assumptions, above all the existence of taxes and transaction costs:

- With a positive inflation rate, private individuals hold lower real money balances than under a situation with price stability ('sub-optimal money holdings'). This effect is due to the implicit inflation tax on money balances and requires more time-consuming economic transactions so that households have less time for leisure and for work.
- If prices change continuously, the unit of account function is impaired. In a world with correctly anticipated inflation, this causes transaction costs for price marking ('menu costs').
- Tax laws frequently operate with nominally fixed magnitudes and the assumption that nominal values are identical with real values ('nominalism'); this causes microeconomic distortions that reduce economic growth and the amount of goods available for consumption.

Sub-optimal money holdings   In the literature the costs of inflation are very often associated with sub-optimal money holdings. Such holdings result from the fact that cash and sight deposits are normally non-interest-bearing. Under such circumstances, an increase in the inflation rate is identical with higher opportunity costs of holding money and thus leads to a reduction in the real quantity of money held by private individuals.

The welfare loss of sub-optimal money holdings can be illustrated by means of the concept of the *consumer surplus* (Bailey 1956; Fischer 1981). Figure 5.1 plots a downward-sloping demand curve for real money

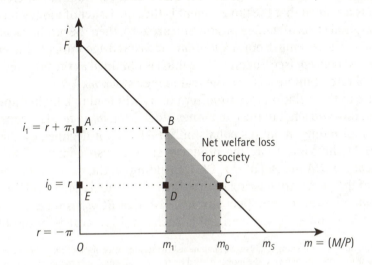

Figure 5.1. *Welfare costs of inflation*

balances which depends on the nominal interest rate. The diagram assumes a constant real interest r. At the starting point C there is price stability; i.e., the inflation rate is zero. According to the Fisher equation (see Appendix A8.1), the nominal interest rate i_0 is calculated as the sum of the real interest rate and the expected inflation rate. Assuming that the expected and the actual inflation rates are identical, the nominal interest rate equals the real interest rate r.[5] The real money stock demanded (m) amounts to m_0. In such a situation, holders of money obtain a consumer surplus equal to the area CEF. The consumer surplus is calculated as the difference between

1. the *value* that those demanding money ascribe to the holding of an additional unit of money—this can be obtained from the money demand function; and
2. the *price* that those demanding money must pay in equilibrium conditions for holding a unit of money.

The latter is determined by the opportunity costs of holding money, measured in terms of the nominal interest rate. The higher the rate of interest on an alternative form of investment (e.g. securities) and the lower the rate of interest on money holdings, the higher will be the opportunity costs and the greater the welfare losses of inflation. In Figure 5.1 it is assumed that no interest whatsoever is paid on money holdings.

The issuers of money obtain a producer surplus, analogous to the consumer surplus accruing to private individuals, that is equal to Om_0CE. This is calculated as the difference between the marginal costs of money production and the price obtained in the amount of the nominal interest rate i_0. If it is assumed that the government is the sole issuer of money and that the marginal costs of money production are zero, then the producer surplus is equal to the revenue from *seigniorage*—measured according to the *opportunity cost concept* (see Chapter 11)—which is obtained as the product of the nominal rate of interest i_0 and the real money stock m_0.[6]

A rise in the inflation rate from zero to π_1 will lead to a higher nominal interest rate and a fall in the real money stock from m_0 to m_1. The consumer surplus on money holdings equals only FAB; i.e., it declines by the area $ABCE$. At the same time, the producer surplus also changes. This now stands at Om_1BA instead of Om_0CE. Depending on the quantitative importance of the monetary base relative to the money stock, there will thus also be a reduction in the producer surplus. The area BCm_0m_1 remains the net welfare loss for society. Clearly, this social welfare cost is borne by the

---

[5] Throughout the following analysis we shall be using the simplified form of the Fisher relation.

[6] If bank deposits are added to the money issued by the central bank, the producer's surplus will be divided between the central bank and commercial banks (Lange 1995: 1).

holders of money, whose consumer surplus has been reduced. The net effect for the money producers is ambivalent. On the one hand, as a result of the lower level of real money holding, they lose income from the money issue equal to DCm_0m_1. On the other hand, as a result of the higher nominal rate of interest, they gain additional income equal to $ABED$.[7]

The calculation of the welfare costs of inflation using such a concept assumes not only that the inflation rate is correctly anticipated, but also that inflation has no other effects on the real output and that at least one alternative type of tax—e.g. a poll tax—exists which does not generate any negative welfare effects (Driffill *et al.* 1990). Otherwise, a positive effect must be contrasted with the calculated negative welfare effect.

This theoretical analysis of the welfare costs of inflation can now be used to derive an optimal rate of inflation which is associated with an optimal level of real money holdings in an economy. As can be seen from Figure 5.1, this level is reached when the consumer surplus is at its maximum, i.e. when real money holding is expanded as far as the *level of saturation* (m_s). This requires that the nominal rate of interest should be zero. For an exogenous real interest rate (r), this situation is realized if the price level is falling. The 'optimum quantity of money' derived in this way by Milton Friedman (1969) is thus achieved only under conditions of deflation with $-\pi = r$, so that the nominal interest rate of bonds will be zero. Then the holding of (non-interest-bearing) money will produce the same return as the holding of fixed-income securities (with a nominal interest rate of zero). Thus, there are no longer any opportunity costs of holding money. This conclusion can be explained by logically applying the rule of marginal costs to the supply of money. This rule states that the optimal allocation of a good is always found when its price is equal to the marginal social costs. Since it can be assumed that the marginal social costs of manufacturing money are negligible, the price of holding money must also be zero.[8]

What is really meant by the welfare costs of too low a level of money holding? In its function as means of payment (Chapter 1), money reduces the costs of economic transactions. In a country with a positive nominal rate of interest, enterprises and households must spend an unnecessary amount of time on managing their real transactions with a level of cash holding lower than m_s. Real money holdings are substituted by an increased time input for the carrying out of real transactions, which reduces either the amount of available leisure time or the time spent on the production of goods (McCallum and Goodfriend 1987). Hence consumers will either try

---

[7] In terms of seigniorage, this is an expression of the above-mentioned contrary effect, which leads to the Laffer curve for seigniorage (see Chapter 11).

[8] For a detailed discussion, see Woodford (1990).

to shorten as much as possible the time between earning and spending income by spending more time on disbursing the money more rapidly, or they will seek to change their money holdings into interest-bearing forms of investment for the period during which the former are not needed. This will require more frequent bank visits. In addition, the sellers of goods will reduce their stocks in order to increase the velocity of circulation of the money. The result of all this is that consumers must spend more time look-ing for and buying the desired goods ('shopping time') or they must visit their bank more often. This is why people often talk of the 'shoe leather costs' of inflation caused by a low level of money holding.

This substitution relationship between real money holdings and the time input for the carrying out of transactions becomes particularly clear in the context of the *Baumol–Tobin model* of real money demand (see Chapter 2). The constant costs per withdrawal assumed therein can easily be inter-preted as costs of the time input. The central conclusion of this model is that the optimal average level of economic agents' cash holdings depends negatively on the interest rate i. On the other hand, the optimal number of withdrawals increases with a rising interest rate. This requires more time for economizing cash holdings (Lucas 1994, Driffill *et al.* 1990).

For countries with low inflation rates, the costs of 'sub-optimal money holdings' should not be overrated. If one assumes that an average house-hold holds an average amount of non-interest-bearing money (M1) of €2,000, an inflation rate of 2%, and a real interest rate of 3% imply costs of €100 per annum or €8.33 per month. If these costs are regarded as a fee for using the network of a universally accepted currency, they are cer-tainly not high enough to induce barter transactions or more frequent bank visits.

This is completely different when inflation rates are very high. As the example of the CIS countries in the 1990s shows, high inflation can revert an economy to a barter economy (Bofinger 2000). At the same time, eco-nomic agents may replace the domestic currency with a foreign currency ('currency substitution' or 'dollarization').

In order to be able to determine empirically the welfare costs of sub-optimal money holding, a concrete money demand function is needed. Lucas (1994) uses a semi-logarithmic real money demand function with a constant semi-elasticity of interest-rates (α) and an income elasticity of 1:

$$\frac{M_t}{P_t} = \beta e^{-\alpha i} Y_t. \tag{5.4}$$

Lucas determines the parameters of this function so that they best represent the empirical combinations of the US nominal interest rate and real money supply relative to other parameter values. For the United States he obtains a value of around 0.27 for β and a value of 7 for the interest rate semi-elasticity (α). For an interest rate of 6%, an inflation rate of 4%, and a real interest rate of 2%, Lucas estimates

1. the welfare costs of *sub-optimal money holdings* (i.e. a too-low level of money holdings compared with a deflation of 2%) to 0.3% of GDP in the USA;
2. the welfare costs of *inflation* (i.e. a too-low level of money holdings compared with an inflation rate of 0%) to 0.2% of GDP in the USA.

Lucas (1994) also shows that the level of welfare losses calculated depends critically on the choice of the money demand function. If, instead of the semi-logarithmic demand function, a function with a constant interest rate elasticity (ζ) and an income elasticity of 1 is used, i.e. if

$$\frac{M_t}{P_t} = \chi i_t^{-\zeta} Y_t, \tag{5.5}$$

a root function ($\zeta = 0.5$) best represents the empirical values.[9] The root function also has the advantage that it is compatible with the Baumol–Tobin model (Section 2.2.2) for explaining money holdings. The value of χ here comes to around 0.04. For the same values of the inflation rate, the real interest rate, and the nominal interest rate, the welfare costs of sub-optimal money holdings are calculated at around 1% of GDP. This is three times more than the above estimate. The welfare costs of inflation come to 0.4% of GDP, twice the inflation costs for the first money demand function.

Other studies of the welfare costs of inflation arrive at quantitatively similar results. For the United States, Cooley and Hansen (1991) find that an inflation rate of 10% is associated with costs amounting to 0.6% of GDP. In 1990 for the member countries of the European Community, the welfare costs of an inflation rate of 10% were estimated at between 0.1% and 0.3% of the Community's GDP (Commission of the European Communities 1990: 99). However, with inflation rates now down to around 2% in most industrial countries, the welfare effects are much smaller. In the event of *hyper-inflation*, Bailey (1956: 99) has calculated much higher inflation effects, amounting on average to 30% of GDP.

---

[9] This applies not only in relation to other functions with constant interest-rate elasticity, but also in comparison with all functions with constant interest-rate semi-elasticity. The value for χ, like that for β, is set so that all functions of the type represented in (5.5) pass through the geometric mean of the observed data pairs of real money demand and nominal interest rate. For the USA a value of around 0.04 is obtained (Lucas 1994: 3).

Menu costs The concept of 'menu costs' includes all costs of correctly anticipated inflation arising from the fact that inflation requires a permanent adjustment of all nominal magnitudes. Such costs arise even in a fully indexed economy, since, as long as money is used as a means of payment, real prices must always be converted into nominal prices (Fischer and Modigliani 1978).

The term 'menu costs' originates from the fact that in inflationary conditions restaurant menus need to be reprinted more often. More generally, menu costs include, for example, the costs of producing new price lists, renegotiating wages and salaries in wage settlements, converting vending machines (coin machines), and—when inflation rates are very high—printing new banknotes. If it is assumed that any change in price entails fixed costs, when inflation rates are low prices will not be changed very often. On the other hand, high inflation rates increase the incentive to change prices quickly. Therefore, there is generally a positive relationship between the level of the 'anticipated' inflation rate and menu costs (Caplin 1992). When inflation rates are very high, menu costs can be considerable and there is a tendency to choose another accounting unit or even to cease marking items in nominal prices in the domestic currency. For example, in Russia in the 1990s many prices were quoted in 'accounting units', which is simply another word for the US dollar. Thus, while the costs of suboptimal money holdings refer to the function of money as a means of payment, menu costs are related to the function of money as a unit of account.

Costs of inflation caused by the tax system Because of the way tax law is framed, inflation has important consequences even when it is correctly anticipated. Tax scales, upper limits, and allowances are set mostly in nominal terms. Since adjustments to actual price changes usually take place after a time lag, inflation means that, especially when taxation is progressive, the tax burden may be increased without the need for parliamentary legislation (so-called 'cold progression').[10] In addition, tax laws are normally based on the principle of *nominalism*, which assumes that nominal values are always identical with real values. In Germany this principle has been named the 'Mark-gleich–Mark Prinzip' ('A Mark equals a Mark' Principle: Stützel 1979). It implies that nominal interest payments are fully treated as costs or income although in an inflationary situation they also contain a compensation for inflation that is related neither with costs nor with income.

---

[10] This is seen in the Federal Republic of Germany, for example. The USA, by contrast, has indexation of nominal taxes bases. Adjustment takes place in accordance with the movement in the cost-of-living index (Koren 1989: 55).

The fact that companies are allowed to set off their nominal interest payments against their taxable income has negative effects on the allocation of resources. This can be demonstrated by a simple example. Assume that the real interest rate is 3%. In a situation without inflation, the nominal interest rate is also 3%. Thus, for an enterprise that plans an investment, the yield of the investment has to exceed 3%. This is different if the inflation rate is 10%. The nominal interest rate is now 13%. The enterprise can set off the nominal interest payments against its taxable income. With a tax rate of 50%, the deduction is 6.5%. As the debt is reduced in real terms by 10%, this leads to negative net real costs of borrowing of −3.5%. Thus, an investment becomes profitable as long as its yield is not lower than −7%.

Similar distortions are created by the effects of inflation on interest incomes. With positive inflation rates savers pay too much tax, since they are fully taxed on that portion of the nominal interest that only serves to compensate for the inflation rate. In practice, they can even suffer a capital loss in real terms (see Table 5.3).

The empirical relevance of these effects depends on the impact of inflation on the real interest rate. The net real interest rate (r_N) can be calculated as

$$r_N = (r + \pi)(1 - t) - \pi. \tag{5.6}$$

The tax rate is t. r_N is greater than 0 as long as the real interest rate is

$$r > \frac{\pi^* t}{1 - t}. \tag{5.7}$$

For $t = 0.5$, this implies a real rate that is identical with the inflation rate. A more general analysis of these effects is presented in Box 5.1.

For the previously high-inflation countries Spain and Italy, the net real rate was negative until the mid-1980s, after which time it remained positive and fairly stable (Figure 5.2). This indicates that, after inflation was anticipated, the effects of the tax system were somehow compensated by a strong increase in the real interest rate. However, as individual tax rate can diverge substantially, severe allocative distortions remain. Thus, the

Table 5.3. *Net real interest rates with different inflation rates (%)*

	$\pi = 0$	$\pi = 3\%$	$\pi = 6\%$
Real interest rate	3	3	3
Nominal interest rate	3	6	9
Net nominal rate ($t = 0.5$)	1.5	3	4.5
Net real interest rate	1.5	0	−1.5

Box 5.1. *The effect of inflation on enterprises' cost of capital*

The effects of taxation and inflation are analysed by Cohen *et al.* (1999). Applying equation (5.6) to companies (*C*) that represent the demand side of the capital market and on households (*H*) that represent the supply side of capital leads to the following two equations:

$$r_C = (r + \pi)(1 - t_C) - \pi, \tag{B5.1}$$

$$r_H = (r + \pi)(1 - t_H) - \pi. \tag{B5.2}$$

Rearranging (B5.2), we get

$$(r + \pi) = \frac{r_H + \pi}{1 - t_H}, \tag{B5.3}$$

and substituting (B5.3) into (B5.1) yields

$$r_C = \frac{r_H + \pi}{1 - t_H}(1 - t_C) - \pi, \tag{B5.4}$$

or

$$r_C = r_H \frac{1 - t_C}{1 - t_H} + \pi \frac{t_H - t_C}{1 - t_H}. \tag{B5.5}$$

If we now assume r_H to be exogenous, two cases have to be distinguished in order to demonstrate the effects of the tax system on enterprises' cost of capital:

1. if $t_H = t_C$, the distorting effect disappears ($r_C = r_H$);
2. if $t_H < t_C$, inflation reduces the net real costs ($r_C < r_H$).

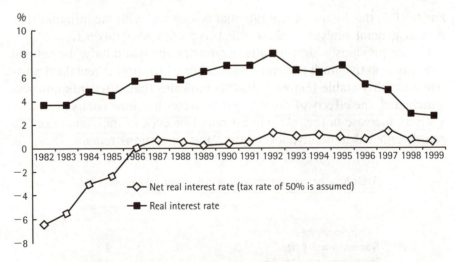

Figure 5.2. *Real and net real interest rates in Italy, 1982–1999*
Source: Own calculations based on data from OECD, *Economic Outlook.*

nominalism in tax laws (together with the 'cold progression'), particularly in periods with unanticipated inflation, can have the effect of

1. subsidizing unprofitable investments, and
2. reducing the incentives for those receiving incomes from interest payments and also from all activities that are not related with debt finance.

For the United States, Feldstein (1999) shows that even low inflation rates exacerbate the distortions created by the tax system. Such distortions are due mainly to the different treatment of capital incomes and the implicit rental return on the capital invested in housing. Feldstein estimates that a reduction of the inflation rate from 2% to 0% would entail a welfare gain equal to about 1% a year.

Another distortion of the tax system is created by the effect of nominalism on tax deductions. Depreciation is normally allowed only in respect of acquisition and production costs and not in respect of replacement costs. In conditions of inflation, the sum of the depreciation amounts fixed in nominal terms in this way thus reflects only a portion of the actual erosion of value. Posted profits are too high and the tax liability is too high. However, when valuing stocks companies are free to choose their valuation method. With inflation they will therefore prefer the LIFO method (last in first out) to the FIFO method (first in first out), since the latter results in the above-mentioned fictitious profits.

Finally, inflation can also have a negative impact on government receipts. This is due to the time lag between the assessment period, the date on which the tax return is filed, the tax decision, and the date on which the tax is finally paid. Especially when inflation rates are very high, this lag can substantially reduce the real value of the actual tax payment. The empirical observation that rising inflation rates lead to a decline of tax receipts in relation to GDP is known as the *Olivera-Tanzi effect*.[11] Its consequences have been particularly drastic in the case of Bolivia. In the years 1980–1, when inflation was running at the rate of 25% p.a., state revenue amounted to just under 10% of GDP. In 1985, with an inflation rate of 10,000%, tax receipts came to only 1.3% of GDP (Sachs and Larrain 1993: 737).

5.2.1.2. *Effects of incorrectly anticipated inflation*
In reality, there is no such thing as perfect indexation or correct anticipation of future price movements. In addition to the costs of inflation described so far, it is therefore also necessary to consider those allocative distortions and redistribution effects that result from the fact that, in the

---

[11] Tanzi (1977) credits Olivera (1967) with discovering this relationship.

context of both existing and new contracts, economic agents' inflation expectations are often wrong.

In practice, forecasting the inflation rate is always an uncertain business. It can be shown empirically that inflation rates become more variable the higher is the average level of inflation. Thus, a high inflation rate is normally associated with greater forecast errors (Barro 1997: 93).

The positive relationship between the average level of inflation and the variability of inflation can be explained first by the fact that when inflation has reached a high level governments normally feel compelled to introduce macroeconomic stabilization programmes. Such measures are usually quite effective in bringing down inflation in the short term, but their chances of long-term success are often small, especially if nothing has been done to tackle the underlying causes of inflation (e.g. insufficient control of public spending). A new stabilization programme will be necessary after a while. In the 1980s many countries in Latin America (especially Brazil and Bolivia) pursued such a 'stop and go' policy. Another reason for the positive correlation between the level and variability of inflation is suggested by the *expectation channel* of monetary policy transmission (described in Section 4.5). An increase in the inflation rate will increase the costs of price rigidity; private individuals will therefore adjust prices and wages more frequently or even adopt indexation or dollarization; this will reduce the stabilizing effect that price rigidities have on the inflation rate in a low-inflation environment.

Thus, the negative effects of incorrectly anticipated inflation are encountered mostly in countries with fairly high inflation rates. Nevertheless, over longer periods of time even small forecast errors have a strong impact on the profitability of investments. In a market economy, the main problems caused by incorrectly anticipated inflation are that the central signal function performed by the price mechanism is impaired and this leads to a misallocation of resources.

If a supplier is no longer able to distinguish between absolute and relative price changes, she may wrongly interpret the fact that she is able to sell larger quantities of a good at the price set by her in nominal terms as an indication of a shift of demand in favour of her product, whereas the only reason for the consumer's apparent increased willingness to pay is that the prices for all other goods have risen on average (general price level). Such a misinterpretation could result in companies increasing their capacity although the real demand for their products has not changed. The increased supply would then be sellable only at a lower relative price. The central signal function that the system of relative prices performs in a market economy can thus be distorted by incorrectly anticipated inflation. These effects play a central role in neoclassical macroeconomics (Section 4.5.6). In reality, however, such costs of inflation should not be overestimated, since statistical information on the actual inflation rate is published with a very short time lag (about two weeks in the euro area).

The costs of incorrectly anticipated inflation are more serious in the case of long-term contracts. This applies first to the labour market, where collective pay agreements are usually concluded a year in advance. As mentioned in Section 4.5.3, the level of nominal wages set in such agreements is determined largely by the expected inflation rate, but, unlike in the case of goods market, there is no possibility of a nominal wage adjustment during the contracting period. Thus, if the inflation rate turns out higher than expected, employees are obliged to offer their labour at a real wage that is lower than what they had intended at the time the collective pay agreement was concluded. The result can be short-term positive employment effects and a redistribution from wage-earners to recipients of profit income. On the other hand, an unexpectedly low inflation rate will lead to unemployment. Divergences between the inflation rate assumed in collective pay agreements and the actual inflation rate form the basis for all models that are based on the Phillips curve (see Section 4.5).

Serious allocative problems arise above all for the intertemporal allocation process, especially for long-term financial contracts. When such contracts are concluded, in nominal terms, expectation errors lead to unpredictable distribution effects between debtors and creditors, which increase the risk attached to long-term capital investments and the incurring of long-term liabilities to an equal extent.

- If the actual inflation rate turns out higher than expected, this is harmful to the creditor's interests, but benefits the debtor. This is the central message of the so-called *creditor/debtor hypothesis*.
- If, on the other hand, the actual inflation rate is lower than the expected inflation rate, an unforeseen capital transfer takes place from debtors to creditors.

Thus, it is not generally true that that an incorrectly anticipated inflation rate—or simply rising prices—is harmful to creditors and beneficial to debtors. Instead, the creditor/debtor hypothesis considers only the special case of inflation expectations that are lower than the actual inflation rate. Therefore, the direction of the distribution effect is determined not by the level of the inflation rate, but solely by the relationship of the expected to the actual inflation rate. This uncertainty about the long-term effects of inflation on the real value of financial contracts is the main reason for the

Table 5.4. *Real value of a nominal payment of €1,000 which is due in 10 years*

Inflation rate per annum (%)	2	6	10	20	25	100
Real value after 10 years (€)	820	558	385	162	107	1

costs of incorrectly anticipated inflation. Table 5.4 shows that the real value of a nominal payment of €1,000 that is due in ten years differs considerably depending on the actual inflation rate.

As a result, in an environment with a very unpredictable inflation rate, creditors are willing to lend money only if they are compensated with a 'risk premium'. This increases the real interest rates and the financing costs for enterprises and reduces the amount of investments. The impressive reduction in nominal and real interest rates that could be observed in several EMU member countries prior to their EMU entry shows that such risk premia can become quite high (see Figure 5.2). For the enterprise sector, the effect of high real interest rates is somewhat mitigated by the possibility of deducting the full nominal rate as costs. As this possibility is not available for loss-making enterprises, they are fully confronted with the problem of inflation-induced risk premia.

Uncertainty over the future inflation rate also results in a shortening of maturity periods for new issues and a 'flight into real assets', in which investors favour physical assets when making their investment decisions (*asset price inflation*). Accordingly, in the course of the 1990s, when there was a more or less steady decline in the inflation rate, a process of lengthening maturity periods was in operation.

5.2.1.3. *Empirical evidence*

The costs of inflation are difficult to assess empirically. Many studies look at real GDP growth rates in order to identify these costs. However, as the costs of inflation are costs of changing prices (menu costs) or of using banking services, they are also included in GDP. In so far as inflation implies a reduction of leisure, its costs cannot be measured at all. The costs of suboptimal money holdings can be compensated if they allow the government to reduce other distorting taxes.

Thus, the results of studies that analyse the impact of inflation on real GDP growth are not always very clear-cut. This applies above to the large group of OECD member countries. Even for the high inflation period from 1972 to 1982, with a strong variance of average national inflation rates (from 4.8% in Switzerland to 20.3% in Portugal), no negative correlation between inflation and real GDP growth or total capital formation can be detected (Figure 5.3). The same applies for the longer period from 1950 to 1981 (Grier and

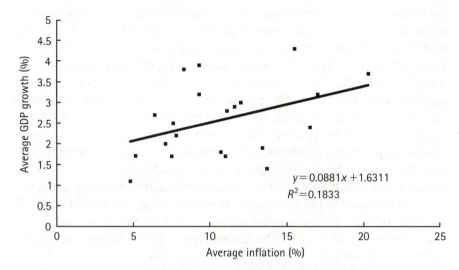

Figure 5.3. *Average inflation and real GDP in OECD countries, 1972–1982*
The countries include all OECD countries with the exception of East European and Asian countries, Iceland, and Turkey.
Source: Own calculations based on data from OECD, Economic Outlook.

Tullock 1989: 265).[12] These results are compatible with calculations by Barro (1995, 1997), who comes to the conclusion that significant growth losses are likely only with annual inflation rates of more than 15%. In fact, in recent decades all OECD countries (with the exception of Turkey and Iceland) were able to keep their inflation rates under this threshold.

Thus, significant negative growth effects can be found only if the studies include high-inflation countries. While these overall results are in line with the theory of the costs of inflation, cross-section analyses of similar scope show quantitative divergences. Barro (1997) finds, for a population of 117 countries, that a 10-percentage-point rise in the inflation rate causes a decline in the growth rate of 0.29 percentage points. Fischer (1993: 498) comes to a decline of 0.39 percentage points.[13] As regards the qualitative direction, however, all studies agree that there is a negative relationship between inflation and growth.[14] The output losses associated with inflation

[12] On the other hand, Grimes (1991: 636), who looks at a selection of OECD countries (excluding Portugal, Mexico, Turkey, and Greece) in the period 1961–87, finds a significant negative relationship.

[13] A range of between 0.2 and 0.4 percentage point is obtained by Motley (1993), depending on the number and selection of countries considered. For the group of OECD countries with more than a million inhabitants (excluding Mexico), he even obtains a value of 1.5. Motley suggests that the reason for this not very plausible result may lie in the small number of observations (Motley 1993: 17).

[14] This result is obtained by Barro (1991, 1995), De Gregorio (1993), Fischer (1993), Grier and Tullock (1989), Grimes (1991), Gylfason (1991), Kormendi and Meguire (1985), and Motley (1993). On the other

can assume sizeable proportions. For example, assuming a steady increase in the inflation rate of ten percentage points leading to a decline in the annual growth rate of 0.2 to 0.4 percentage points, output will fall by 6% to 11% in thirty years. However, caution is needed when drawing such conclusions. Firstly, the possibility of a non-linear relationship[15] must be borne in mind and, secondly, a basic problem of regression analyses is that they give no information about causalities (Cornwall 1987: 839). For example, it could be possible that countries where the real economy is affected by particular problems (high unemployment, low real growth) will tend to try and solve these by pursuing an inflationary monetary policy. However, since such an approach is counterproductive in the long run, not only will the country fail to solve the problems in the real economy, it will also end up with a serious inflation problem. However, this causality is denied by Barro (1995: 173), who finds effects of past inflation rates on the current growth rate.[16]

The influence of the inflation rate is often determined in connection with the capital input. It is clear that this not only concerns the effects of inflation on net investment ('investment channel'), it also affects the efficiency of the available capital ('efficiency channel'). For the *investment channel* of inflation, Fischer (1993: 499) obtains a very marked negative effect.[17] He calculates an investment elasticity of the inflation rate of -0.037, which means that a rise in the inflation rate of 100 percentage points would reduce the growth rate in the capital stock by 3.7 percentage points. Assuming that (net) investment amounts to 20% of the gross national product and that the capital–output ratio in the economy is 2.5, the capital stock would grow at an annual rate of 8%. Thus, with the above-mentioned elasticity, the rise in the inflation rate would result in the annual growth rate in the capital stock being reduced by almost a half. This implies that, once an inflation rate of 210% was reached, there would be no new investment (Fischer 1993: 499).

hand, the negative relationship revealed by Levine and Renelt (1992) is not significant. This also applies to the majority of the other possible macroeconomic explanatory variables considered by them (Levine and Renelt 1992: 959).

[15] However, the hypothesis of nonlinearity is not so obvious from the empirical data as intuition might suggest. Barro (1995: 171) rejects the hypothesis, and Fischer (1993: 503) even concludes that the negative relationship becomes weaker with a rising inflation rate.

[16] Another possibility is that the negative correlation between inflation and growth is due to a series of negative supply shocks. Thus, in order to avoid erroneous interpretations, Fischer (1993: 505) divides his investigation period into a phase in which demand shocks predominate (1960–72) and one characterized by supply shocks (1973–88). However, since a negative correlation also exists in the first phase, Fischer (1993: 507) concludes that the negative relationship is not only the result of negative supply shocks.

[17] Here Fischer (1993) confirms results already obtained by Kormendi and Meguire (1985) and Levine and Renelt (1992). Whereas in Kormendi and Meguire the growth rate is influenced mainly via the investment channel (Kormendi and Meguire 1985), in Levine and Renelt (1992) this effect is seen to be not very robust with respect to the choice of the regression variables additionally included.

On the other hand, the *efficiency channel* of inflation is less marked. For the negative relationship between the productivity gain and the inflation rate, Fischer calculates a regression value of 0.018. However, his productivity measure covers not only changes in capital productivity, but all factors that do not operate on the growth rate through the increase in the labour and capital input. Therefore, if one studies only the efficiency channel of capital, it is found that the inflation rate also has a significant negative influence on the efficiency of the capital input (De Gregorio 1993: 287).

In sum, as inflation impairs or even destroys the functions of money, it leads to negative effects on growth and leisure in an economy. While it is more difficult to identify the economic costs of low inflation empirically, it is obvious that as soon as inflation reaches high rates it causes serious allocative distortions which reduce economic growth. It is important that these effects manifest themselves mainly in the longer term. Very high inflation is associated with a de-monetization of an economy and barter transactions, both associated with high transaction costs (see Chapter 1).

5.2.1.4. *The policy assignment in the long run*

In sum, the long-term perspective shows very clearly that price stability is not a goal *per se*, but an important contribution of monetary policy to an efficient functioning of the market mechanism which fosters investment and growth. Thus, from the microeconomic analysis of the costs of inflation, it seems problematic to define a *nominal income target* as a long-term goal of monetary policy. As such a target includes inflation and growth, it would lead to a double counting of the costs of inflation. A similar problem is associated with the approach of defining intertemporal loss functions, including inflation and output growth in a loss function. However, the problem of double counting is avoided by equation (5.1), since the output gap is used instead of output growth (Svensson 1999*b*). In this formulation the inflation term represents the long-term output losses, while the output gap measures the short-term deviations from an equilibrium growth path.

In the following sections we do not address old-fashioned theories that postulate a positive effect of inflation on real growth, even in a long-term perspective. The problems that are associated with a long-term downward-sloping Phillips curve have been discussed in Section 4.5.6. In the 1960s James Tobin (1965) developed a growth model that postulates a stimulating effect of inflation on economic growth. This model is based on very specific assumptions. First, Tobin assumes an exogenous savings ratio. Second, in his model private agents have only two investment alternatives: money and real assets. Thus, it is not difficult to show that with an increase in inflation it becomes more attractive to save in the form of real assets, so that investment is positively related to the inflation rate. Of course, this implies the absurd result that an economy without any money would achieve the highest growth rate.

5.3. INFLATION AND OUTPUT GROWTH IN THE SHORT RUN

In this section the short run is defined as a period during which demand and/or supply shocks occur. As Table 5.2 has shown, in the G7 countries output shocks with a persistence of four or five years are not unusual.

In this context, the choice between a nominal GDP target and a target for price stability is more complicated than in a long-term view. This section considers the comparative advantages of the two different targets for a demand and a supply shock. For the sake of simplicity, the targets are defined as *level targets*, i.e. for the target of price stability as $P = P^*$ and the target for nominal income as $PY = (PY)^*$.

5.3.1. *An analysis for demand and supply shocks*

The short-term relationship between inflation and output growth is presented in all standard macroeconomic textbooks. In these simple models, a decline in output is always associated with a negative output gap and a reduction of employment. In the context of macroeconomic supply and demand analysis, the nominal GNP rule can be represented as a hyperbola in the AD/AS diagram (Bradley and Jansen 1989: 33).[18] For a target value of $PY = \overline{K}$, we get

$$P = \frac{\overline{K}}{Y}. \tag{5.8}$$

The starting point A is an equilibrium with price stability (P_0) and a full-employment output (Y_f) with an output gap of zero (see Figure 5.4). A *negative demand* shock, e.g. falling investment (the IS curve shifts from IS_0 to IS_1), means a downward shift in the macroeconomic demand curve (from AD_0 to AD_1), assuming that the central bank initially takes a wait-and-see attitude. In the new equilibrium B, as a result of the decline in the price level from P_0 to P_1, the real money supply increases and there is a shift in the LM curve (from LM_0 to LM_1).

---

[18] The graphic representation of the effects of shocks on efforts to manage nominal GNP originates with Bean (1983). The nominal GNP target $(\overline{K} = PY)$ can be represented as an equilateral hyperbola $(P = \overline{K}/Y)$. Only such an isoelastic function type, which at every point has an elasticity of value -1, is compatible with a constant nominal GNP. The elasticity can be calculated simply as: $\varepsilon_{P,Y} = (dPY/dYP) = (-\overline{K}/Y^2)[Y/(\overline{K}/Y)] = -1$.

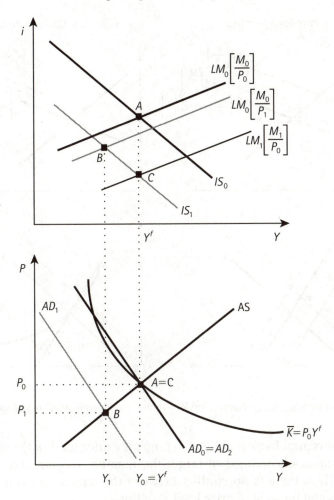

Figure 5.4. *Demand shocks*

In the case of the *nominal GNP target*, then, the central bank must, by pursuing an expansionary monetary policy, cause the macroeconomic demand curve to shift upwards until it again intersects the supply curve at the latter's point of intersection (point *A*) with the nominal GNP hyperbola (from AD_1 to AD_2). This thus requires an expansion in the money supply from M_0 to M_1 (a shift in the LM curve from LM_0 to LM_1), resulting in a restoration of full-employment output Y^f and the original price level P_0.

It is obvious that a *price-level target* would have required an identical response of monetary policy. This means that in the event of demand shocks both targets lead to the same stance of monetary policy. In other

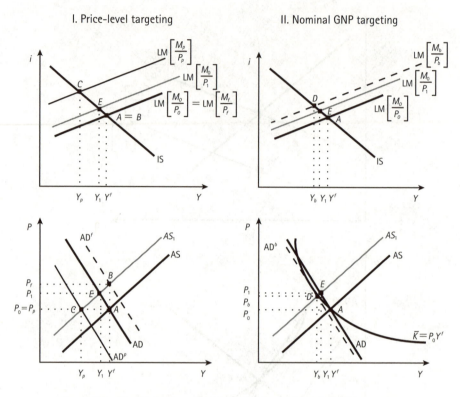

Figure 5.5. *Supply shocks: price-level targeting and nominal GNP targeting*

words, if a central bank is obliged to target the price level *in the short run*, it is automatically obliged to target the nominal income and also real income. Thus, there is no conflict between the output and employment objectives and the goal of price level stability.

However, the situation is different with a *supply shock* (see Figure 5.5). Assuming now a positive supply shock (a leftward shift in the AS curve to AS_1), first the price level will rise to P_1 and output will fall to Y_1; i.e., both ultimate targets are negatively affected. If the central bank tries to return to the correct target position on one of these two aggregates, it will be found that this is possible only at the cost of an even greater target deviation on the other aggregate. An *expansionary* monetary policy $(M = M_f)$ may restore full-employment output Y^f, but it will also cause the price level to rise to P_f (point of intersection B in graph I). Instead, a *restrictive* monetary policy will be needed in order to ensure price-level stability $(P = P_p = P_0)$. However, a strict *price-level target* will lead to a further decline in output $(Y = Y_p)$ and an even more marked undershoot of the full-employment target (point of intersection C in graph I). *Nominal GNP targeting* (graph II in Figure 5.5) represents a compromise between these two extremes in that it distributes the negative effects of the shock equally between the two ultimate targets. It seeks to ensure that the percentage by which prices rise will be exactly equal to the percentage by which output falls (Kahn 1988: 26).[19] When the aggregated demand and supply curve is as represented in Figure 5.5, nominal GNP targeting (point of intersection D in graph II) means that the central bank must pursue a slightly restrictive monetary policy ($M = M_b$). The consequence of this is that the rise in the price level is less sharp ($P = P_b$) than in the case of a 'non-interventionist' central bank ($M = M_0$), but there would be an additional fall in output ($Y = Y_b$).[20]

The intuition of this advantage of a nominal income rule is rather simple. A positive supply shock means that the nominal wages that had been agreed before the shock was realized have become too high. If the central bank allows a temporary increase in the price level, a partial reduction of real wages is possible so that the output decline can be mitigated. This correction is prevented if the central bank holds the price level constant. As the nominal wage can be adjusted in the next wage round, the duration of such shocks is very limited.

If realistic policy lags (of two years) are taken into account, there is in general very little scope for a strict price-level targeting in the short run (see Section 4.4).

5.3.2. *Policy implications*

The short-term analysis of demand and supply shocks shows a clear advantage of the nominal income target over a price-level target. It leads to the same performance in the situation of a demand shock, but it allows a more flexible reaction in the situation of a supply shock. Together with the long-term analysis in Section 5.2, this would call for a definition of the goals of monetary policy that prescribes

1. price stability as a long-term goal, and
2. a stable nominal income as a short-term goal.

---

[19] A stable nominal GNP means $\bar{K} = PY$ and, expressed in growth rates, $0 = Y (dP/dt) + P(dY/dt) = (dP/dt)/P + (dY/dt)/Y$, with the result that $\pi = -\dot{Y}$ (Taylor 1985: 75).

[20] There is then a solution at point E. However, it should be stressed that such a monetary policy implication of nominal GNP targeting is by no means automatic. If the supply shock results in a point of intersection of the (new) supply curve and an unchanged demand curve to the left of the GNP hyperbola, an expansionary monetary policy is required. This will result in a more marked deviation from the price stability target and a less marked one in the case of the full-employment target.

While this looks quite attractive from theoretical considerations, in practical monetary policy such a dual target would be difficult to implement, for the following reasons.

1. As we already mentioned, the dividing line between the short term and the long term is difficult to draw. Thus, with an explicit nominal income target, it cannot be excluded that monetary policy is held responsible for mistakes in other areas of economic policy (fiscal policy, wage policy) that cause a permanent decline in the growth rate of real GDP. This could lead to a less clear-cut policy assignment than under a price level target. For example, the supply shock described above (Figure 5.5) could have been caused by wage increases. In this case monetary policy would have to take some of the blame for the errors of collective pay policy. Unions and management would thus be discharged of their responsibility in the area of employment policy.

2. A short-term nominal income target, e.g. an annual nominal income target, would require very high technical skills of the central bank. As the example has shown, such a target can be met with precision only if monetary policy is able to react even to very short-term supply shocks. Hence it must have sufficiently precise forecasting values for nominal GNP. In contrast to an inflation target, which as a general rule is largely facilitated by the sluggishness of the 'expectations channel' (see Section 4.5), it is now necessary to identify at an early stage, and take account of, possible fluctuations in the real national product. There is thus a danger that such a fine-tuning of nominal GNP will in fact exacerbate cyclical fluctuations instead of ironing them out.

3. With an obligation to target nominal GDP on a permanent basis, the central bank would no longer be able to break inflationary expectations with the means of a restrictive monetary policy. For instance, in 1992/3 the Bundesbank followed a policy of high real interest rates in order to dampen the inflationary process that had been generated by German unification (Figure 4.3). As a result, nominal GDP growth was 2.2% in 1992 and -1.1% in 1993. With a nominal GDP target, the Bundesbank would have been criticized for not fulfilling its legal duties.

Thus, in spite of the theoretical attractiveness of a nominal income target, it seems problematic to define an explicit short-term nominal income target in a central bank constitution, or for such a definition to be announced by a central bank or in joint agreement between the government and the central bank. In reality, most central banks have found a different and quite efficient solution for coping with short-term supply shocks. As we shall discuss in detail in the following section, this approach relies on a long-term goal for price stability which is defined flexibly enough to allow an accommodation of supply shocks in the short run. Compared with an explicit nominal income target, this approach has the advantage and disadvantage that the short-term orientation of monetary policy is decided by the management of the central bank under its own discretion. This implies the risk that a central bank

1. is not reacting, or is not sufficiently reacting, to *demand shocks* which are associated with changes in the price level in the short and medium run, or
2. is pursuing short-term *employment targets* because of political pressure.

In Chapter 7 we will see that this scope for discretion is least problematic if a central bank is efficiently insulated from political influences.

5.4. OPERATIONAL ISSUES OF A 'STABILITY-ORIENTED MONETARY POLICY'

So far we have discussed the target of price stability without a precise definition. As the last section has demonstrated, such a definition is of crucial importance for practical monetary policy.

The expression 'price stability' might suggest that all prices are constant in a given economy. However, since in a market economy relative prices act essentially as a scarcity indicator, it is inevitable that they will be continually undergoing adjustments in response to changes in real conditions. An economically meaningful interpretation of 'price stability' therefore can only mean that prices for the various goods that are produced or consumed in a given economy do not change *on average*. If the price level in an economy is taken to mean the weighted average of the various prices of goods, 'price stability' will then mean stability of the price *level*. In that case, a rise in the price level indicates that the purchasing power of money is declining: a given unit of money will on average buy fewer goods. The price level and the value of money always move in precisely opposite directions.

5.4.1. *The choice of a price index*

The main indicator of whether an economy enjoys price stability, therefore, is the change in the price level over time. An indication of whether there has been a rise in the price level is given by a *price index*. A price index that rises over several periods is a sign of inflation, and the rate of increase in the price index is known as the *inflation rate*.

Any effective measure of the change in the price level must fulfil a number of essential conditions.[21] For example, the price index must show an increase between two periods—the period under review and the base period—if the price of at least one product goes up during the period considered without the prices of other goods falling (*strict monotonicity*). This also means that the price index must change by the factor *k* if all prices have changed by this factor during the period under consideration (*proportionality*). On the other hand, the price index must not change if prices have not changed (*identity*), or if there has only been a change in the currency unit in which the prices are measured (*invariance* with respect to the unit of measurement).

However, inflation measurement must take into account not only the performance of the index. It must also reflect the fact that in a highly developed economy a very large number of very different goods are on offer. Since it is impractical to include all these goods at the same time, there may be very many different price indices. The actual prices included in a given index will depend on the exact nature of what is being investigated (Edey 1994: 122). If it is argued, for example, that the purpose of all economic activity is to satisfy consumer wants, the price index should cover only consumer goods. But here, too, only a selection of consumer prices can be used for the purposes of such a price index. The index may be constructed by category of product or by social group. In order to be able to make meaningful long-term comparisons of prices, not only the selection, but also the weighting, of the selected products in the index must remain constant. The weightings are often derived from the volume of goods consumed in a base period. These constitute the so-called basket of goods (the *Laspeyres index*). If the basket of goods makes no distinction according to social group, the index is known as the *cost-of-living index*.

For the euro area a completely new price index has been constructed: *the harmonized index of consumer prices* (HICP). In order to measure inflation in all member countries in the same way, the HICP is based on a selection of goods and services that are identical throughout the European Union. Because of the harmonization, these national HICPs are less comprehensive than the traditional national cost-of-living indices. However, the harmonization does not imply that the national HICPs all use exactly the same baskets of goods or the same weighting schemes: from the national HICPs the Statistical Office of the European Union (Eurostat) calculates the HICP for the euro area as a weighted average. It is important to note that

---

[21] Many conditions for index formulae are discussed in index theory; the most important of these are summarized in e.g. Diewert (1992).

the HICP is not based on the theory of the cost-of-living index. Thus, Wynne states:

At the time of writing there is no fully articulated theoretical framework for HICPs, although there is a relatively well-defined price concept, namely 'final household monetary consumption.' (Wynne 1999: 1)

From a theoretical viewpoint, it may be objected that to include only consumer goods narrows the scope too much and that therefore the cost-of-living index is not an appropriate measure for price stability. On this argument, it would be preferable to measure price stability in terms of the price-level stability of all monetary transactions (Edey 1994: 122). A broader definition of this sort would have the advantage of including not only prices of current consumables, but also, indirectly, prices of future consumer goods. This would be achieved in particular through the inclusion of prices of securities (fixed-income paper and shares) and real estate. The idea of such an all encompassing index goes back to Irving Fisher:

Perhaps the best and most practical scheme is that which has been used in the explanation of P in our equation of exchange, an index number in which every article and service is weighted according to the value of it exchanged at base prices in the year whose level of prices it is desired to find. By this means, goods bought for immediate consumption are included in the weighting, as are also all durable capital goods exchanged during the period covered by the index number. What is repaid in contracts so measured is the same general purchasing power. This includes purchasing power over everything purchased and purchasable, including real estate, securities, labour, other services, such as the services rendered by corporations, and commodities. (Fisher 1920: 217–18)

In practice, however, such an all-embracing 'cost-of-life' price index (Edey 1994: 122) would be almost impossible to construct, since the data required for it are not available. One of the main problems is the weighting of current consumption and indirectly determined future consumption. In addition, share prices move so erratically that it is more than questionable whether they ought to serve as a guide for monetary policy.

The *gross domestic product (GDP) deflator* could be regarded as a sort of compromise solution. This includes all prices of goods produced by domestic manufacturers and prices of goods for which there is a demand on domestic markets. However, although it is more comprehensive than the cost-of-living index, it still does not include securities. In addition, it uses the product structure of the current period as the weighting schema; thus, it compares the current nominal GDP with the goods produced in the previous period measured in current prices (*Paasche index*). As a result

there is a continually changing weighting scheme, and so the comparability of the rates of change in this price index is rather limited.

A more recent approach for the measurement of inflation is the concept
of *core inflation*. This plays an important role in the monetary policy concept of inflation targeting (see Section 8.4). Wynne describes the rationale
of such indices as follows:

The common point of departure for almost all analyses of core inflation is the idea
that there is a well-defined concept of monetary inflation that ought to be of
concern to monetary policy makers and that this type of inflation, being conceptually different to the cost of living, is not adequately captured by the standard
price statistics. Thus it is argued that central banks ought to target a price index
whose rate of increase corresponds to the inflation that generates the costs that
central banks are seeking to avoid by focusing on an inflation-control objective.
(Wynne 1999: 2)

We have already seen that the costs of inflation are difficult to define
and measure. Therefore, we can understand that it is certainly not easy to
construct a price index on this concept.[22] In practice, several central banks
are working with indices of core inflation, which are derived from cost-
of-living indices by excluding

1. *food and energy prices*: e.g., in addition to the standard HICP, Eurostat
   publishes an HICP excluding food, energy, tobacco and alcohol;
2. *changes in interest rates*: this approach has been adopted by the Bank
   of England with its *RPIX* (retail price index excluding mortgage interest
   payments) and by the Reserve Bank of New Zealand with its *CPIX* (all-
   groups consumer price index excluding credit services);
3. *changes increases in indirect taxes*: this approach has been adopted by
   the Bank of England in its *RPIY*, which is the RPIX minus the first-round
   effects of indirect taxes;
4. *first-round effects of supply shocks*: this index, excluding these effects
   plus the other items already mentioned, was calculated earlier by
   the Reserve Bank of New Zealand on an *ad hoc* basis (Bernanke *et al.*
   1999: 87).

In Canada the central bank focuses on the CPI excluding food, energy,
and the effects of indirect taxes. Indices of core inflation are important
indicators for conduct of monetary policy, especially if they allow a better
forecast of future price developments than the 'headline' CPI. For the
communication with the public, core inflation rates have the disadvantage
that they are not necessarily regarded as a relevant information, since they

---

[22] For a theoretical analysis of these issues, see Wynne (1999).

are not always related to changes in the cost of living. Thus, for the HICP the ECB has decided not to adopt the concept of a core inflation rate.

In the context of discussion on nominal income targeting versus price-level targeting, the focus on core inflation provides a good compromise. It allows the final goal of monetary policy to be defined exclusively in terms of the inflation rate, but at the same times provides the flexibility to cope with temporary supply shocks which have very often been caused by shocks in energy prices.

5.4.2. *Price-level targeting versus inflation targeting*

In the academic discussion, a conceptual distinction between a price-level target and an inflation target is made (Svensson 1999*a*). In view of the algebraic relationship between the definitions of a level and its rate of change, a distinction between the two approaches does not seem obvious: the objective of a constant price level must always be identical with an inflation rate of 0%.

What then could be the reason for making a distinction between price level in the sense of a constant price index and 'zero inflation' (Edey 1994: 118; Goodhart 1994: 1428)? It can be explained with the widespread convention whereby a price-level target is understood to represent a medium- to long-term objective, whereas an inflation target is normally assumed to imply a short-term realization period (Edey 1994: 118). In the words of Svensson,

I shall refer to a monetary policy regime as price-level targeting or inflation targeting, depending upon whether the goal is a stable price level or a low and stable inflation rate, where the latter allows base drift of the price level. (Svensson 1999*a*: 277)

The difference can be explained with a simple example. Assume that a central bank can define its target for a 'stability-oriented monetary policy' in three different ways:

1. by a stable price level for the next four years (price-level target);
2. by an *average* inflation target for the period of the next four years (multi-annual inflation target);
3. by an *annual* inflation target of 0% (annual inflation target).

If the inflation rate is 3% in the first year, the price-level target and the multi-annual inflation target require a deflation in the following three years, as they do not allow a base drift. This is different from the annual inflation target. If it is not met, a base shift is made so that a corrective deflation in the following years is avoided. Thus, a multi-annual inflation target is identical to a price-level target.[23]

In practice, no central bank has ever announced a price-level target or a multi-annual target of zero inflation. As we have already seen, most central banks aim at inflation rates with a midpoint of 1.5%–2%. This practice is mainly related to statistical measurement problems (Section 5.4.3). Thus, a strict price-level targeting would not be a practical solution. Nevertheless, the question of a base drift remains, even with inflation targets that are higher than zero.

The experience of the Deutsche Bundesbank shows that even this ambitious central bank has always been willing to accept base drifts in its monetary policy. In periods with major supply shocks, it even went so far as to adjust its annual inflation target upwards (Table 8.1). It is obvious that price-level targeting or multi-annual inflation targeting requires a more active fine-tuning of the economic process than annual inflation targeting. Instead of simply treating an unanticipated shock to the price level as a one-off occurrence, the former require an active offsetting of the shock. With a limited knowledge about the short-term transmission process, the risk of additional instability arising from such compensating actions is high.

All central banks with declared inflation targets have avoided precise statements about their willingness or otherwise to accept base drifts. But by focusing on core inflation and including escape clauses for 'exceptional circumstances', most inflation-targeting central banks seem to have a preference for allowing base drifts when the inflation target was not met.

5.4.3. *Defining concrete target values*

The experience of the last fifty years indicates that price stability defined in terms of a constant price index is virtually impossible to achieve by means of practical monetary policy measures. Even in countries where the central bank has a high degree of independence (see Chapter 7) and is especially committed to promoting stability, the cost-of-living index has risen significantly over the past fifty years; for instance, in Germany from 1950 to 1998 (the last year the Bundesbank was responsible for monetary policy in Germany) the average annual inflation rate was 2.9%.

In addition to the empirical arguments, the problems connected with the actual calculation of indices suggest that it is impractical to set an inflation

---

[23] See also Mervyn King (2000: 5): 'An average inflation target is, therefore, akin to price level targeting'.

target of zero. In view of the arbitrariness (discussed above) in the choice of the goods to be included, and also the inaccuracies resulting from the index formula used, statistically determined inflation rates of between 1% and 2% can still be regarded as compatible with the objective of price stability. Statistical measurement problems are the result, above all, of four factors (see OECD 1994: 34):

1. *Quality bias*: Although statisticians endeavour to take account of quality improvements in goods in their price index calculations, it is possible to do this only to a limited extent in the case of significant technical advances and innovations.
2. *Product substitution bias*: Consumers replace goods whose relative prices are rising with goods whose relative prices are falling. Since, in order to ensure comparability, consumer price indices have to use fixed weighting systems, they cannot reflect such effects over time and therefore overstate the effective loss in purchasing power.
3. *New goods bias*: When comparing prices over the long term, there is also the practically insoluble problem that many of the items that are common today (such as mobile phones, personal computers, use of internet services) were either unobtainable or inordinately expensive in earlier years. A long-term comparison of prices based on today's basket of goods would show a much less marked erosion in the value of money.
4. *Outlet substitution bias*: Consumers are always keen to buy goods from dealers offering the lowest prices. This important phenomenon, too, can be only partially reflected in the official statistics.

All the above factors mean that the inflation figures tend to overstate the effective inflation rate. Intensive research in the United States (above all the so-called 'Boskin Report'–Boskin *et al.* 1996; Moulton 1996; Shapiro and Wilcox 1996) and Canada estimates the effect of such distortions at 0.2%–2% per annum (OECD 1994: 34). As Table 8.1 shows, the Bundesbank regarded an inflation rate of 2% compatible with price stability. The measurement bias for the euro area is still difficult to estimate. In the words of the European Central Bank,

Eurostat has expended considerable effort to reduce or eliminate the measurement bias in the HICP. It is therefore probable that the bias in the HICP is smaller than that observed in national CPIs of the countries comprising the euro area. Moreover, the available empirical evidence suggests that the measurement bias in national CPIs for euro area countries is smaller than that which has been estimated in a number of prominent studies of consumer price indices in other countries. The success of these attempts to minimise the measurement bias in the HICP is as yet unknown. Furthermore, the size of the measurement bias is likely to change over time as the structure of the economy evolves and statistical methods change, partly in response to these changes in economic structure. (ECB 1999a: 46)

As Table 5.1 shows, the midpoints of the inflation targets published by central banks are in a range between 1.5% and 2%. Thus, they reflect the upper bound of the empirical estimates of the measurement bias.

In addition to these statistical problems, there are also economic arguments that could speak against an inflation target of 0%. Akerlof *et al.* (1996) argue that a slightly positive inflation rate makes it easier to achieve changes in the structure of real wages. This argument is based on the assumption that workers are unwilling to accept a decline in nominal wages. Thus, without inflation, a required adjustment in the wage structure cannot be realized that could lead to an increase in the natural rate of unemployment. Also, an inflation rate close to zero could impair the macro-economic demand management as it implies a 'neutral' nominal interest rate of 3%; as nominal interest rates cannot become negative, there is relatively little scope for an expansionary monetary policy in a period of recession (Summers 1991). As Bernanke *et al.* (1999: 29) point out, real interest rates, which can become negative, are economically more relevant than nominal interest rates. However, it is often found in practice that with negative inflation rates nominal interest rates do not fully adjust in accordance with the Fisher equation, and as a result real interest rates are too high and investment too low (Laidler 1992: 606). In the view of Bernanke *et al.* (1999: 29), the main argument against aiming for an inflation rate of zero is that this 'risks tipping the economy in deflation'.

5.5. SUMMARY

As far as the final goals of monetary policy are concerned, there is today a broad consensus among almost all central banks in the world. In contrast to some popular views of the 1970s, it is completely uncontroversial that inflation is detrimental in the long run, since it impairs an effective use of money in its main functions. In the medium and short run, a trade-off between price stability and nominal (and real) income growth is possible, but it is limited to supply shocks. In the case of demand shocks, a stabilization of output contributes to a stabilization of the price level, but, because of the long and variable lags in the transmission process, such an approach should be limited to more persistent shocks.

This consensus approach is reflected in concrete inflation targets that many central banks, with notable exception of the Federal Reserve, have announced in the last few years. The targets are often defined for 'core inflation', which leaves some scope for supply shocks. In the case of the

ECB, which targets 'headline inflation', its focus on the medium term leaves it room for dealing with temporary supply shocks. As no short-term targets are announced, there is no obligation to react to short-term demand shocks, but persistent demand shocks require a monetary policy response in order to achieve the inflation targets over the medium term.

Appendix 5.1. Different variants of the nominal GDP targeting

In the same way that the objective of price stability can be defined as an inflation or price-level target, nominal GNP targeting offers a choice between

1. *growth-rate targeting*, which aims to ensure that nominal GNP grows by a particular amount in any period, and
2. *level targeting*, which aims to ensure that nominal GNP follows a set course over several years (Taylor 1985; Hall and Mankiw 1994).

There is also a third approach, whereby the central bank is meant to react differently if it misses the target for price stability or full employment. Whereas, in the event of output divergences in the preceding period, the target growth rate in nominal GNP needs to be adjusted by the same amount, a too high inflation rate in the preceding period has no effect on the target growth rate in nominal GNP. Hall and Mankiw (1994: 77) call this '*hybrid targeting*'.

Nominal GNP is equal to the product of the price level (P) and real output (Y). In the simplest case, the objective is a constant price level (P_0) at a reference point of time t_0 and constant full-employment output (Y^f). In this case the *level target* ($\overline{K}$) is obtained as follows:[24]

$$\overline{K} = P_0 Y^f. \tag{A5.1}$$

A target level for nominal GDP can also be formulated in the form of a target path that, starting from an optimal state, grows at a rate of e^{kt}. Here the level target is obtained as

$$\overline{K} = P_0 Y^f e^{kt}. \tag{A5.2}$$

In growth-rate targeting, on the other hand, a target value is derived for the desired growth rate in nominal GNP. In accordance with the definition of nominal GNP, such a growth target (k) for nominal GNP is composed of an

---

[24] In practice, P_0 will correspond to the price-level ruling when full-employment output and actual output are equal, i.e. when the output gap is zero. A reference year is thus needed on which to base the target.

inflation target π^* and a target value for the real growth rate $\hat{Y}^*$. If it is also assumed here that the aim is always to maintain full employment, this means that the target value for real growth must equal the trend growth or the growth in productivity λ:[25]

$$k = \pi^* + \hat{Y}^* = \pi^* + \lambda. \tag{A5.3}$$

Here too a difference between level targeting and growth-rate targeting arises only if it is assumed that

1. the level targeting applies to a period of several years, while
2. in the case of growth-rate targeting only annual targets are used.

Thus, in the case of growth-rate targeting, missing the target in the preceding period has no effect on the following period(s), whereas such 'base drift' is not possible in the case of level targeting (Hall and Mankiw 1994). A growth-rate target is thus less ambitious.

Appendix 5.2. Calculating the welfare losses of sub-optimal money holdings

If one uses the above semi-logarithmic money demand function from Chapter 2 (equation (2.38)), the social costs of a positive nominal interest rate i_1, in relation to the national product Y, are equal to the area Bm_1m_s in Figure 5.1 above. This area is obtained as the difference in the area to the left of the money demand curve between interest rates zero and i_1, less government revenue from seigniorage ABm_10:

$$\frac{C(i_1)}{Y} = \int_0^{i_1} \beta e^{-\alpha i} di - i_1 \beta e^{-\alpha i_1} = \left(-\frac{\beta}{\alpha} e^{-\alpha i} \right)_0^{i_1} - i_1 \beta e^{-\alpha i_1}$$

$$= \frac{\beta}{\alpha} [1 - (1 + \alpha i_1) e^{-\alpha i_1}]. \tag{A5.4}$$

In the context of Figure 5.1, the welfare costs of the inflation rate π_1 are obtained as the area BCm_0m_1. Therefore the area Cm_sm_0 must be deducted from the social costs of a positive nominal rate of interest. If the nominal rate of interest is formed from the sum of the real rate of interest r and the inflation expectation π^e (Fisher relation: $i = r + \pi^e$), and assuming

---

[25] The production function represents the relationship between employment and production. When observing a dynamic situation, this is known as *Okun's Law* and means that the unemployment rate rises (falls) if the actual growth rate in production is lower (higher) than the trend growth.

steady-state conditions so that the inflation expectation is always equal to the actual inflation rate π, then the welfare costs of an inflation rate π_1 are

$$
\frac{L(\pi_1)}{Y} = \int_0^{i_1} \beta e^{-\alpha i} di - i_1 \beta e^{-\alpha i_1} - \left\{ \int_0^r \beta e^{-\alpha i} di - r\beta e^{-\alpha r} \right\}
$$

$$
= \left[-\frac{\beta}{\alpha} e^{-\alpha i} \right]_r^{i_1} - \pi_1 \beta e^{-\alpha i_{1+r}} (\beta e^{-\alpha r} - \beta e^{-\alpha i_1})
$$

$$
= \frac{\beta}{\alpha} e^{-\alpha r} [1 - (1 + \alpha(r + \pi_1)) e^{-\alpha \pi_1} + \alpha r]. \tag{A5.5}
$$

If the government increases the growth rate of the nominal money supply (μ)–and thus in steady-state conditions causes a rise in the inflation rate (π)–then the welfare costs of inflation in relation to the national product also rise (assuming r is a constant real interest rate):

$$
\frac{d(L(\pi)/Y)}{d\pi} = \frac{\beta}{\alpha} [\alpha e^{-\alpha(r+\pi)} + \alpha^2(r + \pi) e^{-\alpha(r+\pi)} - \alpha e^{-\alpha(r+\pi)}]
$$

$$
= \alpha(r + \pi)\beta e^{-\alpha(r+\pi)}. \tag{A5.6}
$$

6

The Institutional Framework
for Monetary Policy I:
'Rules versus Discretion'

What this chapter is about

- It will discuss whether it is necessary to limit the room for manoeuvre of central bankers by 'rules' that are laid down in the central bank constitution and which prescribe the setting of important policy variables (i.e. the final, intermediate, or operating targets) or the use of certain instruments.
- The traditional debate on this issue is based on the assumptions of policy-makers either pursuing targets other than social welfare, or having a very limited knowledge about economic processes. The following chapter will show that a well-designed central bank constitution is a better solution to these problems than a monetary policy guided by rigid rules.
- The more recent debate argues that rules are necessary even if policy-makers are extremely competent and interested only in social welfare. The concrete rule calls for an inflation rate that at all times equals zero. We will see that this surprising result rests on very artificial assumptions, above all that the central bank targets an unemployment rate that is lower than the natural rate of unemployment. Thus, the more recent approach is not very different from the traditional debate. Its main merit is a precise analytical discussion of the main issues.

6.1. OVERVIEW

In order to fulfil its macroeconomic and microeconomic tasks, a central bank needs an adequate institutional framework. This framework is formally laid down in the central bank constitution.

This and the following chapter will start with a normative approach and ask how a central bank constitution should be designed, given the macroeconomic targets that were discussed in the previous chapter. This normative framework makes it possible to analyse the concrete constitutions of important central banks throughout the world.

6.2. RULES VERSUS DISCRETION IN MONETARY POLICY

A natural starting point for all discussions about an optimum institutional framework for monetary policy is the traditional debate on 'rules versus discretion'. This focuses on the very general question of

1. whether central banks should be given the 'power of deciding or acting without other control than one's own judgement',[1] or
2. whether it is not preferable to lay down some procedural 'rules' (in the sense of 'an established guide or regulation for action'[2]) in a central bank's statutes, which could in effect turn the decision-makers at the central bank into little more than 'semi-automatons' (Issing 1993*a*: 7).

The origins of the 'rules versus discretion' debate can be traced back to the debate that was being conducted in the early nineteenth century between the adherents of the 'Banking School' and those of the 'Currency School'. Economists belonging to the former argued that the issue of paper currency should be closely tied to the gold reserves of the central bank, while followers of the latter held the view that, even without such a strict rule, the supply of paper money would increase in a manner that was compatible with macroeconomic stability (see Appendix 6.1).

In the following paragraphs it is important to note that the term 'rule' has very different meanings today.

- In this chapter, a 'rule' is defined as a regulation that is imposed on a central bank *from outside* under statutory provisions (usually the Central Bank Act). Its main function is to limit the discretion of policy-makers.
- In Chapter 8, a 'rule' is defined as an heuristic which facilitates the decision processes of central bankers. In this sense it helps to reduce the complexity of the world to a simple and frugal heuristic. In contrast to the above definition of a 'rule', this one is normally adopted voluntarily by the management of a central bank.

6.3. THE MAIN ARGUMENTS FOR LIMITING THE DISCRETION OF CENTRAL BANKERS

A good example of a central bank constitution that provides a high degree of discretion is the US Federal Reserve Act. As already mentioned (Section 5.1.2), this Act simply enumerates different macroeconomic targets and leaves it up to the discretion of the members of the Board of Governors and

---

[1] This is the description of 'discretion' in *Webster's New Universal Unabridged Dictionary*.
[2] See also *Webster's New Universal Unabridged Dictionary*.

the Federal Open Market Committee (Section 7.2.5) to give specific weights to these targets and to decide on a concrete policy strategy. The performance of the US monetary policy in the period 1950–66 and again in 1985–2000 shows from the very outset that such a discretionary policy can lead to good results.

What are the arguments of the adherents of 'rules'? We have to differentiate between a traditional debate, which is based on the assumption of policy-makers who are either not well qualified or not interested in maximizing social welfare, and a more recent debate, which tries to show from a game-theoretic basis that rules are needed even with perfect policy-makers. In this section we will focus on the traditional debate; the more recent debate will be discussed in Section 6.6.

The traditional arguments for monetary rules are set forth very concisely by Henry Simons (1936) and the German economist Walter Eucken, who was in favour of restricting the central bank's margin of discretion,

because experience shows that a monetary constitution which gives those responsible for monetary policy a free hand implicitly credits them with greater powers than is generally justifiable. Lack of knowledge, weakness in the face of pressure from interest groups and public opinion, false theories can all influence their judgement and prove a major obstacle to achieving the task assigned to them. Particularly nowadays there is a serious risk that an insufficiently structured monetary constitution could be abused and result in inflation.[3] (Eucken 1952: 257)

This statement makes two important assumptions which are essential to the traditional justification of the need for a monetary rule (Blinder 1987: 400):

1. The central bank might be unable to use its margin of discretion so as to achieve the desired macroeconomic target in a satisfactory manner.[4]
2. Even if a central bank were able to manage the economy perfectly, it cannot in principle be expected to take its decisions with the economy's welfare as a whole in mind. It would thus be wrong to assume automatically that a central bank will be a 'benign dictator'. Instead, it must be supposed that the content of monetary policy decisions will bear the

---

[3] What Eucken actually had in mind (1952: 263) was a 'commodity reserve currency' acting as an 'automatic mechanism designed on rational principles which would allow "rational control of the money supply in accordance with certain fixed rules"'. This is basically the gold standard, except that a single commodity would be replaced by a batch of commodities.

[4] See Milton Friedman (1968:15): 'As a result, we cannot predict at all accurately just what effect a particular monetary action will have on the price level and, equally important, just when it will have that effect.'

imprint of those interest groups which are in a better position than others to influence the political process. This is the political-economy justification for rules.

Given this justification for strict rules, it seems obvious that such an institutional arrangement has to meet very different requirements.

1. A rule must be *simple*. Since it is to be enshrined in a law, it must at least be easy enough to be understood by some of the legislators and—in the event of its contravention—by the judges.
2. A rule must be *stable*; that is to say, it must be drafted so as to last. Frequent adjustments would make excessive demands on Parliament's legislative time, and the necessary amending legislation might not always come at the right time.[5]
3. At the same time, the uncertainties about the transmission process require that a rule should be *flexible* enough to cope with various shocks.[6]

6.3.1. *Limited knowledge about the transmission process*

Whether central banks are really able to control economic processes in line with their final target(s) has been the subject of intense discussion and argument in the past. Chapter 4 has already mentioned the influential study of the monetary history of the United States in the period 1867–1960, produced by Milton Friedman and Anna Schwartz (1963), which comes to a very sceptical view regarding the possibilities of an economic fine-tuning by a central bank. But the limited theoretical knowledge of such mechanisms is not an obvious argument for rules so much as an exogenous limitation on a central bank's room for manoeuvre. The limited knowledge about the structure of the transmission process and the variability of lags would also make it difficult to design a rule for monetary policy that could be followed in a strict way. Moreover, as central bankers are well aware of the difficulties of macroeconomic management in the short run, one can expect that they will avoid policy actions that would destabilize the economy. In other words, if there were an efficient rule, central bankers would have a strong incentive to adopt it voluntarily as a 'simple rule' (Chapter 8). In contrast to a legally set rule, this approach would allow a suspension of

---

[5] Henry Simons (1936: 13) puts this as follows: 'In a free-enterprise system we obviously need highly definitive and stable rules of the game, especially as to money. The monetary rules must be compatible with the reasonably smooth working of the system. Once established, however, they should work mechanically, with the chips falling where they may.'

[6] In the words of Simons (1936: 29), 'They [the rules] should be designed to permit the fullest and most stable employment, to facilitate adjustment to such basic changes (especially in technology) as they are likely to occur, and secondarily, to minimize inequities between debtors and creditors.'

the rule whenever an economy was confronted with completely unforeseen shocks.

As far as the risk of unqualified decision-makers is concerned, we will see that most central banks are equipped with relatively large decision-making bodies (Table 7.1). This provides a diversification against the risk of an unqualified central banker ever being appointed.

6.3.2. *The principal–agent problem of monetary policy*

Even if central banks are highly qualified, it cannot be assumed *a priori* that they will in fact take action to this end. For example, it is easy to imagine the central bank adopting a sharply expansionary policy shortly before the end of a parliamentary term in order to improve the current government's chances of re-election by giving a short-term boost to the economy. This would inevitably lead to increased inflation expectations and so would threaten the goal of price stability. These threats to macroeconomic stability are intensively discussed in the literature on 'political business cycles' (Nordhaus 1975).

In such circumstances, subjecting monetary policy to strict rules has the advantage that the central bank is no longer susceptible to such outside pressures. On the other hand, it is questionable whether those responsible for deciding monetary policy really need to be stripped of all essential powers, especially since there is a danger that any given rule can prevent the authorities from responding with sufficient flexibility when shocks occur.

Logically, this situation can be analysed in terms of a typical *principal–agent problem* (Fratianni *et al.* 1997).[7]

- The *principal* is society as a whole (or Parliament), whose priority, as far as monetary policy is concerned, is a low rate of inflation in the long run combined with stable macroeconomic conditions in the short and medium run.
- The *agent* is the central bank, to which society assigns the task (under the Central Bank Act) of realizing these goals. Through its expertise and its direct contacts with the banks and financial markets, the central bank has access to privileged information ('asymmetric information') which also enables it, at least to a limited degree, to pursue a goal different from that formally assigned to it.

It appears, from the business management literature on this subject, that when problems of this sort arise there is certainly no need for the agent to

---

[7] For a survey see Rees (1985) and Stiglitz (1987).

be deprived of all decision-making powers or to be constrained by rigid rules. At the level of the individual company, drawing up binding rules for all-important business decisions would be a fairly hopeless undertaking from the start. Instead, what normally happens is that contractual arrangements are devised which structure the incentives for the agent in such a way that she uses her discretionary powers as far as possible in the interests of the principal. If such mechanisms can be found, they prove to be far preferable to rigid rules, since they allow the agent to react flexibly in the event of unforeseen shocks. In the relationship between society and the central bank, such a system of incentives can be created both by the central bank statutes and by 'performance contracts' for those in charge of the central bank. These aspects will be discussed in detail in Chapter 7.

In sum, the traditional case for limiting the discretion of central bankers with strict rules is not very convincing, at least from the present perspective.

6.4. RULES THAT ARE IMPOSED ON CENTRAL BANKS FROM OUTSIDE

The above assessment is also supported by the fact that there are very few concrete examples of strict externally imposed rules in monetary policy.

At the level of *final targets*, we have already seen that in many countries price stability is regarded as the main target of monetary policy. As a result many central bank constitutions explicitly state the dominance of this target (Section 7.2.3). However, there are no examples where a central bank constitution defines a concrete target value for a concrete price index and a concrete target period. In fact, our discussion in Chapter 5 has shown that such a strict rule would not be advisable. Thus, the price stability rules that are laid down in central bank constitutions do not constitute a very strict limitation of a central bank's room for manoeuvre. For instance, when the Deutsche Bundesbank, while operating under the obligation of the former Article 3 of the Bundesbank Act to 'safeguard the currency', accepted an inflation rate of 7.0% in 1973 and 1974, it was never criticized for doing so.

At the level of *intermediate targets*, a rule could be defined for either a monetary target or an exchange rate target. In the late 1960s and early 1970s, monetarists pleaded for a strict monetary targeting:

My own prescription is still that the monetary authority go all the way in avoiding such swings by adopting publicly the policy of achieving a steady rate of growth in a specified monetary total. The precise rate of growth, like the precise monetary total, is less important than the adoption of some stated and known rate. (Friedman 1968: 16)

However, no country has ever decided to formulate a central bank law that obliges a central bank to follow a concrete target value for a concrete monetary aggregate. Above all, this would raise the issue of continuous financial innovation, which not only can change the demand for money but also can necessitate a reformulation of the target aggregate (Bernholz 1986). Thus, even a sturdy champion of monetary targeting such as the Deutsche Bundesbank admits:

The search for the 'correct' monetary policy indicator or the 'optimal' intermediate target magnitude will never lead to a situation in which the central bank's task becomes a purely automatic exercise in management. (Deutsche Bundesbank 1995: 80)

This does not apply, however, when exchange rate targeting is adopted. Here, we can find many historical examples of targets that were externally imposed on a central bank.

- The *International Gold Standard* (1876–1914)[8] constituted a worldwide fixed exchange rate system in which individual currencies were set in the national coinage legislation in terms of their equivalent in gold.[9]
- The international exchange rate system of *Bretton Woods* (1946–73)[10] obliged member countries to maintain a fixed parity for their own currency *vis-à-vis* the US dollar. This obligation was based on international law. The national authorities were only allowed to make small parity changes; larger adjustments required the approval of the International Monetary Fund (Article IV (5) of the IMF Articles of Agreement).
- In the *European Monetary System I* (1979–98),[11] the parities were decided by the finance ministers of the member countries. Thus, the central banks had to adjust their policy to meet these targets. Above all, however, in the 1980s the parities were adjusted quite regularly,

---

[8] See the 'classical' analysis by Bloomfield (1963), also Bordo and Schwartz (1984) and Bofinger (1991).

[9] For example, the German Law on the Minting of Imperial Gold Coins of 1871 stated: 'An Imperial gold coin will be minted, 139 items of which will be produced from 1 pound of pure gold' (§1). 'The 10th part of this gold coin will be called a Mark and divided into 100 pfennigs' (§2). Thus, according to the German standard of coinage, the value of a kilogram of fine gold was equal to $139 \times 2 \times 10$ marks $= 2,780$ marks. The French coinage legislation of the same period provided that, from one kilogram of gold bullion of a fineness of 900 parts per thousand, coins in the value of 3,100 francs were to be minted. One kilogram of fine gold was thus equivalent to $3,100$ francs $\times 1000/900 = 3,444$ francs. National legislation thus implicitly set a fixed exchange rate between currencies. In the case of the franc and the mark, the exchange rate was 100 francs $= 81$ marks.

[10] See Bordo and Eichengreen (1993) and Bofinger (1991).

[11] The European Monetary System II started with the beginning of the European Monetary Union. It presently includes the ECB and Denmark.

so that this constraint was not very binding (Gros and Thygesen 1998; De Grauwe 2000).

- Under a *currency board arrangement,* a central bank is obliged by national law to maintain a fixed exchange rate between the national currency and an 'anchor currency' (Box 6.1). In order to enhance the credibility of the commitment to a fixed rate, a Currency Board is—in a similar way as under the gold standard—required to ensure that the monetary base is fully covered by foreign exchange reserves (Walters and Hanke 1987). Thus, a rule geared to an intermediate target is extended to include a rule concerning the actual monetary policy instruments (see below).

While rules based on the exchange rate worked well for prolonged periods of time in many countries, especially smaller countries, there are also many examples of currency crises that resulted from too rigid exchange rate targets (Chapters 12 and 13).

For externally imposed rules at the level of *operating targets* (the monetary base or the money market rate), no historic examples can be found. Although as a rule of thumb for the money market rate the Taylor rule performs very well (Section 8.5), it would be very problematic to make it absolutely binding by writing it down in the central bank constitution.

A very stringent variant of a monetary policy rule relates to the exogenous specifications for individual items of the central bank balance sheet, which limit or exclude the use of certain *instruments.*

1. Provisions to prevent central banks from lending to domestic public authorities are now very common. In EU countries these take the form of an 'overdraft prohibition' in the EC Treaty (Article 101).[12]
2. A very strict limitation is provided by the arrangement of a *currency board* (Box 6.1). As this arrangement stipulates 100% cover of the monetary base by foreign currency reserves, a central bank is directly or indirectly forbidden to engage in any form of lending to domestic borrowers and hence is prevented from using any of the traditional monetary policy instruments. Changes in the monetary base are therefore possible only if surpluses are generated in the foreign exchange account of a country's central bank. The money supply is thus completely tied to movements in the balance of payments.

---

[12] Article 101 of the EC Treaty reads as follows: 'Overdraft facilities or any other type of credit facility with the ECB or with the central banks of the Member States ... in favour of Community institutions or bodies, central governments, regional, local or other public authorities, other bodies governed by public law, or public undertakings of Member States shall be prohibited, as shall the purchase directly from them by the ECB or national central banks of debt instruments.'

Box 6.1. *Currency boards*

The currency board is a commitment technology that was introduced in the last century for the British colonies, but has since been introduced in many other countries (see Table 6.1). It issues its own bank-notes, for which it maintains 100% cover by foreign currency reserves. It also maintains a statutorily fixed exchange rate between the national currency and a foreign currency. (In the case of the British colonies this was sterling.) Full cover of the banknote issue by foreign assets also implies that any form of lending to domestic borrowers is prohibited. As an example of the regulations of a currency board, excerpts from the 'Law of the Republic of Estonia on Security for Estonian Kroon' are reproduced below.

In the British colonies the advantages of a currency board, compared with the use of sterling notes, were in the first instance of a purely technical nature. Banknotes that were no longer suitable for circulation did not have to be sent to London, but could be replaced on the spot. But there were also economic advantages. The foreign exchange reserves could be held in interest-bearing form, and so seigniorage was earned in the colony and not in England. In the event of a loss of banknotes, the colony still retained its sterling claims. Today currency boards are particularly interesting from the point of view of monetary policy credibility. The commitment to a fixed exchange rate is given extra credibility not only because the exchange rate is statutorily fixed, but also because the central bank is deprived of almost all margin of discretion. In the countries of Eastern Europe and the CIS undergoing transformation to a market economy, where it is still very difficult to draw the line of demarcation between the State and the private sector, currency boards have the additional advantage of preventing the public sector from circumventing the restrictions on lending to it. On the other hand, the extremely stringent nature of the system's operation means that it can make excessive demands on the domestic banking system's capacity to adapt. This point is made by Walters and Hanke (1987: 561), who regard this as less problematic in the case of the British colonies, since the banks operating there were mostly subsidiaries or branches of British banks; in the event of a major liquidity problem they could always have recourse to the Bank of England as 'lender of last resort' (see Appendix to Chapter 7). The money supply process under a currency board system is determined exclusively by changes in the central bank's net external assets. This aggregate is in its turn determined by the current account of the balance of payments and the capital transactions of banks and non-banks.

Excerps from the Law of the Republic of Estonia on Security Estonian Kroon (20 May 1992)

Clause 1   Security for Estonian kroon
The Estonian kroon (cash in circulation, currency in current accounts and in accounts of a fixed date) is issued fully secured by the gold and convertible foreign exchange reserve of Eesti Pank [Estonian central bank].

Clause 2   Rate of Estonian kroon
The official rate of Estonian kroon will be determined by Eesti Pank with respect to German mark. Eesti Pank has no right to devalue Estonian kroon. The limit of technical fluctuation of Estonian kroon is 3%.

Clause 3   Exchangeability of Estonian kroon
Eesti Pank guarantees to the Republic of Estonia the free exchange of the Estonian kroon to convertible foreign currencies for current needs of customers, according to the official rate of Eesti Pank.

Clause 4   Changing the amount of currency in circulation
Eesti Pank has the right to change the amount of Estonian kroons in circulation only according to a change in its gold and foreign exchange reserve.

Clause 5   Informing on the security of Estonian kroon
Eesti Pank, at least once a month, makes public information about the amount of its gold and convertible foreign exchange reserve as well as the amount of Estonian kroon in circulation.

Table 6.1. *Existing currency boards*

Country	Begin	Anchor currency	Exchange rate	Reserve assets	Minimum coverage ratio
Hong Kong	1984	US$	7.8 HK$ = 1 US$	Foreign currencies and bonds	105% of currency in circulation
Argentina	1991	US$	1 peso = 1 US$	2/3 foreign currencies and gold, 1/3 Argentine government bonds denominated in US$	100% of the monetary base
Estonia	1992	DEM€	8 crowns = 1 DEM	Foreign currencies, bonds, and gold	100% of the monetary base
Lithuania	1994	US$	4 lita = 1 US$	Foreign currencies, bonds, and gold	100% of the monetary base and other obligations of the central bank
Bulgaria	1997	DEM€	1 lev = 1 DEM	Foreign currencies, bonds, and gold	More than 100% of the monetary base
Bosnia/Herzegovina	1997	DEM€	1 marka = 1 DEM	Only DEM-denominated assets, with the exception of 50% of the central bank's own capital	100% of the central bank's liabilities

Source: Molitor (2000).

6.5. SUMMARY OF THE TRADITIONAL DEBATE

In the present debate on monetary policy, the traditional arguments for rules do not play an important role. We will see in Chapter 7 that the incentive problems can be solved by an adequate design of the central bank constitution. As far as the problem of limited knowledge about the transmission process is concerned, most central banks rely voluntarily on relatively simple and robust rules (Chapter 8) which have the advantage that they can be overridden when unexpected shocks occur.

Thus, the only example at present for a strict externally imposed rule is the arrangement of a currency board. This can be regarded as an emergency solution for countries where the reputation of monetary policy-makers is so low that it becomes worthwhile to bear the costs of a very inflexible regime.

6.6. 'TIME INCONSISTENCY': A NEW ARGUMENT IN SUPPORT OF RULES?

A seemingly new argument in support of monetary rules was developed in the early 1980s. Based on the so-called 'time inconsistency' of optimal monetary policy strategies, it did much to stimulate the whole debate on monetary theory throughout the 1980s.[13] Today, some economists are more sceptical about the merits and the scientific productivity of this very intensive debate.

The main argument of this more recent discussion on the subject of 'rules versus discretion' is that rules are preferable even where the underlying circumstances would argue against their strict imposition. It is assumed that

1. the central bank is at all times perfectly able to manage the economy (the price level and national income)—the lag problems associated with an countercyclical policy are thus ignored;
2. the central bank's decisions are geared exclusively to a social welfare function; that is to say, those responsible for deciding monetary policy are regarded as 'benign dictators'.[14]

Under such conditions, the arguments for rules in the traditional debate on 'rules versus discretion' would no longer exist. However, in the more recent 'rules versus discretion' debate it is concluded that even under such ideal conditions it is advisable for a discretionary monetary policy to contain strict rules for the monetary policy authorities: 'even a knowledgeable

---

[13] See the summary article by Blackburn and Christensen (1989).
[14] For this reason this is also known as the 'social welfare approach' (Cukierman 1986: 6).

government intent on serving the public interest may systematically do the wrong thing' (Blinder 1987: 401).

This conclusion, which may appear surprising, is due mainly to the phenomenon of the 'time inconsistency' of optimal strategies.[15] In general terms, a strategy is time-inconsistent if it is optimal at a point of time t_0 but no longer optimal at a point of time t_1. According to such a general definition, however, the time inconsistency of optimal strategies does not appear to be a particularly significant phenomenon, since it is clear at once that a strategy which is optimal at t_0 will not necessarily be optimal at t_1 if the basis on which the parties involved take their decisions has changed. Similarly, a time-inconsistent strategic choice will also occur when new information becomes available.

However, the phenomenon of time inconsistency as has been used in the more recent debate on 'rules versus discretion' is based on a problem structure that arises in *game theory* (Blackburn and Christensen 1989). This modelling originates with Kydland and Prescott (1977), but is also particularly featured in the well-known studies of Barro and Gordon (1983*a,b*).

6.6.1. *A simple example of time inconsistency*

The game-theoretic explanation of the phenomenon of time inconsistency can best be illustrated by a simple example which was first used by Alan Blinder (1987: 407) and is taken from university life. Blinder imagines a professor who wishes to encourage his students to study as hard as possible without his having to spend time marking examination papers. What is his optimal strategy?

The professor first of all announces—as usual—that he intends to set an examination at the end of the academic year. This (he hopes) will provide the students with an incentive to acquire the necessary knowledge. However, on the day before the examination he cancels it, since he has already achieved his own particular goal, which is to impart knowledge. All the students receive a certificate without having to take an examination. The time expended on his marking examination papers is equal to zero. Where does the time inconsistency lie?

- At time t_0, i.e. before the students have studied, it is optimal for the professor to set and to announce the examination.
- At time t_1, i.e. after the students have acquired their knowledge, it is optimal for the professor to cancel the examination.

---

[15] The origin of the debate on time inconsistency is to be found in a study by Strotz (1956), which analyses the effects of preference changes on buyers' decisions.

The strategy of setting the exam is therefore not optimal over time; i.e., it is *time-inconsistent*.

This simple example illustrates the general conditions that must exist in order for time-inconsistent strategies to arise in a game with two players.

1. At least one of the two players must be completely free to choose her strategy, while the other player must be committed to a strategy at one point in time during the game; e.g., the students must decide at an early stage to learn their course material.[16]
2. The game cannot be repeated too often, if at all. If the professor tries it more than once, he must be prepared for the students to give up studying, as they will no longer regard his initial announcement to set an examination as credible. In this event, the professor will no longer achieve his main goal of imparting knowledge. Hence the credibility of announcements is a key factor in determining whether the player who is pursuing a strategy (in this case the professor) will achieve his goal.[17]

Finally, this example also demonstrates the advantage of an exogenous rule. Since there is the risk (after the first time) that the professor's announcements will lose credibility, students will tend to study too little. Therefore, the universities' examination statutes stipulate that in general students will be required to take an examination in order to receive a certificate. Such a rule thus deprives professors of the margin of discretion assumed in the above example.

The phenomenon of time inconsistency occurs in many areas of economic life. An important example in the field of monetary economics is the possibility of increasing seigniorage in the short term beyond the maximum by means of surprise inflation (see Chapter 11).[18] Outside the area of monetary policy, the phenomenon of time inconsistency has received particular attention in the context of patent protection, taxation, and government borrowing.

6.6.2. *The basic Barro–Gordon model (BGM)*

In order to demonstrate the advantages of rules even under ideal conditions for a discretionary policy, a seminal model developed by Barro and Gordon (1983a), (henceforth BGM) describes a game that is played between

[16] It is this early commitment on the part of one of the two players that makes the time inconsistency debate relevant to the 'new institutional economics'. The fact that one of the contractual partners is bound by long-term contracts, owing to the 'asset specificity' of investments, is of fundamental importance in this theory (Furubotn and Richter 1997).

[17] The importance of credibility will be discussed in detail at the end of the chapter.

[18] See Auernheimer (1974).

the central bank and the private sector in an economy. This section presents a slightly modified version of the model.

The model assumes that the central bank is perfectly able to manage the economic process and gears its decisions to a social welfare function which also corresponds to the preferences of private individuals. In this game private individuals have only the action parameter of their inflation expectations. The element of time inconsistency arises from the fact that

1. private individuals must, in an early phase of the game, form and disclose inflation expectations to which they are then committed until the end of the game, whereas
2. the central bank has complete discretion in its choice of strategy at all times.

This 'lock-in' effect in the case of private individuals derives principally from the fact that they normally conclude collective pay agreements for one year or longer, in which the nominal wages are agreed on the basis of inflation expectations prevailing at the time the agreement was concluded. In order to influence inflation expectations, the central bank announces at time t_0 (before inflation expectations have been fixed) a strategy that is optimal for it at that time, but which it is not obliged to adhere to once private individuals are bound by their commitment (at time t_1). Time inconsistency then occurs if the (optimal) strategy announced at t_0 is no longer optimal at t_1.

The key components of the model are a *social welfare function* as the target function of the central bank and private individuals, and the *expectations-augmented modified Phillips curve* (Section 4.5.3.2) as the restriction under which the target function has to be minimized. The social welfare function is rather similar to equation (5.1):

$$Z = [b(U - U^*)^2 + \pi^2] \qquad \text{with } b > 0. \tag{6.1}$$

The welfare function is formulated as a cost function, in which social costs may have two causes.

1. *The actual unemployment rate* (U) deviates from a target unemployment rate (U^*). This gives rise to social costs, irrespective of whether the deviation is positive or negative. For this reason, the deviation is squared in equation (6.1). If the unemployment rate is too high, this means that output is too low, which results in a loss in social welfare. Too low an unemployment rate can be achieved only at the price of expectation errors, which private individuals also evaluate negatively.[19] The squaring of the

---

[19] Expectations are not included in the social welfare function. Cukierman (1986: 6) takes explicit account of this negative evaluation of expectation errors by private individuals.

deviation in the social welfare function also implies that large deviations are more heavily weighted than small ones.

2. *The actual inflation rate* (π) deviates from a target inflation rate π^* (here assumed to be zero). It is again assumed that both positive and negative deviations are similarly detrimental to welfare. Positive inflation rates give rise to the welfare costs described in Section 5.2.1. Negative inflation rates (deflation) also lead to social costs, since here too price labels need to be altered at regular intervals (menu costs), and if the deflation is incorrectly anticipated this leads to distortions in the allocation process. However, these social costs arising from the 'non-negativity of nominal interest rates'[20] are captured in the form of the deviation of the actual from the natural unemployment rate.

Welfare is therefore maximal (and the social costs are minimal) when neither of the two deviations referred to above occurs. Thus, in an ideal world social costs are equal to zero. Deviations from the unemployment target ($U - U^*$) give rise to social costs that are different from those associated with deviations from the inflation target ($\pi - 0$), if the two targets are weighted differently, i.e. if the weighting factor b deviates from unity. Hence when b is high, this means that the unemployment target is given a high priority, whereas a low value for b indicates a high preference for stability on the part of the central bank and private individuals.

Graphically, the social cost function can be represented as social indifference curves (Figure 6.1).[21] Since social costs arise for the central bank

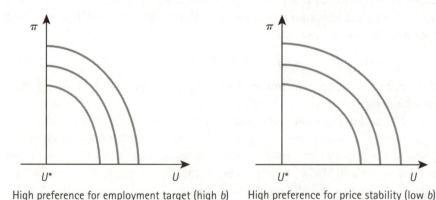

High preference for employment target (high *b*)   High preference for price stability (low *b*)

Figure 6.1. *The social loss function of the Barro–Gordon model*

---

[20] Tobin (1995: 236) calls this the 'floor of zero on nominal rates'.
[21] See De Grauwe (2000: 46) and Jarchow (1998: 282).

and private individuals in accordance with equation (6.1) precisely when the inflation rate or the unemployment rate deviates from its desired target value, the axes should represent the target deviations. However, a representation is chosen here that focuses directly on inflation and unemployment. In order to make the two forms of representation compatible, the origin must be located precisely in the combination of the two target values for the inflation rate ($\pi^* = 0$) and the unemployment rate ($U = U^*$). With the above target function, social indifference curves are then generated in ellipse form around $(0, U^*)$. However, since in the following discussion the only cases that are of interest are those in which positive deviations from the inflation target are accompanied by positive deviations from the desired rate of unemployment, in Figure 6.1 only one sector of the indifference curves will be considered. Here, social costs increase with the distance from the origin.

The concave curvature of the indifference curves in this area is explained by the fact that, in accordance with the social welfare function (see equation (6.1)), the central bank (and private individuals) will show a stronger preference for a reduction in unemployment at the expense of a higher inflation rate, the higher the unemployment rate is. In that case, the weighting factor b will determine the actual shape of the indifference curves. The more weight the central bank (and private individuals) give to the deviation from the desired unemployment rate, the lower will be the unemployment rate that together with the inflation rate occasions a given welfare loss. In Figure 6.1, the higher b is, the closer to the origin lie the points of intersection of the indifference curves with the x-axis.[22]

As a restriction on the central bank's decision process, the model uses the expectations-augmented Phillips curve. According to this, the actual unemployment rate (U) deviates from the natural rate (U^n) only if the actual inflation rate (π) is incorrectly anticipated by private individuals ($\pi^e \neq \pi$). In the context of the BGM, a linear specification of (4.19) is used:

$$U = U^n - a(\pi - \pi^e) \qquad \text{with } a > 0. \tag{6.2}$$

The assumption that the unemployment rate aimed at by the central bank (and private individuals) in the social welfare function (U^*) is lower than the natural rate (U^n) is of crucial importance for the model. Thus, in the BGM it is assumed that

$$U^* = kU^n, \qquad \text{with } 0 < k < 1. \tag{6.3}$$

---

[22] The point of intersection of the elliptical indifference curve for cost level Z_0 with the x-axis is obtained in the relevant areas as $U^* + \sqrt{Z_0/b}$. The point of intersection with the y-axis is independent of the weighting factor b and lies at $\sqrt{Z_0}$. For $b = 1$ circular indifference curves are obtained.

The reason for this value of k is not obvious. It is argued that the natural rate of unemployment can be too high because of *allocative distortions*, so that it should not be considered as a target value of monetary policy. Barro and Gordon (1983a: 593) therefore also refer to k as an 'efficiency criterion' for the economy as a whole, since, as soon as such external effects occur, k will no longer be equal to unity. Thus, for example, the imposition of income tax or the payment of unemployment benefit will usually mean that, from the point of view of individual job suppliers, labour will become dearer relative to consumer goods and there will be a corresponding increase in the amount of leisure time consumed. It is assumed here that in the labour supply decision an individual does not take account of the associated increase (in the case of income tax) or decrease (in the case of unemployment benefit) in the supply of public goods; therefore, the aggregate supply of labour is lower than it would be without the corresponding state interventions in the labour market. A similar justification of the need to pursue an ambitious unemployment target is premissed on the different power positions of the parties to the collective pay negotiations. Canzoneri (1985) argues, for example, that real wages are too high because of the power of the trade unions, and therefore that employment is too low in comparison with the level regarded as desirable by the central bank and private individuals.

A further assumption of the most simple variant of the BGM is *perfect information* of all players. In the first place, this implies that private individuals know precisely that the central bank is pursuing a target function which corresponds to its own macroeconomic target function. Second, the assumption of perfect information means that unpredictable (real and monetary) shocks are disregarded: this implies the perfect control of the central bank over the price level, expressed in an exact correspondence between the inflation rate (π) and the growth rate in the nominal money supply (μ) (Barro and Gordon 1983a: 594; 1983b: 101):[23]

$$\pi = \mu. \tag{6.4}$$

The perfect control of the price level is often assumed for the sake of simplification.[24] However, an important implication of the assumption of perfect information and the resulting identity of the ultimate target (π)

---

[23] Because of the assumed identity of the inflation rate with the growth rate in the nominal money supply, many model variants operate exclusively with the monetary growth rate (Cukierman 1986, 1992). On the fundamental problems arising from the fact that the BGM considers only the money supply as an economic policy variable, see Neumann (1995).

[24] Blackburn and Christensen (1989: 11) describe the perfect control of the inflation rate as a 'heroic assumption', which, however, 'for the most part, serves as a useful abstraction'.

with the intermediate target (μ) is that there seems to be no distinction between a rule geared to an ultimate target and one geared to an intermediate target.

If (6.2) and (6.3) are incorporated in the social welfare function, one obtains

$$Z = \{b[(1 - k)U^n - a(\pi - \pi^e)]^2 + \pi^2\}. \tag{6.5}$$

The central bank calculates the optimal inflation rate by differentiating Z in terms of π and setting the first-order condition equal to zero.[25] The social costs are minimal when the following applies:

$$\pi^* = \frac{ab(1 - k)U^n}{1 + a^2b} + \frac{a^2b}{1 + a^2b}\pi^e = \phi(\pi^e). \tag{6.6}$$

It can be seen immediately from (6.6) that the value of the optimal inflation rate is dependent on the expected inflation rate. If private individuals expect a positive inflation rate, the central bank will in any case also aim at a positive inflation rate. But even when the expected inflation rate is zero, the optimal inflation rate is positive, since as a result of the assumptions made–that the two parameters a and b and the natural unemployment rate U^n are positive and the factor k lies between 0 and 1–the first term of the optimal inflation rate is always greater than zero. The central bank will thus in principle always seek to achieve positive employment effects by means of a positive inflation rate.

It is of crucial importance how inflation expectations are formed in this model. If it is assumed that the central bank announces an inflation rate of zero and that private individuals consider this to be credible ($\pi^e = 0$), the actual inflation rate will, in accordance with equation (6.6), be

$$\pi_S = \frac{ab(1 - k)U^n}{1 + a^2b}. \tag{6.7}$$

As already indicated, the optimal inflation is now positive and so exceeds the expected value of zero. Thus, the commonly used term for this outcome is *surprise inflation*. If the inflation rate for the situation of surprise inflation (π_S) is inserted in the target function (6.4), positive social costs Z_S are obtained for the amount of

$$Z_S = \frac{b}{1 + a^2b}[(1 - k)U^n]^2. \tag{6.8}$$

---

[25] The second-order condition for a cost minimum is fulfilled.

However, under perfect information, private individuals know the central bank's underlying loss function as well as the Phillips curve. Thus, they will take this information into account and set their inflation expectations as *rational expectations* equal to the central bank's optimal inflation rate ($\pi^e = \pi^*$). The central bank's announcement that it wishes to achieve an inflation rate of zero is then not credible. Under the assumption of rational expectations, the optimal inflation rate (π_{rat}) is then obtained as

$$\pi_{rat} = ab(1 - k)U^n. \tag{6.9}$$

Equation (6.9) shows that the optimal inflation rate is also positive in the event of rational expectations. This deviation from zero shows the so-called 'inflation bias'. The inflation rate is also higher than with surprise inflation (equation (6.7)). In that case, owing to the correct anticipation by private individuals of the actual inflation rate, it is not possible to reduce the unemployment rate below the 'natural rate'. Both the inflation rate and the unemployment rate (i.e. the natural rate) will be higher than in the case of surprise inflation. The social costs are therefore necessarily higher. The *a priori* notions are confirmed by the formal findings, since the social costs amount to

$$Z_{rat} = b(1 + a^2 b)[(1 - k)U^n]^2. \tag{6.10}$$

Barro and Gordon (1983*a*) now argue that with rational expectations the social costs can be reduced by subjecting the central bank to the strict rule that the inflation rate (π)—and hence the growth rate in the nominal money supply (μ)—must equal the target value of zero:

$$\pi_{rule} = 0. \tag{6.11}$$

In order to serve as an exogenous rule, the rule must be formulated in such a way that it is absolutely binding. Although commitment to a rule deprives the central bank of the possibility of bringing the unemployment rate down to below the natural rate, no social costs of inflation are involved. Generally speaking, therefore, the social costs are lower than in the case of rational expectations:

$$Z_{rule} = b[(1 - k)U^n]^2. \tag{6.12}$$

If one compares the three variants, there is a clear hierarchy of solutions. The social costs are lowest in the case of surprise inflation and highest in the case of rational expectations. Rules represent a midway solution:

$$Z_S < Z_{rule} < Z_{rat}. \tag{6.13}$$

Thus, the model comes to the conclusion that an exogenous monetary rule is the preferable institutional arrangement, even when in principle optimal conditions exist for a discretionary policy. This conclusion depends crucially on the fact that, in the context of this non-cooperative game between the central bank and private individuals, the optimal solution, namely surprise inflation, will not occur. As private individuals know the central bank's optimization process (rational expectations), they know from the outset that monetary policy will in any case be aiming at a positive inflation rate—irrespective of whether the inflation rate they expect is equal to or greater than zero. Hence for private individuals it is always the dominant strategy to expect the precise (positive) inflation rate that the central bank will actually choose on the basis of the model. At the same time, the central bank will assume that private individuals have correctly anticipated this rate ($\pi^e = \pi = \pi_{rat}$). Rational expectations thus result in the expected inflation rate equalling the actual inflation rate ($\pi^e = \pi_{rat}$) in conditions of equilibrium, since private individuals will anticipate that the dominant strategy from the central bank's point of view is always the realization of π_{rat}. This equilibrium is therefore also known as the *Nash solution*.[26] Any other inflation rate would lead to higher social costs.

If, despite rational expectations, the central bank achieves a stable price level ($\pi = 0$), such a *disinflation* has social costs of

$$Z_{dis} = b(1 + a^2b)^2[(1 - k)U^n]^2. \tag{6.14}$$

Although the actual inflation rate equals the optimal rate of zero, the fact that inflation is too low compared with the expected inflation rate means that the actual unemployment rate is well above the natural rate. Private individuals have assumed a positive inflation rate in their collective pay agreements, with the result that, in a situation of price stability, real wages are now higher than intended. Because the collective pay agreements run for a fixed period, this relative increase in the price of the labour factor will lead to redundancies.

---

[26] In game theory a *Nash equilibrium* occurs when each player chooses precisely that strategy which is optimal irrespective of the chosen strategies of the other players ('dominant' or 'evident' strategy: Kreps 1990). The existence of a Nash solution as a combination of dominant strategies ('strategy profile': Kreps 1990) thus requires that each player has at least one dominant strategy. However, when determining Nash equilibria it is assumed that the players have to decide simultaneously on the strategy they will adopt. If we consider the set of problems described above, where private individuals have to fix their inflation expectations early (otherwise the assumed short-term Phillips curve trade-off would not materialize), the above equilibrium assumes the character of a *Stackelberg equilibrium*, in which the central bank maximizes its target function with given inflation expectations on the part of private individuals. However, since rational expectations are assumed, i.e. that private individuals anticipate the optimal solution for the central bank, the Stackelberg equilibrium and Nash equilibrium coincide (Blackburn and Christensen 1989: 7).

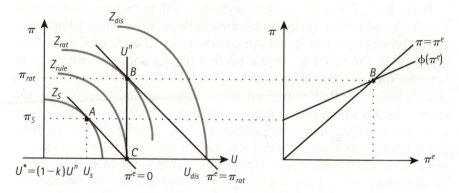

Figure 6.2. *Different solutions to the Barro–Gordon model*

The Barro–Gordon model provides an example of the typical *prisoner's dilemma,* in which the strategies that are optimal for the two individual players (central bank and private sector) lead to a result that is detrimental to both of them (Cukierman 1986: 7). Figure 6.2 shows the Nash equilibrium (π_{rat}) as the intersection of the reaction function of private individuals ($\pi^e = \pi$) with that of the central bank ($\pi = \phi(\pi^e)$). The left-hand side of this figure takes account of the possibility of the different expected inflation rates of the private sector.[27]

If the private sector is expecting an *inflation rate of zero* ($\pi^e = 0$), the intersection of the short-term Phillips curve with the *x*-axis (actual inflation rate $\pi = 0$) lies precisely at the natural unemployment rate, since the latter occurs when there are no expectation errors on the part of private individuals and the expected rate is equal to the actual rate. The central bank will realize surprise inflation (π_S), since in this case the short-term Phillips curve trade-off (for $\pi^e = 0$) is tangent to precisely the social indifference curve that lies furthest at the origin (point A). Social costs arise amounting to Z_S.

On the other hand, if one assumes *rational expectations,* private individuals will expect the positive rate π_{rat}, which is obtained as the intersection of the reaction functions of the central bank and private individuals. The short-term Phillips curve now lies further to the right. The natural unemployment rate U^n again occurs precisely when the actual is equal to the expected inflation rate (i.e. π_{rat}). For the central bank it is now rational to realize π_{rat}, which is already expressed by the intersection of the reaction functions of the central bank ($\pi = \phi(\pi^e)$) and of private individuals

---

[27] See Cukierman (1992: 30).

$(\pi = \pi^e)$. Thus, the natural rate of unemployment will occur and social costs will arise for the amount of Z_{rat}. Z_{rat} is again obtained graphically as the tangential point of the short-term Phillips curve (for π_{rat}) with the indifference curve that lies furthest at the origin (point B).

A *rule-based arrangement* $(\pi = 0)$ means that the natural unemployment rate will be achieved without inflation (point C). The social costs Z_{rule} will be determined by the indifference curve that passes through point C $(U^n, 0)$, so that the social costs for the rules (Z_{rule}) necessarily lie between those for surprise inflation (Z_s) and for rational expectations (Z_{rat}).[28]

Thus, at first sight the model looks impressive, since it seems to be able to derive very stringent conclusions from a simple theoretical framework. This is certainly the main reason why it has been used and refined by so many theoretical papers in the 1980s and 1990s. But the model's extreme simplicity also has the disadvantage that its main policy conclusions have to be treated carefully. The implications of more realistic assumptions will be analysed in the following section.

6.6.3. *Limitations of the basic Barro–Gordon model*

A detailed analysis of the BGM poses three key questions:

1. Is it realistic to assume that a central bank will pursue an employment objective that implies a lower unemployment rate than the natural rate? Can it be assumed at the same time that a social welfare function formulated in this way is identical with the preferences of private individuals?
2. Do the results that have been derived for a one-shot game also occur when the game is played repeatedly?
3. Are rules still preferable if the private agents do not know the central bank's target function and if the economy is confronted with shocks?

6.6.3.1. *Problems with the target function*
The most astonishing feature of the model is its claim that the phenomenon of time inconsistency can be derived despite identical preferences of private individuals and the central bank (Calvo 1978: 1421). Equation (6.7) shows that the inflation bias under rational expectations is entirely due to a value of $k \neq 1$. With $k = 1$, an inflation rate of 0% is the optimal outcome even under discretion so that a rule would not be necessary. $k < 1$ implies

---

[28] If private individuals form their inflation expectations rationally and the central bank realizes an inflation rate of zero, the unemployment rate U_{dis} occurs. This implies social costs amounting to Z_{dis}, which depend on the indifference curve that passes through this combination of unemployment and inflation $(U_{dis}, 0)$. They are by far the highest.

that the central bank targets an unemployment rate (U^*) that is lower than the natural unemployment rate (U^n). In other words, the inflation bias is a direct outcome of the model's very specific assumption that the central bank is trying to lower unemployment below the natural rate. It implies a policy assignment according to which monetary policy is made responsible for the negative allocative effects of other areas of economic policy.

Thus, the *first-best solution* to the problem of inflation bias would be a new policy assignment which obliges the government to remove the causes of the allocative distortions on the labour market and thus enables it to achieve the desired increase in employment. This would allow it to define an employment target of U^n in the loss function of the central bank: the factor k in the above social welfare function would be equal to 1, the welfare-maximizing inflation rate according to equation (6.6) would be equal to 0, and social costs would similarly be equal to 0.

The whole approach of the BGM, therefore, rests on the implicit assumption that monetary policy is able to generate permanent output effects. In the specific context of Barro and Grossman's model, this could be regarded as a *second-best solution* for situations where the government is unable to remove the allocative distortions. For practical monetary policy, it seems *a priori* very problematic to use a model that is based on an extremely flawed policy assignment.

Another problem of the specific social welfare function of the model is that it can hardly be regarded as a welfare function for private individuals. On the one hand, Barro and Gordon (1983*a*: 592) argue that in labour supply decisions private individuals ignore the positive external effects that accompany public goods financed by taxation. On the other hand, private individuals are said to take account of such externalities in the context of their social welfare function, as is reflected in their efforts to achieve an unemployment rate lower than the natural rate. Thus, an essential assumption is being made that in their labour supply decisions private individuals systematically ignore relevant information which they take account of when formulating their social welfare function. This contradiction is then reflected in the main result of the model, that the welfare of private individuals can be increased by systematically deceiving them. It becomes particularly clear how flawed this implication is if one assumes that the economy consists of just one representative agent (Blackburn and Christensen 1989: 16).

If the employment level is too low—not because of labour market distortions, but because real wages are too high owing to the power of the trade unions—the target function according to equation (6.5) cannot reflect the preferences of private individuals. These are expressed in the realized natural unemployment rate. If the central bank none the less pursues a welfare function where the target unemployment rate is lower than the natural rate ($k < 1$), this brings us back to the traditional debate in which rules are explained *inter alia* by diverging target functions between the central bank and private individuals. In this case, although the central bank is pursuing a *macroeconomic welfare function* (Z^{Nbk}) in accordance with equation (6.5), this cannot have been derived from the individual utility functions and should not therefore be confused with a social welfare function (Z),

$$Z = [b(U - U^n)^2 + \pi^2], \tag{6.15}$$

which is based on the target of the natural unemployment rate. In the last resort, any alleged 'welfare improvement' obtained by a systematic deception of private individuals (surprise inflation) can come about only if a social welfare function other than one based on individual utility functions is taken as the point of reference and basis of measurement (Blackburn and Christensen 1989: 16).

Thus, contrary to its main assertion, the BGM does not offer a completely new argument in favour of rules. As it implicitly rests on a divergence between the target function of the central bank and the target function of the private sector, it is very much in line with the traditional debate on rules versus discretion. Nevertheless, it still has the important advantage that it provides a clear analytical framework to that discussion.

This leads to an interpretation of the model as an analysis of political interaction, where the central bank is exposed to pressure from different interest groups. Unlike in the social welfare approach, rather than postulating the existence of homogeneous preferences of private individuals, such a 'political approach' (Cukierman 1986: 9) explicitly takes account of the possibility of diverging interests on the part of the individual actors. The macroeconomic welfare function (Z^{Nbk}) in the form of equation (6.5) can then be interpreted as the political compromise sought by the central bank between the positions of the interest groups that are exerting their influence on the central bank.

6.6.3.2. *The multi-period game*
A second major problem of the very simple variant of the BGM is the neglect of the time dimension. However, as has been demonstrated in the example of the university examination, the results that are achieved in a single-period game cannot automatically be expected to recur if a game is played repeatedly and—in an extreme case—has no ultimate time horizon. The above model must therefore be translated into an intertemporal context. Thus, the central bank has to optimize an intertemporal welfare

function which is obtained using equation (6.1):

$$Z = \sum_{t=0}^{\infty} \frac{1}{(1 + r)^t} Z_t = \sum_{t=0}^{\infty} \frac{1}{(1 + r)^t} [b(U_t - U^*)^2 + \pi_t^2]. \qquad (6.16)$$

The total costs (Z) are thus obtained as the sum of the social costs of the individual successive periods discounted by the real discount rate $r(Z_t)$. The costs of each individual period are determined in the same way as in the single-period game (Barro and Gordon 1983a: 594).

In an intertemporal context, the expectations-augmented Phillips curve has to be formulated with a time dimension:

$$U_t = U^n - a(\pi_t - \pi_t^e). \qquad (6.17)$$

A crucial factor in the central bank's choice of strategy is now the present value of all likely future social costs. However, in the intertemporal problem structure represented here, the future values of the variables are independent of those already realized, and so a multi-period game formulated in this way becomes a single-period game. In each period, therefore, the central bank will maximize the target function only in relation to the current inflation rate (Barro and Gordon 1983a: 595). However, this total lack of relevance of past monetary policy to likely results in the future applies only in the case of rational expectations.

Hence in the literature repeated games are often characterized by interdependencies between the current strategy and the results of the past (Blackburn and Christensen 1989: 6). Such a 'supergame' (Friedman 1971) is found in the present context if it is assumed that private individuals take account of past inflation rates when forming their expectations ('trigger mechanism'). Thus, they can 'punish' the central bank for surprise inflation in period t by forming higher inflation expectations in the following periods, while the central bank has an opportunity to gain a reputation for a clear commitment to price stability by deliberately not pursuing an inflationary policy.

What is crucial, therefore, is private individuals' 'memory' (Blackburn and Christensen 1989: 17) of past monetary policy and the degree to which this prompts them to punish a central bank for pursuing an inflationary policy. Let us assume a simple mechanism for the formation of expectations which can be found in Barro and Gordon (1983b: 108):[29]

$$\pi_t^e \begin{cases} = \pi_{rule} = 0, & \text{if } \pi_{t-1} = \pi_{t-1}^e, \\ = \pi_{rat} = ab(1 - k)U^n, & \text{if } \pi_{t-1} \neq \pi_{t-1}^e. \end{cases} \qquad (6.18)$$

---

[29] This trigger mechanism is a particular expression of the more general 'tit-for-tat' rule, which is often employed in non-cooperative game theory. When applied to the present problem, this rule states

The rationale for this approach can be described as follows. Let us assume that the central bank announces at the beginning of each period an inflation target $\pi^* = 0$. Private individuals will regard the announcement in the current period as credible if their expectations have been confirmed in the preceding period, $\pi^e_{t-1} = \pi_{t-1}$, i.e. if the central bank has not produced surprise inflation. If on the other hand expectations in the preceding period have been disappointed, private individuals will assume an inflationary monetary policy for the current period, too. They will expect π_{rat}, and the Nash equilibrium occurs (π_{rat}). The central bank has thus lost its credibility.

If the central bank wishes to optimize its target function (equation (6.16)), it will no longer achieve this solely by minimizing the social costs of the current period ('piecewise optimization'), but must also now take account of the effects of its policy on the costs in the following periods. The optimal inflation rate for this variant of the game (π_{trig}) is called *trigger strategy equilibrium* (Rogoff 1987: 149), or *reputational equilibrium* if it coincides with the expected inflation rate. Whether or not the central bank realizes a positive inflation rate will depend on whether the positive effect of surprise inflation that occurs in the short term in the form of the reduction in the unemployment rate (the 'incentive effect') is higher or lower than the costs in the following periods that result from the rise in private individuals' inflation expectations ('deterrent effect').[30]

The actual trigger mechanism is of prime importance in determining the two effects. First, it determines the inflation rate that optimizes the central bank's target function (π_{trig}). Second, it determines the reaction of private individuals and thus future costs. If the private individuals' punishment mechanism described above is assumed, the trigger strategy equilibrium corresponds to either an inflation rate of zero $(\pi_{trig} = 0)$ or the surprise inflation derived above $(\pi_{trig} = \pi_s)$. If in period t the central bank produces a positive inflation rate instead of the announced rate of zero, the central bank is punished in accordance with the short-term orientation implicitly assumed in equation (6.18) *only* in the following period, $t + 1$. Private individuals will expect π_{rat} and the central bank will realize π_{rat} (Nash equilibrium). In period $t + 2$ inflation expectations (π^e) are again equal to zero, as the central bank has confirmed private individuals' inflation expectations in $t + 1$. With such a trigger mechanism, the multi-period game thus becomes a *two-period game* (Barro and Gordon 1983*b*: 109), and the social costs in the following period $t + 1$ are fixed and equal to the above costs

that at the start of the game private individuals adopt a 'benign' attitude and are willing to cooperate ($\pi^e_t = 0$) and that thereafter they precisely imitate the behaviour of the central bank (Axelrod 1984).

[30] See Fischer (1990: 1175). The presentation given here is based on Jarchow (1998: 290–3).

under rational expectations (Z_{rat}). Thus, if the central bank decides to realize an inflation rate other than zero in period t, it minimizes the costs in the current period t—and hence also the sum of the social costs influenced by its decision—by opting for surprise inflation ($\pi_{trig} = \pi_s$).

Whether or not the central bank aims at a positive inflation rate here ($\pi_{trig} = \pi_s$) depends on the relationship between the incentive and deterrent effects. The *incentive effect* of surprise inflation (i.e. the reduction of costs) in period t is obtained as the difference between the costs under conditions of price stability (Z_{rule}) and surprise inflation (Z_s):

$$Z_{rule} - Z_S = b[(1 - k)U^n]^2 \frac{b}{1 + a^2b}[(1 - k)U^n]^2$$

$$= \frac{a^2b^2}{1 + a^2b}[(1 - k)U^n]^2. \tag{6.19}$$

The *deterrent effect*, which covers the additional costs in period $t + 1$, is obtained as the discounted difference between costs under rational expectations (Z_{rat}) and under conditions of price stability (Z_{rule}):

$$\frac{(Z_{rat}) - (Z_{rule})}{(1 + r)} = \frac{b(1 + a^2b)[(1 - k)U^n]^2 - b[(1 - k)U^n]^2}{(1 + r)}$$

$$= \frac{a^2b^2}{(1 + r)}[(1 - k)U^n]^2. \tag{6.20}$$

The central bank will thus pursue a policy of surprise inflation in period t, if the incentive effect (equation (6.19)) is greater than the deterrent effect (equation (6.20)):

$$\frac{a^2b^2}{1 + a^2b}[(1 - k)U^n]^2 > \frac{a^2b^2}{(1 + r)}[(1 - k)U^n]^2. \tag{6.21}$$

Thus, there will be surprise inflation only if $r > a^2b$, i.e. if the discount rate r is greater than the term a^2b. The probability that a central bank enjoying a margin of discretion will pursue a policy of surprise inflation will thus depend essentially on the following factors.

1. *The central bank's time preference*: a high discount factor (r) will mean that the deterrent effect will be assigned only a very small weighting in the central bank's calculation. This increases the probability of surprise inflation.
2. *The central bank's preference for the employment target (b) and the slope of the short-term Phillips curve (a)*: it is somewhat astonishing that high

values of a and b reduce the incentive to engineer a surprise inflation. As (6.19) and (6.20) show, this result is due to the fact that the incentive and the deterrent effects increase with a and b. However, the incentive effect increases less than the deterrent effect. The explanation for this seeming paradox are rational expectations, which implies that with a high a and b private agents expect a high inflation rate if they do not expect $\pi^e = 0$.

The trigger mechanism represented in (6.18) may be criticized on a number of grounds. First, the pronounced short-term orientation of this approach is problematic. It has the curious result that an inflation rate that is expected and actually realized in period t (reputation equilibrium) is, irrespective of its level, rewarded by an inflation expectation of zero in period $t + 1$. This can lead to a continuous alternation between surprise inflation (π_s) and a Nash equilibrium (π_{rat}), without the involving consequences for the trigger mechanism. Second, the simplified representation of expectations formation can be criticized. Private individuals expect the Nash solution (π_{rat}), regardless of how far the central bank has missed the target announced for the preceding period. This is not likely to be the case in practice.

It would therefore be desirable to find a mechanism in which the expected inflation rate for the following period is a continuous function of the current inflation rate (Rogoff 1987: 153). In particular, private individuals may punish the central bank by not setting their inflation expectations back to zero immediately after one period. By reducing π^e very gradually, they can cause future social costs to shoot up and increase the deterrent effect. A problem exists in so far as there are in theory an infinite number of trigger mechanisms that are all equally plausible, and in the last resort it is virtually impossible to determine empirically which is the 'correct' one (Backus and Driffill 1985: 532).

Nevertheless, by transforming the simple one-shot game into a repeated game, the case for 'rules' is no longer obvious. Depending on the concrete trigger mechanism, the central bank's time preference and the values of a and b, it is possible that the central bank will opt for price stability even if it is not constrained by a rule. In fact, it might very well of its own accord even aim over a period of years at an inflation rate that is below private individuals' expectations (*disinflation*), in order to reduce high inflation expectations to zero.

An interesting feature of the repeated game is the question of whether the game has a finite or infinite time horizon, since the assumption of a backward-looking trigger mechanism makes sense only if the game has no finite time horizon. For the case of a finite time horizon, it is more plausible to assume that private individuals' expectation formation is forward-looking. The reason for this is as follows. If there is a last period that is known to private individuals, the central bank can pursue an inflationary policy in this period without being punished. Since private individuals anticipate this, they will form their inflation expectation for this period accordingly and the Nash solution will occur. However, the positive inflation expectation in the last period deprives private individuals of the possibility of punishing the central bank for an inflationary policy in the penultimate period. Therefore the central bank can also pursue an inflationary policy in this period. Since private individuals anticipate this, too, their inflation expectations will also be positive for the penultimate period, with the result that the Nash solution occurs again here. If the train of this argument is followed back to the initial period, the Nash solution can even occur for this period (the 'chain store paradox'). Thus, with a finite time horizon, rational expectations always lead to the unsatisfactory Nash solution in all periods (Blackburn and Christensen 1989: 18).

6.6.3.3. *Imperfect information*
Up to now it has always been assumed that all actors (central bank and private individuals) possess complete information. This implies in particular that

1. private individuals know the central bank's target function, and
2. no stochastic shocks occur.

Ignorance of the central bank's target function   Private individuals cannot be expected to have precise knowledge of the central bank's target function, above all when the above-mentioned BGM is interpreted in terms of the political approach, whereby the central bank pursues a macroeconomic welfare function that does not correspond to a social welfare function—however derived from the individual utility functions of private individuals. But even if it is supposed that the central bank seeks to maximize the same target function as private individuals (social welfare approach), it is in no way imperative that private individuals are informed about this.

In the case of the *single-period game*, private individuals' ignorance of the central bank's target function prevents rational expectations that are endogenous to the model. Now the welfare effects depend essentially on what actual inflation rate private individuals will be expecting, and so, unlike in the case of perfect information, nothing useful can be said about the relative advantage of one or the other regime (discretion or rules). Therefore the problem of lack of knowledge about the central bank's target function is always discussed in the context of a repeated game.

Following Backus and Driffill (1985: 532), we assume that there are (only) two types of a central bank: 'strong' and 'weak'. The distinguishing feature of 'strong' central banks is that they single-mindedly pursue the goal of price-level stability ($\pi = 0$), without worrying about the employment situation. In the model described above, this means assigning to the employment target (b) a weighting factor of zero. 'Weak' central banks, on the other hand, are those that have a macroeconomic welfare function in the form of equation (6.4) and thus may yield to the temptation of achieving welfare gains by surprise inflation ($\pi = \pi_S$). For private individuals there is now the problem that they do not know which category their central bank belongs to. In other words, they do not know whether to expect an inflation rate of zero or of π_{rat} for the coming period. To enable them to choose their strategy, it is now essential that private individuals form a subjective probability (p) that theirs is a 'strong' central bank, since, the greater this probability, the more they will expect an inflation rate of zero.

This probability need not be constant over time. The central bank can, for example, seek to increase it by announcing a stability-oriented strategy ($\pi = 0$). However, private individuals will not automatically regard such an announcement as credible, as has already been clearly demonstrated in the above discussion of rational expectations. Instead, the credibility and hence the value of p will depend, above all, on the monetary policy pursued in the past. In fact, private individuals' ignorance of the central bank's target function enables 'weak' central banks to build up a reputation—as in the multi-period game with certainty—by appearing 'strong' and avoiding surprise inflation for as long as possible (a 'wolf in sheep's clothing'), but then revealing their true nature and delivering surprise inflation when inflation expectations are zero. From the private individuals' point of view, it is therefore essential that they take account of the possibility of strategic behaviour on the part of the 'weak' central bank when forming their expectations. For this reason, the probability p_t will feature in their deliberations as a conditional probability whereby they assign their central bank to the 'strong' category, provided that it has not pursued an inflationary policy in the preceding period. If the central bank pursues a continuing policy of price stability, such an optimal backward-looking (Bayesian) learning process is characterized by the fact that it takes account of all relevant information from the past in such a way that the value of the probability p_t increases the longer price stability is maintained (Backus and Driffill 1985: 533). However, as soon as the central bank creates surprise inflation, even if this happens only once, its reputation ($p_t = 0$) is destroyed for ever, since then will have revealed its true identity and private individuals can assume with certainty that they are dealing with a 'weak' central bank. Henceforth only the equilibrium with rational expectations will occur.

The results of this variant of the model are not very much different from those of the repeated game discussed in the previous section. The only difference is that private agents are now confronted with two possible scenarios.

1. The case of the 'weak' central bank is identical with the game discussed under the assumption of perfect information.
2. The case of the 'strong' central bank simply reduces the risk of $\pi > 0$ compared with the situation of perfect knowledge about the central bank's target function.

For the central bank, this implies that, depending on p, inflation expectations are lower than in the case where the private sector knows its target function. Thus, uncertainty about the target function has the effect of increasing for the 'weak' central bank the incentive to pursue a policy of surprise inflation. Again, the result is not clear. It might still be possible that the 'weak' central bank refrains from inflation because of the trigger effects, so that price stability be realized even without a rule.

Stochastic shocks   So far, the game between the central bank and the private sector has been discussed without mentioning shocks. As the model is specified only for the supply side, in the following paragraphs only supply shocks can be discussed while demand shocks have to be neglected.

In the literature this variant of the model is discussed under the assumption of *asymmetrically distributed information*, which means that the central bank knows sooner than private individuals when the macroeconomic disturbance will arise and how severe it will be. In spite of its popularity in the literature, this assumption is not very realistic, since today all relevant macroeconomic information is available to the private sector very shortly after it has been produced by official institutions.

In the model, a real disturbance can affect only the Phillips curve equation (6.2), which needs to be expanded by a term for disturbance (ε). It has an expected value of zero and a constant variance over time (σ_ε^2) ('white-noise' process). The Phillips curve equation will then be:

$$U = U^n - a(\pi - \pi^e) + \varepsilon \qquad \text{with } a > 0 \text{ and } E[\varepsilon] = 0. \qquad (6.22)$$

It is now assumed that the actual value of this disturbance term (ε) is not available to private individuals when they conclude collective pay agreements. But, supposing it is known to the central bank early enough, monetary policy can counteract the employment effect of the shock. Thus, in this setting the central bank has to minimize an *expected* welfare loss (Z^e), i.e.

$$Z^e = E\{b[(1 - k)U^n - a(\pi - \pi^e) + \varepsilon]^2 + \pi^2\}. \tag{6.23}$$

Then,

- when ε is positive, the central bank will realize a higher than expected inflation rate, in order to mitigate in the negative employment impulses associated with the shock;
- when ε is negative, the central bank will pursue a less inflationary or even a deflationary policy, since the shock will tend to produce the desired unemployment rate U^* even without an intervention by the central bank.[31]

On the assumptions made, there is a clear trade-off between 'rules' and 'discretion'.

- A rule requiring $\pi = 0$ avoids the danger of surprise inflation and thus helps to ensure that inflation expectations do not systematically deviate from zero ($\pi^e = 0$). At the same time, however, it prevents a temporary deviation from price stability which would help to compensate the employment effects of the shock.
- Discretion provides flexibility in the case of shocks, but is associated with the disadvantage of systematically positive inflation expectations ($\pi^e = \pi_{rat}$).

The choice between the two options depends on the variance of the disturbance term, i.e. the probability and severity of the stochastic shock, and on the values of the parameters a and b (Persson and Tabellini 1990: 25). Rules are superior to discretion if, because of the inflation bias, the expected 'costs of flexibility' under discretion are higher than the expected welfare gain that is realized by compensating the employment effects of the negative supply shock (Lohmann 1992: 277).

Formally, this result can be obtained as follows. It is assumed that under discretion the central bank behaves in accordance with the reaction function

$$\pi(\varepsilon) = \bar{\kappa} + \kappa\varepsilon, \tag{6.24}$$

which implies that the inflation rate can be split up into a component that is independent of shocks and a component that is dependent on them.

---

[31] Note that this result depends on the assumption that the central bank is pursuing a target unemployment rate U^* that is lower than the natural rate U^n. Otherwise flexibility assumes the character of a 'free lunch'.

The term $\bar{k}$ takes account of the fact that under discretion the inflation rate will be systematically higher than zero, since inflation expectations will be positive. If this reaction function is inserted into the central bank's target function (equation (6.23)), the following equation is obtained:

$$Z^e = E\{b[(1 - k)U^n - a[(\bar{\kappa} + \kappa\varepsilon) - \pi^e] + \varepsilon]^2 + (\bar{\kappa} + \kappa\varepsilon)^2\}. \quad (6.25)$$

Taking account of the fact that the expected value of the shock is equal to zero, this equation gives

$$Z = b[(1 - k) U^n]^2 - 2ab(1 - k)U^n(\bar{\kappa} - \pi^e) + b\sigma_\varepsilon^2 - 2ab\kappa\sigma_\varepsilon^2$$
$$+ a^2b(\bar{\kappa}^2 - 2\bar{\kappa}\pi^e + \kappa^2\sigma_\varepsilon^2 - \pi^{e2}) + \bar{\kappa}^2 + \kappa^2\sigma_\varepsilon^2. \quad (6.26)$$

In order to determine the value of the central bank's policy parameters κ and $\bar{k}$, it is necessary to derive the welfare loss calculated in (6.26) in terms of them. If one then assumes rational expectations on the part of private individuals, where the latter are able to predict only $\bar{\kappa}$, i.e. the component that is independent of shocks ($\pi^e = \bar{\kappa}$), one obtains the optimal inflation rate $\pi_{disc}(\varepsilon)$ as follows:

$$\pi_{disc}(\varepsilon) = ab(1 - k)U^n + \frac{ab}{(1 + a^2b)}\varepsilon. \quad (6.27)$$

In periods without stochastic shocks ($\varepsilon = 0$), the central bank will realize the inflation rate with rational expectations ($\bar{\kappa} = \pi_{rat}$).[32] If shocks occur, it will deviate from this rate depending on the shock ($\kappa = ab/(1 + a^2b)$).

The advantage of the situation-related monetary policy now is that in the case of negative disturbances the central bank can prevent the unemployment rate U rising by the full amount ε. This is demonstrated if the optimal inflation rate $\pi_{disc}(\varepsilon)$ (equation (6.27)) is inserted into the Phillips curve (equation (6.22)). It is again assumed that inflation expectations equal the non-shock-dependent component of this inflation rate:

$$U_{disc}(\varepsilon) = U^n + \frac{1}{(1 + a^2b)}\varepsilon. \quad (6.28)$$

Thus, the expected welfare costs of a monetary policy under discretion amount to

$$Z_{disc}(\varepsilon) = b(1 + a^2b)[(1 - k)U^n]^2 + \frac{b}{1 + a^2b}\sigma_\varepsilon^2. \quad (6.29)$$

---

[32] As the expectation value of the shock is zero, the non-shock-dependent component exactly equals the inflation rate with rational expectations.

The social costs of a monetary policy governed by rules are

$$Z_{rule}(\varepsilon) = b[(1 - k)U^n]^2 + b\sigma_\varepsilon^2. \tag{6.30}$$

A rule is advantageous over discretion if it is associated with lower costs than discretion (i.e. if $Z_{rule} < Z_{disc}$); that is,

$$\frac{1}{1 + a^2 b}\sigma^2\varepsilon < [(1 - k)U^n]^2. \tag{6.31}$$

Thus, the attractiveness of a rule increases with the values of a and b, and decreases with the variance of the shock and with U^* approaching U^n. In the situation with $k = 1$, where there is no inflation bias, discretion is always superior to rules.

The price of discretion therefore lies in the fact that, with $k < 1$, inflation expectations systematically deviate from zero. In these circumstances, an optimal solution would be a rule framed in such general terms that it takes account of shocks from the outset and so allows an automatic reaction without leading to inflation expectations that systematically deviate from zero. Such 'flexible rules' (Rogoff 1985: 1170) could be formulated in such a way that deviation from the target inflation rate ($\pi^* = 0$) is possible only in the event of an exogenous shock. The inflation rate that the central bank should aim for under a flexible rule (π_{flex}) is thus

$$\pi_{flex}(\varepsilon) = \kappa\varepsilon. \tag{6.32}$$

The rule now sets the reaction coefficient κ for the central bank (Persson and Tabellini 1990: 20). Its value can be determined in exactly the same way as above. If it is assumed that the rule is regarded as credible by private individuals, they will expect an inflation rate of zero, since the expected value of the stochastic disturbance is zero. If the flexible rule (equation 6.32)) is now inserted into the target function (equation (6.23)) and the expected inflation rate is replaced by the value zero, one obtains the welfare loss Z as

$$Z = b[(1 - k)U^n]^2 + (1 + a^2 b)\kappa^2\sigma_\varepsilon^2 + b\sigma_\varepsilon^2 - 2ab\kappa\sigma_\varepsilon^2. \tag{6.33}$$

In order that the flexible rule minimizes the social costs, the value of κ must be determined from the first-order condition. The optimal inflation rate is then obtained as follows:

$$\pi_{flex}(\varepsilon) = \frac{ab}{(1 + a^2 b)}\varepsilon. \tag{6.34}$$

The theoretical advantage of the flexible rule over a discretionary policy lies in the fact that such a rule is able to realize the partial compensation of the undesirable employment effects of a negative supply shock as represented in (6.28) without causing systematically higher inflation expectations.

In the very simple framework of the BGM, which completely fades out the demand side and international linkages, the design of a flexible rule looks quite simple. However, in reality it is certainly not possible to write an exogenous rule for monetary policy that is at the same time 'simple' and 'stable' (Section 6.3) and which also provides an optimum reaction to all possible contingencies.

So far we have discussed only a supply shock. But monetary policy can also be confronted with shocks that affect the relationship between the money supply and the price level. Thus, contrary to (6.4), a distinction needs to be made between rules that focus on an *intermediate target* and those geared to a *final target*, since they imply different welfare losses. If we assume a monetary shock ξ, (6.4) becomes

$$\pi = \mu + \xi \qquad \text{with } E[\xi] = 0. \tag{6.35}$$

A rule that prescribes a constant growth rate of the money stock implies $\mu = 0$, while a rule that prescribes price stability requires that $\pi = 0$. If it is again assumed that the distribution of information is asymmetric and that the central bank has early knowledge of the occurrence of a monetary shock ξ, the central bank can compensate the shock if it operates under a rule that prescribes price stability. It simply allows for a suitable variation in the money supply (Rogoff 1985: 1176). On the assumptions of the BGM, this means that the social welfare loss is exactly equal to the social welfare loss under a rule-bound monetary policy (Z_{rule}):

$$Z_{rule} = b[(1 - k)U^n]^2. \tag{6.36}$$

A money supply rule prevents the central bank from being able to react to such shocks. Thus, it leads to stochastic deviations in the inflation rate from zero and thereby, in accordance with the Phillips curve trade-off, to fluctuations in employment. Even if the fluctuations have an expectation value of zero, they lead to a systematically higher welfare loss (Z_{money}):

$$Z_{money} = b[(1 - k)U^n]^2 + (1 + a^2b)\sigma_\xi^2. \tag{6.37}$$

In this very simple setting, a money supply rule is therefore inferior to a price-level rule. However, such a conclusion requires that the central bank is able to react promptly to the monetary disturbance and that a perfect direct control of the price level is possible. This superiority of the price-level rule is not surprising, since intermediate target rules have been designed explicitly as a solution for the problems that are associated with an *imperfect* direct control of the price level.

6.6.4. *Economic policy implications*

The starting point of the BGM was the attempt to derive a rationale for (exogenous) rules in monetary policy that went beyond the traditional debate. An essential element of this was the assumption that the central bank and private individuals are guided by the same target function. However, upon closer scrutiny we have seen that here, too, private individuals and the central bank pursue different targets. This can be verified intuitively, since if one assumes fully identical targets it is difficult to imagine that the central bank will be able to achieve a result that is 'better' for both sides by deceiving private individuals. Seen in this light, there is in principle no reason to evaluate the BGM any differently from the traditional debate. However, it has the merit of having developed a clear analytical framework for the traditional argument that policy-makers follow final targets which differ from those of the society. In that case, its main policy recommendation is a rule that obliges a central bank to pursue price stability even in the short run.

Thus, the model provides above all a good description of the problems that arise if monetary policy follows an *activist employment policy*. While this is normally not made explicit, it is obvious that the whole inflation bias depends on $k \neq 1$ or on an unemployment target of monetary policy $U^* < U^n$. Given the central importance of this assumption for the policy conclusions of the model, it is surprising that it has not been discussed more intensively. An important exception is Alan Blinder:

Well, I can assure you that my central banker friends would not be surprised to learn that academic theories that assume that they seek to push unemployment below the natural rate then deduce that monetary policy will be too inflationary. They would doubtless reply, 'Of course. That's why we don't do it.' Therein lies the solution: direct the central bank to set $k = 1$—that is, not to seek unemployment lower than the natural rate. In the world of practical central banking, this 'solution' is, I submit, adopted as if it were second nature. (Blinder 1997: 14)

Of course, this is true only for central banks that are efficiently insulated from the general political process (see Section 7.2). If myopic politicians who are always under the pressure of elections have a say in monetary policy, the BGM with $k < 1$ provides a very important description of economic reality. In fact, in the early 1980s, the period when the model was developed, many central banks were under a very tight control by the government. Thus, the model can be regarded as a very important justification for central bank independence. As this arrangement guarantees $k = 1$, it is no longer necessary to prescribe a rule that forces a central bank to follow price stability even in the short run.

The disadvantage of such a rule is evident and has already been discussed in Chapter 5. Whenever an economy is confronted with a supply shock, either it forces the central bank to magnify the output shock (the AS/AD model), or it prevents the central bank from compensating the shock (BGM), although there is no economic rationale for such a policy. Inequality (6.31) shows that for $k = 1$ rules are always a sub-optimal solution.

Related to the myopia of politicians is another important result of the model. The analysis of repeated games shows that a *long-term perspective* of the decision-makers can also contribute to a policy that avoids an inflation bias. We will see in the next chapter that a well-designed central bank law will ensure that central bankers have such a long-term perspective.

The discussion of shocks has also made clear that the BGM provides no argument in support of *monetary targeting*. This is not surprising, given that their work assumes that the central bank is able to perfectly control the ultimate target at all times. The rationale for controlling the money supply, however, is based on the premises that monetary policy is not able to control ultimate targets directly. In the BGM, which assumes that the central bank has early knowledge of the degree and timing of stochastic disturbances, a money supply rule prevents the possibility of complete compensation of monetary shocks through an adjustment of the money supply.

It is one of the main strengths of this discussion initiated by the BGM that, regarding the concept of *credibility*, it identified an important determinant of the real economic effects of monetary policy. Although 'credibility of monetary policy' might in very general terms be understood to mean that monetary policy announcements are regarded as credible by private individuals, to the extent that they base their inflation expectations on them, a narrower definition of the concept has become accepted in the literature. A central bank is generally described as 'credible' if its declared policy of *pursuing price stability* (or, more precisely, the concrete numerical value of its inflation target) is taken by private individuals to be the basis of their expectation formation (Cukierman 1986: 6).

Once a central bank has lost this credibility, in the last analysis it has little alternative but to feed inflation expectations, even if this means pursuing an inflationary policy. The economy is then in the unfortunate position, which has been designated by Z_{rat}, in which, in spite of high inflation rates, monetary policy produces no positive employment effects. Such 'stagflation' was a worldwide phenomenon in the first half of the 1980s, the period in fact when the basic research on monetary policy credibility was conducted.

The only way in which a central bank can regain its lost credibility by its own efforts is by accepting a policy of *disinflation* over several years. That is to say, despite positive inflation expectations ($\pi^e > 0$), it must pursue a policy of price stability ($\pi = 0$). This means that the central bank must temporarily accept a decline in output and employment—i.e. the worst solution, Z_{dis}—as the price for gradually convincing private individuals once again that its announcement of a policy of price stability is meant to be taken seriously. By being prepared to accept Z_{dis} from time to time, the central bank is, so to speak, investing in its own credibility. The more rapidly the central bank can regain a satisfactory level of credibility, the sooner will it be able to achieve welfare values of the order of Z_{rule} instead of Z_{rat}.

Since, as a general rule, the restoration of credibility is never an instantaneous process, but can be achieved only by pursuing a disinflationary policy ($\pi < \pi^e$) over several years, it is worthwhile asking whether less costly ways of improving a central bank's credibility are available. This is where *commitment technologies* become important, that is those methods whereby a central bank can convince private individuals as rapidly as possible that it is determined to pursue policy aimed at price stability.

An example of a particularly drastic method is *currency reform*, where a government withdraws from circulation entirely a currency that has lost its value through inflation, in the hope that the new currency will be the subject of significantly lower inflation expectations. The German currency reforms of 1923 and 1948 prove that this is possible in principle. On the other hand, many failed currency reforms in Latin America and also in the Ukraine make it clear that currency reform is not of itself sufficient to eliminate acute inflation expectations (Bruno 1993).

A similarly very far-reaching measure is *monetary union* with a country (or group of countries) whose central bank enjoys a high degree of credibility. Thus, the former German Democratic Republic, for example, managed to replace the unpopular East German mark with the internationally respected Deutschmark almost overnight. The basic problem with such a strategy, however, is that countries with stable currencies (and generally also a stable fiscal policy) will usually be rather reluctant to form a common currency area with countries that have shown themselves unable in the past to keep their domestic economy under control. This also explains why membership of the European Monetary Union has been open only to those countries that could meet the criteria of convergence (De Grauwe 2000).

The remarkable decline of the long-term real interest rate in countries with high inflation records (Spain, Italy) in the years 1994–8 shows that such an institutional arrangement can be quite effective.

Examples of less spectacular forms of a commitment technology are all attempts of central banks to make monetary policy more transparent for private individuals. In principle, this allows them to identify a policy of surprise inflation more quickly and reduces the possible advantage that a central bank can derive from such a policy, as the punishment by private individuals (an increase in their inflation expectations) will come sooner. As a result, such a strategy becomes less attractive to the central bank and so is regarded as less likely by private individuals. Chapter 8, which discusses different conceptual frameworks for monetary policy, will examine these points in detail.

Appendix 6.1. The debate between the Banking School and the Currency School[33]

The issue of 'rules versus discretion' dates back to the early nineteenth century, when a fierce debate was raging in England over the constitution of the Bank of England. It originated in a decision taken in 1797 to suspend the practice of honouring Bank of England notes with gold, a measure made necessary by the war with France. The technical arguments focused on the reasons for the inflation that arose in this period and the regulatory action that was most suited for restoring price stability.

The adherents of the *Currency School*—most notably McCulloch, Lloyd (later Lord Overstone), Longfield, George Warde, Norman, and Torrens—believed the main cause of inflation to be the excessive note issue by the Bank of England. They therefore pressed for a monetary constitution formulated in such a way that it made no difference to the price level whether the only money used was gold coins ('gold circulation standard') or banknotes circulated alongside them. They argued that, under a gold circulation standard, flows of gold to and from abroad always exert a direct influence on the domestic money supply. A current account deficit would result in an outflow of gold abroad, leading to a fall in the domestic money supply and thus in the price level. This would result in an improvement in international competitiveness and hence in the current account balance. A current account surplus would have the exact opposite effect. According to

---

[33] This account of the debate between the Banking School and the Currency School follows closely Anna Schwartz (1987: 182–6).

the Currency School, such a self-regulating mechanism should also operate in a system in which the money supply was composed of gold coin
and banknotes. To this end, the proponents of this doctrine held that the
banknote circulation should be fully covered by gold, or in other words
that monetary policy should be bound by strict rules.

The *Banking School* (Tooke, Fullarton, John Stuart Mill) regarded such
rules as superfluous, since they believed that an expansion in the money
supply beyond the demand for money was not in principle possible, provided the banks confined themselves to lending exclusively against 'real
bills'. In this way, the money circulation would be firmly tied to trends in
the real economy and this would prevent the development of inflationary
pressures. However, the supporters of this view overlooked the fact that
when the volume of money is tied to the nominal amount of bills it is no
longer possible to determine the price level. The 'real bills' doctrine would
thus be compatible with a process of hyperinflation, in which a continuous
growth in the nominal demand for credit to businesses (and an increase in
the nominal amount of outstanding bills) would always be met by an
expansion in the volume of lending by banks (and hence in the nominal
money supply). Moreover, the Banking School failed to recognize that
there is no strict relationship between the demand for credit and production by businesses. The demand for credit is essentially determined by the
interest-rate level and the marginal efficiency of capital. Thus, if interest
rates are low, the demand for credit can expand much faster than the volume of production. It is therefore not possible to assume, as the Banking
School did, that the (nominal) demand for money constitutes an exogenous
upper limit on the money supply. This undermines another premise of the
Banking School, the so-called 'law of reflux', according to which an excess
issue of banknotes would at most lead to private individuals repaying their
outstanding loans, meaning that the quantity of money could not in the
last resort exceed the given money supply. The adherents of the Banking
School again overlooked the influence of interest rates. As any macroeconomic textbook will demonstrate, an expansionary monetary policy has
the effect of lowering the level of interest rates in the short term, leading to
an increase in the demand for money.

In the case of the Bank of England in the first half of the nineteenth century, the reflux principle was relevant only in so far as an expansionary
monetary policy necessarily caused the country's balance of payments current account eventually to move into deficit. When there is an obligation
to honour English banknotes with gold (*convertibility*), this causes gold to
flow out of the country. However, the resulting reduction in the country's
domestic money supply will not be felt until a considerable time later, and

so this mechanism is not a reliable defence against the inflationary effects of excessive note issue.

The Currency School eventually won the political debate. Peel's Bank Charter Act of 1844 laid down that any issue of Bank of England notes above a certain amount must be fully backed by gold reserves.

7

The Institutional Framework of Monetary Policy II: The Design of the Central Bank Legislation

What this chapter is about

- The central bank constitution determines the incentive structure of central bankers. Given the long lags of monetary policy, it is important that the central bank constitution guarantees a long-term horizon of the central bank management. Such a 'conservatism' is generated by insulating monetary policy from the political process and by long terms of office for the members of a central bank's decision-making body.
- Differentiating between goal, instrument, and personal independence, it becomes possible to construct an index of central bank independence. According to this index, the ECB is currently the most independent central bank in the world. In the past, central bank independence contributed to a lower inflation rate. In the current low-inflation environment, such a causation is not evident.
- A natural corollary of independence is accountability: *ex post* accountability compares performance in the past with the targets of a central bank; *ex ante* accountability uses forecast values in order to find out whether a central bank will be able to meet its targets. For *ex ante* accountability it is important that economic processes are sufficiently transparent, so that outside researchers can make qualified forecasts.
- Direct sanctions play no role in most central bank constitutions. But there are informal sanctions for unqualified central bankers, and parliament can always change the central bank constitution. 'Performance contracts' are a theoretical possibility which relies on the assumptions of the Barro–Gordon model.

7.1. OVERVIEW

Our discussion of 'rules versus discretion' has led to the fundamental conclusion that monetary rules cannot be treated separately from the incentives of policy-makers. This chapter discusses how the central bank legislation should be designed in order to induce those who are in charge of monetary policy to behave as if they were following a rule that aims at price stability in the long run with due regard for supply and demand shocks in the short and medium run. As Fischer puts it,

The trick is to attain the appropriate balance between the need to be responsive to short-term pressures and the need to ensure that those pressures are exerted in a system that safeguards the long-term interest of the population. (Fischer 1995: 205)

These institutional aspects of monetary policy received little attention from academic economists in the 1970s and 1980s, but more recently have been the subject of intense discussion, not least as a result of the debate about the creation of the European Central Bank in the 1990s.

The previous chapter has led to the main lesson: that an inflation bias is due mainly to a short-term time horizon of politicians. This calls for a central bank legislation that provides central bankers with independence from politicians and with long terms of office. We will see that long terms of office are at the same time a very efficient means of insulating central bankers from the government.

The very independent status that central banks have been granted in many countries raises the question of how such an institution can be effectively monitored by the public and above all by the respective parliaments. Such a monitoring seems necessary since there is always a risk that the managers of a central bank are incompetent or are following goals that are incompatible with the central bank legislation. We will discuss how a central bank can and should be made accountable and what limitations to such accountability are unavoidable. In order to be effective, accountability has to be supplemented by sanctions if central bankers are unable to fulfil their mandate. In central bank legislation today, the triad of independence, accountability, and sanctions is rather unbalanced. While independence is now very well developed, accountability is often weak and direct sanctions are almost always absent.

Finally, Appendix 7.1 considers the various functions that have historically been assigned to central banks at a very much earlier date than the macroeconomic objective of price stability:

- the (exclusive) right of note issue (as 'bank of issue');
- safeguarding the stability of the financial sector (as 'banker to the banks' or 'lender of last resort');
- providing specific financial services to the public sector (as 'banker to the government').

7.2. INDEPENDENCE OF MONETARY POLICY

7.2.1. *'Conservatives take a long-term view'*

The discussion of the basic Barro–Gordon model has shown that costs of discretion increase with the value of b, which is the weighting for unemployment in the central bank's target function. In order to reduce the costs of discretion, Rogoff (1985) suggested the solution of a 'conservative' central banker, which is characterized by an individual target function that weights unemployment less than society or the 'non-conservative' central banker would. The target function of a conservative central banker with a value of b reduced by ξ can be written as

$$Z^{kNbk} = (b - \xi)[(1 - k)U^n - a(\pi - \pi^e)]^2 + \pi^2$$

$$\text{with } 0 \le \xi \le b. \tag{7.1}$$

Since the conservative central banker assigns the employment target a lower weighting than would be implied by the pursuit of the macroeconomic welfare function, the resulting inflation rate will, assuming rational expectations, turn out lower than in the basic BGM:

$$\pi_{rat}^{kNbk} < \pi_{rat}^{Nbk}.$$

The reduction of social costs is maximal when ξ assumes the value b; i.e., the conservative central banker is solely concerned about price-level stability and no longer pays any attention to the employment target. The social costs, which society can achieve by the appointment of such an ultra-conservative central banker, are then precisely those that were obtained above in the case of rules:

$$Z^{kNbk}\big|_{\xi = b} = b[(1 - k)U^n]^2 = Z_{rule}. \tag{7.2}$$

Thus, although the cost difference between the two strategies can be reduced by the appointment of a conservative central banker, with each positive weighting of the employment target in the central banker's target function ($b - \zeta > 0$), the solution of a conservative central banker is inferior to the rules solution and so is at best a *third-best solution* (Rogoff 1985: 1170).

Although this solution to the problem of time inconsistency is sometimes regarded as providing a theoretical justification for central bank independence[1] (Haldane 1995; Fischer 1995), it suffers from the fact that it

---

[1] See Briault *et al.* (1996: 64): 'Such a model comes closest to matching what many people think of as central bank independence: delegation of monetary policy to an inflation-averse authority with instrument independence.'

is basically designed for a *single-period game*. In this narrow framework, the concept of a 'conservative central banker' is possibly the only way to model central bank independence. But it is evident that the whole approach lacks a convincing microeconomic explanation of why some central bankers should be 'conservative' and others not.

If it is assumed more realistically that monetary policy decision-making is to be modelled as a *repeated game*, the figure of the 'conservative central banker' can be dispensed with altogether. What matters then is not that a central banker assigns a high weight to the goal of price stability in his target function, but that he is operating under a long-term time horizon.[2] Cukierman in particular emphasizes this point, defining 'conservative' central bankers not only in terms of the higher priority they give to certain objectives, but also in terms of a lower rate of time preference:

Conservatives usually take a longer view. (Cukierman 1992: 351)

Seen in this light, monetary policy independence is not necessary primarily in order to protect a 'conservative' central banker (with a low b, according to Rogoff's definition) from the influence that a less 'conservative' government might seek to bring to bear, but rather to enable central bankers with a longer-term decision horizon (and/or a lower rate of time preference) to assert their authority when faced with a government with a shorter planning horizon (and/or a higher rate of time preference). Then, when the government 'by a conscious act relinquishes its own power' (Issing 1993*b*: 30), this does not mean that the institution to which the power of decision-making is transferred has different inflation and employment preferences from the population, but simply that it is operating with a longer time horizon than the government.

Thus, it is quite possible that the central bank will react appropriately to temporary output shocks, if it is of the opinion that such a policy can be pursued without long-term disadvantages for price stability. From this standpoint, the economic rationale for independence is, that it enables those deciding monetary policy to conduct their policy without being always scrutinized by the government for short-term results. The longer-term time horizon in their decision-making implies that they make full allowance for the long time-lags to which monetary impulses are subject before they take effect.

---

[2] It is also necessary to ensure that the decision-making body consists of several persons whilst staggering the terms of office so that the problem of a 'last period' (see Section 6.3.3.2) does not arise.

This interpretation of central bank independence is much more consistent with empirical evidence than is the Rogoff approach, which is based exclusively on the different weightings. In the words of Briault *et al.*,

So the two most important implications of Rogoff's model are that an independent central bank should attenuate inflation biases (lower inflation) and accentuate stabilisation biases (raise output variability). Empirical evidence ... lends strong support to the first of them: in cross-section, greater (goal and instrument) independence does tend to be associated with lower inflation, both in mean and (to a lesser extent) variance. ... The second of the model's predictions has fared less well. Most empirical studies have failed to find any significant link between independence and the mean or the variability of output growth or employment. (Briault *et al.* 1996: 65)

Of course, Rogoff's concept of the conservative central banker would also become obsolete if one abandoned the completely arbitrary premises of a *k* factor of less than 1. But then, as has already been pointed out, the whole conceptual structure of the BGM collapses.

7.2.2. *Different definitions of 'independence'*

Thus, it must be the most important aim of central bank legislation to create an incentive structure that guarantees a long-term time horizon of central bankers. As most politicians are characterized by rather myopic behaviour, this implies above all that the monetary policy decisions taken in the central bank have to be insulated from the general political process as far as possible. This explains why central bank independence is now widely regarded as a prerequisite for an efficient monetary policy. In the literature, differing definitions of central bank independence can be found.

- Debelle and Fischer (1995: 197) define independence by differentiating between 'goal independence' and 'instrument independence'. A central bank enjoys *goal independence* when it is free to choose its goals or at least free to decide the actual target values for a given goal. A central bank has *instrument independence* when it 'is given control over the levers of monetary policy and allowed to use them' (Fischer 1995: 202).
- Grilli *et al.* (1991) offer an alternative definition, which distinguishes between political and economic independence. By *political independence* they mean a central bank's ability to pursue the goal of price stability unfettered by formal or informal instructions emanating from the

politicians.[3] *Economic independence* means that a central bank has unlimited freedom to determine all monetary policy transactions that lead to changes in its operating targets (Grilli *et al.* 1991: 367).

As these definitions have both merits and shortcomings, it seems useful to make a synthesis of both approaches, which distinguishes three different notions of independence.

1. *Goal independence* requires that the government has no direct influence on the goals of monetary policy. In the definition by Grilli *et al.*, this issue is not explicitly addressed.
2. *Instrument independence* requires that the central bank be able to set its operating targets (interest rate, exchange rate) autonomously. This notion of instrument independence is identical with the concept of 'economic independence' by Grilli *et al.*
3. *Personal independence* requires that the decision-making body of a central bank be in a position to resist formal directives as well as informal pressure from the government. This element, which goes back to Issing (1993*b*), is lacking in the definition by Debelle and Fischer. It is, however, almost identical with the notion of political independence by Grilli *et al.*; the only difference concerns the target of price stability, which is included in the definition by Grilli *et al.*, while here it is addressed in the definition of goal independence.

7.2.3. *Goal independence*

Chapter 5 shows that the definition of the goals of monetary policy includes not only the choice between price stability and nominal GDP, but also a definition of the time horizon for their realization, the definition of concrete indices, their numerical target values, and the definition of escape clauses. Thus, 'goal independence' can take very different forms. It can include a framework wherein the central bank has complete freedom on all these issues, as well as a framework wherein it can decide on only some of these issues. In reality, one can find three main solutions for the definition of goal independence.

The highest degree of goal independence is found in the *United States*. As already mentioned, Section 2A of the Federal Reserve Act specifies that the Federal Reserve System and the Federal Open Market Committee should

---

[3] Grilli *et al.* (1991: 367) identify independence with 'autonomy to pursue the goal of low inflation. Any institutional feature that enhances the central bank's capacity to pursue this goal will, on our definition, increase central bank independence.'

seek 'to promote effectively the goals of maximum employment, stable prices, and moderate long-term interest rates'. Thus, it only enumerates the goals of monetary policy without assigning a specific weight to them. This leaves it up to the Federal Reserve to decide on the weights that it attaches to employment (which in the short run can be regarded as a proxy for real GDP) and price stability. The mention of 'stable long-term interest rates' is not compatible with the standard definition of the goals of monetary policy. Long-term interest rates are at best an intermediate target.

The *European Central Bank* is granted a somewhat more limited degree of goal independence. As already mentioned, Article 105 of the EC Treaty prescribes price stability as the main goal of the ECB's policy. But as this formulation does not specify a time horizon, the ECB has the option to follow other targets in the short run. This has been made explicit by the ECB's statement that it regards this target as a medium-term target (see Chapter 5). As far as the influence of the political sphere is concerned, the EC Treaty explicitly excludes any influence of politicians (from national governments, from the EU Commission or the European Parliament) on the goals of the ECB's policy. This is explicitly stated in Article 108 of the Treaty:

When exercising the powers and carrying out the tasks and duties conferred upon them by this Treaty and the Statute of the ESCB, neither the ECB, nor a national central bank, nor any member of their decision-making bodies shall seek or take instructions from Community institutions or bodies, from any government of a Member State or from any other body.

Similar arrangements can be found in Japan[4] and in a somewhat less explicit form in Sweden.

A low degree of goal independence characterizes the central bank legislation of the *United Kingdom, Canada*, and *New Zealand*. In these countries, the central bank legislation defines price stability as the main goal of monetary policy, but gives the government the right to determine the concrete target values.

- In New Zealand, price stability is defined in a Policy Targets Agreement that is negotiated periodically between the Minister of Finance and the Governor of the Bank.
- The Bank of England Act states in Section 112(1) that the Treasury is responsible for defining and publishing what it means by price stability.[5]

---

[4] Article 3 of the Bank of Japan Law states: 'The Bank of Japan's autonomy regarding currency and monetary control shall be respected.'

[5] 'The Treasury may by notice in writing to the Bank specify ... what price stability is to be taken to consist of ... .'

- In Canada, the Bank of Canada and the Government of Canada jointly announce 'inflation control targets'.

The virtues of goal independence are discussed differently in the literature. Several authors are opposed to goal independence. As Fischer puts it,

The most important conclusion of both theoretical and empirical literatures is that a central bank *should* have instrument independence, but *should not* have goal independence. (Fischer 1995: 202)

A similar conclusion can be found in the study by Bernanke *et al.*, who argue in favour of policy dependence for purely political reasons:

Because ultimately policy objectives in a democracy must reflect the popular will, they should be set by elected officials. (Bernanke *et al.* 1999: 312)

A completely different argument can be derived from the analysis of the BGM as well as from the traditional debate on 'rules versus discretion'. As politicians are typically dominated by a short-term time horizon, they will be always tempted to use any influence on monetary policy for a policy of surprise inflation. In Chapter 5, the discussion of the goals of monetary policy has shown that there are no *permanent* trade-offs between price stability and other macroeconomic targets. Therefore, there is no real choice that 'elected officials' could make for the population in the long run. In the short term, supply shocks make it necessary to allow for deviations from a medium-term inflation target. But entrusting the government or the parliament with this decision (Lohmann 1992) would clearly lead to the risk of an inflation bias. This leads to a possible trade-off between

- a more flexible response of monetary policy in the case of supply shocks, but only if the central bank is overly committed to price stability, and
- a reduced political independence of monetary policy with all the risks that are described in the BGM.

The experience with the Bundesbank, which was certainly a very 'conservative' central bank, indicates that the willingness to respond flexibly to supply shocks is in general very strong. In fact, the Bundesbank has even been willing to accept an implicit inflation target of more than 2% for several years (see Table 8.1). Thus, the risk of an inflation bias seems more relevant than the risk of an independent central bank that is not willing to accommodate a supply shock in the short run.

The different forms of goal independence that can be found in reality clearly reflect these two different views on the role of 'elected officials' in the determination of the goals of monetary policy. In the following, especially for constructing an index of central bank independence, I regard goal independence as a positive feature of a central bank legislation. I will make no distinction between the first two forms of goal independence, since a long-term perspective of monetary policy will automatically lead to a preference for price stability as the main goal. This is confirmed by the preference of the Federal Reserve Board for the target of price stability. Thus, a score of 2 is given for goal-independent central banks and score of 0 to goal-dependent central banks. For goal-dependent central banks with a clearly defined target of price stability in the central bank constitution, the score is 1, as this limits the governments' potential to generate a policy of surprise inflation.

7.2.4. *Instrument independence*

The notion of instrument independence implies that a central bank is able to set its operating targets without any interference from the government. It includes three important elements:

1. the *control of the short-term interest rate* as the most important operating target of monetary policy;
2. the *control of the exchange rate*, which can be used as an additional operating target especially in a relatively open economy (see Chapter 12);
3. *restrictions of central bank credits* to the government, which could undermine the control over the monetary base and thus over short-term interest rates.

Compared with the discussion on goal independence, all authors agree that instrument independence constitutes an indispensable element of a stability-oriented central bank legislation.[6]

If we look at concrete central bank acts, we can see that in almost all cases monetary policy can determine *interest rates* in an autonomous way. However, as in the case of goal independence, there are countries where the government can still override the central bank's decisions. This is the case in Canada (Paragraph 14(2) Bank of Canada Act), in the United Kingdom ('Treasury reserve powers', Section 19 of the Bank of England Act), and in New Zealand. In our index of central bank independence, such override provisions lead to a score of 1 instead of 2.

As far as the control over the *exchange rate* is concerned, there is at present no central bank that has unlimited responsibility for this target of monetary policy. The most far-reaching provision can be found for the ECB

---

[6] See Fischer (1995) and Bernanke *et al.* (1999: 322): 'We believe that inflation targeting is most effective and leads to the most democratically accountable policy-making when the central bank is instrument independent but not fully goal dependent.'

in Article 111 of the EC Treaty, which makes a distinction between formal exchange rate arrangements and a policy of managed floating. For *formal arrangements*, the European Council (i.e. the finance ministers of the EU member countries) has the main responsibility:

1. ... the Council may, acting unanimously on a recommendation from the ECB or from the Commission, and after consulting the ECB in an endeavour to reach a consensus consistent with the objective of price stability, after consulting the European Parliament, ... conclude formal agreements on an exchange rate system for the ECU in relation to non-Community currencies. The Council may, acting by a qualified majority ... adopt, adjust or abandon the central rates of the ECU within the exchange-rate system.[7]

For a system of *managed floating*, the Treaty limits the responsibility of the Council very strictly:

2. In the absence of an exchange-rate system in relation to one or more non-Community currencies as referred to in paragraph 1, the Council, acting by a qualified majority either on a recommendation from the Commission and after consulting the ECB, or on a recommendation from the ECB, may formulate general orientations for exchange-rate policy in relation to these currencies. These general orientations shall be without prejudice to the primary objective of the ESCB to maintain price stability.

Compared with the ECB, the central banks in all other countries have very limited responsibilities in the field of exchange rate policy. All central bank acts that we have discussed so far assign this responsibility without qualifications to the government. As no central bank has complete independence in this regard, our index gives a score of 1 to the ECB and a score of 0 to all other central banks.

A third element of instrument independence concerns the explicit limitations for central bank *lending to the government*. As already mentioned, this is stipulated by Article 107 of the EC Treaty. There is a problem, though, in so far as this rule relates exclusively to direct lending to the public sector. It is therefore perfectly compatible with the EC Treaty if the ECB purchases government bonds from the commercial banks as part of their open-market policy. In this way a central bank can easily bypass the prohibition on deficit financing, by conducting its money-market management essentially on outright open-market operations (see Chapter 10). In other central bank Acts, no similar regulations can be found. However,

---

[7] When the Treaty was formulated in 1991, it was planned that 'ECU' (European Currency Unit) should be the name of the common currency.

it is conceivable that a monetary policy geared to price stability might be guaranteed simply by giving a politically independent central bank the power to decide of its own accord when and how much to lend to public-sector borrowers (Swinburne and Castello-Branco 1991: 34). But then there is always the danger of a central bank giving in to political pressure and thus promoting inflationary state financing. Thus, a score of 1 is given for the EC Treaty's limitation. A score of 2 would require a complete prohibition of such lending, as is the case under a 'currency board' (see Chapter 6).

7.2.5. *Personal independence*

Even if central bankers are granted instrument and/or goal independence, the government could try to exert some informal pressure on monetary policy. For instance, if the central bank governor could be dismissed at any time, and without specific reasons at the discretion of the government, he or she would be in a rather weak position *vis-à-vis* the minister of finance or the head of government. A strong informal influence on the central bank can also be exerted if only one person, i.e. the governor, is in charge of monetary policy decisions. In this case it is sufficient that the government sends a dedicated partisan to the top of the central bank. The importance of these influences is confirmed by Cukierman (1992: 383–6), who takes the average number of changes of governors at the central bank each year as an approximation for actual independence. This figure varied, in the period 1950–89, between 0.03 in the case of Iceland and 0.93 in Argentina, where the average period of office came to only 13 months.[8]

Grilli *et al.* (1991) have tried to capture these issues in their definition of 'political independence'. On the basis of their work, the following issues will be included in the index of 'personal independence' of a central bank's governing body for monetary policy. (The names and the members of these bodies are shown in Table 7.1.)

- The *terms of office* of the members of the central decision-making body: for terms of office of five years and more the score is 1; for ten years and more the score is 2.
- The *number of members* in the decision-making body: for six or more members the score is 1; for ten and more the score is 2.

---

[8] This problem is especially serious with developing countries, where there is a significantly greater gap between what is provided for in law and *de facto* independence. Here the average number of changes of governor has a dominant and significant influence on the level of the inflation rate (Cukierman 1992: 419–22). This suggests that, in the case of developing countries, either the law is not being put into practice, or the index used for institutional independence does not take sufficient account of the absence of essential aspects of central bank independence (Fischer 1995: 205).

Table 7.1. *Governing bodies of central banks*

Central bank	Governing body	Number of members
ECB	Governing council	6 on Executive Board; 11 governors of member central banks
Federal Reserve System	Federal Open Market Committee	7 on Board of Governors, 5 presidents of Federal Reserve Banks
Bank of Japan	Policy Board	Governor and 2 deputy governors, 6 deliberative members
Reserve Bank of New Zealand	Governor	—
Bank of England	Monetary Policy Committee	Governor, 2 deputy governors, 6 other members
Sveriges Riksbank	Executive Board	6 members
Bank of Canada	Executive Committee (Governing Council)	Governor, deputy governor, presently 5 directors

- The *degree of political diversification* in the nomination process: if different legal bodies (e.g. lower and upper houses of the parliament; national governments and the European Council in the case of the ECB) are involved in the nomination process the score is 2; if the parliament appoints the members, the score is 1; if the government is the only institution with the right of appointment, the score is 0.
- As the BGM model shows that a finite time horizon leads to incentive problems (see Chapter 6), a central bank legislation gets a score of 2 if it explicitly prescribes *staggered terms of office*.
- Finally, as a ruling party could always threaten a central bank with a change of the central bank act, it is sometimes demanded that the central bank legislation should have a constitutional status (Neumann 1992: 20). Thus, a score of 2 is given for central bank legislation that has such a *special legal status*; otherwise the score is 0. The only central bank with such a special legal status is the ECB, as its legislation is defined in the EC Treaty, which can be changed only by a ratification in each of the 15 member countries.

7.2.6. *Empirical evidence*

In their study on central bank independence, Grilli *et al.* (1991) come to the conclusion that both political and economic independence are negatively correlated with the level of the inflation rate. While the various forms of independence may be more or less significant in relation to the inflation rate, the authors could find no significant correlation between the indexes of political and economic independence and the growth rate in real GNP. For this reason, they conclude: 'having an independent central bank is almost like having a free lunch, there are benefits, but no apparent costs in terms of economic performance' (Grilli *et al.* 1991: 375).

This finding is supported by many further studies. Independence always shows a negative correlation with the level of the inflation rate, without having a significant effect on real growth.[9] Graphically, this is demonstrated in Figure 7.1, which shows a clear negative correlation between the average inflation rate and the independence index used by Alesina and Summers (1993) for the most important Western industrial countries in the period 1955–88.[10] By contrast, there is no systematic correlation between the average real growth rate and central bank independence (see Figure 7.2).

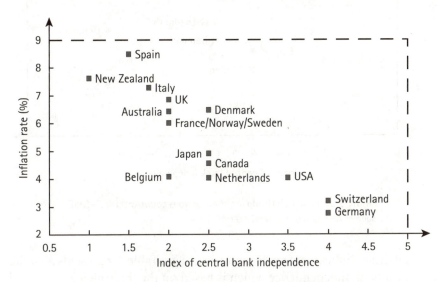

Figure 7.1. *Inflation and central bank independence, 1955–1988*
Source: Alesina and Summers (1993: 160).

[9] See also Alesina and Summers (1993); Cukierman (1992); Cukierman *et al.* (1992, 1993); De Haan and Sturm (1992); De Haan *et al.* (1993); De Long and Summers (1992); Eijffinger and Schaling (1993, 1995).

[10] A major problem of their analysis is that it includes the long period with fixed exchange rates under the Bretton Woods system (until 1973) whereby all central banks outside the United States had to operate under a strict exogenous rule of fixed exchange rates. Therefore it makes sense to analyse the putative negative correlation between independence and inflation only for the period after 1973. Siklos (1994: 9) shows that the negative correlation between central bank autonomy and the inflation rate is very much more marked in periods of flexible exchange rates than under a fixed exchange rate system.

Policy

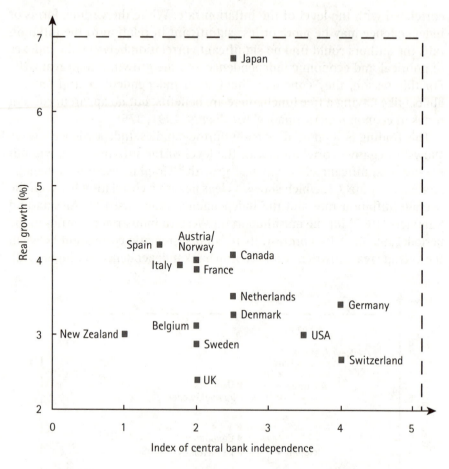

Figure 7.2. *Real growth and inflation, various countries, 1955–1988*
Source: Alesina and Summers (1993: 160).

As all these studies were made many years ago, Table 7.2 presents an index of central bank independence which is based on the three elements of goal, instrument, and personal independence. It should be clear that any attempt to define an index of central bank independence is confronted with the problem of choosing the criteria that it includes and of weighting the different elements of independence and the different criteria with each category. It is therefore not surprising that the central bank independence 'league tables' found in the literature give strikingly different results. As weightings are always associated with value judgements, we simply give an equal weight to each of the three elements of independence and to each of the criteria that make up the three elements. The result of this index shows that the ECB is by

Table 7.2. *Indices of central bank independence*

Central bank	ECB	Fed	BoJ	SR	BOC	BoE	RBNZ
Goal independence	2	2	2	2	1	1	1
Instrument independence							
Interest rate policy	2	2	2	2	1	1	1
Exchange rate policy	1	0	0	0	0	0	0
Explicit limitation of credit to government	1	0	0	0	0	0	0
Total instrument independence	1.33	0.66	0.66	0.66	0.33	0.33	0.33
Political independence of the decision-making body							
Terms of office	1	2	1	1	0.29	0.3	1
(Years)	(5;8)[a]	(14)[b]	(5)	(6)	(7;3)[c]	(5;3)[d]	(5)
Diversification	2	2	1	1	1	1	0
(No. of members)	(17)	(12)	(9)	(6)	(7)	(9)	(1)
Diversified nomination	2	0	2	1	0	0	0
Staggered appointments	2	2	0	0	2	0	0
Specific status of central bank legislation	2	0	0	0	0	0	0
Total personal independence	1.8	1.2	0.8	0.6	1.1	0.26	0.2
Total independence	1.7	1.3	1.2	1.1	0.8	0.5	0.5

[a] 5 yrs' minimum for the 11 national central bank governors; 8 yrs' minimum for the 6 members of the ECB Board.
[b] 7 yrs for members of the Board of Governors.
[c] 7 yrs for the governor and deputy governor; 3 yrs for the 5 directors.
[d] 5 yrs for the governor and 2 deputy governors; 3 yrs for the 6 other members.

Source: See text.

far the most independent central bank, followed by the Federal Reserve and the Bank of Japan. The independence is relatively less in the three inflation-targeting countries (Canada, United Kingdom, and New Zealand).

In contrast to earlier studies, these indices of central bank independence show absolutely no correlation with the inflation performance of the respective countries in the years 1996–2000 (Table 7.3). However, the results have to be treated very carefully. As most of the actual central bank laws have been introduced only in the last few years, it is not possible to rely on longer-term comparisons. In addition, the period 1996–2000 was characterized by worldwide price stability, so that it is possibly not a good test for the quality of different central bank legislation in a more difficult environment.

Table 7.3. *Inflation and central bank independence, 1996–2000*

Central bank	Index	Inflation (%)
European Central Bank	1.8	1.6
Federal Reserve System	1.3	2.1
Bank of Japan	1.2	−0.4
Sveriges Riksbank	1.1	1.2
Bank of Canada	0.81	1.0
Bank of England	0.53	2.7
Reserve Bank New Zealand	0.51	1.5

Source: Own calculations based on Table 7.2 and on OECD, *Economic Outlook.*

A theoretical problem with all studies of the correlation between independence and inflation is that central bank independence is required only for situations where the government is tempted to pursue an inflationist policy in order to reduce the unemployment rate. Thus, an 'inflation bias' under a politically dependent central bank will exist only if

1. the country suffers from an unemployment problem,
2. inflation is not regarded as an equally serious problem, and
3. the government is afraid of not being re-elected so that it will take recourse to myopic strategies.

In other words, in countries with low unemployment, a high preference for price stability among the population, and a very stable political environment, an inflation bias is not very likely even with a completely dependent central bank. Good examples of such a constellation are Japan and France, which followed very stability-oriented policies in the 1980s and 1990s although their central banks were not independent until 1993 (Banque de France) and 1998 (Bank of Japan).

As the preference for price stability is very high today in almost all countries of the world, this could lead to the conclusion that central bank independence is no longer necessary. But the experience of the last fifty years shows that, even after long periods of very low inflation (the 1950s and 1960s), an outburst of inflation cannot be excluded. Therefore, it is always good to be prepared.

7.3. ACCOUNTABILITY OF CENTRAL BANKS

As many central banks in the world are now given a high degree of independence, it is necessary that the principals, i.e. the population and above all the parliament, are able to monitor the actions of the central bankers that act as their agents. A consequent application of the principle of political accountability would imply a liability of the members of a central bank's governing body which could even include the dismissal of incompetent central bankers.

7.3.1. Ex post *and* ex ante *accountability*

In the last few years the issue of central bank accountability has been intensively discussed, very often together with the concept of transparency. In a general sense, the management of a central bank can be held accountable only for reaching or missing the stated targets of monetary policy. Thus, for an understanding of transparency and accountability it is important to recall the main result of Chapter 5, which discusses the goals of monetary policy. In addition, it is useful to differentiate between two forms of accountability.

- *Ex post accountability* implies that a central bank has to justify *ex post* if it has been unable to reach its targets. The ECB seems to interpret accountability mainly in this way.[11]
- *Ex ante accountability* implies that a central bank should also be compelled to justify deviations of forecast values from target values. Such a forward-looking perspective is warranted above all because of the long lags in the monetary policy transmission process.

If we start with *ex post* accountability, Figure 7.3 gives a rough survey over possible outcomes, based on the analysis of supply and demand shocks in Section 5.3.1. The unproblematic cases are marked with a square, the problematic cases with a circle. Accountability implies that a central bank would have to justify why it was unable to avoid one of the following negative outcomes:

- a positive or negative *demand shock* associated with a higher (lower) inflation rate than the inflation target;
- a positive or negative *supply shock*, with price stability but associated with a positive or negative output gap.

In the case of a supply shock, which is associated with an inflation rate higher (lower) than the target and a negative (positive) output gap, there would be a presumption that the central bank did react correctly (see Section 5.3.1),

---

[11] See Duisenberg (1999c): 'Thus, publication of the forecasts cannot contribute to accountability. Rather its performance in maintaining price stability in the medium term should be used by the public to judge the success of the Eurosystem.'

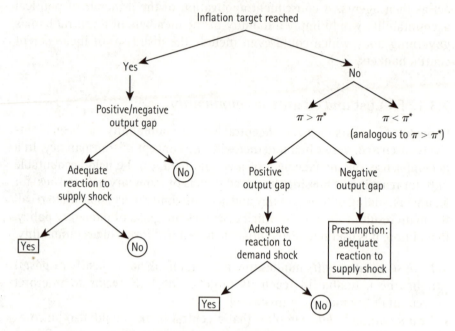

Figure 7.3. Ex post *accountability*

Note: A square indicates a successful monetary policy.

but the assessment would depend on the size of the output gap and the deviation between actual inflation and the inflation target.

A similar exercise could be applied for *ex ante* accountability. In this case, forecast values for the inflation rate and the output gap would have to be used. As in the case of inflation targeting, a forecast horizon of two years would be useful. The analytical structure would be identical with the case of *ex post* accountability. Again, the central bank would be under an obligation to justify situations where negative outcomes are forecast.

Analytically, *ex ante* accountability is more difficult to exercise since it relies on forecast values. These data could be provided either by the central bank or by outside forecasters. For an evaluation of the central bank, it seems obvious that outside forecasts are more objective than the forecast produced by the central bank. This is especially the case if one sees a risk that the central bank could have an incentive to engineer a policy of surprise inflation (Section 6.3), which implies that a central bank would produce an inflation forecast that is downward-biased.

The question whether outside forecasters are able to produce useful forecasts for an *ex ante* accountability of central banks leads to the closely related concept of transparency.

7.3.2. *Transparency*

The two dimensions of accountability provide a good basis for a discussion of 'transparency'. Above all, they make clear that it would be misguiding to regard transparency as a value in itself by implying that a central bank should always supply a maximum amount of information to the public. As Issing puts it,

It is not quite obvious to my mind that the legitimate and important cause of transparency would be advanced if central banks were to make available to the public the maximum amount of information at their disposal. You could perhaps imagine all data and records continuously being put on the Internet. You could, in addition, imagine live broadcasts of all Governing Council meetings, committee meetings, perhaps including the coffee breaks and all words uttered in the halls and corridors of power. George Orwell in reverse, if you will. (Issing 1999a)

If accountability is regarded as the main goal of a central bank's information policy, what matters is information that allows the public to assess on an *ex post* and an *ex ante* basis whether a central bank is able to meet its targets. As far as *ex post* accountability is concerned, there is no reason to assume that a central bank would possess information that is unavailable to the public. For this purpose, mainly national accounts data are required that are generally accessible. This is somewhat different for *ex ante* accountability, which requires forecasts for the relevant macroeconomic data. Again, such information is common knowledge today since there are many public and private institutions that regularly produce comprehensive forecasts for all important data of all major countries. In addition, institutions like Consensus Economics provide a synthesis of these forecasts; the ECB publishes a 'Survey of Professional Forecasters' regularly in its *Bulletin*. Thus, in principle, each citizen and each member of the parliament can relatively easily obtain the data that are needed to find out

1. whether the central bank is able to reach its main target within the next two years, and
2. what implications for real growth and employment are associated with the central bank's policy.

From this perspective, the academic debate on transparency[12] seems somewhat out of touch with reality. It is often based on the assumption that the central bank possesses private information that it could hide from the public. However, in spite of the strong interest in that debate, there is little discussion on whether such information asymmetries are also an empirical fact.

---

[12] For a survey see Winkler (2000).

As far as economic shocks are concerned (Geraats 1999), there is no reason to believe that a central bank could be better informed than institutions
like the IMF, OECD, national research institutes or private institutions like
Deutsche Bank Research, which all make the results of their analyses public. As central banks also publish a vast amount of data, their information
advantage would have to rest on some secrete data concerning the financial sector of the economy. It seems very unlikely that such data, if they are
really relevant for economic analysis, would be kept secret by central
banks for a longer period of time.

The only important information advantage that a central bank has over
the public is the knowledge about the intended path of short-term interest
rates. Thus, all outside forecasts rest on an assumption about this path,
which can differ from the true intentions of the central bank. However, for
the process of accountability, outside forecasters can always try to identify
an interest rate path which—starting from the actual level of interest rates—
is required for achieving the inflation target within the forecasting horizon. After some months, they can observe whether or not the central bank
is following this path. Interest rates that are too low compared with the target path are a clear indication that a central bank is either incompetent or
no longer committed to its inflation target. Of course, in the case where the
central bank is no longer on such a path, it can be difficult to estimate
the inflation rate. But for *ex ante* accountability, it is already sufficient if
the public knows that the central bank will fail to meet its target.

The literature also assumes that the public is not informed about the central bank's true preferences for inflation and employment. While this is
true, there is no reason why a lack of such information would prevent an
effective *ex ante* accountability. As long as outside forecasts can be made
that show whether or not an inflation target can be reached, it makes little
difference for the process of *ex ante* accountability whether this is due to
incompetence or to specific preferences of the central bank. In both cases,
the central bank management will be exposed to strong public pressure to
explain its reasons for failing to reach its target.

Thus, the academic discussion is very much shaped by a somewhat naive
view of the competencies and information of the central bank and of the
general public.[13] This view is nicely presented in a quote by Willem Buiter:

Mr Duisenberg's accountability model, which suggests that as long as daddy
brings home the bacon, mummy and the children ought not to ask where he got it,

---

[13] See also Issing (1999*b*: 507): 'I am rather sympathetic to the view that central banks have only
limited information advantage over sophisticated market participants, both with respect to the
available data and—perhaps—also with respect to the understanding how the economy works.'

is not viable as a modern model for the relationship between the citizen and the state. (Buiter 1999: 6)

Given the available data and the technical skills of forecasters in the private sector and in international institutions, who are often much better paid than their colleagues in the national central bank bureaucracy, it seems odd to use the analogy of an omniscient 'daddy' and a completely ignorant 'mummy' and children. If instead one regards both sides as equally competent, transparency becomes much less of an issue, since there is very little that the central bank could hide from the public.

We can see this in greater detail if we look at the communication technologies that are centrally applied in the efforts to become transparent (see Table 7.4).

1. For most central banks, the announcement of a *monetary policy strategy* plays an important role in their communication strategy. A notable exception is the Federal Reserve, which makes no explicit statements on this topic. We will see in Chapters 8 and 9 that the information content of such announcements is relatively low. The most impressive example is the Bundesbank, which for more than two decades announced monetary targets that never played a major role in its interest rate policy (Section 9.1). As far as the inflation-targeting countries are concerned (Section 8.4), their strategy is of such a general nature that the public can infer very little from this information about the central bank's 'view of the world' (Winkler 2000: 13). The same applies to the ECB's two pillar strategies (Section 9.2), where the first pillar is only a 'reference value' for the money stock M3 and the second is kept extremely vague ('broadly based assessment of the outlook for future a rather price developments'). Thus, outside analysts have to rely on their own 'view of the world' if they want to forecast the relevant macroeconomic variables.

2. The announcement of a *concrete target* value for price stability is useful, but even without this information there is a general consensus among economists that a rate of about 2% is compatible with this goal (Section 5.4.3).

3. The publication of a central bank's *inflation forecasts* constitutes one of the core elements of inflation targeting. While this strategy will be discussed in more detail in Chapter 8, it seems obvious that for the process of accountability outside forecasts are more suitable. A survey of external evaluations has the advantage of being more objective and more diversified. The central bank's own forecast is important only if it comes to the conclusion that outside forecasts are incorrect.

4. Many economists regard the *publication of the minutes* of the meetings of the central bank's decision-making body as an important piece of

Table 7.4. *Instruments of monetary policy transparency*

	US Federal Reserve	Bank of Japan	Eurosystem	Bank of England	Memo item Bundesbank
Objectives					
Specification of an overriding ultimate goal	No	Price stability	Price stability	Price stability	Price stability
Quantification of ultimate goal	No	No	Quantitative definition by Governing Council of the ECB	Inflation target of the government	Medium-term price assumption[a]
Strategy					
Announcement and substantiation of the monetary policy strategy	No	No	Two-pillar strategy	Inflation targeting	Monetary targeting
Announcement of an intermediate target	No	No	No	Inflation projection as intermediate target proxy	Monetary target
Announcement of prominent indicators	Monitoring ranges for money and credit growth[b]	No specific indicators	Reference value for M3 growth	No specific indicators	–
Data and forecasts					
Publication of data on intermediate targets/indicators and explanation of possible deviations	Yes[b]	No	Yes	Yes	Yes
Publication of an inflation forecast and explanation of deviations from target	Twice a year[c]	No	Inflation projection by ECB staff	Quarterly	No

Decisions					
Announcement of monetary policy decisions	Yes	Yes	Yes	Yes	Yes
Statements concerning direction of future interest-rate policy	Interest-rate bias of the FOMC; meanwhile superseded by risk assessment	No	Occasionally	No	No
Means of communication					
Parliamentary hearings	At least twice a year	At least twice a year	At least four times a year	Regularly[d]	No
Reports on economic conditions and monetary policy[c]	Semi-annual report (Monthly report)	Monthly report	Monthly bulletin	Quarterly Inflation Report	Monthly report
Press conferences on economic conditions and monetary policy	No	Monthly[f]	Monthly[g]	Quarterly Inflation Report	On specific occasions[h]
Publication of minutes of meetings	After 6–8 weeks	After about one month	No	After 2 weeks	No
Publication of voting behaviour of individual members	After 6–8 weeks	After about one month	No	After 2 weeks	No

a As part of the derivation of the monetary target.
b Prescribed by law, but now of minor relevance for practical monetary policy.
c As part of reports which the chairman of the Federal Reserve Board has to make under the Humphrey Hawkins Act to Congress.
d In addition, reporting requirement of the central bank governor to the government if inflation leaves the target band.
e All central banks mentioned here also publish an annual report.
f On the second working day after the first Policy Board meeting each month.
g Immediately following the first meeting each month of the Governing Council of the ECB.
h To announce and review the monetary target, and after major monetary policy decisions.

Source: Deutsche Bundesbank (2000a).

information (Buiter 1999; Svensson 2000*b*). However, whenever discussions of a committee are made public, there is a natural tendency that the more controversial issues are discussed informally. As a result, the minutes of the Bank of England consist mainly of a broad analysis of the current economic situation while the description of the discussion is kept in rather vague and general terms. In this regard, it differs little from the monthly press conference statement by the ECB's president. Both pieces of information are of some interest since they convey some information about the future interest rate path.

5. Related to the publication of minutes is the publication of the *voting behaviour* of individual members. This information can be useful for an assessment of the future interest path. But in a supranational institution like the ECB there is also the risk that the national central bank governors might be exposed to domestic political pressure whenever the overall economic stance of the euro area differs from the situation in individual countries.

All in all, for *ex ante* accountability the value of these communication technologies is rather limited. They are of some interest for the outsider's assumption about the central bank's future interest rate path. However, there is so far no empirical evidence that central banks with very intensive information technologies like the Bank of England have achieved a better performance than central banks like the Federal Reserve or the ECB, which both offer only parts of the whole set of possible communication tools.

Compared with the intensive discussion on transparency, astonishingly few efforts have been made so far to develop a *structured process* for *ex post* and *ex ante* accountability as it has been laid down in Figure 7.3. The annual reports and monthly bulletins of most central banks are rather descriptive and do not systematically discuss the reasons for *ex ante* and *ex post* deviations of inflation from target values, nor do they analyse the interplay of inflation and output gaps.

7.4. LIABILITY OF INCOMPETENT CENTRAL BANKERS

While there has been much discussion about the monitoring of central banks, very little has been said about how to sanction an incompetent central banker or even an incompetent governing body of a central bank. The only central bank legislation that entails such a sanction is the Reserve Bank of New Zealand Act.

7.4.1. *Country models*

7.4.1.1. *The model of New Zealand*
The power to dismiss the central bank governor without notice if the inflation rate is out of line with the target is a particularly drastic form of sanction mechanism. In New Zealand, the central bank governor may be
dismissed by the finance minister if his performance does not live up to the
target agreed in the Policy Targets Agreement (PTA) (§49 (2) of the Reserve
Bank of New Zealand (RBNZ) Act). Dismissal is not an automatic procedure, though, but has to be decided by the government or the finance minister (§49 (3) of the RBNZ Act). This is necessary if only because the PTA
provides for various exemptions which release the central bank governor
from strict adherence to the target. The basic idea behind these exemptions
is to ensure that the central bank governor is punished for poor performance only where he is to blame and must bear the responsibility for it
(Issing 1993*b*: 27). According to the PTA of 16 December 1999, a deviation
from the target rate is possible in the case of 'unusual events' which include
shifts in the aggregate price level as a result of

- exceptional movements in the prices of commodities traded in world
  markets;
- changes in indirect taxes;
- significant government policy changes that directly affect prices;
- 'a natural disaster affecting a major part of the economy'.

If he believes that circumstances have arisen in which the exemptions ought
to apply, the central bank governor is required to report them and to provide
a justification of his view. Ultimately, it is his report that will enable the
finance minister to decide whether the justification is a sound one or whether
a sanctioning breach of the target has taken place. The governor of the Reserve
Bank of New Zealand is therefore required to report regularly—at least every
six months—in the form of an interim report ('Monetary Policy Statement') on
the conduct and results of monetary policy (§15 of the RBNZ Act). He must
also explain any deviations from the target to the finance minister.

In the 1990s the target was missed twice (in 1995 and 1996), but the
sanction of a dismissal was not applied (Bernanke *et al.* 1999: 109). Instead
of firing the governor, the government decided to widen the target range,
from 0%–2% to 0%–3%.

7.4.1.2. *Liability in other countries*
Without direct sanctions, accountability, which in principle always entails
liability, is always limited, especially if the members of a governing body are

employed under long terms of office. Thus, in almost all countries it would be practically impossible to dismiss central bankers who are obviously incompetent. This unsatisfactory state of affairs could be improved by introducing direct sanctions that are based on a framework of outside evaluation. For instance, if a central bank decides not to raise interest rates, although outside forecasts indicate a serious target violation because of a demand shock (*ex ante* accountability), and if it turns out that the central bank was wrong (*ex post* accountability), an 'admonition' could be decided by the parliament. If a similar mistake happens a second time, the parliament could have the right to dismiss the central bank governor or the whole governing body with a majority of two-thirds of its votes. Such a measure, combined with liability, would enhance accountability much more than an excessive transparency.

But the absence of explicit sanction mechanisms does not mean that the officials of an independent central bank can operate entirely free of sanctions. If they pursue a policy that in the longer term runs counter to the interests of the population, they could at all events suffer a serious loss of reputation or fail to be reappointed. An extreme solution would be a change of the central bank constitution which would deprive the central bank of its independent status.

A main disadvantage of indirect sanctions, on the other hand, is that they operate with long lags, as they will become effective only if a central banker can be appointed for a second term or if he is a candidate for a responsible position in the public or private sector. For the reason of assessing the competence of individual members, Buiter (1999) recommends publishing the track record of individual votes and on-the-record explanations of these votes.

However, in the political sphere, informal information on the competence of individual central bankers is always available. Compared with this small advantage, the costs of publishing the votes would be very high in the case of the ECB. It would certainly expose the national governors to strong pressure from their national governments which could threaten their independence. While Buiter (1999) argues that the voting behaviour would become public anyhow—'Leaks, and even open breaches of confidentiality arrangements will be the rule rather than the exception'—this has so far not been confirmed by evidence. Thus, the costs of publishing the individual votes would be high, while the advantages would be very limited.

7.4.2. *A purely theoretical solution: performance contracts*

The lack of efficient direct sanctions in central bank legislation has led to theoretical approaches aiming at incentive-compatible contracts for central bankers. The models are based on the BGM and on its rather arbitrary assumption that central bankers tend to pursue an unemployment target that is lower than the natural rate of unemployment. The main idea is that the contract between the government and the central bank governor must remove any systematic incentive for surprise inflation, without reducing monetary policy flexibility. What is required, therefore, is a solution that corresponds to the flexible rule, since this also reduces inflation expectations to zero, but in addition allows scope to counteract supply shocks.[14] Then the optimal inflation rate from society's point of view will depend on the real disturbance:

$$\pi_{flex}(\varepsilon) = \frac{ab}{(1 + a^2 b)} \varepsilon. \tag{7.3}$$

However, as has already been discussed in detail, it is not really possible in practice to formulate a rule that depends on circumstances in this way. If on the other hand a strict price level target is chosen, no stabilization of output takes place ('stabilization bias'). If therefore one does without rules altogether, this provides flexibility, but then the problem of inflation bias arises, which characterizes discretionary solutions in the context of the time inconsistency model. If the central bank pursues the same macroeconomic target function as society or the government, i.e. if

$$Z^{Nbk} = Z = [b(U - kU^n)^2 + \pi^2], \tag{7.4}$$

a central bank with discretion will produce the inflation rate

$$\pi_{disc}(\varepsilon) = \underbrace{ab(1 - k)U^n}_{\text{inflation bias}} + \frac{ab}{(1 + a^2 b)} \varepsilon \tag{7.5}$$

if private individuals form their expectations rationally and random real shocks occur.

The permanent component of the inflation rate (inflation bias) depends exclusively on the central bank's employment target and preference ($b(1 - k)U^n$) and on the slope of the short-term Phillips curve (a).

The contractual approach is now based on the recognition that the inflation bias can be removed by a suitable formulation of the contract between the principal (government) and a responsible agent (central bank). For this purpose, the marginal welfare gain from an increase in inflation (the marginal return) must be exactly offset, in the central banker's calculations, by

---

[14] For a derivation of this and the following results, see Walsh (1995a) and Waller (1995).

marginal welfare costs.[15] This would solve the time inconsistency problem. Since, moreover, the inflation bias is independent of the magnitude of possible shocks, it is now possible to pursue a monetary policy that is not only credible, but also flexible.

Contracts that allow the inclusion of incentives always take as their starting point the individual utility of the persons involved. It is therefore in the government's interest only to appoint a central banker who takes responsibility for meeting his objectives. It is now assumed that the utility function of the responsible central bank governor V^{Nbk} incorporates not only employment and the inflation rate in the form of the above target function, but also the governor's income or the central bank's budget (T). Marginal costs of inflation can then be created by causing the amount of this payment (T) to fall as the inflation rate rises. A central banker who maximizes his utility,

$$V^{Nbk} = T(\pi) - Z^{Nbk} = T(\pi) - [b(U - kU^n)^2 + \pi^2], \tag{7.6}$$

depending on the inflation rate achieved, will then take into account not only the effects on the welfare of society, but also the change in income flows. If one again assumes rational expectations on the part of private individuals, the central banker will obtain the following level of inflation:

$$\pi_{contr}(\varepsilon) = \frac{1}{2}\frac{\partial T}{\partial \pi} + ab(1 - k)U^n + \frac{ab}{1 + a^2b}\varepsilon. \tag{7.7}$$

This solution bears a strong similarity to the discretionary solution. However, it adds an extra element, namely the change in the payment flow. By choosing an appropriate value for this term, the government can induce the central banker to eschew surprise inflation and, in the event of stochastic (supply) shocks, to react only in the optimal manner described above. If π_{contr} and π_{flex} are made equal, this means that the payment flow must be reduced linearly for the amount of the dual inflation bias:

$$\frac{\partial T}{\partial \pi} = -2ab(1 - k)U^n. \tag{7.8}$$

For the total payment (including a constant payment T and variable payment T_0) to the central banker, the following equation will then apply:

$$T(\pi) = T_0 - [2ab(1 - k)U^n]\pi. \tag{7.9}$$

Since the payment is a function of the inflation rate, the contractual approach is also referred to as the *performance contract approach*. Here, the

---

[15] The 'marginal return on inflation' is here understood to mean the net return. If the central bank increases the inflation rate, there may be a short-term rise in employment, but the higher level of inflation decreases welfare, so that the difference between the two components corresponds to the 'marginal return on the increase in inflation'. The welfare costs referred to here are thus additional costs.

constant income payment T_0 must be at least equal to the social welfare expectation value, since otherwise the central banker would receive a negative utility from his job and be unlikely to sign the contract. It can also be seen that the 'optimal' linearity factor again depends on the employment preference of the central banker and the slope of the short-term Phillips curve. If the k factor is again equal to unity, there is no need at all for an income component that is dependent on inflation ($T(\pi) = T_0$).

If the target inflation rate is not zero, but any positive figure π^*, this requires an adjustment of the deduction factor by the positive difference between the actual and the target inflation rate.[16]

$$T(\pi) = T_0 - [2ab(1 - k)U^n] (\pi - \pi^*). \tag{7.10}$$

In periods without shocks, such a contract offsets the incentive for surprise inflation. If shocks occur, the optimal tax means that the central banker achieves exactly that combination of inflation and employment that society prefers. In this solution, the inflation bias and stabilization bias are equal to zero.

The central condition for this is that the central banker actually derives utility from the monetary payment flow *and* at the same time makes his decisions dependent on the government's macroeconomic target function (Walsh 1995a: 158–60).[17] If, on the other hand, one assumes an exclusively income-dependent utility function for the central banker, then it is not sufficient to gear the tax solely to the level of the inflation rate, but it is necessary to take account of other important macroeconomic variables in accordance with society's (the government's) target function. Otherwise, the central banker would profit from the pursuit of a *deflationary policy*, which would lead to a real increase in his income payments. In the context of the model discussed here, the income payment would therefore need to be determined not only by the inflation rate, but also by the employment level or unemployment rate. A credible monetary policy that also produced the optimal stabilizing effect is achieved only when the payment is made dependent on the level of the social welfare, i.e. when the income function is as follows:

$$T(\pi, U) = T_0 - (2ab(1 - k)U^n)(\pi - \pi^*)$$
$$- b(U - U^*)^2 - (\pi - \pi^*)^2. \tag{7.11}$$

---

[16] See Walsh (1995a: 157). This result is also obtained by Persson and Tabellini (1993) and by Fratianni *et al.* (1997).

[17] Strictly speaking, however, it is only necessary that the central banker and the government should agree on the weighting of the employment target in their target functions, since it is only this component, together with the slope of the short-term Phillips curve, that determines the optimal (shock-dependent) inflation rate π_{flex} (Waller 1995: 8–10). A k factor of less than 1 is not necessary here.

This payment function means that the central banker ultimately maximizes the utility function, which is designed to operate as if he had the same inflation and employment preferences as society (Walsh 1995a: 158–60).

In spite of its analytical merits, the whole approach is hardly applicable to practical monetary policy. Like the BGM, the approach of performance contracts depends on the rather dissimilar assumption of $k \neq 1$, i.e. the assumption that central bankers normally pursue an activist employment policy. Only for this very specific case do performance contracts make sense. As can be seen from equation (7.9), for $k = 1$, the variable payments component of the contracts becomes zero.

An analytically less demanding, but easier-to-implement, variant of a direct microeconomic sanction mechanism is that in which the central bank governor has his salary fixed in nominal terms. Then the real value of his income falls in proportion to the inflation rate. In order to avoid a deflation, a reduction of the nominal income by the deflation rate could also be envisaged. This form of sanction was actually considered in New Zealand, but ultimately was rejected in favour of a central bank budget fixed in nominal terms (Haldane 1995: 19). This was due to the requirement of setting the budget for five years in advance (§§159–61 of the RBNZ Act).

Appendix 7.1. The functions of central banks and the technology of the payments systems

It was already mentioned that, in addition to their macroeconomic functions, central banks have always been responsible for important additional tasks. They include, above all,

- the (exclusive) right of note issue (as 'bank of issue');
- safeguarding the stability of the financial sector (as 'banker to the banks' or 'lender of last resort');
- providing specific financial services to the public sector ('banker to the government').

In a very systematic analysis, Giannini (1994) has shown how the central bank functions that we can observe today have evolved historically. The main result of his study is that there was always a very clear relationship between the technology of the payments system and the functions of a central bank.

1. As a consequence of the increasing importance of banknotes (which had been convertible into gold) in the nineteenth century, many countries decided to grant the right of note issue to only very few banks (or even a monopolistic bank), which were often private banks.

2. The gradual substitution of banknotes by bank deposits that started in the second half of the nineteenth century created a problem of financial instability which overburdened the private banks of issue. As a result, the private banks were transformed in state banks which were assigned the responsibility of a 'lender of last resort'.

3. In the twentieth century convertible money was replaced by 'definitive money', i.e. paper money which promises no convertibility into any other medium. This process ended with the introduction of flexible exchange rates in 1973. It had its corollary in the increasing macroeconomic responsibility of central banks which was definitively acknowledged with acceptance of price stability as the main target of monetary policy by almost all central banks in the course of the 1990s.

The right of note issue

The beginning of modern central banking dates back to the first half of the nineteenth century. In that period it was for the first time officially acknowledged that the government has an important role to play in setting an institutional framework for the monetary sphere of an economy. A model for many countries become the 'Bank Charter Act Model' (BCAM), which was decided for the Bank of England in the Peel Bank Act of 1844. It includes the following elements:

- Note issuing banks are private, profit-maximizing banks
- The note issue is determined by a strict rule
- The number of banks that are entitled to issue notes is limited, but from the beginning one bank is privileged, and over time it becomes the central bank.

The BCAM can be regarded as the institutional solution to the financial innovation of the 'banknote'. In contrast to the view of the adherents of the 'banking school' (see Appendix 6.1), the BCAM is based on the view that a pure *laissez-faire*, i.e. unrestricted competition among the issuing banks, would not guarantee a stable financial system.

1. From a microeconomic perspective, the need of a rule was justified by the fact that an individual bank customer is not able to assess the quality of the banknotes of different issuers. This would make it possible for some banks to over-issue banknotes without being sufficiently restricted by the requirement to convert their banknotes into gold.

2. From a macroeconomic point of view, for the same reason the banks altogether could over-expand the note issue. Such an inflationary process could be corrected only with a substantial lag, thereby leading to a deficit

in the current account which causes an outflow of gold for the country as a whole.

These fears were confirmed by banking crises in many countries. As Giannini (1994: 21) shows, the BCAM was often introduced as an immediate reaction to a banking crisis.

The central bank as the 'banker to the banks' ('lender of last resort')

As soon as a bank was granted the monopoly of note issue, it was automatically in a privileged position in relation to all other banks. Banks that were not able to issue notes were forced to keep deposits with the issuing bank as a liquidity reserve. In situations with a general increase of cash holdings—e.g. because of a distrust of the soundness of the whole banking system—only the note-issuing bank was able to provide a sufficient supply of banknotes. This leads to function of the 'lender of last resort', which implies that the note-issuing bank is willing to grant credit to the other banks in a general liquidity crisis. This function is therefore related directly to the monopolistic issue of banknotes.

While this central bank function is undoubtedly very important, it was not clear from the beginning whether a private issuing bank would be willing to perform it. In the first half of the nineteenth century private central bank institutions were preferred, but in the second half of the twentieth century the increasing amount of bank deposits led to the view that only a public institution would be willing to provide the necessary refinancing for the other commercial banks.

Again, this function is clearly related to an innovation in the payments technology. As the BCAM restricted the issue of bank notes, banks develop deposits as a substitute. In connection with cheques, they could be used as a means of payment almost like banknotes. If deposits were not regulated in the same way as banknotes, this is due to the fact that transactions with deposits lead to a more immediate loss of gold than transactions with banknotes.

- When a payment is made with a *cheque*, the seller credits the cheque to his bank account. His bank presents the cheque immediately to the bank of the issuer. This bank has to transfer gold (or a deposit with the central bank) to the bank of the seller. As a result, the bank of the issuer is confronted with an immediate loss of reserves, which restricts its future lending. Of course, this restriction does not apply if the seller is a customer of the same bank as the issuer of the cheque.

- When a payment is made with a banknote, the seller can use the banknote for his transactions so that a reserve loss of the issuing bank is not a necessary consequence.

However, with a growing amount of bank deposits, the banking system was confronted with the problem that the amount of deposits exceeded by far the amount of banknotes and of available gold reserves. In fact, this was the main reason why deposits were invented. Thus, the stability of the whole financial system depended on a two-corner solution. When everybody had faith in the soundness of the banking system, the withdrawal of cash from deposits was a relatively small and stable percentage of all deposits (see Chapter 3). However, in crisis situation everybody wanted to withdraw their deposits and convert them into gold. And as the total amount of gold available was much smaller than the sum of banknotes and deposits, a complete convertibility was no longer possible.

Such a crisis could be observed in England as early as 1847. It could be overcome because the Bank of England was empowered by the government to grant credits to the other banks and to supply them with banknotes even if this implied that the additional banknotes were no longer covered by gold reserves. This ability to deviate from the BCAM was sufficient to satisfy the increased demand for banknotes and to avert the crisis. In the end, the Bank of England did not even fall below the gold coverage required by law. This experience made it clear the BCAM was no longer compatible with a banking system that is allowed to issue a substantial amount of deposits. To avoid a general banking crisis, it was necessary

1. that the note-issuing bank had the right to deviate from the strict coverage requirements set by the BCAM and
2. that the bank felt a responsibility to perform this task for the whole banking system.

This implied that the function of 'the banker to the banks' could be fulfilled neither by a multitude of banks nor by a single bank that is a private business. This paved the way for central bank institutions as we know them today. In 1876 the Deutsche Reichsbank was established as a private company, but the members of its board were already appointed by the government. The prototype for the future became the US Federal Reserve System, which was founded in 1913. This was from the beginning a public institution with a clear mandate for financial stability.

In the EC Treaty no explicit mention of a lender of last resort function of the ECB is made, but the Treaty does also not rule out such function.

The central bank as the 'banker to the government'

Very often, the list of central bank functions also includes the function of the 'banker to the government'. The history of central banking shows that, indeed, many of the central banks that are still active today were created for that purpose. The establishment of the Bank of England in 1694 and of the Banque de France in 1800 were clearly related to the high financing needs of the government during periods of war. But this function was very different from the financing of government deficits as we would understand it today. In the past, state banks acted mainly as intermediaries between private investors and the government. Since non-convertible banknotes were not accepted as a regular instrument[18] at that time, the government could not automatically rely on 'seigniorage' (see Chapter 11) as a means of finance.

Thus, the birth of central banking took place much later than the establishment of the Bank of England or Sveriges Riksbank (1668). As already mentioned, the starting point is the year 1844, when the Bank Charter Act was enacted by the British parliament.

Macroeconomic functions of the central bank

During the period of the international gold standard (1876–1914) the macroeconomic functions of the central bank were very limited. The obligation to maintain a fixed relation between gold reserves and the monetary base was identical with the rule that prohibited a deliberate use of standard instruments of monetary policy (see Chapter 6). Thus, monetary policy was focused mainly on preserving the gold convertibility of its banknotes. In a seminal article by Bloomfield (1963), the rules of this game (and their limitations) are described in detail. Some form of gold convertibility remained in the gold standard during the years 1925–1931 and even under the Bretton Woods System. Under this system the United States was obliged to guarantee the gold convertibility for all dollar reserves that were held by foreign central banks. Thus, in a somewhat indirect way, the banknotes of all countries in the world still had a link to gold until 1973.

After the breakdown of the Bretton Woods System, all currencies became 'fiat currencies', i.e. currencies that are completely inconvertible into gold or any other commodity. The lack of the dollar anchor created the need for

---

[18] It should be noted that gold convertibility was suspended from time to time, e.g. in England in the period 1797–1821 (Capie *et al.* 1994: 128).

all central banks to decide their own monetary policy geared to macroeconomic targets. Chapters 8,9, and 13 will discuss which solutions were adopted. Again, a financial innovation—the creation of 'fiat currencies'—led to a new central bank function: the management of macroeconomic targets, above all the price level.

8

Strategies ('Simple Rules') for a Stability-Oriented Monetary Policy

What this chapter is about

- Given the complexity of the monetary policy transmission process, it is not surprising that central bankers and academics have been engaged in a constant search for 'simple rules'. Ideally, such a rule allows one to determine the adequate level of the operating target by focusing on a small number of relevant variables (or even just a single relevant variable).
- A prototype of such an 'heuristic' is monetary targeting, which in theory should function as follows: by comparing actual monetary growth with a target value, a central bank can easily assess whether short-term rates are too high or too low. In practice, however, this rule is difficult to apply.
- Inflation targeting is often regarded as a substitute for monetary targeting. It relies on the comparison of an inflation forecast with an inflation target. However, since it leaves completely open how to produce an inflation forecast, it can at best be regarded as a 'framework', but cannot be used as a 'simple rule'.
- The Taylor rule comes relatively close to the ideal of an heuristic, providing a simple formula for the short-term interest rate that is quite robust under different shocks and different models.
- Nominal GDP targeting is in many respects similar to inflation targeting, but is very different from monetary targeting. A simple rule for this approach has been provided by McCallum. This rule has some parallels to the Taylor rule, but, as it is based on the monetary base, it would be very difficult to implement in practice.

8.1. THE FUNCTION OF SIMPLE RULES

In the present chapter we are looking at a central bank which by its statute is obliged to pursue price stability as its main goal, but which is left with a sufficient discretion to cope with supply and demand shocks. Using the terminology of Chapter 6, we can say that it is constrained by an exogenous final target rule,[1] which by its very nature is not very binding, and can determine intermediate targets, operating targets, and instruments at its

---

[1] Or, in the terminology of Svensson (1999*b*), a 'targeting rule'.

own discretion. We also assume that the central bank legislation provides the decision-makers at the central bank with a high degree of goal, instrument, and personal independence (see Chapter 7).

These assumptions coincide with the actual situation in many industrial countries today. As we saw in Chapter 7, the world's most important central banks (ECB, Federal Reserve System, Bank of Japan) are nowadays based on such central banking legislation. Formal independence is weaker for those industrial countries that explicitly follow the strategy of 'inflation targeting' (Australia, Canada, New Zealand, Switzerland, United Kingdom); but so far the governments of these countries seem also to be interested in a long-term orientation of monetary policy, so that the risk of an inflation bias seems very low.

The key question for such central banks is how to frame their monetary policy so as to achieve the ultimate goal of low inflation while at the same time being flexible enough to accommodate supply shocks and to compensate demand shocks (Chapter 5). This is certainly a very difficult task.

Those responsible for deciding monetary policy are continually being confronted with an abundance of new macroeconomic information (data on GDP, new orders, industrial production, unemployment rate, inflation rate, exchange rate, movements in the foreign exchange reserves, exports and imports, balance of payments figures, money stock, long-term interest rates). On the basis of these data, they then have to decide, at the regular meetings of their governing bodies, the concrete values for their *operating targets*, i.e. the aggregate over which they have direct control. While in theory this could be either the monetary base or a money market interest rate (see Chapter 10), all the central banks in the world are at present targeting short-term interest rates.

Ideally, to help a central bank to do this, it will have a comprehensive and reliable macroeconomic model, which will enable it to:

1. identify, out of the wealth of available data, those aggregates that are relevant for monetary policy purposes;
2. determine what effect the observed changes in such variables will have on the ultimate goal of price stability;
3. ascertain what changes to the operating target are necessary in order to avoid any deviations from the ultimate goal.

In fact, many central banks have large econometric models,[2] which are, however, of limited use as a tool for monetary policy decision-making and

---

[2] For the Bank of England, see Bank of England (1999); for the Bundesbank, see Deutsche Bundesbank (1994).

need to be complemented by judgemental decisions. John Vickers, chief economist of the Bank of England, states that

good forecasting generally entails use of off-model information and hence off-model models. Precisely how this is done seems to me to be literally indescribable in detail. (Vickers 1998: 371)[3]

However, as all the 'off-model information' has to be processed in some way, a central bank needs some relatively simple rules of thumb that enable it to check the plausibility of the results that have been produced by a large econometric model. The last few years have seen an intensive discussion of such 'simple rules', ignited primarily by a pioneering paper by Taylor (1993).

It is obvious that even a 'simple rule' needs a theoretical background. The rules that will be discussed below rely on the different theories of the transmission process that were presented in Chapter 4. As already mentioned, rules can also be classified according to the level of the transmission process for which they are designed.

- *Inflation targeting* provides a rule for an ultimate target of monetary policy. It can be interpreted as inflation-forecast targeting, which is based on the aggregate demand channel, or as inflation-expectations targeting, which is based on the expectations channel.
- *Nominal income targeting* is in important respects very similar to inflation targeting. It is often but incorrectly regarded as a close substitute for monetary targeting.
- *Monetary targeting* provides a rule for an intermediate target; it is based on the quantity theory of money.
- *Exchange rate targeting*, which will be discussed in Chapter 13, uses the theoretical frameworks of purchasing power parity and uncovered interest rate theory. Depending on the concrete strategy adopted, it can be regarded as an intermediate target rule or as an operating target rule.
- The *Taylor rule* is designed for the level of operating targets and relies on the aggregate demand channel and the transmission via changes in the interest rate structure.

This chapter discusses advantages and disadvantages of each of these rules. The most important question is whether there exists such a thing as a 'simple rule' that can be used as the main navigation system of a stability-oriented monetary policy. This question is of interest for two reasons.

1. If such a rule does exist, it would greatly facilitate the daily or weekly internal decision processes within a central bank. This would be especially

---

[3] See also Haldane (1997).

useful in central banks with a large number of members in their governing bodies.

2. A reliable 'simple rule' could also help in the bank's communication with the public. It would make it possible not only for the experts (who can produce their own forecasts), but also for interested citizens, to monitor whether monetary policy is still on a stability-oriented path. This would create transparency and increase the central bank's credibility. In addition, by committing itself to such a rule, the central bank would enhance transparency and credibility, as this would provide a clear framework for its dialogue with the public.

It is important to make a distinction between two different forms of a rule.

- The term *explicit rule* is used for rules that define the concrete setting of a target variable.
- As far as the explicit rule relates to an intermediate or a final target, it is usually combined with an *implicit rule*, which defines how an operating target has to be adjusted in order to keep the target variable close to the target value.[4] As far as an intermediate target rule or an operating target is concerned, we will see that they also imply an implicit rule for a final target.

It is important to note that the use of the term 'rule' in this chapter is more restrictive than in other literature. It comes close to the notion of an 'heuristic', which is defined as a simple, generally applicable rule which allows decisions to be taken even under difficult situations in a reliable and fast way. For an understanding of an heuristic, Gigerenzer, Todd *et al.* (1999: 7) distinguish four visions of rationality. The left branch of Figure 8.1 describes 'models that assume the human mind has unlimited demonic or supranatural reasoning power', the right branch describes models 'that assume that we operate with only bounded rationality'. At the next level, four different visions of rationality can be summarized as follows.

1. *Unbounded rationality* assumes that there are no limits for information search, while the three other approaches assume that search must be limited because real decision-makers have only a finite amount of time, knowledge, attention, or money to spend on a particular decision.

2. *Optimization under constraints* assumes that the mind should calculate the costs and benefits of searching for each further piece of information and stop as soon as the costs outweigh the benefits. Gigerenzer,

---

[4] See also Rudebusch and Svensson (1998: 8): 'By a *targeting rule*, we mean that the central bank is assigned to minimize a loss function that is increasing in the deviation between a target variable and a target level for this variable. The targeting rule will, as we shall see, imply an *implicit* instrument rule.'

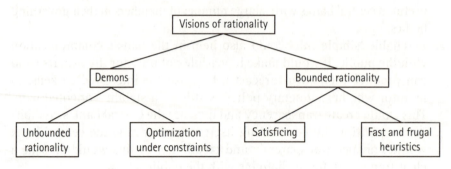

Figure 8.1. *Four visions of rationality*
Source: Gigerenzer, Todd *et al.* (1999).

Todd *et al.* regard this vision of rationality as something that comes very close to unbounded rationality:

The paradoxical approach of 'optimization under constraints' is to model 'limited' search by assuming that the mind has essentially unlimited time and knowledge with which to evaluate the costs and benefits of further information search. ... constrained optimization invites unbounded rationality to sneak in through the back door. (Gigerenzer, Todd *et al.* 1999: 11)

3. *Satisficing* is a method for making a choice from a set of alternatives which takes the shortcut of setting an adjustable aspiration level and ending the search for alternatives as soon as is encountered that exceeds the aspiration level (Gigerenzer, Todd *et al.* 1999: 13),

4. *Fast and frugal heuristics* 'make their choices with easily computable rules' (Gigerenzer, Todd *et al.* 1999: 14). 'A computational model of an heuristic specifies the precise steps of information gathering and processing that are involved in generating a decision such that the heuristic can be instantiated as a computer program' (p.16).

Thus, when discussing 'rules' in this chapter, we will need to check whether such rules are able to serve as an heuristic for policy-makers in the sense of providing a relatively simple and reliable recipe for interest rate decisions. As a consequence, very complex 'rules' such as the 'targeting rule' proposed by Svensson are excluded from the very outset:

The staff at the central bank can generate a collection of feasible inflation and output gap paths for different instrument paths for the MPC [monetary policy council of a central bank] (or the Board). In this way, the staff shows the set of feasible conditional forecasts ... to the MPC. The MPC then selects the conditional forecasts of inflation and the output gap that 'look best', that is, that return inflation to the inflation target and the output gap to zero at an appropriate rate. If this selection is done in a systematic and rational way, it is approximately equivalent to minimising a loss function ... over the set of feasible conditional forecasts. The corresponding instrument path then constitutes the basis for the current instrument setting. (Svensson 1999*b*: 628)

It is obvious that such a fairly general description of a decision-making process is unable to serve as a 'rule' in the sense of an heuristic. Thus, the rules that are discussed below come close to what Svensson (1999*b*: 616) calls 'base-lines, that is comparisons and frames of reference, for the actual policy and evaluation'.[5] We will see that most monetary rules are shaped by the attempt to aim for 'simplicity' and 'frugality'. Unfortunately some of them only pretend to be simple and frugal, while others rely on cues that are not the 'most important cues' (Gigerenzer, Todd *et al.* 2000).

8.2. 'SIMPLE RULES', INTERMEDIATE TARGETS, AND INDICATORS OF MONETARY POLICY

The topics in the actual debate on 'simple rules' are not completely new. In recent decades similar questions were discussed under the headings of 'intermediate targets' or 'indicators' of monetary policy.

8.2.1. *Indicators of monetary policy*

The search for monetary policy indicators can be interpreted as an attempt to reduce the multitude of available data to a set of 'most important cues'. Following Issing (1994), we can distinguish two different definitions of an indicator.

One set of indicators can be used as an early warning system, which signals the existence of inflation risks in good time. Issing describes the indicators that give such signals as 'leading indicators' (in German, *Frühindikatoren*).

---

[5] The difference between Svensson's approach and the approach that is used in the following is neatly described by Gigerenzer, Todd *et al.* (2000): 'Leibniz' universal calculus exhibits the aesthetics and the moral virtue of this lofty ideal, as does Laplace's omniscient superintelligence. Cognitive scientists, economists, and biologists have often chased after the same beautiful dreams by building elaborate models endowing organisms with unlimited abilities to know, memorize, and compute. These heavenly dreams, however, tend to evaporate when they encounter the physical and psychological realities of the waking world: mere mortal humans cannot hope to live up to these standards, and instead appear nightmarishly irrational and dysfunctional in comparison. In the face of this dilemma, many researchers have still preferred to keep dreaming that humans can approximate the exacting standards of optimality, rather than surrendering to an ungodly picture of human irrationality and stupidity. The choice, however, is not between an unrealistic dreaming rationality and a realistic nightmare irrationality. There is a third vision that dispenses with this opposition: rationality through simplicity, and accuracy through frugality.'

A second set of indicators shows what adjustment will need to be made to the operating target in order to put the economy back on the path for price stability when disturbances arise that have been signalled by the 'leading indicators'. Accordingly, Issing (1994: 4) refers here to the 'policy indicators' (in German, *Wirkungsindikatoren*). This use of the term 'indicator' is to be found mainly in the earlier literature (Saving 1967). Basically, it refers to an aggregate that provides evidence as to whether monetary policy is having an expansionary or restrictive effect on the overall economy.

Both of these aspects are broadly covered by a definition proposed by Davis (1990):

the recent technical literature has tended to focus on intermediate 'indicators' ... not as measures of the stance of policy, but as measures of the present or prospective state of the economy. (Davis 1990: 73)

In much of the earlier literature (early 1960s), the term was interpreted in the sense of indicators of the stance of monetary policy. That is, as measures that could provide in some sense an index of monetary 'ease' or 'restraint'. (Davis 1990: 72)

When considering this dual interpretation of the term 'indicator', it is clear that 'policy indicators' are usually a *subset* of leading indicators, since the former at all events belong to that class of aggregates that, functioning as an early warning system, can provide evidence of the existence of inflationary risks. From this point of view, indicators of monetary impulse are those leading indicators that can be influenced by the central bank directly as an operating target, or at least indirectly as an intermediate target. Important indicators that are widely used are the short-term real interest rate and the term structure of interest rates (see Appendix 8.1).

8.2.2. *Intermediate targets of monetary policy*

As the expression suggests, intermediate targets are aggregates that, in the monetary policy transmission process, occupy an intermediate position between the operating targets, which can be controlled by the central bank, and the ultimate macroeconomic objectives. Basically, if an aggregate is given the status of an intermediate target, it can be regarded as an attempt to reduce the decision process to a single cue.

The justification that economists usually give for using intermediate monetary policy targets is that it is difficult for a central bank to control the ultimate goal of price stability directly.

The relationship, it is argued, between the operating target and the ultimate target is extremely complex, and our understanding of this relationship is incomplete (Neumann 1974).

Because of time lags between a change in the operating target and the effects of this on the ultimate target, a central bank that gears its policy directly towards the ultimate target might not react, with the instruments at its disposal, until a disturbance has already occurred. This effectively rules out the possibility of a prompt monetary policy response.

As a solution to these problems, economists have suggested an indirect management of the ultimate target by means of an intermediate target. It is generally agreed that such an aggregate should, above all, meet two criteria.

1. It must be *susceptible to control by the operating target*; that is to say, there must be a stable relationship between changes in money market rates (or the monetary base) and the aggregate used as the intermediate target.
2. There must, furthermore, be a *close relationship between the intermediate target and the ultimate target*; in other words, the intermediate target must provide a good forecast of the ultimate target.

Only when a macroeconomic aggregate fulfils both of the above conditions will it be suitable as an intermediate target aggregate for money policy purposes. An aggregate that is related to the ultimate target but cannot easily be controlled by the central bank will be as useless as a variable that can be perfectly controlled by the central bank but shows no stable relationship with the ultimate target. It is also important that an intermediate target should be precisely measurable without any significant time lag.[6]

A certain inconsistency in the traditional reasoning concerning the question of intermediate targets becomes apparent at the outset. It is illogical to argue that an intermediate target is needed because of our lack of knowledge about macroeconomic relationships, and at the same time to expect to be able to find an intermediate target that can be reliably managed by the central bank and that has a close relationship with the ultimate target. This would imply the existence of a stable relationship between the operating target and the ultimate target which would enable the ultimate target to be controlled directly.

Ideally, therefore, an intermediate target aggregate serves as a compass, which the central bank can consult at any time in order to determine precisely how it should use its operating target. An intermediate target aggregate that fulfils the above-mentioned criteria also serves as monetary policy's most important leading indicator and indicator of the monetary impulse.

---

[6] On the criteria that need to be fulfilled, see Saving (1967), who was the first to deal comprehensively with the question of intermediate monetary policy targets and indicators.

1. It acts as a *leading indicator* because it registers changes in advance of changes in the ultimate price stability target.
2. It can also be used as a *policy indicator*, since it is controlled largely by monetary policy and so reflects the intentions of the central bank.

The decision concerning which actual aggregate to choose as the intermediate target will again depend essentially on which theory the central bank adopts to explain the transmission process. It will become clear in the analysis below that the following aggregates could be considered as intermediate targets:

1. a *monetary aggregate* such as M1, M2, or M3 (see Section 8.3);
2. the *exchange rate* or an exchange rate basket (see Section 13.3);
3. an *inflation forecast* by the central bank and *inflation expectations* by the private sector (see Section 8.4).

If the conditions for using such an intermediate target do not exist in a given economy, monetary policy will have to try to control the ultimate target directly with the instruments at its disposal.

8.3. MONETARY TARGETING

The *explicit rule* provided by monetary targeting can be stated as follows: the growth rate of the money stock should follow a medium-term path that is determined by the quantity theory. In practical monetary policy, the *implicit rule* for achieving the target is often understood as follows: if monetary growth exceeds (falls short of) the monetary target, short-term interest rates have to be increased (reduced). If monetary growth is in line with the target, the interest rate should be kept constant.[7]

Thus, this approach reduces the monetary policy decision process to a single cue. As already mentioned in the discussion of intermediate targets, both rules make sense only if there is a stable relationship between monetary growth and inflation and if it is possible to control monetary growth with short-term interest rates.[8] In the literature it is often assumed that the stability of demand for money is identical with this requirement (European Central Bank 1999*a*: 44). This will be discussed in detail.

[7] A more complex variant of the implicit rule that includes the demand for money is presented by Svensson (1999*b*). I will not discuss his proposal in detail because it has so far played no role in the political discussion on monetary targeting.

[8] There are also economists who favour the monetary base as the operating target for monetary targeting (Neumann 2000). But as this approach is impractical, I will discuss it only in the context of monetary policy instruments (see Chapter 10).

8.3.1. *Introduction*

The concept of monetary targeting was developed by economists of the Monetarist School during the 1950s and 1960s (Friedman 1968; Brunner and Meltzer 1964; Brunner 1968). It became attractive for policy-makers after the breakdown of the Bretton Woods system in 1973. In the postwar period that fixed exchange regime (see Chapter 6) had provided a simple and stable monetary policy rule which the central banks outside the United States were expected to follow: each central bank was required to direct its monetary policy in such a way as to preserve the parity set for its currency against the dollar without major outflows from its foreign exchange reserves. With the collapse of this system in March 1973, most central banks were forced to design a new monetary policy strategy almost overnight.

The monetary policy of the Deutsche Bundesbank will be of particular interest to us in this chapter, not only because this approach has been applied in Germany without interruption from the end of 1974 until the end of the Bundesbank's autonomy in 1998, but also because the Bundesbank was particularly keen to make the method whereby it derives its monetary targets as transparent as possible.

8.3.2. *The explicit rule of monetary targeting*

Monetary targeting is based on the simple theoretical framework described in quantity theory (see Sections 2.1 and 4.3). It is characterized by the neo-classical view that the economic process is inherently stable because of strong self-stabilizing tendencies of the flexible prices. Thus, the main task of monetary policy is to increase the money supply over time in accordance with trend rate of real growth. In other words, the best thing monetary policy can do is to prevent money becoming a source of economic instability (Friedman 1968).

Monetary targeting, therefore, is basically a medium-term or even long-term strategy which has the main advantage of defining a neutral path for the money stock. We will see in what follows that monetary targeting includes an implicit rule for the final target of monetary policy which is defined as medium- to long-term stabilization of the price level.

In spite of this medium-term orientation, the practical rules for monetary targeting are mostly formulated on an annual basis. The whole approach can most clearly be demonstrated with the Bundesbank's practice of deriving the numerical values for its monetary targets. The ECB has adopted exactly the same approach for the calculation of its reference value for the money stock M3.

8.3.2.1. *The 'potential formula'*

The starting point for the derivation of the annual target rate for the money stock is based on the quantitative equation for money:

$$MV \equiv PY. \tag{8.1}$$

If the quantitative equation is transformed into growth rates and solved in terms of the money stock, one obtains

$$\hat{M} \equiv \pi + \hat{Y} - \hat{V}. \tag{8.2}$$

Thus, the rate of change in the money stock is equal to the sum of the rate of change in the price level (inflation rate), the real growth rate in the national income, and the rate of change in the velocity of circulation of money.

This identity can be transformed into the so-called 'potential formula', which replaces the actual values of the right-hand side by normative or trend values so that the three determinants of the growth target for the money stock M3 (*M3**) reflect the medium-term orientation of monetary targeting:

$$\hat{M}3^* = \pi^{norm} + \hat{Y}^{pot} - \hat{V}^{trend}. \tag{8.3}$$

The value for the inflation rate is a *normative inflation rate,* which is chosen in the way that it reflects the measurement problems of the cost-of-living index (see Section 5.4.3). As Table 8.1 shows, from 1984 to 1996 the Bundesbank set a normative inflation rate of 2%; for 1997 and 1998 the rate was 1.5%. The ECB has not published a normative inflation rate, but we will see that it too uses a rate of about 1.5%. In the early years of monetary targeting, the Bundesbank calculated the normative inflation rate on the basis of an 'unavoidable increase in prices', which, although higher than a normative value of 2%, was less than the actual inflation rate at the time. The justification for this approach, which is linked to the expectation channel (see Section 4.5), was that inflation expectations would be adjusted downwards only gradually after the inflation phases of the years 1971–4 and 1980–3. Any attempt to bring inflation down in one go from, say, 7% in 1974 to 2% would have involved a high 'sacrifice ratio', i.e. unjustifiable production and employment losses.

For the *real growth component* in the potential formula, the trend rate of real GDP growth is used which in principle is identical with the growth rate of potential output. By taking a trend rate of real GDP rather than its actual forecast value for GDP, the formula ensures that monetary policy is geared to the medium term. The European Central Bank also emphasizes that this approach provides a built-in-stabilizer:[9]

In this respect, assuming trend growth for real GDP would tend to impart a counter-cyclical property to monetary policy, as GDP growth below trend would

---

[9] This advantage was already emphasized by Friedman (1959).

Table 8.1. *The 'potential formula' and the Bundesbank's monetary targets*

Year	Normative inflation rate (%)	Growth rate of potential output (%)	Change in velocity	Monetary target[a] (%)
1975	5–6	—	—	8
1976	4–5	2	'An increase of velocity is to be expected'	8
1977	$\leqslant 4$	3	'Slight increase'	8
1978	3	3	—	8
1979	'Moderate price increase'	'About the same rate as the year before'	'Declining'	6–9
1980	$3\frac{1}{2}$–4	3	'Continuous decline'	5–8
1981	$3\frac{1}{2}$	$2\frac{1}{2}$	'Increasing' (about 1%)	4–7
1982	$3\frac{1}{2}$	$1\frac{1}{2}$–2	—	4–7
1983	3	$1\frac{1}{2}$–2	—	4–7
1984	2	2	—	4–6
1985	2	2	—	3–5
1986	2	$2\frac{1}{2}$	—	$3\frac{1}{2}$–$5\frac{1}{2}$
1987	2	$2\frac{1}{2}$	—	3–6
1988	2	2	$-\frac{1}{2}$	3–6
1989	2	2–$2\frac{1}{2}$	$-\frac{1}{2}$	5
1990	2	$2\frac{1}{2}$	$-\frac{1}{2}$	4–6
1991	2	$2\frac{1}{2}$	$-\frac{1}{2}$	3–5[b]
1992	2	$2\frac{3}{4}$	$-\frac{1}{2}$	$3\frac{1}{2}$–$5\frac{1}{2}$
1993	2	3	-1[c]	$4\frac{1}{2}$–$6\frac{1}{2}$
1994	2	$2\frac{1}{2}$	-1	4–6
1995	2	$2\frac{3}{4}$	-1	4–6
1996	2	$2\frac{1}{2}$	-1	4–7
1997[d]	$1\frac{1}{2}$–2	$2\frac{1}{4}$	-1	$3\frac{1}{2}$–$6\frac{1}{2}$
1998	$1\frac{1}{2}$–2	2	-1	3–6

[a] 1975–87 central bank money stock, since 1988 M3; 1976–8 targets for annual average; for all other years targets were on a year-on-year basis for the fourth quarter and for December in 1975.
[b] Adjustment of the target corridor from originally 4%–6%.
[c] The surcharge of $\frac{1}{2}$ percentage point was attributed to the normative inflation rate and to the trend in velocity.
[d] In December 1996 a 2-year target of 5% from 1996 (IV) to 1998 (IV) was announced.

Source: Deutsche Bundesbank monthly and annual reports.

normally be associated with lower monetary growth relative to a reference value derived. (ECB 1999*a*: 48)

Thus, in periods of recession this approach tends to produce an excess of money in the economy, which prevents a contraction in the economic process from being accompanied by a decline in the money supply, as happened most notably in the Great Depression of 1929–33 in the United States and Germany. On the other hand, in boom conditions the growth rate in real GDP is higher than the growth in the production potential. In this case the fact that the money supply is geared to potential growth has a dampening effect and so similarly helps to smooth out the course of the cycle. For Germany the Bundesbank has calculated trend rate of real GDP growth in a range between 1.5% and 3%. The ECB has started with a rate of 2%–2.5%.

For a change in the velocity of circulation, the potential formula uses a value that is obtained as the long-term *trend in the velocity* of money. A completely different approach would result if actual forecast values were used instead (see Section 8.6). In Germany a falling trend has been observed in the velocity of circulation for a long time now.[10] Since 1994, the trend value in the velocity of circulation has been unambiguously estimated at −1% . The ECB also assumes a trend decline in the velocity of money which it estimates at −0.5% to −1%.

Table 8.1 shows the target values that the Bundesbank has derived since 1975 based on the potential formula. An interesting feature is the stability of the values of its three determinants. It also demonstrates that the ECB, with a 'reference value' of 4.5% for the money stock M3 (Section 9.3), has come to astonishingly similar values for the euro area.

8.3.2.2. *The time horizon of the explicit rule*
An important feature of the Bundesbank's and the ECB's monetary targets is that they are set on an annual basis (with the exception of the period 1997–8). Especially given the constancy of the determinants of the potential formula, multi-annual targets would seem much more compatible with the medium-term orientation of the whole approach (Neumann 1986: 595).[11] Annual targets are problematic above all for two reasons.

In the first place, the determination of the inflation rate by the money stock requires above all a stable velocity of money, or at least a stable trend of the velocity of money. This is the main assumption of all variants of the quantity theory (see Section 2.1). While most econometric studies come to the conclusion that the demand for money is stable in the long run, this is not the case in the short run. Thus, short-term deviations of the money stock from its target rate can simply reflect this instability and are not necessarily an indication of inflationary pressure.

---

[10] For an explanation of the surprising fact, see Section 2.5.

[11] This issue was taken up again in Germany at the beginning of 1994 and at the end of 1995 as a consequence of the extremely high rates of money supply growth during the first few months of 1994 (von Hagen 1994) and the below-average growth rates in the money supply in the course of 1995 (Mayer and Fels 1995).

In addition, the quantity theory completely neglects the impact of interest rates on the demand for money. However, as interest rates play a decisive role in all empirical money demand functions, a practical application of the quantity theory can lead to serious problems if monetary targets are set on an annual basis. The derivation of monetary targets by the Bundesbank, and of the reference value by the ECB, shows that the 'potential formula' completely disregards interest rates. Thus, if relevant interest rate(s) in the demand for money function (see Section 2.5) change during the target period, the money growth rate will automatically be stronger or weaker than the rate calculated by the potential formula. This could be observed for instance in Germany in the years 1992–3, when the spread between the long-term and the short-term interest rate was very low and money growth far exceeded its target value. Again, such interest rate induced changes in money growth do not indicate an inflationary pressure, but simply a reallocation of portfolios from bonds to the interest-bearing components of M3.

Thus, a stable money demand function does not by itself justify the use of monetary targeting as a 'simple rule', as it has been used by the Bundesbank and is now used to some extend by the ECB. A deviation of actual monetary growth from an annual target or reference value does not always require a correction, since it could be related to a short-term instability in the demand for money, or to a deviation of the relevant interest rate in the demand-for-money function from a neutral value or from the value of the period before.

The use of annual targets is especially problematic if the new target path is based not on the normative target value but on the actual outcome in the preceding year. Such 'base shifts' have been very common in the conduct of monetary policy in Germany, where except in 1995 the corrections have always been for an excessively high starting base. As a result, the essential orientation that is intended by monetary targeting is lost. Instead of monetary policy following the direction set by a long-term compass, the compass is adjusted when the deviations from the original setting become too great.

8.3.3. *Monetary targeting and shocks*

While monetary targeting may be helpful for the identification of a neutral line of monetary policy in the medium term, it is interesting to see how this strategy works if an economy is confronted with demand or supply shocks. As the potential formula shows, such shocks are not explicitly addressed by monetary targeting. In fact, its supporters even regard this as an advantage, since it avoids any reaction of monetary policy to such shocks, which would always bear the risk of additionally destabilizing the economic process. For instance, ECB president Duisenberg declared:

A monetary policy reaction to inflationary or deflationary pressures may cause short-run fluctuations in real output (Duisenberg 1999*b*: 4)

and:

It would be overambitious and therefore risky to steer the economy in the short term. Fine-tuning would more likely lead to instability than to stability. (Duisenberg 1999*a*: 3)

The IS/LM–AS/AD model provides a relatively simply analysis of monetary targeting in situations with supply and demand shocks. Of course, this assumes that a central bank can perfectly control the money stock. If an economy is confronted with a negative *demand shock*, monetary targeting implies that a central bank will keep the money stock constant. In the IS/LM model the result is a decline in the interest rate that is not sufficient to restore full-employment output. This result is better than the outcome of a monetary policy, which would aim to keep the interest rate constant (see the discussion of the Poole model in Appendix 4.1). This shows the automatic stabilizing properties of monetary targeting, already mentioned. But as the AS/AD model shows (Figure 8.2), the ideal response would be a discretionary reduction of the interest rate that fully compensates the demand shock, so that the aggregate demand function, which is shifted to the left, is brought back to its initial position. In other words, monetary targeting is better than a policy of stubbornly holding the interest rates constant, but worse than a policy that actively manages interest

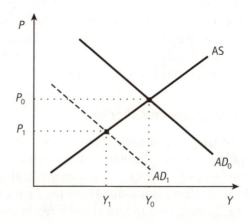

Figure 8.2. *Monetary targeting and demand shocks*

rates. Of course, such an active monetary policy is limited by the well-known policy lags, so that it would seem advisable only if an economy is confronted with a more persistent demand shock.

In a situation with a *supply shock*, the AS/AD model shows that monetary targeting comes close to a nominal GDP rule. As Figure 8.3 shows, the passive attitude of monetary policy implies that the aggregate demand curve remains constant. Thus, no active attempt is made to keep the price level constant in the short run. A policy of constant interest rates would completely compensate the output effects of the shock but would increase its effects on the price level so that it would amount to a real income rule.

Thus, although monetary targeting has not explicitly been designed to cope with supply and demand shocks, one can see that it provides a partial stabilization of demand shocks and a partial accommodation of supply shocks. But compared with an activist interest rate policy, monetary targeting entails a passive attitude to short-term changes in the price level. In other words, monetary policy entails an *implicit final target rule* that price stability is to be maintained over the medium and long term. As monetary targeting is not a strategy that allows a short-term control of the price level, its usefulness for inflation forecasts in the short and medium run is limited.

Although the ECB has not adopted monetary targeting, but only the weaker form of a 'reference value' for monetary growth (see Section 9.3), therefore, it has explicitly adopted the implicit final target of monetary targeting.

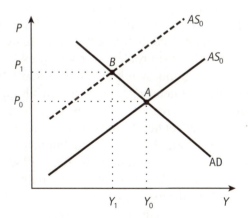

Figure 8.3. *Monetary targeting and supply shocks*

8.3.4. *The implicit rule of monetary targeting*

While an explicit rule simply defines the target level of an aggregate, an implicit rule describes how the central bank can control the target aggregate so that it can reach that target. In political discussions, the implicit rule of monetary targeting is normally understood as follows: if monetary growth (μ) exceeds (falls short of) the target (μ^*), the central bank has to increase (decrease) short-term interest rates in order to dampen (speed up) monetary growth. Thus,

$$i_t - i_{t-1} = \gamma(\mu_t - \mu^*) \qquad \text{with } \mu > 0. \tag{8.4}$$

This implicit rule constitutes the second main criterion for an intermediate target. Again, the applicability of this rule depends mainly on the stability of the money demand function. As already mentioned, in the short run such a stability cannot be taken for granted, which means that the central bank can control monetary growth on an annual basis only imperfectly.

But even if the money demand were stable, the control of monetary growth tends to be difficult. This is due to the interest variable that is used in a demand function. We have seen in Section 2.5 that for the money stock M3, which was targeted by the Bundesbank and is also targeted by the ECB, the interest variable is represented by the *spread* between a long-term and a short-term interest rate. This raises above all the problem that the ECB cannot fully control this spread, since it can control only the short-term rates, which also affect long-term rates. In addition, as money demand has a negative elasticity in relation to this spread, control of the M3 with a short-term rate implies a very odd approach: whenever the money growth is too high (low), which signals an inflationary (deflationary) process, interest rates have to be lowered (increased) in order to decelerate (accelerate) the monetary growth. This problem was also present in the era of the Bundesbank. In fact, the Bundesbank lowered its short-term rates in the period 1992–4 although monetary growth was much higher than targeted. As a result, the monetary growth decelerated. In the case of the ECB, this problem has obviously not yet been observed by its decision-makers. Thus, they argued in 1999 and 2000 that in order to dampen monetary growth it would be necessary to increase short-term interest rates.

In sum, for the money stock M3 the implicit rule could even be formulated in the opposite direction: if monetary growth exceeds (falls short of) the target, the central bank has to reduce (increase) short-term interest rates in order to dampen (speed up) monetary growth.

These problems of the implicit rule of monetary targeting are discussed theoretically in the Poole model (see Appendix 4.1 above), which analyses the effects of an unstable demand for money.

8.4. INFLATION TARGETING

For a consideration of inflation targeting this section will discuss the approach of the Bank of England (BoE), which has played a similarly pioneering role for this approach as the Bundesbank did for monetary targeting.

- The *explicit rule* of the BoE's inflation targeting can be formulated as follows: Keep the conditional inflation forecast of the retail price index (excluding mortgage interest payments) for a target horizon of two years close to the target value of 2.5%.
- The *implicit rule* is less specific but can be formulated as follows: If the conditional forecast exceeds (falls short of) the inflation target, an increase (reduction) in interest rates is required. The example of the Reserve Bank of New Zealand shows that an inflation forecast can be also conditional upon an interest rate path.

Inflation targeting looks similar to monetary targeting, since it too reduces monetary policy decisions to a single cue: the central bank's inflation forecast. But, while this rule looks simple at first sight, we will see that it is very different from a 'fast and frugal heuristic'.

8.4.1. *Introduction*

Since 1988, a number of countries have explicitly adopted a monetary policy approach which is generally described as 'inflation targeting'. New Zealand was the first to do so in 1989, followed by Canada (1991), Israel (1991), the United Kingdom (1992), Sweden (1993), Finland (1993), Australia (1993), and Spain (1994). While monetary targeting had been drawn up after an intensive academic discussion, inflation targeting was developed mainly as an *ad hoc* solution. In Canada and New Zealand, it was, above all, the unsatisfactory experience with monetary targeting that prompted the change of approach. In the European countries the decision to try a new strategy was triggered by the fact that their exchange rate target *vis-à-vis* the Deutschmark or the Ecu had become obsolete following the unexpected collapse of the Exchange Rate Mechanism (ERM) in the 1992–3 crisis. In these cases a new strategy had to be found almost overnight. This explains the quite pragmatic approach of inflation targeting, for which a theoretical framework was developed only many years after its first application (Leidermann and Svensson 1995; Svensson 1997).

We shall begin with an attempt to identify the specific elements of inflation targeting, above all in comparison with monetary targeting. We will then consider the concrete application of inflation targeting by the Bank of England. Finally, we will discuss the 'simple rule' that can be deduced from inflation targeting and will compare it above all with monetary targeting.

8.4.2. *Genuine elements of inflation targeting*

In their comprehensive study, Bernanke *et al.* give the following definition of 'inflation targeting':

Inflation targeting is a framework for monetary policy characterised by the public announcement of official quantitative targets (or target ranges) for the inflation rate over one or more time horizons, and by explicit acknowledgement that low, stable inflation is monetary policy's primary long-run goal. Among other important features of inflation targeting are vigorous efforts to communicate with the public about plans and objectives of monetary authorities, and in many cases, mechanisms that strengthen the central bank's accountability for attaining those objectives. (Bernanke *et al.* 1999: 4)

This definition more or less circumscribes what in Germany, above all, has long since been understood as a 'stability-oriented monetary policy'. It is much less demanding than a definition that can be found in Svensson:

Inflation targeting is characterised by, first, an explicit numerical inflation target. The inflation target is pursued in the medium run, with due concern for avoiding real instability, for instance, in the output-gap; that is, inflation targeting is 'flexible' rather than 'strict'. Second, due to the unavoidable lags in the effects of instruments on inflation, the decision framework is in practice 'inflation-forecast targeting' .... Third, communication is very explicit and to the point; policy decisions are consistently motivated with reference to published inflation and output (-gap) forecasts. (Svensson 2000*b*: 95)

An additional element of 'inflation targeting' as it is presented in the study by Bernanke *et al.* is a preference for an inflation target that is set by 'elected officials':

Because ultimately policy objectives in a democracy must reflect the popular will, they should be set by elected officials. (Bernanke *et al.* 1999: 312)

As far as the execution of the inflation target is concerned, Bernanke *et al.* favour 'instrument independence', which means that the central bank should have the sole responsibility for the setting of interest rates. This topic and the problems of a lack of goal independence have already been discussed in Chapter 6.

The different elements of inflation targeting according to the definitions by Bernanke *et al.* and Svensson are summarized in Table 8.2. If we start with the definition by Bernanke *et al.*, it would be very difficult to identify the specific features of inflation targeting. As we will see in Section 9.3, the ECB's approach matches almost all parts of the definition by Bernanke *et al.* The same applies to the Bundesbank, which, although it did not explicitly publish an inflation target, announced a numerical normative inflation target on an annual basis when setting its monetary target (Section 8.3). In spite of this accordance, however, Bernanke *et al.* classify these two central banks not as inflation targeters but as ' "hybrid" inflation targeters and monetary targeters' (Bernanke *et al.* 1999: 41). The main reason for this seems to be that both central banks attach an importance to monetary targeting. Thus, the definition by Bernanke *et al.* implicitly includes as a negative criterion that a central bank can only be regarded as an inflation targeter if it does not follow traditional intermediate targets like the money stock or the exchange rate. This criterion becomes more explicit in the definition by Svensson, who defines inflation targeting as 'inflation forecast targeting', which he regards as a rule that is completely different from monetary targeting (Svensson 1999*b*). Thus, we shall follow this definition in the following and interpret inflation targeting as an

Table 8.2. *Alternative definitions of inflation targeting*

Criterion	Bernanke *et al.* (1999)	Svensson (2000*b*)
(1) Price stability as the main target of monetary policy	Yes	Yes
(2) Announcement of a numerical target	Yes	Yes
(3) Medium-term target	Unclear ('one or more time horizons')	Yes
(4) Intensive communication with the public	Yes	Yes
(5) Specific monetary policy rule	Unclear	Inflation forecast targeting
(6) Published inflation and output forecasts	Not required	Yes
(7) Target set by government ('goal dependence')	Yes	Not required
(8) Instrument independence	Yes	Yes, but not explicitly addressed

approach to monetary policy in which a central bank pursues the ultimate target of price stability *without* taking recourse to traditional intermediate target aggregates such as the exchange rate or the money supply.

A somewhat unclear issue in the classification of inflation targeting is the importance of publishing a central bank's internal inflation forecast. While Bernanke *et al.* are not very specific about this question, Svensson regards the publication of internal forecasts as essential. However, the Bank of Canada and the Bank of Australia are widely regarded, and regard themselves, as inflation targeters, although they provide only rather non-technical forecasts that are hardly different from statements that can be found in the ECB publications.[12]

In the context of this chapter, the elements (1)–(4) of Table 8.2 will not be discussed in detail. As they are not a specific feature of inflation targeting, they have already been described and analysed in the preceding chapters. In this chapter we will focus on the interesting issue of whether inflation targeting can be regarded as a 'simple rule' for the setting of a central bank's short-term interest rates.

8.4.3. *The explicit rule of inflation targeting*

The explicit rule of inflation targeting requires that a central bank keeps its inflation forecast close to its inflation target. Thus, the determination of the target value and the forecast value of inflation play a crucial role in the whole concept.

We have already seen that inflation targets can be formulated quite differently. In the United Kingdom, the inflation target is set by the chancellor of the Exchequer. The present target, which was determined on 12 June 1997, is a rate of 2.5% for the RPIX, i.e. the index for retail price inflation excluding mortgage interest payments. The target is surrounded by a threshold of ±1%. When the threshold is reached, the chancellor expects an explanatory letter from the Bank.

While the definition of the *target* is relatively simple, the determination of the *forecast* is quite complicated. The Bank of England publishes this forecast, which it calls its 'inflation projection', in a quarterly *Inflation Report* together with a projection for real GDP. As already mentioned, the forecast is presented as a *conditional forecast;* i.e., it is based on the

---

[12] See e.g. European Central Bank (1999c: 6): 'Available forecasts suggest that, despite the expected rise in the rate of increase in the HICP in the coming months, price increases will nevertheless remain below 2% in 2000 and 2001.' In December 2000 the ECB published an inflation projection that was prepared by its staff, but it maintained that this does not entail a switch to inflation targeting (ECB 2000d).

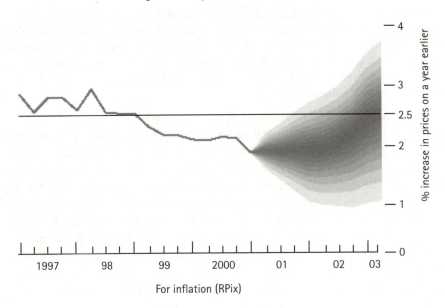

Figure 8.4. *The Bank of England's 'fan-chart' for inflation (RPIX)*
Source: Bank of England: www.bankofengland.co.uk.

assumption of a constant short-term interest rate. A different approach is followed by the Reserve Bank of New Zealand, which makes its forecast conditional upon an interest rate path (i.e. it forecasts the annual average for the three-month money market rate). The Bank of England forecast is made for a time horizon of two years in advance. As Figure 8.4 shows, the inflation projected is presented in the form of the so-called 'fan chart'. It can be read rather like a contour map. The Bank of England states:

At any given point during the forecast period, the depth of the shading represents the height of the probability density function over a range of outcomes for inflation. The darkest band includes the central (single most likely) projection and covers 10% of the probability. Each successive pair of bands is drawn to cover a further 10% of the probability until 90% of the probability is covered. The bands widen as the time horizon is extended, indicating increasing uncertainty about outcomes. (Bank of England 2000*b*: iv)

Haldane describes how the Bank's inflation projection is produced:

The general point here is that the Bank's published inflation projection is not a mechanical extrapolation from a single macro model. Rather, it draws upon a much wider and richer set of information variables—quantitative and qualitative, real and monetary. Indeed, increasingly, the Bank's published projection is also drawing on a wider set of models, as well as information variables .... The eclectic approach to the use of models mirrors the approach when using indicators .... Using a 'portfolio' of models offers insurance against model uncertainties. Diversification applies as much to policy-makers when choosing among uncertain indicators and macro models as it does to investors when choosing among uncertain securities and asset-pricing models. (Haldane 1997: 21)

If we compare this with the concept of monetary targeting (which is different now from how it used to be practised–see Section 9.2), we can see that inflation targeting entails a completely different approach. While monetary targeting (and other 'simple rules') intends to reduce the complexity of the economic process to a 'fast and frugal heuristic' that can be easily implemented by the central bank and easily monitored by the public, the 'eclectic approach' favoured by inflation targeting leaves it completely open how such a reduction should be achieved. While monetary targeting uses only the money stock to predict inflation, inflation targeting implies that almost all available information is used. In other words, inflation targeting can certainly not be regarded as a 'simple rule'. Bernanke *et al.* put this as follows:

First, at a technical level, inflation targeting does not provide simple, mechanical operating instructions to the central bank. Rather inflation targeting requires the central bank to use structural and judgmental models of the economy, in conjunction of whatever information it deems relevant, to pursue its price-stability objective. In other words, inflation targeting is very much a 'look at everything' strategy, albeit one with a focused goal. (Bernanke *et al.* 1999: 22)

As a result, the targeting process is also difficult for the public to monitor. Monetary targeting requires a comparison of two relatively objective data: the monetary target derived by the 'potential formula', and the actual monetary growth. Inflation targeting requires a comparison of a target value, which is also easy to derive, with an inflation forecast, which is very difficult to verify, at least by the public.

Because of these completely different approaches, it is also problematic to regard the central bank's inflation forecast as an intermediate target of monetary policy (Haldane 1995; Svensson 1999*b*). Of course, this analogy can be derived from a comparison with monetary targeting, where the money stock serves as the main forecast for inflation and at the same time as the intermediate target of monetary policy. But our discussion of intermediate targets has shown that they were designed for an indirect targeting process, i.e. as alternative to a *direct* targeting of ultimate goals. As inflation targeting implies such a direct targeting, it must lead to confusion if the inflation forecast is treated as an intermediate target.

8.4.4. *The implicit rule of inflation targeting*

The implicit rule of inflation targeting, as it is understood in the policy debate, is relatively simple: if the conditional forecast leads to a value that is higher (lower) than the target, an increase (decrease) in the short-term interest rate is required. Thus,

$$i_t - i_{t-1} = \gamma(\pi_{t+T|i_{t-1}} - \pi^*) \qquad \text{with } \gamma > 1. \tag{8.5}$$

The interest rate in t has to be higher than the interest rate in $t - 1$, if the conditional forecast in t for T quarters ahead on the basis of the interest rate in $t - 1$ exceeds the target value. This rule looks compatible with the practice of the Bank of England, which Haldane (1997: 22) describes as follows:

the constant interest rate assumption is useful in helping the Bank decide on the appropriate *direction* for future interest rate moves .... (Haldane 1997: 22)

However, this 'simple rule' leaves open

1. by how much the interest rate has to be adjusted if the forecast deviates from the target, which depends on the value of γ, and
2. whether any deviation from target is already a cause for an interest rate adjustment which depends on the nature of macroeconomic shocks.

Alternatively, the implicit rule could also be formulated as:

$$i_t = \hat{i} + \gamma(\pi_{t+T|i_t} - \pi^*) \qquad \text{with } \gamma > 1. \tag{8.6}$$

This variant which comes relatively close to a Taylor rule can be found in Svensson (1999*b*: 615), but so far the Bank of England has not made any statement on an average short-term interest $\hat{i}$, which would be necessary for the implementation of such a rule.

8.4.5. *Inflation targeting and macroeconomic shocks*

While monetary targeting has been designed as a medium-term or even long-term strategy defining a passive role of monetary policy, inflation targeting leads to a more activist approach based on a short- to medium-term orientation of interest rate policy. We will describe this using the IS/LM–AS/AD apparatus.

The main difference between monetary targeting and inflation targeting can be shown in the situation of a (e.g. negative) *demand shock*. If the shock is persistent enough to affect the two-year time horizon of the inflation forecast, the central bank has to react by adjusting its interest rates with the aim of completely offsetting the shock. In the AS/AD model this implies that the aggregate demand curve that was shifted to the left by the shock is shifted back to its original position by an expansionary monetary policy (back to AD_0 in Figure 8.2). With monetary targeting, the aggregate demand curve would not have been readjusted. Thus, inflation targeting with a two-year horizon requires a fine-tuning of economic activity which is absent in monetary targeting.[13] If the time horizon were extended to, say, four years, inflation targeting would also lead to a more passive attitude of monetary policy.

In the situation of a *supply shock* that affects the forecast, inflation targeting seems to prescribe a completely non-accommodating policy stance. If interest rates are set so that the forecast of inflation rate remains always identical with the target, a supply shock would require a much stronger interest-rate increase than under monetary targeting or a nominal income rule. In practice, however, inflation targeting is much more flexible. As mentioned in Section 5.4, the targets are often defined for core inflation, which means that they exclude energy and food prices. In the case of the Bank of England, the threshold of $\pm 1\%$ offers some additional flexibility.

8.4.6. *Inflation targeting: a framework, but not a 'simple rule'*

So far, we have seen that inflation targeting as it is recommended by academics and applied by central banks is very different from a 'simple rule' for policy-makers and the public at large.

With its 'eclectic approach', it does not prescribe a specific set of variables and a specific model with which an inflation forecast can be produced. Thus, the explicit rule leaves ample room for discretion in producing an inflation forecast.

The implicit rule that can be derived from inflation targeting is not specific enough either, as it leaves it open by how much the interest rate has to be adjusted if a deviation from the inflation target is expected. Nor does it give any clear advice in the case of supply shocks.

Thus, if a stability-oriented central banker were to seek guidance from such a policy rule, she would soon realize that there is little to learn from inflation targeting except that she should

1. pursue a forward-looking approach (but she might know this already);
2. not rely solely on traditional intermediate targets like the money stock or the exchange rate (but, at least in the case of monetary targets, nobody did that anyway—see Section 9.2);

[13] As Svensson (1999*b*) shows, monetary targeting could be also designed for an inflation targeting approach. In this case, the money stock would have to be permanently readjusted in order to generate an interest rate level that is compatible with the attainment of the inflation target. But this implies a completely different framework from the Bundesbank approach presented in Section 8.2.

3. use different macroeconomic models; but also
4. rely on her judgement (which is another term for an 'eclectic approach').

In other words, although inflation targeting is often understood a 'rule' facilitating a stability-oriented monetary policy, it comes relatively close to pure discretion. Also, an approach that is 'indescribable in detail' (Vickers 1998) is not very helpful for communicating with the public. For those observers who are unable to produce their own forecasts, there is no other 'rule' by which they could at least check the plausibility of the central bank's forecast. This is especially problematic if the central bank forecast is conditional on a given interest rate level and external forecasts are made under the assumption of a certain interest rate path, which means that a comparison of internal and external forecasts is impossible.

Thus, in spite of its seeming transparency, inflation targeting is a rather intransparent approach, as far as the realization of the ultimate targets of monetary policy is concerned. It can be compared to a cookery book that, instead of providing concrete recipes, only contains pictures of the prepared dishes and the advice to buy the best ingredients and prepare them as skilfully as possible. This does not mean that inflation targeting is useless as a policy framework for a stability-oriented monetary policy. It clearly has its merits, by providing numerical targets for the inflation rate which serve as the main benchmark for the evaluation of central bankers.

The limited contribution of inflation targeting to the transparency of monetary policy is confirmed by the evidence of its concrete effects. In the view of Svensson (2000a: 155), inflation targeting can be regarded as an 'apparent success'. Bernanke *et al.* (1999: 6) come to the result that inflation targeting 'has had important benefits for the countries that have used it'. Upon closer scrutiny, however, the benefits of inflation targeting are much less clear-cut. Even Bernanke *et al.*, contains a rather sceptical assessment:

Overall, though, we must admit that the economic performance of the non-targeters over the period considered is not appreciably different from that of inflation targeters. (Bernanke *et al.* 1999: 283)

Lane and van den Heuvel (1998), Siklos (1999), and Jonsson (1999) come to rather similar results. Jonsson shows that inflation has become less volatile after the introduction of inflation targeting, but the same effect can be observed in many other industrial countries.

8.4.7. *Inflation expectations as an intermediate target aggregate*

In the discussion of inflation targeting, relatively little attention has been paid to the role of private-sector inflation expectations. This is somewhat astonishing, as several central banks now provide intensive information on different indicators of such expectations. Four different groups of indicators can be distinguished.

1. Surveys of the results of *inflation forecasts made by professional researchers*. For instance, the ECB has conducted a quarterly survey of inflation expectations in the euro area: the Survey of Professional Forecasters (SPF).[14] In its *Monthly Bulletin* the ECB publishes the SPF together with other survey-based indicators of future price developments (e.g. from Consensus Economics).
2. Surveys of *inflation expectations of households, managers, trade union officials*. Such data are published by, e.g., the Reserve Bank of Australia or the Bank of England.
3. Indicators of *inflation expectations derived from financial market data*, above all long-term bond yields and the difference between such yields and the yields of index-linked gilts. Such data are regularly published by the ECB and other central banks.
4. In addition, the *results of wage settlements* can be used as very important indicators of inflation expectations and of future cost pressure.

The theoretical basis for the specific role of private inflation expectations is provided by the 'expectations channel' (see Section 4.5). As already mentioned, its main feature is that market participants' inflation expectations provide a link between the instruments available to the central bank and the ultimate objective of monetary policy:

Instruments ⇒ Operating target ⇒ Inflation expectations
⇒ Inflation target.

Compared with the highly complicated process of producing an internal inflation forecast, the four sets of data on inflation expectations provide a relatively simple rule for monetary policy. As long as inflation expectations are identical with the inflation target, the risk of missing the inflation target is relatively low, especially if the currency area is relatively large so that it is not very much exposed to the disturbances of exchange rates.

This does not necessarily imply that interest rates will be held constant. If private inflation expectations are made under the assumption of an interest rate path, e.g. with increasing rates, this rule implies that the central

---

[14] For details, see ECB (2000a: 28): 'The inflation expectations obtained from the SPF are based on the responses to a questionnaire submitted to a sample of 83 forecasters throughout the EU. Respondents are asked to provide estimates of the expected rate of change in the euro area HICP, looking one and two years ahead. Once a year, in February, the SPF also requests expectations for five years ahead.'

bank will also follow this path. In its quarterly *Inflation Report*, the Bank of England presents a survey of twenty-eight forecasters who, in addition to their inflation forecasts, provide a survey of their forecasts for the repo rate. In case of inflation expectations that diverge from the inflation target, the rule calls for a change in interest rates or for an interest rate path that differs from the forecasts for interest rates.

This use of inflation expectations in a 'simple rule' does not imply that the central bank is reacting mechanistically to inflation expectations. In the same way as the proponents of monetary targeting always envisage the possibility of a deviation as long as the central bank can justify it, a monetary rule based on private inflation expectations can be suspended as long as the central bank has convincing arguments for such a procedure (Bernanke and Woodford 1997: 682).

Important reasons for not reacting to private inflation forecasts that differ from the inflation target could be

- a supply shock;
- a demand shock of a very short-term nature;
- a wrong assumption of outside forecasters about the future interest rate path.

In order to serve as an *intermediate target*, inflation expectations must be controllable by the central bank, and they must also have a close correlation with the ultimate goal of price stability. The second of these conditions seems relatively unproblematic (see Deutsche Bundesbank 2001). As is discussed in detail in Section 4.5.2, because of price rigidities, the inflation rate is in the short run essentially determined by inflation expectations in the previous period. This correlation is especially strong in a large economy or in a smaller economy that is able to maintain a fixed exchange rate *vis-à-vis* an anchor currency (e.g. Austria and the Netherlands in the 1980s and 1990s).

When considering the suitability of inflation expectations as an intermediate target, it is also important that they can be controlled by the central bank's instruments. This question is discussed in more detail in Section 4.5.7, where it is shown that, when a central bank's reputation is high, low inflation expectations tend to stabilize themselves and there is very little need for active management on the part of the central bank. In the event of a massive inflationary shock which drives inflation expectations up, the central bank will have to raise its real money market rates substantially in order to trigger restrictive impulses in the real economy via the aggregate demand channel. If the central bank uses its instruments in this way, private individuals can deduce from this that the central bank is giving high priority in its target function to the objective of price stability (relative to the employment objective). They will therefore adjust their inflation expectations downwards. Such management of inflation expectations thus takes place as follows:

Nominal money market rates ↑ ⟹ (assuming short-term price rigidities) Real money market rates ↑ ⟹ Macroeconomic demand ↓ ⟹ Unemployment ↑ ⟹ Inflation expectations ↓

In the case of the Federal Reserve Board's monetary policy, Goodfriend describes this mechanism in the context of disinflation as follows:

Inflation scares appear to be central to understanding the Fed's management of short-term rates. ... Sharply rising long rates in the first 9 months of 1981 indicated that the Fed had yet to win credibility for its disinflationary policy, and probably contributed to the Fed maintaining very high real short rates for as long as it did. (Goodfriend 1995: 137)

As well as exerting influence on inflation expectations 'by deeds' (Briault *et al.* 1996: 67), central banks can also seek to produce a similar effect 'by words'. The main instruments of a central bank's communication policy have already been discussed in Section 7.3.

8.5. THE TAYLOR RULE: A RULE FOR AN OPERATING TARGET

After considering rules for the setting of an intermediate target and an ultimate target of monetary policy, we now come to rules prescribing a concrete value for the short-term interest rate that serves as the operating target for all central banks in the world. We have already discussed two implicit rules for the setting of operating targets that serve as implicit rules for the control of the monetary growth and the central bank's inflation forecast. In this section we will focus on a rule that has been formulated explicitly for the short-term interest rate, the so-called Taylor rule. This was developed by John Taylor (Taylor 1993) and states: keep the real-short-term interest rate constant as a neutral policy stance, and make a surcharge (discount) when the output gap is positive (negative) and/or inflation is above (below) a target rate.

This rule comes very close to the ideal of a 'fast and frugal heuristic', as it reduces the monetary policy decision process to a limited set of relatively easily accessible variables.

8.5.1. *Introduction*

Like inflation targeting, the Taylor rule was not developed from a comprehensive theoretical model or an intensive academic debate. It was the result of an empirical study of the actual monetary policy of the Federal Reserve System during the years 1987–92. In a very general form, the Taylor rule can be formulated as a rule for the short-term real interest rate:

$$i_t - \pi_t = R + \alpha(\pi_t - \pi^*) + \beta\left(\frac{Y_t - Y^*}{Y^*}\right). \tag{8.7}$$

The nominal short-term interest rate has to be set equal to an average short-term real interest rate (R) plus a term that reflects deviations from an inflation target and the output gap; α and β are weights reflecting the impact of the output gap and the deviation of the inflation rate from its target. In his study, Taylor came to the result that the following equation gives a very good description of the Federal Reserve Board's interest rate policy:

$$i_t - \pi_t = 2 + 0.5(\pi_t - 2) + 0.5\left(\frac{Y_t - Y^*}{Y^*}\right). \tag{8.8}$$

This implies

1. an average real short-term interest rate of 2%, which during the period analysed by Taylor was almost identical with the trend growth of real income (2.2% in the period 1984–92);
2. an inflation target of 2%;
3. an equal weighting of the output gap and the inflation deviation by the Federal Reserve Board.

The most important question is whether a rule derived from this empirical observation can serve as a general guideline for monetary policy. On the basis of a comprehensive analysis comparing different models and different rules, Taylor argues that this is the case:

Model simulations show that simple policy rules work remarkably well in a variety of situations; they seem to be surprisingly good approximations to fully optimal policy. Simulations results also show that simple policy rules are more robust than complex rules across a variety of models. Introducing information lags as long as [a] quarter does not affect the performance of the policy rule by very much. Moreover, the basic results about simple rules designed for the United States seem to apply broadly to many countries. (Taylor 1999: 657)

A similar result is presented by Rudebusch (2000), who shows that the simple Taylor rule performs better than a nominal income rule, especially if the autoregressive element in the Phillips curve is very high (see Section 4.5.5).[15]

---

[15] A similar result can be found in Debelle (1999).

8.5.2. *The theoretical framework of the Taylor rule*

Although the Taylor rule was developed empirically, its good performance in a multitude of models indicates that it must be based on some very solid theoretical cornerstones. An important pillar of the whole approach is the notion of a *neutral real short-term interest rate*. Blinder reminds us that this is a difficult concept:

It is therefore most usefully thought of as a concept rather than as a number, as a way of thinking about monetary policy rather than as the basis for a mechanical rule. (Blinder 1998: 31)

The logic of a neutral interest rate can be derived from the two main versions of the interest-rate channel of monetary policy transmission (see Section 4.4). In the flow approach of the IS/LM model, a neutral real interest rate can be defined as a rate that leads to an aggregate demand that equates the full-employment aggregate supply, which is identical with potential output (Figure 8.5). The notion of a neutral real interest rate can also be considered with respect to the stock approach of the balance sheet channel. As firms normally rely on debt financing, their return on equity is determined by the return on their assets, the interest rate on debt, and the debt–equity ratio. As mentioned in Section 4.4.2, this relationship allows a central bank to influence directly the return on equity. In a very general way, a 'neutral' real short-term interest rate can then be defined as an interest rate that is identical to an average long-term real interest rate, which can be assumed to be independent of monetary policy and thus mainly to reflect the average profitability of the economy, minus a risk liquidity premium.

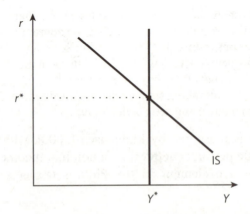

Figure 8.5. *The neutral real interest rate*

Table 8.3. *Historical short-term and long-term real interest rates (% per annum)* [a]

Period	Short-term real interest rate			Long-term real interest rate		
	Euro area	Germany	USA	Euro area	Germany	USA
1960–69	–	2.2	2.8	–	4.2	2.4
1970–79	–	1.9	0.9	–	3.2	0.5
1980–89	–	3.9	5.0	–	4.8	5.5
1990–98	4.5	3.2	2.3	5.2	4.1	3.9
1960–98	–	2.8	2.8	–	4.1	3.1

[a] Short-term real interest rates are calculated by subtracting the contemporaneous 12-month CPI inflation rate from the nominal 3-month interest rate. Long-term real interest rates are calculated by subtracting the contemporaneous 12-month CPI inflation rate from the 10-year government bond yield. The HICP inflation rate is used for current euro area data.

Source: ECB (1999*b*).

Average interest rates for the United States, Germany, and the euro area are shown in Table 8.3. For the whole period from 1960 to 1998 this would imply a liquidity premium of about 1.3 percentage points in Germany and 0.3 percentage point in the United States. The data also show that Taylor's value of 2% (which corresponds with an average of 2.3% in the period 1990–8) is much lower than the average real rate over longer periods.

While the neutral policy stance of the Taylor rule can be explained by the balance sheet channel, its other two components are related to the AS/AD model. As far as the direction of interest changes is concerned, it can be derived from an analysis of shocks in the AS/AD model. In the situation of a negative demand shock,

1. the price level is lower than at equilibrium level; thus, one can assume that the inflation rate is lower than the target;
2. the output level is lower than full capacity output, which is identical with a negative output gap.

As these two determinants have the same sign, the Taylor rule indicates a real interest rate reduction. Thus, it calls for an expansionary monetary policy which is the same policy reaction as required by a nominal income rule or a (short-term) inflation targeting. A specific advantage of the Taylor rule in situations with demand shocks is that it provides a diversification of measurement errors. In principle, a demand shock should affect the price level and the output gap in the same way. Thus, for this shock it would be sufficient to formulate a Taylor rule for either the inflation rate or the output gap. However, as both aggregates have their specific measurement problems, the standard Taylor rule is the superior solution.

In the situation of a positive supply shock (a leftward shift in the AS curve to AS_1) the price level increases while the output level declines. Thus, these two determinants of the Taylor rule have now opposite signs. If one assumes that the shock leads to an identical shift in the price level and the output level, the combined effect of both determinants would be zero, which means that the short-term *real* rate would remain constant. However, as the supply shock leads to a higher inflation rate, the *nominal* interest rate would have to be increased by the increase in the inflation rate.

Unfortunately, the standard IS/LM model does not distinguish between real and nominal interest rates. But it is obvious that the IS curve has been designed for real interest rates.[16] Thus, the nominal interest-rate response of the Taylor rule can be interpreted as a constant (real) interest rate in Figure 8.5. It is therefore identical with a real income rule, as it provides a complete output stabilization at the cost of a strong inflation response. This feature of the Taylor rule does not necessarily lead to a stronger variance of inflation over time. As most models assume that output affects inflation with a one-period lag, a stable output path can also contribute to a more stable inflation path.

8.5.3. *Defining the target values*

In spite of its apparent simplicity, the practical application of the Taylor rule raises some difficult empirical questions. The problem of a *correct definition of the neutral real short-term interest rate* has already been mentioned. At first sight, the spectrum for the euro area is wide. As Table 8.3 shows, the neutral values range from 2.3% to 4.5% depending on the reference area and the reference period, and they all have some plausibility. However, because of German unification and the ERM crises, the values of the 1990s are not a good benchmark for a 'neutral' short-term interest rate. On the contrary, the high unemployment rate in this decade indicates that real interest rates in the euro area were far too high. Thus, it seems more adequate to use the German rates as a benchmark, above all as the monetary constitution of the euro area is very similar to the former German monetary constitution. Taking the average for the period 1960–98, this would lead to a neutral real rate of 2.8%, which is identical with the rate for the United States.

---

[16] See Romer (2000). The LM curve is based on a nominal interest rate, as the demand for money depends on the nominal interest rate. A dynamic version of the IS/LM model is presented by McCallum (1989).

Table 8.4. *Difference between estimates of the output gap (IMF minus OECD)*

	1993	1994	1995	1996	1997	1998	1999	2000
Germany	1.0	0.5	0.2	−0.2	−0.6	−1.1	−1.3	−1.5
USA	−2.1	−2.4	−2.6	−2.6	−2.5	−1.9	−1.5	−1.8

Sources: IMF *World Economic Outlook*, May 2000; OECD *Economic Outlook*, July 2000.

A second problem is related to *choice of inflation rate*. In situations with supply shocks, the core inflation rate and the consumer price index can deviate by a substantial amount. For instance, in the euro area in July 2000, the core inflation rate was 1.3% while the HICP inflation rate was 2.4%. This difference was due mainly to a strong increase in energy prices. The core inflation rate seems the more suitable inflation variable, since enterprises are not profiting from the price increases, which are due to higher energy prices.

A very serious problem is due to the *difficult measurement of the output gap*. As Orphanides (2000) shows, real-time data on the output gap in the United States were seriously flawed in the 1970s, which led to an overestimation of the economy's growth potential. Orphanides regards this as a major cause for the relatively high inflation during that period: 'The evidence points to misperceptions of the economy's productive capacity as the primary underlying cause of the 1970s inflation … ' (2000: *i*). A comparison of the estimates of the output gap for the United States and Germany by the OECD and the IMF shows how much these estimates can differ (see Table 8.4).

In sum, the measurement problems concerning the output gap, the neutral real interest rate, and the correct inflation rate can add up to several percentage points.

8.5.4. *A forecast-based Taylor rule*

While the original Taylor rule was developed to deal with available information, it can be also formulated to deal with forecasted values. In the literature the original rule is labelled an 'outcome-based rule' and the forward-looking one a 'forecast-based rule'. From a theoretical standpoint, the logic of the 'balance sheet channel' (Section 4.4.2) does not call for a 'forecast-based rule'. On the contrary, what matters for the profitability of enterprises is the actual real short-term interest rate, not the completely theoretical concept of an actual short-term interest rate deflated by an inflation rate that is expected for the next year. As far as the impact of the real interest on investment decisions is concerned, the real long-term rate seems more important than a real short-term rate. However, as we have seen that the actual inflation rate is a good predictor of the future inflation rate (Section 4.5.5), the difference between a forecast-based Taylor rule and an outcome-based rule is limited in reality.

In fact, a comprehensive study by Levin *et al.* comes to the following conclusion:

we find that forecast-based rules yield at best only small benefits in stabilizing inflation, output and interest rates relative to optimized outcome-based rules that respond to inflation, the output gap and the lagged interest rate. This is even true in the two large-scale models, which contain literally hundreds of state variables and allow for significant lags until the maximum effect of a policy change on the economy is felt. Thus, as far as the potential advantages of forecast-based rules are concerned, neither the lag- nor the information-encompassing feature turn out to be of quantitative importance. (Levin *et al.* 1999: 24)

8.5.5. *Summary*

In sum, the Taylor rule has the obvious advantage of providing a simple and clear structure for thinking about monetary policy. This is important not only for the internal discussions of a central bank, but also for its communication with the public. For 'policymakers facing real-time policy decisions' (Kozicki 1999: 25) the usefulness of the rule is more limited, since there are considerable problems in defining and measuring the average real interest rate, the output gap, and the inflation rate. Kozicki (1999: 17) shows that these differences lead to a roughly 1½-percentage-point range of rule recommendations.

8.6. A NOMINAL GDP RULE

The explicit rule of a nominal GDP rule can be formulated as follows: monetary policy should target nominal GDP. An implicit rule has been formulated by McCallum (1989) and is often referred to as the McCallum rule. It defines an average growth rate of the monetary base that is adjusted upwards (downwards) when nominal GDP growth is lower (higher) than its target value.

8.6.1. *Introduction*

The proposal of a nominal GDP targeting is to be found in the works of many economists.[17] Chapter 5 discussed the pros and cons of using nominal income as the final target of monetary policy. As it is formulated for a

---

[17] The advocates of this approach are Meade (1978), von Weizsäcker (1978), Tobin (1980, 1983), R. E. Hall (1983), Bean (1983), Taylor (1985), and McCallum (1984, 1987).

final target, this rule is of a similarly general nature as the rule of inflation targeting. We have also seen (in Chapter 8) that inflation targeting in practice comes very close to nominal income targeting.

Nevertheless, it seems important to discuss the nominal GDP rule, since

1. it is often, but incorrectly, regarded as being identical to a monetary targeting rule;
2. it was designed by McCallum as an implicit rule that uses the monetary base as an operating target.

8.6.2. *Money supply versus nominal GDP*

In the following analysis, therefore, we shall examine whether an aggregate that is a simple product of two ultimate targets (the price level and real GDP) can in fact serve as an intermediate monetary policy target. For the proponents of nominal GDP targeting, the suitability of this aggregate as an intermediate target is self-evident from the quantity equation. In terms of rates of change, this is formulated as follows:

$$\hat{M} + \hat{V} = \pi + \hat{Y}. \tag{8.9}$$

If a nominal GDP target is now expressed in terms of growth rates,[18] i.e. if

$$\hat{Y}^n = \pi + \hat{Y}, \tag{8.10}$$

then it might be concluded that nominal GDP targeting is basically identical with the money supply approach, the only difference being that, in the case of nominal GDP targeting, the right-hand side of the quantity equation is controlled whereas with monetary targeting it is the left-hand side (Wagner 1992: 144). This—prima facie surprising—conclusion applies, however, only if it is assumed in the case of monetary targeting that fluctuations in the velocity of circulation are taken account of *ex ante.*

Since the ECB does indeed take account of changes in the velocity of circulation in its potential formula (see Section 9.3),[19] this can easily give the impression that in the last analysis its reference value for the money stock M3 is a disguised form of nominal GDP targeting (Rudebusch 2000):

$$\underbrace{\hat{M} + \hat{V}}_{\substack{\text{monetary targeting} \\ \text{adjusted for the} \\ \text{velocity of money}}} = \underbrace{\pi + \hat{Y}.}_{\substack{\text{nominal GDP} \\ \text{targeting}}} \tag{8.11}$$

---

[18] On the difference between a growth target and a level target, see Appendix 5.1 to Chapter 5.

[19] See also Shigehara (1996: 12): 'In a sense, the nominal income target can be regarded as a velocity-adjusted monetary target for guiding monetary policy.'

However, this would be a false impression. A careful examination of the actual determinants of the quantity equation in the two approaches shows that

- monetary targeting results in a *medium-term stabilization* of monetary growth, whereas
- nominal GDP targeting leads to *countercyclical fluctuations* in the money supply growth.

If we compare the process of deriving a money supply target with that of deriving a nominal GDP target, there is a superficial similarity in so far as in both strategies definite values need to be set for real GDP and the inflation rate. It is clear that for these aggregates a normative value is used for the inflation rate (π^{norm}) and the growth rate of potential output is used for the real growth term ($\hat{Y}^{pot}$). To this extent, therefore, the ECB's reference value for the money supply is indeed equivalent to a nominal GDP target.

The crucial difference between the two approaches lies in the values of the velocity of circulation of money ($\hat{V}$). Whereas the ECB operates with the *long-term trend* ($\hat{V}^{trend}$) in the velocity of circulation (see Table 8.1), a nominal GDP rule requires that the quantity equation should always use the *current forecast value* ($\hat{V}_t$) for the velocity of circulation.

The target value for the money stock in the case of monetary targeting ($\hat{M}_M$) is then calculated from the potential formula as

$$\hat{M}_M = \pi^{norm} + \hat{Y}^{pot} - \hat{V}^{trend}. \tag{8.12}$$

In the event of nominal GDP targeting ($\hat{M}_{GDP}$), the target value of the money stock is derived from the target value for nominal GDP on the basis of the actual velocity of circulation of money:

$$\hat{M}_{GDP} = \pi^{norm} + \hat{Y}^{pot} - \hat{V}_t. \tag{8.13}$$

Differences between $\hat{M}_M$ and $\hat{M}_{GDP}$ are then solely the result of deviations in the actual velocity of circulation from its trend value:

$$\hat{M}_M - \hat{M}_{GDP} = \hat{V}^{trend} - \hat{V}_t. \tag{8.14}$$

In the event of monetary targeting, such deviations are first and foremost cyclically determined. If actual values are included in equation (8.12) and it is assumed that the central bank meets its money supply target, the following equation is obtained:

$$\hat{M}_M = \pi_t + \hat{Y}_t - \hat{V}_t. \tag{8.15}$$

The difference between equations (8.12) and (8.15) gives:

$$\hat{V}^{trend} - \hat{V}_t = \underbrace{(\pi^{norm} - \hat{Y}^{pot})}_{\text{implicit GDP target}} - \underbrace{(\pi_t + \hat{Y}_t)}_{\text{actual GDP}}. \tag{8.16}$$

It can thus be seen that monetary targeting which is geared exclusively to the trend in the velocity of circulation of money cannot ensure that the implicit target value for nominal GDP will always be met.

The resulting practical implications for monetary policy can most easily be illustrated by means of a numerical example. We shall assume that both monetary targeting and nominal GDP targeting are geared to a value for nominal GDP growth of 4.5%. Let this target be based on an inflation rate of 2%, which for statistical reasons is regarded as compatible with price-level stability, and on an empirically determined value for the long-term real growth path of 2.5%. At the same time, for monetary targeting, a trend in the velocity of circulation of -1% will be assumed, giving a target value for the money supply of 5.5% ($\hat{M}_M = 2\% + 2.5\% - (-1\%)$).

In the case of the nominal GDP rule, it is no longer quite so straight-forward to derive the result for the money supply, since the velocity of circulation of money can vary in different cyclical phases. Generally speaking, in cyclical booms the velocity of circulation tends to rise (or declines more slowly than the trend rate), i.e. real GDP increases faster than the real demand for money. The opposite happens in recessions, when the real demand for money generally rises faster than real GDP. Let us assume that the rate of change in the velocity of circulation under boom conditions is $+1\%$ and in a recession is -3%, which means a uniform deviation from the trend of ±2 percentage points. Depending on the individual cyclical phase, the nominal GDP target of 4.5% gives three different rates of change in the money supply:

1. If GDP grows at the *trend* rate, the velocity of circulation similarly does not deviate from its trend growth, and the optimal rate of growth in the money supply, as in the case of monetary targeting, comes to 5.5% ($\hat{M}_{GDP}^{trend} = 2\% + 2.5\% - (-1\%)$).
2. If the economy is in a *boom* phase, the velocity of circulation rises. In order to keep nominal GDP on the target path, the central banks must therefore increase the money supply at a correspondingly slower rate. Thus, the rate of change in the money supply should be only 3.5% ($\hat{M}_{GDP}^{boom} = 2\% + 2.5\% - 1\%$).
3. In the case of a *recession*, with a declining velocity of circulation, the money supply should grow at a more than proportional rate, in order to realize the target value for nominal GDP growth, i.e. by 7.5% ($\hat{M}_{GDP}^{rec} = 2\% + 2.5\% - (-3\%)$).

Thus, whereas in the case of monetary targeting a constant expansion in the money supply is achieved, nominal GDP targeting involves counter-cyclical fluctuations in the money supply. The logic of this approach implies that monetary policy would then be conducted in such a way that all cyclical fluctuations are fully offset. In other words, it is assumed that the following equation holds good at all times:

$$\pi_t + \hat{Y}_t = \pi^{norm} + \hat{Y}^{pot}. \tag{8.17}$$

In the event of recessionary tendencies, the money supply is increased at a correspondingly faster rate, with the result that nominal GDP continues to be kept on the trend path. A boom phase can be prevented by placing a corresponding restriction on monetary growth.

Thus, it is certainly not correct to treat a nominal income rule as a disguised form of monetary targeting. In Section 8.3.3 it was shown that monetary targeting implies an implicit final target rule which aims at a stabilization of the price level in the *medium and long run*. Therefore, it is not surprising that it differs from a nominal income rule if an economy is confronted with *demand shocks*. While the nominal income rule leads to a complete compensation of the shock, monetary requires no compensation at all. In a situation with a supply shock, the two rules arrive at relatively similar results, since we have seen that monetary targeting implies a partial accommodation of a supply shock.

As the analogy with monetary targeting is flawed, so it is also not correct to regard a nominal income target as an *intermediate target* of monetary policy.[20] A multiplication of two final targets (real GDP and price level) makes no intermediate target.

8.6.3. *The control of nominal income*

8.6.3.1. *Nominal income targeting without a defined implicit rule*
Not all proponents of nominal income targeting regard it as necessary to define an implicit rule for the control of this aggregate. In the words of Hall and Mankiw,

Once the Fed is committed to pegging the consensus forecast of nominal income, we see no need to tell it how to go about achieving the peg. The Fed's bond traders should simply buy or sell securities as needed to keep the forecast at the peg. In practice, this would be similar to the way that many central banks today achieve exchange rate pegs. There is a difference in response time, of course. The exchange rate reacts to portfolio changes in a few seconds, whereas the consensus forecast reacts to portfolio changes in a few days or a week. Just as a supertanker needs a

---

[20] For an opposite, see Taylor (1985: 63): 'In this sense nominal GNP is not a *final* target; rather it is an *intermediate* target. Therefore, it should be evaluated as an alternative to other intermediate targets.' Also King (1994: 11): 'Of the alternative intermediate targets that have been suggested, the most serious candidate is a nominal income or GDP target.'

more qualified pilot than a small ship, a central bank pegging a nominal income forecast needs a better technician than one pegging an exchange rate. But the peg is still just a technical issue. (Hall and Mankiw 1994: 14)

Thus, instead of providing policy-makers with a 'fast and frugal heuristic', these authors leave the most difficult part of the decision process to the policy-makers in the central bank.

8.6.3.2. *The McCallum rule*

A notable exception is McCallum (1987, 1988, 1989, 1999), who developed an implicit rule based on the monetary base for nominal GDP targeting which has received a good deal of attention in the monetary debate.[21] What McCallum is basically proposing is to replace the rigid Friedman rule with a feedback rule which takes equal account of the trend growth in nominal GDP, trend changes in the velocity of circulation, and cyclical fluctuations in GDP. McCallum regards his rule as an alternative to the Taylor rule but points out that his rule 'has agreed with Taylor's over many periods' (McCallum 1999: 8). This similarity can be explained by the fact that the monetary base, which consists mainly of currency in circulation, is a highly interest-rate-sensitive aggregate. Thus, if the short-term interest rate goes up, the growth rate of the monetary base declines. In addition, as already mentioned, the determinants of the real interest rate in the Taylor rule are similar to those in a nominal GDP rule.

The McCallum rule, like monetary targeting, is derived from the quantity equation; however, it is subject to certain modifications. Thus, McCallum initially formulates the quantity equation for the monetary base in terms of growth rates:

$$\hat{B}_t = \pi_t + \hat{Y}_t - \hat{V}_t^B. \tag{8.18}$$

Between the rate of variation in the velocity of circulation of the monetary base ($\hat{V}_t^B$) and the money supply ($\hat{V}_t$), the following relationship exists:[22]

$$\hat{V}_t^B = (\hat{V}_t + \hat{m}_t). \tag{8.19}$$

Thus, the two velocities differ if the multiplier ($\hat{m}$) changes. McCallum sets a rate of zero as the normative value for the inflation rate π_t. For Y_t he uses a growth rate of 3% per year, which corresponds to the growth trend in the US economy over the last 100 years if one excludes the Great Depression and the war years (McCallum 1989: 341). When converted to a quarterly

---

[21] See e.g. T. E. Hall (1990), Loef (1989), Judd and Motley (1993), Dueker (1993), and Croushore and Stark (1995).

[22] It is based on the quantity equation for the money supply and for the monetary base and on the multiplier correlation $m = M/B$.

basis, the annual rate for the target value of nominal GDP of 3% comes to 0.74%. When inserted in (8.19), this gives

$$\hat{B}_t = 0.0074 - \hat{V}_t^B. \tag{8.20}$$

Unlike in the nominal GDP rules described above, for the velocity of circulation McCallum uses not the actual value, but the average velocity of circulation of the monetary base for the last sixteen quarters. The reason for using this longish period is to smooth out cyclical fluctuations in the velocity of circulation. The equation for the targeted value of the monetary base is then

$$\hat{B}_t = 0.0074 - \frac{1}{16}\sum_{i=1}^{16} \hat{V}_{t-i}^B. \tag{8.21}$$

In this form, the McCallum rule shows a certain affinity to the ECB's and the Bundesbank's monetary targeting, since both methods use longer-term trend values in the velocity of circulation. However, McCallum's approach differs from that of the ECB and the Bundesbank in so far as he formulates the target directly for the monetary base, while monetary targeting requires a further instrumental realization via interest rate or monetary base targeting.

While equation (8.21) still contains no explicit countercyclical component, McCallum supplements his rule by a term that takes account of temporary fluctuations in real GDP. This is calculated as the difference between the actual level of nominal GDP for the previous period (Y_{t-1}^n) and a standard value calculated with the trend growth rate of 3% $(Y_{t-1}^{n^*})$. Both values are expressed in logarithms, so that the determining equation for the monetary base is

$$\hat{B}_t = 0.0074 - \frac{1}{16}\sum_{i=1}^{16} \hat{V}_{t-i}^B + \lambda(\ln Y_{t-1}^{n^*} - \ln Y_{t-1}^n)$$

with $\lambda = 0.25$. (8.22)

In this formulation of the rule, therefore, the central bank must increase the growth rate in the monetary base if the actual value of nominal GDP in the preceding period is below its trend value, and vice versa. The value chosen for λ determines how pronounced the countercyclical character of this rule will be. When the value is high, there is the risk of an explosive process developing as a result of the phenomenon of instrument instability. Then, if nominal GDP deviates from the target path, the effect on the monetary base could be strong enough to push the economy beyond the target path in the other direction. This would then lead to destabilizing effects which

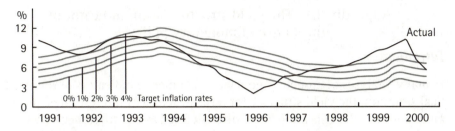

Figure 8.6. *Monetary base growth* and inflation targets in the United States*
*Modified for the effects of sweeps programmes on reserve demand.
Calculated base growth is based on McCallum's rule. Actual base growth is the percentage change from one year before.
Source: Federal Reserve Bank of St Louis, *Monetary Trends.*

would run counter to the intention of nominal GDP targeting. McCallum regards a value of 0.25, which he calculates on the basis of empirical research, as appropriate for λ in the case of the United States.

There is another marked difference with respect to a pure nominal GDP rule, since the latter, if it is applied consistently, requires a monetary policy reaction in period t, i.e. not lagged by a period. Moreover, with this approach monetary policy always needs to ensure that a decline in Y_t is fully offset, while in the McCallum rule an upper limit is imposed by the value set for λ.

Figure 8.6 shows that in the United States the actual growth rate of the monetary base is not too different from the path prescribed by the McCallum rule, at least for a target inflation rate of about 2% with a band of ± 2 percentage points.

For practical monetary policy, the rule is rather difficult to apply. It would above all require that the central bank uses the monetary base as its operating target. While the McCallum rule is based on a long-term average of velocity, monetary policy would have to deal with the actual changes in the base velocity which, in comparison to a four-year moving average, are quite substantial. Given the low elasticity of the demand for monetary base in the short run (Chapter 3), wrong estimates of the monetary base target level would lead to excessive fluctuations of short-term interest rates. As interest rates have a direct impact on banks' and enterprises' profits (because of the balance sheet channel), one can understand why

many central bankers view discussion of the monetary base with about the same enthusiasm as I would have for the prospect of being locked in a telephone booth with someone who had a bad cold, or some other infectious disease. (McCallum 1999: 8)

Appendix 8.1. The yield structure as an indicator of the stance of monetary policy

Introduction

In many analyses of monetary policy and composite indicators of the cyclical situation, the yield structure (or term structure of interest rates) plays an important role. This indicator is often defined as the difference between a long-term and a short-term interest rate:

$$YS = i_{long} - i_{short}. \hspace{4cm} (A8.1)$$

The term structure of interest rates can also be depicted in the form of *yield curves,* which show the interest rate on the *y*-axis and the maturity on the *x*-axis. Thus, for each date a yield curve can be depicted. (Figure A8.1). If the yield curve is upward-sloping, the yield structure is regarded as 'normal'; if it is downward-sloping it is regarded as 'inverted'. A representation of such yield curves over time leads to a three-dimensional graph (Figure A8.2).

It is generally assumed that a 'normal' yield structure is a sign of an expansionary or at least neutral stance of monetary policy, while an 'inverted' yield structure is regarded as an indication of monetary restriction. Figure A8.3 shows that, for instance in the case of the United States, the yield structure has indeed served as a very good leading indicator for all three recessions in the period 1970–99. Similar results can be found for other countries (Estrella and Mishkin 1995).

How can we explain the good explanatory power of the yield structure? For an understanding of the theoretical basis of this indicator, it is important to discuss its two determinants separately.

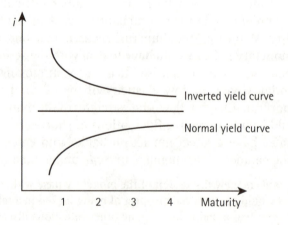

Figure A8.1. *Hypothetical yield curves*

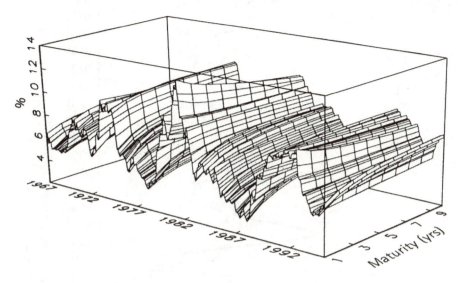

Figure A8.2. *Empirical yield curves*
Source: Gerlach (1995: 6).

As far as the *short-term interest rate* is concerned, it is obvious that it mainly reflects the actions of the central bank. In Chapter 10 we will consider in more detail the fact that all central banks use the short-term interest rate as the operating target of their policy, which they can control reasonably well. In addition, as we will see in Section 9.5, the interest rate policy of many central banks can be traced relatively well with a Taylor rule. This implies *inter alia* that, in situations with increasing inflation rates, central banks raise nominal interest rates by more than the increase in the inflation rate. Thus, the real short-term rate fluctuates considerably.

A8.2 *The long-term interest rate*

The theory of the *long-term interest rate* is more complicated, and it has been the subject of a long debate in the history of economic theory. We will focus on some core issues only. According to classical and neoclassical theory, the capital market interest rate is formed exclusively on the basis of real factors. Its function is to bring about an equilibrium in investment and saving plans. This idea is already to be found in the works of Smith, Ricardo, Jevons, Mill, and von Böhm-Bawerk.[23] Thus, the capital market is where the demand for financial resources to meet the amount of planned

---

[23] For a survey see Panico (1987).

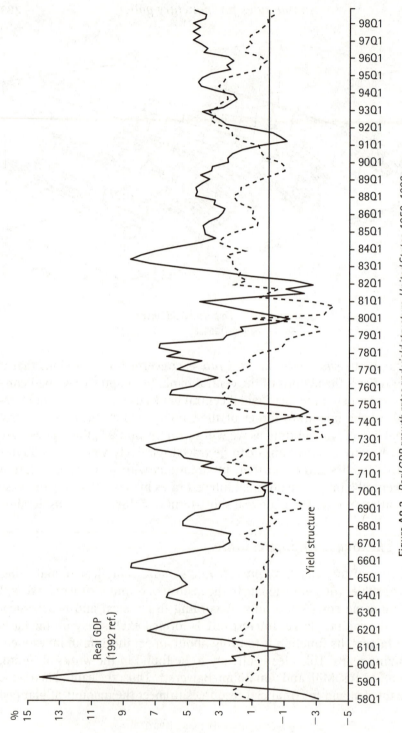

Figure A8.3. *Real GDP growth rates and yield structure, United States, 1958–1998*
Source: Own calculations based on data from IMF, *International Financial Statistics.*

investment and the supply of capital to meet the amount of planned saving come together. The equilibrium market interest rate is derived from the
maximization behaviour of enterprises and consumers, and so is determined by the marginal productivity of capital and also by consumers' rate
of time preference.

The view that the capital market interest rate is determined by the real
economy is also held by economists who, like Wicksell (1898), draw an
explicit distinction between the 'money interest rate' (in German, *Geldzins*
as the market rate of interest for capital, which is not to be confused with
the above-mentioned short-term interest rate) and the 'natural interest
rate' (as the rate of return on real capital). Although Wicksell acknowledges
that in the short-term monetary impulses can lead to divergences between
the 'money interest rate' and the 'natural rate of interest on capital'
(natürlicher Zins), he shows that these can never be of long duration
(Wicksell 1898: 117). For example, if the behaviour of the commercial
banks causes the 'money interest rate' to fall below the 'natural rate of
interest on capital', this will stimulate additional credit demand, which will
continue until such time as the 'money interest rate' once again equals the
'natural rate of interest on capital'.

The importance of inflation expectations for the long-term interest rate
is described in the so-called *Fisher equation*, which explains the relationship between the nominal and real rate of interest. It was developed by
Irving Fisher (1896) and can be derived as follows.[24] At the beginning of a
one-year time horizon, a sum of money M_t will buy the nominal volume of
goods $X_t P_t$:

$$M_t = X_t P_t. \tag{A8.2}$$

Both quantities are now lent for the period of one year. In an equilibrium
situation it is now necessary to ensure that the economic agent that lends
a given volume of goods is in the same position at the end of the year as the
creditor in respect of a money debt. If, for the volume of money lent M_t, the
money interest rate i is paid and for the volume of goods $X_t P_t$ the rate of
interest on capital is r, then at the end of the period the following must
hold true:

$$M_t(1 + i) = X_t P_t(1 + r). \tag{A8.3}$$

If during the year the price of goods rises—at a rate that has been predicted
with certainty—to P_{t+1} (or, expressed in terms of growth rates, if prices rise
by π^e), then at the time of repayment the sum of money required in order

---

[24] Besides the primary source of Fisher (1896: ch. III), see also Monissen (1982: 117–23).

to be able to purchase the same quantity of goods as at the beginning will have increased by $(1 + \pi^e)$:

$$M_t(1 + \pi^e) = X_t P_{t+1} \qquad \text{with } \pi^e = (P_{t+1} - P_t)/P_t. \tag{A8.4}$$

A creditor who lends a given sum of money will therefore demand not only a premium for the intertemporal shift in his consumption, but also a compensation for the rise in the price of goods. Therefore, assuming a rise in prices, at the end of one year, instead of equation (A8.3), the following will apply:

$$M_t(1 + i) = X_t P_{t+1}(1 + r), \tag{A8.5}$$

where the price level P_{t+1} can be expressed as $P_t(1 + \pi^e)$. When incorporated into (A8.5), this gives

$$M_t(1 + i) = (1 + \pi^e) X_t P_t(1 + r). \tag{A8.6}$$

If, in accordance with (A8.2) $P_t X_t$ is replaced by M_t, the following relationship between i and r can then be derived from (A8.6):

$$M_t(1 + i) = M_t(1 + \pi^e)(1 + r); \tag{A8.7}$$

$$i = r + \pi^e + r\pi^e. \tag{A8.8}$$

For small values of π^e and r the product $\pi^e r$ can be ignored. This leads to the more general version of the Fisher equation, which can be described as the nominal interest rate theorem and the real interest rate theorem:

$$i = r + \pi^e \qquad \textit{Nominal interest rate theorem,} \tag{A8.9}$$

$$r = i - \pi^e \qquad \textit{Real interest rate theorem.} \tag{A8.10}$$

Fisher's equations can now quite easily be made compatible with the real view of the classical and neoclassical schools. Assuming perfect foresight, inflation tendencies triggered by changes in the money supply are fully reflected in nominal interest rate increases. The real interest rate is unaffected, and continues to be determined purely by non-monetary factors. To this extent, the real interest rate used by Fisher and the capital market interest rate described above coincide. This explains the parallel movement—often seen in practice—of longer-term interest rates and the inflation rate (see Figure A8.4).[25]

[25] In two studies carried out in 1923 and 1926 Gibson established a correlation between the index for wholesale prices and the average effective rate of interest paid on consols (government stock with no fixed redemption date). Keynes (1930) subsequently attributed this discovery to him and called it the 'Gibson Paradox', the name still current today. It is called a paradox because it was supposed that rising interest rates are an expression of a restrictive monetary policy, which ought to be reflected in falling inflation.

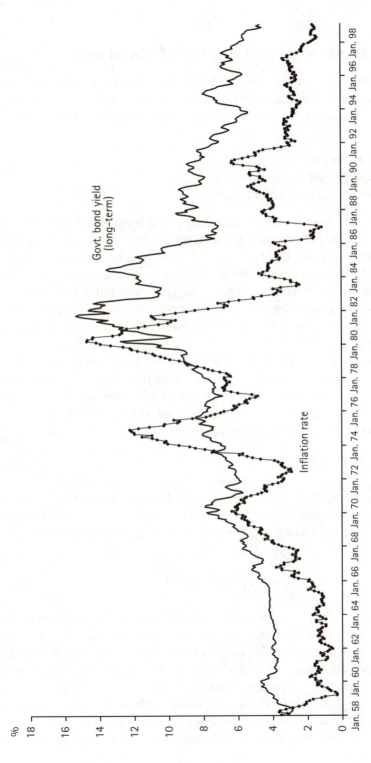

Figure A8.4. *Bond yields and inflation rates, United States, 1958–1998 (first month of each year)*

Source: IMF, *International Financial Statistics.*

A8.3 *Theories of the term structure of interest rates*

On this basis it is now possible to discuss theories of the yield structure. There are essentially three theoretical approaches described in the
literature that seek to explain the relationship between short- and long-term
interest rates (Campbell 1995):

1. the expectations theory;
2. the liquidity premium theory;
3. the market segmentation theory.

The *expectations theory* also originated with Irving Fisher (1930) but the
main development of the theory was done by Lutz (1941) and Hicks (1946).
The backbone of this theory is an arbitrage logic. If short-term and long-
term assets are perfect substitutes, the long-term interest rate must be the
geometric mean of current short-term and expected future short-term
interest rates. Thus, a long-term investment will have the same yield as a
sequence of short-term investments which, when aggregated, equal the
long period.

Formally, this can be illustrated by means of an example in which an
economic agent has to decide between either investing a sum of money X
for a fixed period of three years at a long-term interest rate (i_{long}) or investing for three successive periods of one year at a short-term interest rate
(i_{short}). In the first case, the value at the end of the investment is

$$V_{long} = (1 + i_{long})^3 X. \tag{A8.11}$$

In the case of the short-term investment at the time the decision is made (t),
only the interest rate for the first period (i_{short}) is known. For the remaining
two periods expectations must be formed, so that here earnings are calculated as

$$E_{short} = (1 + i_{short}^t)(1 + i_{short}^{e_{t+1}})(1 + i_{short}^{e_{t+2}})X. \tag{A8.12}$$

If the result of these calculations is that it is more profitable to invest short
term for three separate periods, an economic agent wishing to maximize
the earnings on her portfolio would choose this option. This would result
in an additional supply of capital (demand for securities) at the short end
of the market, causing interest rates to fall there (prices rise). At the same
time, the supply of capital (demand for securities) would tighten at the long
end, leading to an increase in long-term interest rates (prices fall). Both
these movements have the effect of equilibrating the yields on short- and

long-term forms of investment.[26] Thus, in equilibrium the following must apply:

$$(1 + i_{long})^3 = (1 + i^t_{short})(1 + i^{e_{t+1}}_{short})(1 + i^{e_{t+2}}_{short}) \qquad (A8.13)$$

or,

$$i_{long} = \sqrt[3]{(1 + i^t_{short})(1 + i^{e_{t+1}}_{short})(1 + i^{e_{t+2}}_{short})} - 1. \qquad (A8.14)$$

Thus, expectation theory shows that the long-term interest rate is the geometric mean of short-term (expected) interest rates. It is clear that there is no true arbitrage relationship, since the short-term interest rates for periods 2 and 3 are expectation values. Therefore, as with the uncovered interest parity (Section 12.3), there is a price risk.

A central assumption of expectation theory is that short- and long-term financial investments are entirely homogeneous. Different preferences and risks are ignored. At the heart of the *liquidity premium theory*, which was first developed by Hicks (1946), is the view that investors expect to be compensated for not holding cash, and for the associated loss of liquidity, through the payment of a premium. The longer the residual period to maturity of the security, the less liquid it is, and therefore the greater the risk that it may have to be sold at a loss. On the other hand, it is in the borrower's interest to raise capital for as long a period as possible, in order to minimize planning uncertainty. This leads to excess demand for capital at the long end of the market. This 'constitutional weakness' (Hicks 1946: 146) results in a positive liquidity premium for long-term paper, which is proportionately higher, the longer the maturity period. Thus, the 'pure' liquidity premium theory always produces a positive interest rate curve. This problem forms the starting point for a 'weak' form of this theory, which assumes the general possibility of different preferences for securities with different maturities. In combination with expectation theory, this approach, which originated with Modigliani and Sutch (1966), is referred to as *preferred habitat theory*. Long-term interest rates are then obtained as the sum of the mean of (expected) short-term interest rates and the liquidity premium.

A somewhat outdated explanation of the interest rate curve is provided by *market segmentation theory* (Culbertson 1957), which assumes that the markets for securities with different maturities are completely separate from one another. The lack of substitutability among securities means that interest rates are formed in isolation on the sub-markets and that this

---

[26] In the context of the expectations theory, transaction costs, different preferences (risk considerations), and institutional factors are excluded. The last two are the province of the 'liquidity premium theory' and 'market segmentation theory'.

process is not offset by arbitrage. Market segmentation was due to institutional factors, which played an important role in the United States before the radical financial innovation that took place at the end of the 1970s, which was aimed specifically at overcoming such institutional barriers.

A8.4. *The explanatory power of the yield structure*

It was already mentioned that the yield structure is often used for forecasting purposes because of its good leading indicator qualities. Above all, an inverse yield structure (short-term rates exceeding long-term rates) is regarded as a sign of a restrictive monetary policy.

   This evidence can be explained if we look at the policy of a central bank in a period of high inflation. If the central bank is determined to bring inflation down, it must raise short-term rates considerably so that the real short-term rate is relatively high. This exerts a restrictive influence via the interest rate channel (see Section 4.4). Normally the markets regard such a high real and nominal short-term rate as a sign of monetary restriction which will lead to the expectation of lower inflation rates and lower growth (or even a recession). For both reasons, they will also expect lower nominal short-term interest rates for the future. Thus, a negative term structure emerges. This explanation, which relies very much on the impact of short-term rates on the term structure, is compatible with the fact that very often the real short-term rate and the (reciprocal) yield curve move in parallel. This can be explained as follows. The reciprocal yield structure is

$$YS_R = i_{short} - i_{long}. \tag{A8.15}$$

The short-term real interest rate is

$$i_{short}^R = i_{short} - \pi^e. \tag{A8.16}$$

Using the Fisher relation, (A8.15) can be written as

$$YS_R = i_{short} - (i_{long}^R - \pi^e). \tag{A8.15'}$$

If one assumes that the real long-term rate i_{long}^R is a rather stable variable, and that the expected inflation is the same in the short term and the long term, then absolute changes in the reciprocal yield structure become identical with absolute changes in the short-term real interest rate. Figure A8.5 shows that such a parallel development can be observed for periods where the Fisher equation holds for the long-term rate.

   Both indicators have their advantages and disadvantages. The real short-term interest rate, if calculated by deflating the nominal short-term rate with a consumer price index, can be misleading if changes in the inflation

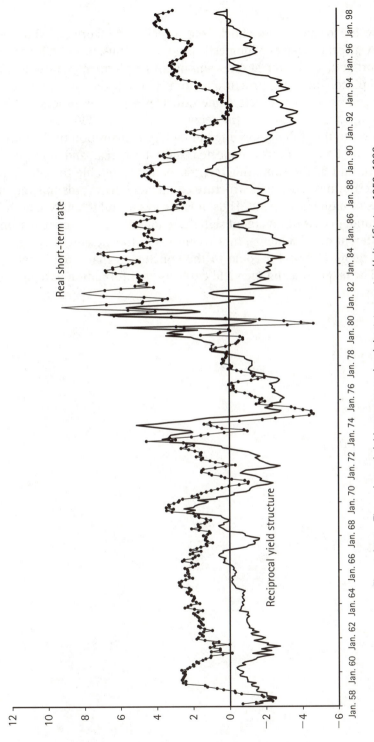

Figure A8.5. *The reciprocal yield structure and real short-term rates, United States, 1958–1998*

Source: Own calculations based on data from IMF, *International Financial Statistics*.

rate are due to supply-side shocks (e.g. a decline in oil prices), which do not directly affect the prices of domestic producers. Thus, in 1987, for example, the short-term real interest rate went up although no monetary restriction was in place. The yield structure is problematic if the long-term real rate and the short-term real rate come down in a parallel process. This was the case in the euro area in the second half of the 1990s. Because of the transition to the stability-oriented monetary constitution of the European System of Central Banks, expected short-term real and nominal rates declined and at the same time central banks were able to reduce actual short-term rates. The yield structure completely disregards this important process of monetary easing. Thus, it is always useful to analyse both indicators and, in case of divergent signals, to identify the concrete reasons for the different developments. In a recent study for the euro area, Berk and van Bergeijk (2000: 18) come to the conclusion that 'considerable care should be taken in using the yield curve as an information variable for the Eurosystem'.

9

The Conduct of Monetary Policy by the World's Major Central Banks

What this chapter is about

- It explains how central bankers in the world's most important central banks have been able to reach the main targets of monetary policy. After the discussion of 'simple rules' in the last chapter, it is especially interesting to analyse the policy frameworks that were used by decision-makers in Germany, Japan, the United Kingdom, and the United States.
- Although it covers the whole period since 1974, i.e. since the breakdown of the Bretton Woods system, the main focus is on the 1980s and 1990s.

9.1. A COMPARISON OF THE PERFORMANCE OF CENTRAL BANKS

Before we start the analysis of individual central bank strategies, it seems useful to compare the performance of important central banks over a longer period of time. Their performance in terms of price stability, the main goal of monetary policy, can be assessed through the average annual CPI inflation rate.

As Table 9.1 shows, no central bank was able to achieve a stable price level in the period from 1960 to 1999 even if we define this target as an annual inflation rate of 2% (see Section 5.4.3). While the Bundesbank

Table 9.1. *Inflation performance (average annual CPI inflation)*

	USA	Germany	Japan	UK	Euro area	Difference between highest and lowest rate
1960–99	4.6	3.2	4.7	6.9	n.a.	3.8
1982–99	3.5	2.3	1.5	4.7	4.8	3.3
1990–99	3.0	2.3	1.2	3.7	3.2	2.5
1993–99	2.5	2.0	0.6	2.6	3.7	3.1

Source: Own calculations based on data from OECD, *Economic Outlook* and IMF, *International Financial Statistics.*

comes relatively close to that benchmark, the three other central banks have clearly missed it. For the three most recent sub-periods a somewhat different picture emerges. Japan had the lowest inflation rate in all sub-periods with a clear indication of a deflationary process, followed by the Bundesbank and the Federal Reserve. The Bank of England almost always comes fourth, and the countries of the present euro area were two times the worst performers. The difference between the best and the worst result differs also very little in the four sub-periods.

For a more comprehensive analysis of the performance of monetary policy, it seems useful to evaluate it via the loss function (5.1) that was presented in Chapter 5 with a weighting factor $\lambda = 1$. The advantage of this function is that its focuses on the most important goals of monetary policy: its long-term goal of keeping inflation low, and its short-term goal of avoiding unnecessary real fluctuations in the form of output gaps. Table 9.2 shows that the outcome of this evaluation depends very much on the period for which a comparison is made.

- If we look at the period 1982–99 (data for the euro area are not available before 1982), we can see that Japan has realized the best outcome, slightly ahead of Germany. The euro area and the UK are the worst performers.
- In the observation period 1983–99 Germany and the United States are leading, which shows that the year 1982 was a especially bad year for the United States.
- In the 1990s Chairman Alan Greenspan clearly outperformed all other central bankers, but the difference between the best and the worst monetary policy is much lower than in the 1980s.
- For an assessment of inflation targeting, the period 1993–99 is of interest as the Bank of England started with this framework in autumn 1992. This brings the United Kingdom to the top and indicates that inflation targeting

Table 9.2. *Annual social welfare loss (according to equation 5.1) (%)*

	USA	Germany	Japan	UK	Euro area	Difference between best and worst performer
1982–99	7.1	5.6	5.5	15.0	18.8	13.3
1983–99	5.0	4.7	5.8	12.4	13.8	9.1
1990–99	4.0	5.0	7.3	9.5	5.1	5.5
1993–99	2.5	3.1	7.5	2.1	3.7	5.4
Memorandum item: average real GDP growth, 1960–99	2.9	2.2	1.7	1.9	n.a.	1.2

has at least improved the performance of the Bank of England. However, this specific period is biased in favour of the UK as that country had started inflation targeting after it had achieved its disinflation process.

An interesting result of this comparison is that a clear ranking of the four central banks is no longer possible. This applies above all to the relative position of the Federal Reserve and the Bundesbank. But even the Bank of Japan is in the first place if the whole period from 1982 to 1999 is considered. As far as the last few years are concerned, the difference between the United States and the United Kingdom is especially low.

The comparison of Tables 9.1 and 9.2 shows above all that Germany, the country with best inflation performance, was not able to stabilize real output in a similar way to the United States.

Thus, in discussing the monetary policy frameworks of these four central banks (plus the strategy of the ECB), it will be interesting to analyse whether the sometimes relatively similar performances can be explained with a more or less identical policy framework.

9.2. THE MONETARY POLICY FRAMEWORK OF THE DEUTSCHE BUNDESBANK

Since start of the European monetary union on 1 January 1999, the Deutsche Bundesbank has become an integral part of the European System of Central Banks. Thus, as all responsibilities were transferred to the ECB, monetary policy in Germany is no longer decided by the Bundesbank's governing body (the Zentralbankrat). If we nevertheless wish to consider the Bundesbank's monetary policy during the period 1974–98, this is because of its specific conceptual approach which has at least partly been adopted by the ECB.

9.2.1. *Experience of monetary targeting*

Jürgen von Hagen summarizes the Bundesbank's experience of monetary targeting as follows:

Money growth targeting served the Bundesbank a number of politico-economic functions. It marked the end of the old regime where the Bank was powerless to control monetary conditions in Germany; it defined the central bank's monetary policy goal and its role in the macroeconomic policy game; and it served as a focal point in council meetings, strengthening the pursuit of a consistent monetary policy geared at price stability over time. (von Hagen 1999: 699)

This positive assessment is not easy to reconcile with the performance of the Bundesbank's monetary targeting (see Table 9.3). In the twenty-three

Table 9.3. *The Bundesbank's performance with monetary targeting*

Year	Target: growth rate of the central bank money stock or M3[a] (%)			Actual growth rate (%)		Target reached[c]
	In the course of the year[b]	Average	Specification during the year	In the course of the year[b]	Average	
1975	About 8	—	—	10.1	—	No
1976	—	8	—	—	9.2	No
1977	—	8	—	—	9.0	No
1978	—	8	—	—	11.5	No
1979	6–9	—	Lower bound	6.3	—	Yes
1980	5–8	—	Lower bound	4.9	—	Yes (No)[d]
1981	4–7	—	Lower half	3.5	—	Yes (No)[d]
1982	4–7	—	Upper half	6.0	—	Yes
1983	4–7	—	Upper half	7.0	—	Yes
1984	4–6	—	—	4.6	—	Yes
1985	3–5	—	—	4.5	—	Yes
1986	$3\frac{1}{2}$–$5\frac{1}{2}$	—	—	7.7	—	No
1987	3–6	—	—	8.1	—	No
1988	3–6	—	—	6.7	—	No
1989	About 5	—	—	4.7	—	Yes
1990	4–6	—	—	5.6	—	Yes
1991	3–5[e]	—	—	5.2	—	Yes (No)[d]
1992	$3\frac{1}{2}$–$5\frac{1}{2}$	—	—	9.4	—	No
1993	$4\frac{1}{2}$–$6\frac{1}{2}$	—	—	7.4	—	No
1994	4–6	—	—	5.7	—	Yes
1995	4–6	—	—	2.1	—	No
1996	4–7	—	—	8.1	—	No
1997[f]	$3\frac{1}{2}$–$6\frac{1}{2}$	—	—	4.8	—	Yes
1998	3–6	—	—	5.6	—	Yes

[a] Since 1988: M3.
[b] 4th quarter of the previous year to the 4th quarter of the target year; 1975: December 1974–December 1975.
[c] The assessment refers to rounded values (Procedure of the Bundesbank).
[d] Assessment for non-rounded values.
[e] Adjusted target of July 1991.
[f] In December 1996 a target for 2 years was set with an average target rate of 5%. The concrete corridor was announced in December 1996 and December 1997.

Source: Deutsche Bundesbank (1995); Schächter (1999).

years for which targets were set, only in ten years could the target be clearly reached. In three years the growth rate was outside the relatively broad corridor, but the Bundesbank widened the target range by rounding off the actual figures: thus, a corridor of 4%–7% actually meant a band width of 3.5%–7.4%. This outcome is not too surprising, as the stability of the demand for money is notoriously unstable in the short run. In addition, the demand for money depends on interest rates which were neglected in the annual targets, although the whole period from 1975 to 1998 saw marked upward and downward trends of short-term rates (Figure 3.4). The failures in the first four years in particular can clearly be explained by a strong decline in money market rates which had a marked effect on the target aggregate at that time: the 'central bank money stock', which consisted in large part of components of the money stock M1.

In addition to the difficulty of meeting the target, the application of monetary policy was flawed by the practice of using the actual outcomes as the starting point for the annual target range in the following year. Thus, after a year of strong overshooting, no correction was made in the new target range. This policy is difficult to reconcile with the medium-term orientation that underlies the quantity theory of money. In other words, the simple rule that could have been provided by monetary targeting was simply suspended. Instead of adjusting monetary policy to the direction that was indicated by that compass, the Bundesbank simple adjusted the needle of the compass.

Also difficult to reconcile with a medium-term orientation of monetary targeting are the permanent changes in the derivation of the target values. As Schächter (1999: 105–6) describes in detail, from 1974 to 1986 almost no year went by without a change in the concrete procedure for setting the target.

Thus, in retrospect one can form the impression that the Bundesbank was simply 'masquerading' (Bernanke *et al.* 1999: 330) its approach as one of monetary targeting. Nevertheless, especially in the German academic debate, monetary targeting still plays an important role. For instance, in its Annual Report 1999/2000, the German Council of Economic Experts urged the ECB to pursue a stringent monetary targeting in the tradition of the Bundesbank.[1]

This performance also raises the question of why the Bundesbank did not give up a strategy where it failed to meet the targets almost every second year. Immediately after the breakdown of the Bretton Woods system, it was understandable that the Bundesbank was looking for a 'simple rule'. But after the failure of the first four years, the continuation of the monetarist experiment is somewhat astonishing. The only plausible answer is that this approach served mainly a 'politico-economic function'. For an understanding of this function, one has to know that in general the Bundesbank was inclined to set its targets too low. From Table 8.1 we can see that the Bundesbank was assuming a decline in the velocity of money of about

---

[1] Sachverständigenrat (1999: para. 270).

½% until 1992, and from 1993 to 1998 the assumption was of a decline of 1%. But as Schächter (1999: 82) shows, the actual decline was 1.35% until 1990 and 2.08% after 1990.[2] Thus, the Bundesbank was systematically setting its targets too low. This is also confirmed by the fact that, in spite of a frequent overshooting of the targets, a sufficient degree of price stability could be attained in Germany.

The advantage of announcing targets with a downside bias is that they provide the central bank with a protective shield against political pressure. As we have seen in Chapter 6, there is always a risk that myopic politicians will exert pressure on central bankers to reduce interest rates. But if the monetary target indicates an overshooting of the money supply, the central bank can always argue that monetary conditions are already too expansionary so that a further interest rate reduction would definitively lead to inflation. While such a strategy provides some protection against external influences on monetary policy, it does not constrain the leeway of the central bank. The example of the Bundesbank shows that a central bank must then be able to point to the presence of 'special factors'. Monetary targeting can therefore be seen as an approach whereby a central bank can obtain additional independence from the politicians.

These reasons were discussed, above all, in connection with the massively restrictive policy pursued by the US central bank in the 1979–81 phase (Bernanke and Mishkin 1992). Monetary targeting in those years enabled the Fed to push through such a policy in the teeth of other political pressures. In fact, the Fed abandoned monetary targeting in 1982, when it had clearly achieved the goal of disinflation.

In Germany this kind of approach was particularly noticeable in the years following German reunification in the 1990s. Despite a sharp rise in the demand for 'transaction balances' in Eastern Germany, the Bundesbank made no significant alterations to the way it derived its money supply targets for the whole of Germany. The protective shield function of the money supply target was particularly evident in 1993, when, on account of the serious tensions that had built up within the EMS in the first half of 1993, the Bundesbank came under pressure both at home and abroad to cut its interest rates: it managed to avoid having to do so by pointing to the excessive expansion in the money supply. On the other hand, one month after the collapse of the system (end-July 1993) the Bundesbank embarked upon a steady series of interest rate reductions, although the money supply was still well above the target corridor.

---

[2] For the 'central bank money stock' which was used as the target aggregate until 1987 the decline was 0.79%, but until 1987 changes in velocity were not included in the potential formula.

There is not necessarily anything wrong with using the money supply approach as a protective shield; after all, it strengthens the political independence of the central bank and thus helps to achieve the ultimate goal of price stability. It is not without problems, however, since it means that

1. money supply targets are systematically set too low, which can create deflationary pressure;
2. targets are frequently missed, which can damage the transparency and—in the longer term—the credibility of monetary policy.

9.2.2. *What the Bundesbank really did*

As monetary targeting was not providing the 'simple rule' for the Bundesbank's policy, there must have been some other heuristic that guided the decisions of the Central Bank Council. As in other industrial countries the Taylor rule seems to have played an important role. The Bank itself presented an analysis which shows that, above all, after 1987 German interest rates followed rather closely a path that was determined by the Taylor rule (Deutsche Bundesbank 1999*a*). From Figure 9.1[3] one can see

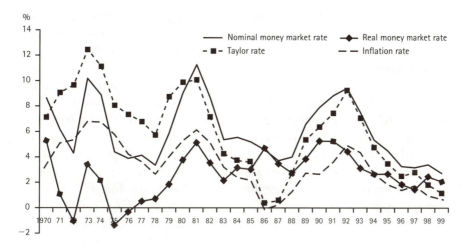

Figure 9.1. *The Taylor rule for Germany, 1970–1999*
Source: Own calculations based on data from IMF, *International Financial Statistics.*

---

[3] Figure 9.1 shows the behaviour of the Taylor interest rate for Germany if it is largely calculated using Taylor's original method. The inflation and output gaps are both given an equally high weighting of 0.5 and are entered simultaneously into the Taylor interest rate. The inflation rate is based on the (western German) consumer price index, and the inflation target is the upper limit of the 'unavoidable rate of inflation' (or, from 1985, the 'normative inflation') used by the Bundesbank in deriving the monetary targets. The output gap is based on the Bundesbank's potential estimation for western Germany.

that, in the 1970s and the first half of the 1980s, the Bundesbank's interest rates were always relatively close to the Taylor rule.

A more systematic analysis of the Bundesbank monetary policy is provided by reaction functions (see above all Clarida and Gertler 1996). A survey by Schächter (1999) shows, as a rather unanimous result of most studies, that the Bundesbank's interest rate decisions have been determined by

1. a high degree of interest-rate smoothing;
2. CPI inflation and inflation forecasts;
3. the exchange rate above all *vis-à-vis* the dollar;
4. US short-term interest rates;
5. real GDP growth or industrial production.

Compared with these factors, the growth rate of the money stock, although significant, did not play a major role in the Bundesbank's interest rate decisions.

9.3. THE MONETARY POLICY FRAMEWORK OF THE EUROPEAN CENTRAL BANK

When the ECB started its operations in January 1999, it was confronted with the difficult task of conducting monetary policy in a completely new environment. This implied an especially high degree of uncertainty about the transmission process (ECB 1999*a*: 45).

In the first place, as the regime shift to a common monetary policy was likely to change the way expectations are formed, there was a risk that empirical relationships between economic variables that have been estimated using data from the past might become unstable. Such changes were expected above all for the financial sector, where the impact of monetary union was most pronounced. As a consequence, the information content of monetary aggregates was lower than under normal conditions.

In addition, the creation of European Monetary Union had led to an entirely new economic area for which comprehensive and harmonized data had not previously been collected. A number of fully, or almost fully, harmonized series become available just at the beginning of monetary union (monetary data, the balance of payments data, the Harmonized Index of Consumer Prices). As these euro area-wide statistics are based, in part, on new concepts, the properties of the series were not well known.

In its own analysis of the Taylor rule, the Bundesbank (1999*a*) uses an average real short-term rate of 3.4%. This value corresponds to the period 1979(I)–1998(IV). Compared with the values in Table 8.3, the Bundesbank's estimates are relatively high.

As the concrete definition of the ECB's final target has already been described (Section 5.1.2), this chapter will focus on the monetary policy framework that the ECB has developed in order to achieve its target. In its own view, the ECB has developed a completely new strategy which it calls 'stability-oriented monetary policy strategy':

The Eurosystem's stability-oriented monetary policy ... is a new and distinct strategy, which reflects the unique circumstances and institutional environment that will face the Eurosystem. (ECB 1999*a*: 50)

Basically, the ECB's approach rests on two pillars:

1. The first pillar is provided by a 'reference value' for the money stock M3, with which the ECB intends to assign a 'prominent role' to money and which can be regarded as a weak form of monetary targeting.
2. As the second pillar, the ECB has established a 'broadly based assessment of the outlook of price developments'. While one could think that this pillar has some affinity to the concept of inflation targeting, we will see that the ECB does not subscribe to this view.

9.3.1. *A reference value for the money stock M3*

In contrast to the Bundesbank, the ECB has not decided to pursue an outright monetary targeting. This can be explained by the fact that, of the two requirements for an intermediate target, only one is met in the euro area. As far as the control of inflation by the money stock is concerned, the ECB states:

... substantial or prolonged deviations of monetary growth from the reference value would, under normal circumstances, signal risks to price stability of the medium term. (ECB 1999*a*: 48)

The problematic issue is the control of the money stock M3 with short-term interest rates.[4] Here, the ECB concedes:

... the euro area monetary aggregate for which the reference value is announced does not need to be controllable in the short run, using a short-term interest rate influenced closely by the Eurosystem. (ECB 1999*a*: 48)

Consequently, the ECB decided to adopt only a weak form of monetary targeting in the form of a 'reference value' for the money stock M3. The

---

[4] This is different for the money stock M1 which, according to the ECB, is 'controllable using short-term nominal interest rates' (ECB 1999*a*:. 48). However, this aggregate has the disadvantage that the second condition for an intermediate is not met. According to the ECB (1999*a*: 48), 'euro area narrow money ... exhibited neither stability nor significant indicator properties for the price level'.

rationale of a 'reference value' is explained by the ECB as follows:

However, the concept of a reference value does not entail a commitment on the part of the Eurosystem to correct deviations of monetary growth from the reference value over the short term. Interest rates will not be changed 'mechanistically' in response to such deviations in an attempt to return monetary growth to the reference value. (ECB 1999*a*: 48)

Thus, one could say that the ECB uses the monetary growth not as intermediate target, but as a 'prominent' indicator of medium-term risks for price stability. However, a main problem of this approach is the low quality of monetary growth rates if they are used as the single indicator of price stability.[5] Figure 9.2 shows that especially since 1995 the growth rate of M3 is not very closely related to the inflation rate in the euro area.

As far as the derivation of the reference value is concerned, we have already seen (Table 8.1) that the ECB has completely adopted the Bundesbank's potential formula and even the concrete values of its determinants. In contrast to the Bundesbank, the ECB does not formulate the reference value in the form of a target corridor: instead, it compares a three-month moving average of annual growth of M3 with its reference value.

While there are some minor differences between the ECB's and the Bundesbank's approach,[6] they both share the problem that they have not been designed as a medium-term benchmark. In the case of the Bundesbank, this was due to annual targets and the practice of the base shifts, i.e. the use of actual values instead of normative values as the starting base for the subsequent year (see Section 9.2). In the case of the ECB, the medium-term orientation gets lost because of the comparison with annual growth rates. As a result, an excessive monetary growth in one year will simply grow out of the data as soon as twelve months have passed. Therefore, the only consequent application of a reference value would be a comparison with long-term monetary growth rates. In other words, the present practice of the ECB is not compatible with the aim of identifying medium-term risks to price stability.

In the actual monetary policy of the ECB, the influence of the monetary pillar cannot be easily identified. As already mentioned, the main problem of this approach is the confusion about the interest rate elasticity of M3. The ECB and many of its watchers erroneously believe in a negative elasticity of M3 in regard to short-term interest rates. But this is simply wrong

---

[5] See Gerlach and Svensson (1999). Svensson (1999*c*: 34) states: 'It is easily shown ... that such a money-growth indicator will be a relatively useless indicator of risks to price stability and, indeed, mostly a noisy indicator of the deviation of current inflation from the inflation target.'

[6] Above all, the ECB's reference value lacks a target range.

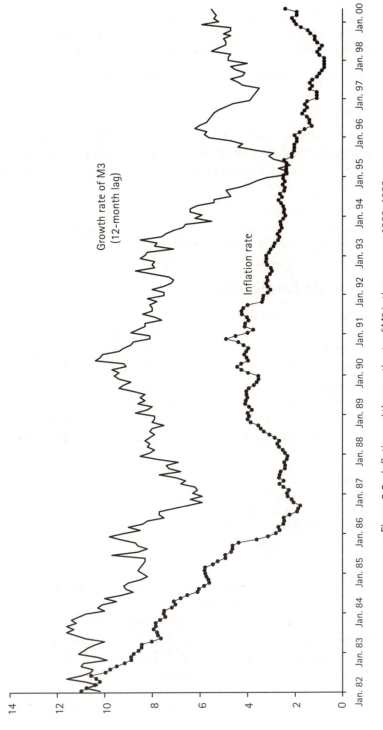

Figure 9.2. *Inflation and the growth rate of M3 in the euro area: 1982–1999*
Source: European Central Bank.

(see Section 2.5). Therefore the first interest rate decision of the ECB, a reduction of interest rates in April 1999, when the monetary growth rate was about one percentage point above the reference value, was

- incorrect as far as the ECB's understanding of the interest elasticity is concerned, and
- correct as far as the true elasticity is concerned.

In the following decisions to increase interest rates, the ECB always emphasized the negative impact of short-term interest rates on the growth rate of money. For instance, at a press conference on 6 July 2000, Duisenberg made the following statement:

The increase in ECB interest rates on 8 June—in conjunction with the interest rate increases made since November 1999—exerts a moderating influence on both money and credit growth. (Duisenberg 2000)

9.3.2. *A broadly based assessment*

At first sight, this second pillar seems to be identical with an inflation forecast by the ECB with a confidence band. However, the ECB tries to avoid that term 'forecast', although it is not clear why an 'assessment of the outlook for price developments' should be qualitatively different from an 'inflation forecast'.

This assessment is based on 'a wide range of economic indicators' which 'will include many variables that have leading indicator properties for future price developments' (ECB 1999*a*: 49). They 'include inter alia':

- wages,
- the exchange rate,
- bond prices and the yield curve,
- various measures of real activity,
- fiscal policy indicators,
- price and cost indices and
- business and consumer surveys. (ECB 1999*a*: 49)

It is somewhat astonishing that this pillar does not include monetary data (money stocks and/or the short-term interest rate). Of course, the ECB could argue that this information is already processed by the first pillar, but it is nevertheless difficult to understand how an assessment of future price developments can be made without such indicators, and how the relationship of the two indicators is to be interpreted.

The presentation of this 'assessment' by the ECB looks very much like a 'look at everything strategy' (Bernanke *et al.* 1999: 22). This would not be objectionable, but in this case this pillar could not be regarded as a major contribution to the transparency of the ECB. It would simply state what is obvious: the ECB wants to take into account all information that is relevant for future price developments.

9.3.3. *The ECB lacks a clear policy framework*

In Chapter 8 we saw that a policy framework serves two main purposes. By reducing the complexity of the reality to a set of relatively 'simple rules', it helps

1. to facilitate internal decision processes of a central bank, and
2. to structure the dialogue with the public which contributes to the transparency, accountability, and hence credibility of monetary policy.

The discussion of both pillars of the ECB's stability-oriented monetary policy strategy shows that this strategy is at the same time both too narrow and too general to serve as a framework that could fulfil these two functions. While the first pillar pays too much attention to monetary growth, the second pillar simply states that the ECB will look at all relevant factors. In addition, it is not clear what has to be done if the two pillars give contradicting signals.

Additional confusion has been created by the publication of the ECB's staff projection for the inflation rate in December 2000 (ECB 2000*d*). In contrast to the practice of inflation-targeting countries, the ECB Board has not endorsed this projection. The Board commented on this projection as follows:

macroeconomic projections do not cover all the information pertaining to the second pillar and do not take into account the information relating to the analysis under the first pillar of the ECB's monetary policy strategy. From this perspective, the staff projections play a useful but limited role in the strategy. (ECB 2000*d*: 6)

This raises the question of what information pertaining to the second pillar is not used in macroeconomic projections and for what reasons. Similarly, if the standard macroeconomic models do not take into account monetary growth rates, one has to ask whether this is a flaw of these models or whether the ECB is paying too much attention to this indicator. In any case, the half-hearted inclusion of an important element of inflation targeting into the ECB strategy has not increased the transparency of its policy.

It seems relatively obvious that the ECB needs a more coherent policy framework. Above all, the monetary pillar should be integrated into the 'broadly based assessment'. As this would lead to a single-pillar approach, the 'broadly based assessment' would have to become more informative

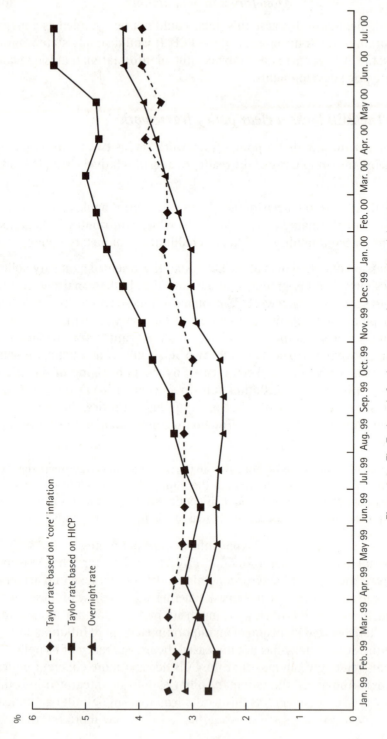

Figure 9.3. *The Taylor rule for the euro area, January 1999–July 2000*
Source: Own calculations based on data from European Central Bank.

than now. While many critics encourage the ECB to adopt the inflation targeting framework of the Bank of England (Buiter 1999; Svensson 2000*b*), this approach would not substantially reduce the transparency deficit. As Section 8.4 has shown, inflation targeting looks like a 'simple rule', but the complexity reappears when the central bank has to produce the inflation forecast. As an alternative, the ECB should consider a framework that attributes a 'prominent role' to private inflation expectations. The ECB is already publishing such data in its *Monthly Bulletin.* In a revamped stability-oriented monetary policy strategy, data on inflation expectations could be surveyed and analysed in a more regular and more systematic way than this is done today.

The ambiguity of the ECB's strategy raises the question of how the ECB takes its interest rate decisions. At the moment the experience with the ECB is still relatively limited, so that no definitive answer can be given. But there are some indications that the Taylor rule—in the same way as in the case of the Bundesbank—provides a relatively good explanation of the level and of the changes in the ECB's interest rates. Figure 9.3 shows that the repo rate in the euro area has always been relatively close to a Taylor rate on the basis of the core inflation rate for the euro area, an inflation target of 2%, and an assumed average short-term rate of 2.8%. As Gerlach and Schnabel (1999: 4) show, with such a policy the ECB does not 'deviate much from past (weighted) interest rate behaviour in the countries forming the EMU area'.

9.4. THE MONETARY POLICY FRAMEWORK OF THE FEDERAL RESERVE SYSTEM

9.4.1. *Lack of an announced policy framework*

Compared with the Bundesbank, the Bank of England (and other inflation targeters), and the ECB, the US Federal Reserve System has made relatively little efforts to provide the public with a clearly defined monetary policy framework. An attempt at monetary targeting in the years 1979–82 had to be given up because of a strong instability in the money demand in a period of rapid financial innovation (see Section 2.6 and Bernanke and Mishkin 1992). Today the Fed openly admits that it pursues an 'eclectic approach':

All of the guides to monetary policy ... have something to do with the transmission of monetary policy to the economy. As such, they have certain advantages. However, none has shown a consistently close enough relationship with the ultimate goals of monetary policy that it can be relied upon single-mindedly. As a consequence, makers of monetary policy have tended to use a broad range of indicators ... to judge trends in the economy and to assess the stance of monetary policy. Such an eclectic approach enables the Federal Reserve to use all available information in conducting policy. This may be especially necessary as market structures and economic processes change in ways that affect the usefulness of any single indicator. However, communicating policy intentions and actions to the public can be more difficult with the eclectic approach than with the approach, for example, of targeting the money stock if the linkage between the money stock and the economy were fairly close and reliable. (Board of Governors 1994: 25)[7]

This does not mean that the monetary policy of the Federal Reserve System has been or is made on a completely ad-hoc basis.

9.4.2. *The implicit rules of the Fed's interest rate policy*

The intensive research on monetary policy rules shows that there are at least rough guidelines that determine the Fed's interest rate decisions. It has already been mentioned that the Taylor rule had been discovered as an attempt to describe the path of short-term interest rates in the period 1987–92 (Taylor 1993). A study by Clarida *et al.* (2000) provides a comprehensive framework for the analysis of the period 1960(I)–1996(IV). The authors use a backward-locking Taylor rule which is formulated as follows:[8]

$$i_t^* = \hat{i} + \beta(\pi_{t-1} - \pi^*) + \gamma\left(\frac{Y_{t-1} - Y^*}{Y^*}\right), \tag{9.1}$$

where i^* is the interest rate target of the central bank. If (9.1) is formulated in terms of real interest rates (which implies that the nominal interest rate is deflated with the inflation rate of one period ahead), we get

$$r_t^* = R + (\beta - 1)(\pi_{t-1} - \pi^*) + \gamma\left(\frac{Y_{t-1} - Y^*}{Y^*}\right). \tag{9.2}$$

Assuming interest rate smoothing (see Section 10.4), the central bank adjusts the actual interest rate i_t to the target value after some delay. Thus,

$$i_t = \rho(L)i_{t-1} + (1 - \rho)i^*, \tag{9.3}$$

where $\rho(L) = \rho_1 + \rho_2 L + \cdots + \rho_n L^{n-1}$, and where $\rho \equiv \rho(1)$. This leads to the following policy reaction function:

$$i_t = (1 - \rho)\left[R - (\beta - 1)\pi^* + \beta\pi_{t-1} + \gamma\left(\frac{Y_{t-1} - Y^*}{Y^*}\right)\right] + \rho(L)i_{t-1} + \varepsilon_t. \tag{9.4}$$

---

[7] See also Greenspan (1997).
[8] Clarida *et al.* (2000) mainly use a forward-looking Taylor rule. But their results are similar for both the forward-looking and the backward-looking rule.

Table 9.4. *A monetary policy reaction function for the United States*

	π^*	β	γ	ρ
Pre-Volcker	5.95	0.86	0.39	0.68
(1960–79)	(1.92)	(0.07)	(0.08)	(0.05)
Volcker–Greenspan	4.08	1.72	0.34	0.71
(1979–96)	(0.56)	(0.28)	(0.19)	(0.05)
Post-1982	2.96	2.55	−0.15	0.89
	(0.27)	(0.56)	(0.28)	(0.03)

Source: Clarida *et al.* (2000, Table VI); standard errors are reported in brackets. The set of instruments include four lags of inflation, output gap, the federal funds rate, the short–long spread, and commodity price inflation.

The estimated results are shown in Table 9.4. The results provide a very instructive description of the Federal Reserve's monetary policy over the 1960s–1990s. They show first of all that there was a significant difference in the way monetary policy was conducted pre- and post-1979. First, the target inflation rate was significantly higher in the first than in the second period. Second, the value of β is significantly less than 1 in the pre-Volcker phase and far greater than 1 in the Volcker–Greenspan phase. This has important implications for the response of monetary policy to inflationary shocks. With $\beta < 1$, the central bank reacted to an increase in the inflation rate with a smaller increase in the nominal interest rate so that the real interest rate was lowered by inflation. Thus, a destabilizing process was set in motion.

This was different in the Volcker–Greenspan period, where the nominal interest rate was raised by more than the increase in inflation so that the real interest rate was increased, too. These results thus 'lend quantitative support to the popular view that not until Volcker took office did controlling inflation become the organizing focus of monetary policy' (Clarida *et al.* 2000: 148).

As far as the stabilization of output gaps is concerned, an activist approach ($\gamma > 0$) can be observed for the pre-Volcker era, while for the post-1982 period the output gap has the wrong sign and is no longer significant. As we already observed for the reaction function of the Bundesbank, the high values for ρ show that interest-rate smoothing has played an important role in the Fed's considerations. This strategy has clearly become more important over time, especially if one excludes the rather turbulent period from 1979 to 1982, where the Fed practised a monetary targeting that lead to a strong interest rate volatility.[9]

---

[9] There is still a controversy whether the Fed used the monetary base or the short-term interest rate as its operating target in that period; see Goodfriend (1991) and Bernanke and Mihov (1998).

The results provide no clear indication that the output gap has been an important determinant of the Fed's interest rate policy after 1979. In fact, there have been major deviations of US interest rates from the normative path set by the Taylor rate, especially before 1987 and 1992, i.e. the period for which Taylor estimated this rule.

9.4.3. *The dangers of activism*

The dismal performance of the Fed's monetary policy in the period before 1979 raises the question of whether a better outcome would have been possible if the Fed had known and followed the Taylor rule. This issue has been discussed intensively by Orphanides (2000). He shows that, with a Taylor rule and the data that are available today, an activist monetary policy would indeed have led to better outcomes, both in terms of inflation and in terms of output stabilization. However, he points out that the data that were available when the decisions had to be made differ considerably from the final data. This concerns above all the output gap data. The very negative output gaps that were recorded in the early 1970s have almost vanished in many revisions of the data. As a consequence, the actual interest rates are more or less compatible with the values that can be obtained from a Taylor rule using real-time data. In other words, in the period of the 1970s, the inflation rate would have been exactly the same. Orphanides therefore comes to the following conclusion:

If policymakers could be confident that they can correctly assess the economy's potential, then activist policies might indeed be sensible. But if policymakers believe the data at present are as likely to yield an unreliable indication of the present economic situation as history over the past thirty years suggests, then it is best to avoid activist policies altogether. (Orphanides 2000: 33)

This raises the question of alternative approaches. A relatively obvious alternative is a Taylor rule with $\gamma = 0$, i.e. a rule that sets the nominal interest without taking into account the output gap. Orphanides calls this *inflation targeting*. This approach avoids a $\beta < 1$ and at the same time is not influenced by output gap measurements. In Section 8.5, we argued that in situations with demand shocks such a rule leads in principle to the same results as the original Taylor rule. Figure 9.4 shows that Orphanides is right if he states that this rule 'would have called for a significantly tighter policy during most of the Great Inflation period'. As a result, the inflation performance would have been much better.

But then, all other alternatives would have also been affected by these measurement problems. As far as *nominal income targeting* is concerned,

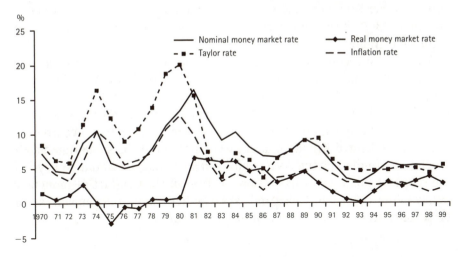

Figure 9.4. *The Taylor rule for the United States, 1970–1999*
Source: Own calculations based on data from IMF, *International Financial Statistics.*

overly optimistic estimates about potential output growth in the second half of the 1960s would have also led to excessive nominal income targets. This problem is completely neglected by Orphanides's analysis of this alternative. The same applies to monetary targeting. From the Bundesbank's potential formula we have seen that the growth rate of potential output is a main determinant of the monetary target. Again, the measurement errors would have led to an overly expansionary monetary policy in the United States.

Thus, if policy-makers are afraid of measurement problems concerning the output, the choice is not between activist and non-activist policies, but between rules that are determined by the real side of the real economy and rules that are determined by the inflation rate only.

9.5. THE MONETARY POLICY FRAMEWORK OF THE BANK OF JAPAN

9.5.1. *The overall performance*

As Table 9.2 shows, the overall performance of the Bank of Japan's monetary policy in the last two decades is more or less in line with the results that were achieved by the Bundesbank and the Federal Reserve. However, this positive outcome is due mainly to developments in the 1980s; in the

1990s the performance of the Japanese economy deteriorated markedly, and in 1993–9 the outcome was worse than in all other areas that are included in Table 9.2.

After the successful and dynamic development in the 1970s and the 1980s, this dismal performance of Japan in the 1990s is especially astonishing. The asset price 'bubble' in the second half of the 1980s is very often regarded as the main reason for the problems of the following years. But this leaves the question why bubbles of similar size that occurred in Finland, the United Kingdom, and Sweden at about the same time had a much more limited effect. As a comprehensive analysis would go beyond the scope of this book, this section focuses on the conduct of monetary policy in the 1980s and 1990s and asks whether major policy mistakes can be detected in this specific area of monetary policy.

9.5.2. *Domestic issues of monetary policy*

The Taylor rule provides a rough description of the main periods of Japanese monetary policy. Figure 9.5 shows that in 1973, immediately after the breakdown of the Bretton Woods system, nominal interest rates were far too low, so that real interest rates became negative for the years 1974–8. As a consequence, inflation reached high levels, especially in the years following the first oil price shock (1973–5). In the 1980s the stance of monetary policy was relatively restrictive, with nominal interest rates above the reference values for the Taylor rule. In the years 1989–95 the

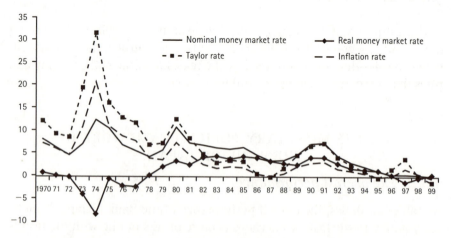

Figure 9.5. *The Taylor rule for Japan, 1970–1999*
Source: Own calculations based on data from IMF, *International Financial Statistics.*

Taylor rule provides a very good explanation of the Bank of Japan's interest rate policy. Since 1995, the level of short-term interest rates has been close to zero ('zero interest rate policy') and below the level of the Taylor rule, which indicates that the Bank of Japan has been trying to exert a strong monetary stimulus to the deflationary economy.

From this purely domestic perspective, it is not clear *a priori* that monetary policy can be regarded as a main cause of the bubble[10] or of the deflation in the 1990s. This becomes obvious if one compares the deviations from the Taylor rule in the three G3 countries. Figure 9.5 shows that the monetary policy in the period 1984–8 cannot be regarded as especially expansionary. The only monetary explanation for the bubble are the historically (at that date) low *nominal* short-term and long-term interest rates. The long-term rates in particular were very low throughout the years 1986–9, at only about 5% in nominal terms and with government bond yields of only 4.2%–4.3% in 1987/8. The low level of long-term rates is also reflected in a negative yield spread (difference between long-term and short-term interest rates) in 1985 and 1986. This can be explained by the swing in the international perception of the G3 currencies in February 1985. From January 1980 until that date, the dollar had been appreciating considerably *vis-à-vis* the Deutschmark and the yen. After February 1985 international investors preferred the yen and the Deutschmark, which reduced bond yields, especially in Japan.

The very small deviation from the Taylor rate during the years 1989–95 is another factor indicating that it was not a policy mistake by the Bank of Japan that was the cause of the deflationary tendencies in the 1990s.

9.5.3. *The exchange rate problem*

While it is difficult to explain the negative performance of the Japanese economy with domestic monetary indicators, a completely different picture emerges if one looks at the exchange rate of the yen. Figure 9.6 shows the real exchange rate on the basis of unit labour costs for the yen, the dollar, pound sterling, and the Deutschmark. By 1985 the yen started to appreciate in real terms. A second and stronger wave of real appreciation occurred in the period 1990–5. A third wave occurred in 1998–9. Figure 9.6 shows that neither Germany nor the United States was confronted with a similarly strong real appreciation. Figure 9.7 shows that the waves of real appreciation were associated with a negative export performance

---

[10] For a comprehensive analysis, see Okina *et al.* (2000) and Hoffmaister and Schinasi (1994).

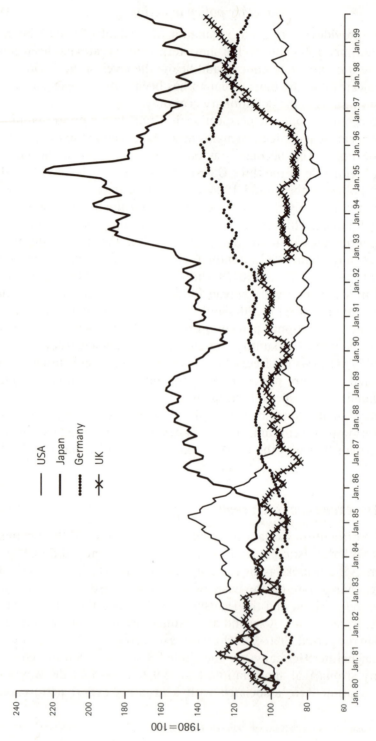

Figure 9.6. *Real effective exchange rates, USA, Japan, Germany, and United Kingdom, 1980–1999, by month: unit labour costs (1980 = 100). Increase shows a real appreciaton*

Source: IMF, *International Financial Statistics.*

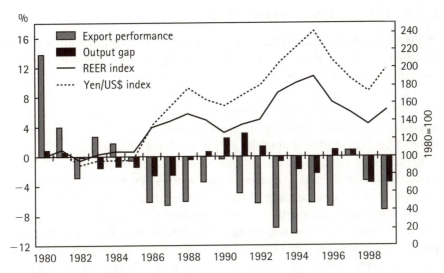

Figure 9.7. *Real exchange rates and export performance in Japan, 1980–1998*
The export performance and the output gap are measured in percentages and are
depicted on the left-hand scale; the indices of the REER based on normalized unit
labour costs and the nominal yen–US$ exchange rate are depicted on the right-hand
scale (1980 = 100). An upward movement corresponds to an appreciation.
Source: OECD, *Economic Outlook.*

(Japanese export growth minus growth of Japanese export markets) and
with the emergence of negative output gaps.

Thus, the negative performance of the Japanese economy in the 1990s
is not so much a problem of an inadequate domestic interest policy, as
the effect of an uncontrolled real appreciation which occurred at exactly
that time.[11] Because of the 'pricing-to-market' strategy of Japanese manufacturing firms (Marston 1990; Klitgaard 1999), profit margins declined
and investment conditions deteriorated. The ongoing exchange rate instability remains a serious impediment to a strong recovery of the Japanese
economy. This exchange-rate-based explanation of the Japanese slump
seems more convincing than an attempt to attribute the dismal performance of Japan throughout the 1990s to an asset bubble that occurred in
1987–90.

In Chapter 13 we will see that it would have been possible to limit the real
appreciation of the yen in the 1990s. In fact, the Bank of Japan has inter-
vened heavily and successfully in 1999–2000 to prevent the yen–dollar
exchange rate falling below the level of 100 yen per dollar.

---

[11] See also McKinnon and Ohno (2000).

9.5.4. *The conceptual approaches*

While the Taylor rule allows us to explain the path of nominal interest rates in Japan, the Bank of Japan has never been very explicit about its concrete conceptual approach to monetary policy. In the last few years, the 'zero interest rate policy' has reflected more the state of emergency in the Japanese economy than a clear concept for monetary policy.[12] Thus, in its conceptual approach the monetary policy in Japan is closer to the model of the Federal Reserve System than to that of the ECB or the Bank of England.

It should be mentioned that in the 1970s and 1980s the Bank of Japan, like other central banks, had operated with a weak form of monetary targeting.[13] The monetary aggregate it chose was money supply M2 + CD,[14] which, empirical studies suggest, best fulfilled the conditions of an intermediate target. There are two features about monetary targeting that were peculiar to Japan. First, the Bank of Japan described the rates it announced not as intermediate targets in the strict sense, but simply as 'forecasts'. In fact, since the forecasts included both past monetary policy measures and future intentions, they accurately reflected the money supply that the Bank of Japan is prepared to allow and therefore, functionally speaking, they are no different from an intermediate target (Suzuki 1987: 331).

The second feature concerns the way in which the forecast was formulated. In the first month of every quarter, the Bank of Japan announced a forecast for the rate of change in M2 + CD in the current quarter compared with that for the same period in the previous year. In other words, at the time of the money supply projection, three-quarters of the growth in the money supply had already occurred. This particular method of formulating the forecast automatically makes it highly probable that the projections will be fulfilled (Argy *et al.* 1990: 45). Added to this, the Bank of Japan set either a corridor of ±0.5 percentage point or an absolute value which was only meant to be met approximately.

It is therefore not particularly surprising that projections of money supply growth have been almost 100% accurate. Since in the last analysis they only reflected the established trend, however, they could not provide the kind of long-term orientation that monetary targeting is intended to achieve.

---

[12] For a survey of the monetary policy in the 1990s, see Mori *et al.* (2000).

[13] 'In order to achieve price stability and to strive for the appropriate development of the economy, it will be necessary to pay sufficient attention in the future to the movements of M2 in the management of monetary policy' (Bank of Japan statement of 1975; in Suzuki 1987: 328).

[14] M2 + CD consists of notes and coin in circulation, sight and time deposits, and certificates of deposit; see also Chapter 1.

Nevertheless, as a result of a strong process of financial liberalization and innovation, the Bank of Japan decided in the 1990s to downplay the role of monetary targeting in its monetary policy framework:

What is required in the final analysis is a thorough examination of a multiplicity of economic data, such as monetary aggregates, lending figures and other quantitative monetary indicators, information regarding actual corporate finances and profits, and information on trends in the asset markets. (Mieno 1993: 11)

9.6. THE MONETARY POLICY FRAMEWORK OF THE BANK OF ENGLAND

9.6.1. *The overall performance*

Compared with the three other central banks discussed so far, monetary policy in the United Kingdom is characterized

1. by an impressive variety of conceptual approaches since 1973 and
2. by the fact that the United Kingdom is a relatively open economy with a foreign trade share of GDP of 21%[15] compared with values of around 10% for the United States, Japan, and the euro area.

As Table 9.2 shows, the overall performance of the Bank of England has not been very good in the last two decades. However, it has improved markedly since 1992. Before describing the most important episodes of the Bank's monetary policy since 1973, it is useful to assess this policy in terms of the Taylor rule. Figure 9.8 shows that in the 1970s nominal interest rates were much too low compared with the reference values calculated by any version of the Taylor rule. The diagnosis of an inflationary monetary policy also becomes evident, by the fact that the real short-term interest rate was negative in almost all of the 1970s. As a result, from 1974 to 1981 inflation was almost always in double-digit figures. A major policy change can be observed only in 1982, when real short-term rates reached a level that was significantly positive. After a long period of rather high inflation, it took more than a decade for the Bank of England to bring inflation definitively down to acceptable levels in 1993.

9.6.2. *The Bank of England's different conceptual approaches*

As in all industrial countries, the collapse of the Bretton Woods system and the high inflation rates of the early 1970s necessitated a reorientation of

[15] Measured as $\frac{1}{2}$(exports + imports)/GDP.

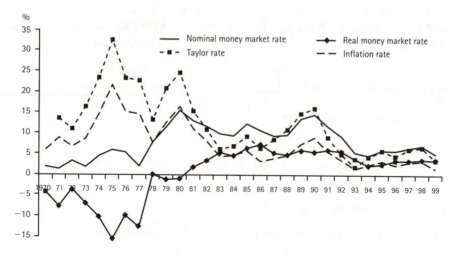

Figure 9.8. *The Taylor rule for the United Kingdom, 1970–1999*
Source: Own calculations based on data from IMF, *International Financial Statistics.*

monetary policy in the United Kingdom. In the first few years of that decade the Bank of England pursued a rather *dirigiste* approach, which was based on the so-called 'Corset' (Supplementary Special Deposit Scheme). This laid down upper limits on deposit growth at the commercial banks and punished banks that exceeded the limit by requiring them to hold non-interest-bearing deposits at the Bank of England (Roth 1989: 143). For those banks seeking to maximize their profits, this drastic regulation of the liabilities side of the banks' balance sheets naturally affected assets side. Until 1979 the UK also maintained restrictive exchange controls.

In July 1976 the Bank of England for the first time announced a target value for the growth in M3.[16] Only a year later, the Bank changed over to the intermediate target aggregate Sterling M3 (£M3), which in contrast to M3 did not include private-sector foreign currency deposits. Despite the strict regulation of credit and money supply growth under the Corset, the money supply targets were almost never reached, and sometimes the deviations were quite high.

In 1979 the incoming Conservative government removed exchange restrictions and the Corset. It also sought to continue monetary targeting

[16] In fact, the BoE first experimented with quantitative targets as far back as 1967, when the UK was forced, as a result of balance of payments difficulties, to utilize short-term drawing facilities at the IMF (Argy *et al.* 1990: 47). These were granted subject to certain conditions regarding domestic credit expansion, which, in the system of fixed exchange rates, was to be accompanied by the required effective control of monetary growth (Minford 1992: 421).

as part of its Medium-Term Financial Strategy.[17] For this purpose the Bank of England, while continuing to announce monetary targets, also introduced the following measures.[18]

1. In addition to the annual intermediate targets, three-to four-year intermediate targets were set, which were, however, revised after two years at the latest.
2. From 1982 to 1984, target values were announced not only for £M3, but also for M1 and PSL2 (private sector liquidity), although this did nothing to increase the success rate in meeting the targets.
3. From 1984 to 1987, the Bank of England again changed the intermediate target aggregates and announced targets for £M3 and the monetary base (M0). From 1987 the monetary base was the only target aggregate used. However, conceptually this is not a true money supply aggregate. Since the monetary base is controlled as an operating target directly by the central bank, it cannot perform the function of an intermediate target.
4. In addition to its monetary targets, the Bank in 1987–8 tried to hold the sterling exchange rate *vis-à-vis* the Deutschmark below a threshold of DM 3. This required a reduction of the real and nominal interest rates, which caused another surge of inflation.

All in all, and in spite of the many adjustments, the monetary targets were quite often missed. Thus, the policy pursued by the Bank of England during these years bears little resemblance to the ideal of a medium-term-oriented strategy. The frequent changes in the target variable, target period, and values and the use of several target aggregates indicate that the Bank's monetary policy operations were not determined by the pursuit of a target path for monetary expansion that was stable over the medium term. But in fact, in a period of far-reaching financial innovation this would not even have been desirable, since there was no longer a stable correlation between the intermediate target—however the particular money supply aggregate was defined—and the ultimate goal of price level stability.

While monetary targeting had little impact on the Bank of England's interest rate decisions in the 1980s, it seems that the Bank—like all other central banks—must have been guided by some form of Taylor rule. Figure 9.8 shows a rather good explanation of the nominal short-term rate by the Taylor rule in the period from 1983 until today.

[17] In addition, the Medium-Term Financial Strategy included reducing the budget deficit and abandoning incomes policy (Minford 1992: 408).

[18] Up to 1992, the BoE's ultimate target included nominal GDP as well as the inflation rate. From 1982 an inflation target of under 5% was aimed at. The authorities rejected a lower rate on the grounds that this would slow down economic growth and the decline in unemployment (Minford 1992: 414).

Officially, the policy of monetary targeting was ended only with sterling's brief membership of the EMS Exchange Rate Mechanism (ERM) from October 1990 to September 1992. In that period the Bank of England had adopted a nominal exchange rate target *vis-à-vis* the Deutschmark as the intermediate target of its monetary policy. Figure 9.8 shows that the years 1990–2 were characterized by an unavoidable disinflation policy in the United Kingdom. In the public perception, the output costs of this disinflation were attributed mainly to ERM membership. Thus, in the ERM crisis of September 1992, which would have required a renewed increase in interest rates, the British government decided to leave the system and to pursue a domestically oriented monetary policy.

The conceptual framework of this policy is inflation targeting, which has been presented in Section 8.4. The inflation target was set for the retail price index excluding mortgage interest rates (RPIX). From December 1992 until the May 1997 elections the target range was 1%–4%. From July 1997 the target has been defined as a point target of 2.5 with a corridor of ±1%. Since December 1992 the Bank has always been able to meet its inflation target.

In the period of inflation targeting, the short-term nominal interest rate path can again be traced with the standard Taylor rule. A major problem of the Bank of England's monetary policy in the second half of the 1990s is its almost complete neglect of the sterling exchange rate *vis-à-vis* the euro. From 1995 to 2000, strong capital inflows led to a real appreciation of the pound by more than 40% (See Figure 9.6), which caused a serious contraction of the manufacturing sector.

10

The Instruments of Monetary Policy

What this chapter is about

- It starts with a general discussion of monetary policy instruments and presents a minimalist set of instruments that is required for the two alternative operating targets: the short-term money market rate and the monetary base.
- On this basis it discusses the toolbox of the European Central Bank, the Federal Reserve System, the Bank of Japan, and the Bank of England. A comprehensive survey for other countries is found in Borio (1997) and BIS (1999).
- It concludes that all central banks are able to control their operating target but that they apply too many instruments and overly complicated operating procedures which make the process of monetary policy unduly intransparent.

10.1. BASIC REQUIREMENTS

It is obvious that the monetary policy instruments have to be designed in such a way as to allow an efficient realization above all of the operating targets. If this is done, the operating targets can be set according to the 'simple rules' discussed in Chapter 9 or according to the values that have been calculated with elaborate macroeconomic models. We have seen that, with the exception of McCallum's rule (see Section 8.6.3.2), in all 'simple rules' the short-term interest rate is regarded as the only operating target. This also applies to the more sophisticated approach of inflation forecasts which has been proposed by Svensson (1999b).

Apart from this general requirement, the set of instruments used by a central bank must also satisfy the following criteria.

1. The banks must be continually supplied with the monetary base (*continuous funding*) that they need for the provision of currency to their customers, for their working balances, and, if required, for their minimum reserves at the central bank.
2. As all central banks operate in an open economy, they cannot be completely indifferent to changes in exchange rates (see Part III). Thus, there will always be occasions when it might be useful to intervene on the foreign exchange market. As such interventions have an immediate

impact on the monetary base, an exchange rate policy can only be compatible with the domestically oriented interest rate policy if a central bank is to be able to 'sterilize' such effects of interventions on the monetary base. Since the amount of foreign exchange market intervention can build up very rapidly,[1] a central bank needs to have as high a 'sterilization potential' as possible.

3. Monetary policy instruments should be designed in a way that they create a relationship of dependency between the banks and the central bank. This is an arguable *raison d'être* for the minimum reserves. It could become especially important if future advances made in the automation of payments ('electronic cash') were to lead to a massive decline in the total amount of cash held.

As a more general requirement, it is important that the free functioning of financial markets is not distorted by monetary policy instruments. Given the negligible transaction costs involved in money and capital market operations, it can be assumed that any monetary policy intervention by the central bank that runs counter to market conditions will result in a substantial switching to other segments of a country's financial market[2] or to foreign markets. This fundamental requirement has been widely acknowledged in the 1980s and 1990s, with the result that most instruments with a distorting character have been abolished or at least reduced.

- *Interest rate ceilings* for deposits or loans were very common in the 1960s and 1970s. The best-known example was Regulation Q in the United States, which was revoked in the early 1980s. In Germany all interest rate controls were lifted as early as 1967.
- *Quantitative restrictions* on the banks' operations, particularly lending ceilings, played an important role in the monetary policy arsenal of the Bank of England until 1979.
- *Minimum reserves* are still in use in some areas, but the reserve ratios have been substantially reduced and the design of the system has become more market-oriented, above all by remunerating minimum reserve balances with a market interest rate.

In many countries this process was accompanied and even furthered by the wide-ranging liberalization of capital movements that took place towards the end of the 1980s. It is clear that monetary policy instruments

---

[1] In the ERM crisis of September 1992, the expansion in the German monetary base caused by intervention operations came to almost DM93 billion. In July 1993 it amounted to DM60 billion (Deutsche Bundesbank 1992, 1993).

[2] This process was often euphemistically referred to as 'financial innovation'.

that run counter to market conditions can work properly only if a country's financial market is effectively sealed off from the outside world. Otherwise, private individuals are able to circumvent domestic regulations by investing their funds on the euromarket[3] or borrowing from foreign banks. If such an avoidance is possible, market-incompatible instruments not only fail to achieve the desired monetary policy effect, but also place the domestic banking system at a considerable competitive disadvantage.

Similarly, all instruments that result in a central bank entering into direct competition with the banks should also be rejected on the grounds that they interfere with market processes. Thus, for example, it would be problematic for a central bank to offer short-term money market paper to non-banks. In order to be sure of selling such paper, the central bank would have to make the terms at least as attractive as those of paper issued by the banks. As soon as the volume of such operations assumed a significant size, they would have a direct influence on the banks' short-term deposit rates, which in normal circumstances ought to be determined exclusively by market mechanisms. The Bundesbank, which began issuing Bundesbank liquidity paper (*Bundesliquiditätspapiere*) or 'Bulis' in March 1993, partly with the intention of selling them to private investors, fairly soon decided to restrict sales to banks and foreign investors, in particular central banks.

10.2. MONETARY BASE TARGETING *V.* INTEREST RATE TARGETING

10.2.1. *The market for central bank money*

The control of the operating target by central bank instruments takes place on the market for monetary base or central bank money. By bank practitioners this market is referred to as the 'money market'. Chapter 3 has already made clear that this market has to be distinguished from the 'money market' that is found in macroeconomic textbooks (see Table 10.1). This chapter deals only with the market for central bank money and uses the term 'money market' for it. The main market participants are commercial banks and the central bank. From time to time large companies also participate in this money market.

For the individual banks, the money market is the place where they can offset temporary surpluses or deficits in their central bank balances. For example, if a bank's (non-interest-bearing) central bank balance exceeds

---

[3] The term 'euromarket' is always used when a bank accepts foreign deposits or grants foreign loans in a currency other than that of the country in which the bank is operating.

Table 10.1. *The market for money in the IS/LM model and the money market*

	Market participants	Assets traded
Money market	Central bank and commercial banks; some large companies	Central bank deposits (reserves) against claims on banks, the State or private domestic non-banks
Market for money in the IS/LM model	Commercial banks and the private non-bank sector	Commercial bank deposits against claims on non-banks

its minimum reserve requirement or the optimum level of its voluntary 'working balance' at the central bank, it can make these funds available to another bank in the form of an interest-bearing loan. Depending on the notice period, such money market loans are referred to as 'overnight money', 'one-month money', 'three-month money', 'six-month money', or 'twelve-month money'.

In addition to smoothing out liquidity imbalances between the banks, which always implies a horizontal shift in a given amount of central bank reserves (*interbank money market*), the money market also serves as the channel whereby the banking system as a whole is supplied with central bank money. This process operates via transactions that take place between the central bank and individual banks. These transactions will be described in detail later. They usually involve the trading of claims (on banks, the State, or private domestic non-banks) against deposits at the central bank.

From the macroeconomic point of view, the technical money market is of interest only to the extent that it balances the supply of central bank funds with the banks' net demand for such funds. Therefore, in the following analysis we shall largely ignore the gross transactions which serve to smooth out liquidity flows between the individual banks.

As already mentioned, banks need central bank balances for two reasons.

1. Depending on the cash holding ratio (cash holdings/total deposits), lending to non-banks implies that the banks must provide non-banks with cash, which they obtain by drawing on their balances at the central bank.

2. In countries with a minimum reserve requirement, banks must hold (non-interest-bearing) balances at the central bank in respect of part of the deposits constituted in the credit creation process, in accordance with the current minimum reserve rate. Even without such a requirement, it can be advisable for the banks voluntarily to hold such funds as a transaction or precautionary balance. They are then known as *working balances*.

It can be assumed here for simplicity's sake that the net demand of the banking system for central bank balances is determined essentially by the interest rate at which the banks obtain such assets from the central bank. Usually this takes place in the form of borrowing from the central bank, and the rate for such borrowing can be regarded as the main determinant for the demand for central bank money.[4] We shall see that this interest rate broadly corresponds to the money market rate for shorter-dated paper.

Since central bank balances are ultimately an input factor for lending by the banks, the banks' demand for monetary base (B^D) can be assumed to stand in an inverse relationship to the money market rate (i_R):[5]

$$B^D = f(i_R) \qquad \text{with } \partial B^D / \partial i_R < 0. \tag{10.1}$$

Graphically, this relationship has already been represented in Figure 3.2 and is reproduced here as Figure 10.1.

The central bank is the sole net supplier of central bank money. It is therefore in the position of a monopolist, which is now able to choose as its target any point on the demand function curve, which when seen in these terms represents a linear inverse demand function. A derivation of a supply function for the technical money market is therefore unnecessary.

As illustrated by the graph, for a given demand for central bank money by the banks, there will always be a fixed relationship between monetary

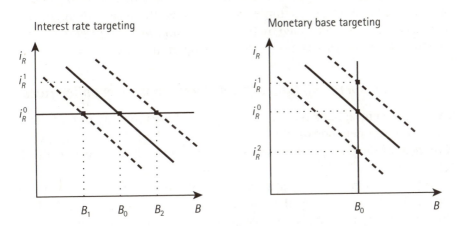

Figure 10.1. *Interest rate and monetary base targeting*

---

[4] In the United Kingdom, Japan, and the United States the banks are provided with liquidity via outright open-market operations (see Sections 10.5–10.7). In that case the interest rate at which the banks obtain central bank money can be deduced—as a *shadow price*—from the interest loss suffered by the banks by selling interest-bearing paper to the central bank and receiving in exchange non-interest-bearing central bank balances.

[5] For a detailed analysis, see Section 3.4.

base and the money market rate. The central bank's decision to aim at a particular target value for the money market interest rate thus directly implies a particular amount of central bank money. For example, if the central bank wishes to increase the money market rate from i_R^0 to i_R^1, it must reduce the supply of monetary base from B_0 to B_1. Conversely, a central bank that is pursuing a fixed target for the level of central bank money is no longer free to determine the interest rate level on the money market. From this point of view, it would appear unimportant whether a central bank aims to use as its operating target

- a target value for the money market rate ('interest rate targeting'), or
- a target value for the volume of central bank money ('monetary base targeting').

As was described in more detail in Appendix 3.1 above, the difference between these two basic targeting methods becomes clear only when it is assumed realistically that the banks' demand for central bank money is not a deterministic aggregate, but is continuously exposed to stochastic shocks which even the central bank is unable to predict.

In the case of monetary base targeting (i.e. a fixed target value for B_0), the money market interest rate will now fluctuate between i_R^1 and i_R^2. In the case of interest rate targeting, the interest rate level will always remain at i_R^0, since the central bank will here adjust the supply (B_1, B_0, or B_2) in such a way that the interest rate target is always met. Because both aggregates can very easily be controlled by the central bank, we shall refer to them in the following analysis as monetary policy operating targets.

10.2.2. *The operating targets for different monetary policy rules*

Whether a central bank opts for the monetary base targeting or for interest rate targeting depends on the specific framework of its monetary policy. For most of the policy rules discussed in Chapter 8, the choice is relatively clear-cut.

Interest rate targeting is always preferable to monetary base targeting when, for at least some of the time, a necessary condition for implementing the chosen approach is stability in the money market rate. This is clearly the case when a central bank pursues a policy in which it seeks to control the price level directly via money market interest rates (*inflation targeting*). Interest rate targeting is also essential when the exchange rate is being used as an intermediate monetary policy target (see Chapter 12). Owing to the interest parity condition, short-term fluctuations in money market rates can have a direct influence on the spot rate. Thus, shocks affecting banks' demand for central bank money could, in the case of monetary base targeting, lead to erratic interest rate movements and hence to destabilizing capital flows and disruptive exchange rate fluctuations. For the Taylor rule (Section 8.5) it is also obvious that a perfect control of short-term interest rates is required.

On the other hand, *monetary base targeting* is clearly superior to interest rate targeting when a central bank has decided to adopt nominal GDP targeting of the kind proposed by McCallum (see Section 8.6.3.2). In this case, interest rate targeting could lead to undesirable fluctuations in the monetary base.

The choice is less obvious when a central bank follows the rule of monetary targeting. Although monetarists often show a preference for monetary base targeting, it can be demonstrated that it is not automatically to be regarded as superior to interest rate targeting. As is shown by McCallum (1989: 55–73) and explained in detail in Appendix 3.1, when targeting the money stock our assessment of which of the two methods is superior will depend essentially on the nature and intensity of the expected shocks.

- *Interest rate targeting* is preferable to monetary base targeting when shocks occur mainly in the money multiplier. These can be caused either by fluctuations in the cash holding ratio or—in a system without minimum reserves—by variations in the voluntary reserves held by the banks. In this case interest rate targeting allows an automatic adjustment in the monetary base, which fully offsets the disturbance in the multiplier.
- *Monetary base targeting* is superior to interest rate targeting when the monetary disturbances principally affect either private individuals' demand for money or bank lending, while the multiplier is relatively stable. When the monetary base is being targeted, an endogenous adjustment in the money market rate helps to prevent such disturbances from having an effect on the money supply.

Thus, a central bank pursuing a policy of monetary targeting would have to consider what types of disturbance are most likely to occur. In reality, the very low short-term interest elasticity of the demand for base money makes it almost impossible to pursue strict monetary base targeting as an operating procedure for monetary targeting.

From the two main targeting approaches briefly outlined here, it is clear what practical criteria the overall range of monetary policy instruments must satisfy when a central bank has to decide between these two options.

- *Monetary base targeting* requires that the central bank should be able at all times to control the assets side of its balance sheet in such a way that it cannot be forced to expand the monetary base involuntarily.
- *Interest rate targeting* requires that the central bank should have access to instruments that set a strict upper and lower limit at all times on market-induced fluctuations in the money market rate. Because of the interdependent relationship (as described above) between the monetary base and the money market rate, this strategy too requires some degree of control over the assets side of the central bank's balance sheet.

It can thus be seen that the traditional classification of monetary policy instruments into 'liquidity policy' and 'interest rate policy' instruments (Deutsche Bundesbank 1995: 98) is in the final analysis not very helpful. As will be outlined below, of far greater importance is the general orientation of the management approach, where the role of the individual instruments cannot be considered in isolation, but must be seen in the overall context of interest rate or monetary base targeting.

10.2.3. *Monetary policy instruments for interest rate targeting*

When a central bank pursues interest rate targeting, it has to equip its toolbox with instruments that allow an efficient control of the short-term interest rate. While the operating procedures of central banks in all industrial countries can be described as interest rate targeting, there are, however, marked differences in the concrete implementation of this policy. The concern above all is the instruments that are used. Many countries target the interest rate with refinancing facilities, although some countries have a preference for open-market operations. The operating target can also relate primarily to the rate for overnight money or to money market rates for longer maturities, such as the one-month or three-month rate. There are also differences regarding the degree of precision with which the money market rate is controlled, i.e. whether a concrete interest rate *level* is targeted or whether fluctuation within a given interest rate *band* is allowed.[6] All this will be discussed in detail below.

Interest rate targeting is often wrongly thought of as an approach in which a central bank keeps the money market rate constant over longish periods. However, its essential aim is simply to exert an influence on economic developments via a money market rate that can be completely controlled by monetary policy. As the example of the Federal Reserve

---

[6] The wider the permitted band, the more closely interest rate targeting resembles monetary base targeting.

demonstrates, this can involve phases when the money market rate is markedly stable (the second half of the 1990s) as well as periods of rapid and abrupt interest rate changes (e.g. the period 1972–5). Another misconception about interest rate targeting is the fear that with this approach a central bank might lose control over the money supply. Such concerns probably reflect a conception derived from the traditional *multiplier model* (see Section 3.3), which in practice would require quantitative restrictions on the monetary base. But the money supply theory discussed in Chapter 3 shows that such concerns are groundless, since with each money market rate there is a clearly determined monetary base and also a clearly determined money stock.

As the specific approaches to interest rate targeting differ from one country to another, we shall first of all consider which instruments are absolutely necessary for pursuing such a policy. In other words, we shall be describing a *minimalist approach* which helps to understand the basic principles. On this basis, we shall then undertake a critical comparison of the armoury of monetary policy instruments available to some major countries.

In principle, only two monetary policy instruments are required in order to ensure perfect control of the money market rate. The first one is needed for the purpose of setting an upper limit on the money market rate and the second one, for setting a lower limit. The upper and lower limits can be separated by a certain distance (*interest rate band*), or they can coincide (*point targeting*).

- The *upper limit* on the money market rate is set by an instrument that the central bank uses to make central bank money available to the banks. In general terms, this can be referred to as a 'refinancing facility'.
- The *lower limit* on the money market rate is set by an instrument whereby the central bank provides the banks with an outlet for the short-term investment of surplus central bank money. In general terms, this can be referred to as an 'absorption facility' or 'deposit facility'.

10.2.3.1. *Refinancing facility*

The upper limit of the interest rate band for the money market rate is determined by the interest rate at which the central bank supplies monetary base to the banks. The banks always require a certain quantity of monetary base for the note and coin circulation and for their reserves. As is explained in detail in Section 3.1, monetary base is supplied by central bank purchases from the banks' interest-bearing assets (foreign claims, claims on domestic public authorities, claims on a domestic credit institution). In order to control the money market interest rate, the central bank needs to set an interest rate at which the banks can acquire monetary base from it at all times.

In its simplest form, a central bank refinancing facility can be thought of as an overdraft facility, whereby the central bank grants to each credit institution a generous credit line (at a given interest rate), which it can draw on as and when it needs to. In order to act as an upper limit for the interest rate band, such a facility, which is also known as a *standing facility*, must be so designed that it can meet the aggregate demand of the banking system at the interest rate targeted by the central bank. As in the case of ECB's marginal refinancing facility (Section 10.4), this can be guaranteed if the facility as a whole is provided free from quantitative restrictions.

The question of the *collateral* that the central bank requires from the banks as security for such funding is frequently discussed in the literature. Many writers, following the tradition of the Banking School (see Appendix 6.1), believe that central bank lending should be secured by assets representing a claim on the real economy. However, we have seen from our discussion of the Banking School that such a real economic basis for central bank funding is neither a necessary nor a sufficient condition for ensuring that money is supplied to the banking system in non-inflationary conditions.

Therefore, in line with our minimalist approach, we might even envisage the possibility of a standing facility in the form of a book credit at the central bank. Even collateral might not be necessary. In order to prevent central bank credit from being granted to insolvent institutions, access to this facility could be made dependent on a bank's complying with all the banking supervisory regulations in force.

The period for which central bank credit is granted is another important factor in how interest rate targeting operates. In addition to one-day loans, periods of one week, one month, or even several months are possible. In order to illustrate how the system works, we shall first of all examine interest rate targeting with a *one-day* borrowing facility.

As with an overdraft facility, changes in the interest rate on the funds borrowed directly affect the total amount of central bank borrowing by banks. Such a facility means that the banks are able at any time to use any liquidity surpluses they might have to reduce their borrowing from the central bank. With a one-day facility, managing the money market rate is extremely simple. The funding rate set by the central bank automatically becomes the upper limit on the rate for overnight money in money market dealings between the banks, as no bank will be willing to acquire central bank money from another bank if it is asked to pay a rate for overnight money above what it would have to pay for borrowing from the central bank. Because of its one-day notice period, such a standing facility also sets a lower limit on the money market rate. For example, if foreign exchange market interventions with foreign currency purchases lead to an increase in central bank balances that are not required by a bank, it can use them directly to reduce the amount of its borrowing from the central bank. Therefore it will not be willing to lend central bank money to other banks at a rate that is below the central bank borrowing rate. If a bank has already reduced its central bank borrowing to zero, it can lend surplus central bank money to other banks, which will then use it to reduce their own central bank borrowing.

Thus, provided that the aggregate amount of outstanding central bank funding is greater than the amount of intervention on the foreign exchange market, the interest rate on such a facility will act both as an upper and a lower limit on the money market rate. Therefore, large fluctuations in the rate for overnight money should be eliminated. Small fluctuations cannot, however, be ruled out, since it will be profitable for a bank to borrow on the money market only if this can be done at an interest rate that is lower than the central bank borrowing rate. Given the low transaction costs and relatively large amounts dealt with on the money market, very small interest rate advantages (e.g. 0.10 percentage point) should be sufficient to make such transactions profitable between banks.

Thus, as long as a central bank is free from the need to intervene on the foreign exchange market (flexible exchange rates), or the total amount involved in its funding operations is very large (meaning that it has a *large sterilization potential*), a single monetary policy instrument is sufficient to enable it to achieve complete and virtually infallible control of the money market rate.

10.2.3.2. *Absorption facility*
From the above, it is clear that the need for an absorption facility mainly results from

- official intervention obligations under a fixed exchange rate system, which require a central bank with a strong currency to purchase foreign currency or grant stand-by credits in domestic currency to central banks with a weak currency, or
- interventions within the framework of a managed float, where a central bank follows an informal exchange rate target and tries to prevent the domestic currency from appreciating (Chapter 12).

If a central bank in such a situation wishes to continue to keep the money market rate under control, it must be able to offset the expansion in the monetary base caused by foreign currency inflows by means of compensating measures. This is known as *sterilization*, and interventions whose effect on the monetary base is offset in this way are known as *sterilized interventions*.

Against such an institutional background, an absorption facility will always be needed when the level of foreign exchange market intervention is so high that the total amount of central bank funding of the banking system falls to zero. Such a situation arises when the banks use the liquidity that they build up as a result of foreign currency purchases by the central bank to reduce their borrowing from the central bank. Once such borrowing is fully repaid, any additional foreign currency purchases (and the associated increase in the monetary base) cause supply-side pressure on the money market, which drives the money market rate below the central bank borrowing rate. In order not to lose control over the money market rate in such a situation, a central bank needs an instrument with which to take liquidity out of the money market.

The absorption facility must be designed so as to enable the banks to invest central bank balances in the short term at a fixed rate of interest. As with the central bank borrowing facility, here too a deposit facility of one day's notice might be the standard arrangement. The rate of interest paid on funds invested in this way could be identical to the interest rate on the central bank borrowing facility. In that case the money market rate would be controlled with perfect precision. Another option would be to set the rate of interest paid on funds invested under the absorption facility 0.5 or 1 percentage point below the central bank borrowing rate, in which case the money market rate could fluctuate within a band. Because both the borrowing and the absorption facilities are at one day's notice, the money market rate would always be either at the band's upper margin (amount of outstanding central bank borrowing positive) or at its lower margin (amount of central bank borrowing equal to zero).

10.2.3.3. *Interest rates for different maturities on the money market*
The two facilities described above allow perfect control of the rate for overnight money from the central bank. However, with the overnight money rate fixed in this way, the money market rates on longer maturities (one-month money, three-month money) can fluctuate upwards or downwards. Therefore, in accordance with the expectation theory of the yield curve (see Appendix 8.1), the rate for, say, three-month money will be higher than the rate for overnight money if there is a general expectation among the banks that the central bank will be adopting a tighter stance in its interest rate targeting. The opposite will be the case when banks are expecting interest rates to fall. Thus, a central bank that focuses its money

market management on overnight money can exert some control over longer-term rates, but is not able to control them perfectly.

An alternative might be for the central bank to make a funding facility available only for longer periods (e.g. one week, two weeks, one month), in order to be able to directly influence money market rates in this range of maturities. If the banks are offered an unlimited facility of this kind, the central bank can perfectly control the money market rate on funds for these periods. However, a side-effect of the longer maturity period for such borrowing is that the banks can no longer repay it in the short term. Temporary liquidity surpluses will then result in excess supply on the market for overnight money. Also, in the event of a short-term demand for central bank money, the rate for overnight money can rise sharply if the banks are not willing to utilize a longer-term facility.

Generally speaking, therefore, the maturity period of the central bank funding facility will determine which actual money market rate a central bank is able to control. If the facility falls due after one day, the operating target will be the rate for overnight money; if the maturity period is one month, it will be the rate for one-month money; and so on.

10.2.4. *Pure monetary base targeting*

If a central bank is pursuing the approach of monetary base targeting, then at all times it should be able to control as accurately as possible the outstanding amount of central bank balances held by the banks. To ensure this, it must be prepared to accept sizeable fluctuations in the money market rate.

The kind of instruments that are suitable for monetary base targeting are therefore exactly the opposite of those used in interest rate targeting. Since the key feature of both the facilities described above is that they allow the banks in principle *unlimited* access to central bank money or *unlimited* absorption of central bank money for a certain period, they would be quite incompatible with monetary base targeting.

The most suitable instrument in a *minimalist approach* to monetary base targeting are open-market operations in fixed income securities, where the central bank makes available to the banks a certain amount of monetary base by way of an auction. The money market rate is then derived as an endogenous variable from the rates bid by the banks. From the point of view of managing the operating target, it is of secondary importance whether the open-market operations entail

- a definitive purchase of paper by the central bank (*outright operation*), or
- a purchase with a simultaneous agreement to repurchase at a later date (*securities repo*).

From the economic point of view, the above variants are equivalent if the residual maturity period of the paper purchased in an outright operation is the same as the period separating the purchase and repurchase dates in a securities repo. For practical purposes, therefore, the outright purchase of government securities with a residual maturity of one month is regarded as equivalent to a one-month securities repo.

This can be illustrated by means of an example in which we shall imagine an economy in which only one commercial bank is operating. Suppose that at the beginning of the month the bank owns public-sector bonds worth €1 million falling due at the end of the month and that the bank also needs an additional €1 million on its central bank account for the whole month. It can choose to raise these additional funds either through a securities repo or through an outright operation concluded with the central bank.

In the case of the *outright operation* the central bank makes a definitive purchase of the paper. The commercial bank's balance at the central bank increases at the beginning of the month by €1 million. At the end of the month the State must redeem the securities at the central bank. In order to do this it will sell new paper to the commercial bank, which accordingly sees its central bank balance reduced by €1 million. If the commercial bank continues to need additional liquidity, it will have to conclude another open-market operation.

In the case of the *securities repo*, the commercial bank again receives an additional €1 million of central bank money at the beginning of the month. At the end of the month it receives the securities back and its central bank balance is reduced by a corresponding amount. The initial expansion in liquidity is thus offset again. The State must now redeem its securities at the commercial bank. In the simplest variant, this can take place through the commercial bank replacing the old securities by new paper for the same maturity period (known as a 'revolving' operation). This time there is no additional effect on the commercial bank's balance at the central bank.

The essential point is that in both these transactions there is a *self-liquidating* element. In the case of the outright operation, this is because when the securities fall due the State has to pay the central bank and, in order to do this, it needs to borrow again. In the case of the securities repo, it arises from the fact that the commercial bank repurchases the paper, as agreed at the time the operation is concluded.

From the point of view of monetary base targeting, this self-liquidating effect is crucial. The central bank must first decide on the time-scale of its operating target, i.e. whether it is to run for one week, one month, one quarter, or one year. For example, if the monetary base is to be managed over a monthly period, it would make sense to set a period of one month for the open-market operations to self-liquidate. The central bank could then set a new monetary base target at the beginning of each month and offer open-market operations with this maturity for the appropriate amount.

Thus, as in the case of interest rate targeting, the maturity period for which these facilities are concluded is the central bank's main action parameter. In the case of monetary base targeting, it determines the period over which the operating target can be controlled. In the case of interest rate targeting, it decides which actual money market rate is to be targeted.

However, this relationship need not apply to the whole amount of the funding facility. For example, a central bank can still control the monetary base over a monthly period even if it offers a substantial portion of its funding facilities by way of longer-dated outright operations, provided that the amount involved in the revolving facilities at any given time is sufficient to adjust the monetary base to the target set by the central bank. In that case, the increase in liquidity could be offset by mopping-up operations on the open market.

Additional aspects need to be taken into consideration if a central bank pursuing a policy of monetary base targeting is also a member of a fixed exchange rate system. In such a situation the purchase and sale of foreign currencies can cause the monetary base to deviate from the target value. The sterilization that would then be required would make it necessary to engage in additional open-market operations between the regular dates for such transactions. Here it is also helpful if, in addition to existing government securities in circulation, the central bank is able to mobilize other paper which can be offered to the banks as an investment outlet for their surplus liquidity. Such a reserve supply would then be used specifically for the absorption of liquidity. With monetary base targeting, it is important to

Table 10.2. *Minimalist approaches to monetary base targeting and interest rate targeting*

Strategy	Operating target	Concrete definition of the operating target	Feature of the instrument that is required to control the operating target
Interest rate targeting	Money market rate	Maturity of the interest rate (i.e. overnight rate, 1-month rate, 3-month rate)	Maturity of the refinancing or absorption facility
Monetary base targeting	Monetary base	Period during which the monetary base is kept constant (i.e. 1 day, 1 week, 1 month, 3 months)	Residual maturity period of the assets purchased in an open market; maturity of a repurchase agreement

concentrate exclusively on holding the monetary base to its target value at all times. This means that the whole of the adjustment burden is borne by the money market rate.

The main aspects of the two minimalist approaches are summarized in Table 10.2.

10.3. SIGNIFICANCE OF INDIVIDUAL MONETARY POLICY INSTRUMENTS

We have so far considered the minimalist approaches to targeting in very abstract terms. Now we shall take a detailed look at some of the main monetary policy instruments, though still concentrating on their general characteristics. Their actual use will be discussed in individual country studies.

In the armoury of instruments available to the central banks, there are five main instruments:

1. standing facilities for refinancing purposes;
2. standing facilities for absorption purposes;
3. outright open-market operations, i.e. operations in which securities are bought or sold outright;
4. securities repos, i.e. open-market operations in which securities are bought (sold) by the central bank for subsequent resale to (or repurchase from) a bank on an agreed date;
5. minimum reserve requirements.

Since standing facilities have already been discussed in some detail, this section focuses on the other three instruments.

10.3.1. *Outright open-market operations*

In true open-market operations the central bank purchases (sells) securities outright from (to) the banks. They differ fundamentally from standing facilities, since:

1. the initiative for such operations always comes from the central bank;
2. the interest rate at which monetary base is made available is not fixed exogenously, but is derived as the 'shadow price'. A bank that acquires (non-interest-bearing) central bank money through the sale of an (interest-bearing) security to the central bank incurs an interest loss.

As already noted, this instrument is the appropriate choice, above all, when a central bank is pursuing a policy of *monetary base targeting*. For example, if the central bank sets monthly target values for the monetary base, it should conduct the necessary open-market operations at the beginning of each month via paper with a residual maturity period of one month. In practice, however, outright open-market operations are always used in the context of *interest rate targeting*, and usually in combination with other instruments, since interest rate targeting carried out exclusively via true open-market operations would involve relatively high transaction costs. In the event of unstable demand among the banks for monetary base, a central bank must, in order to be sure of always meeting the interest rate target, buy or sell securities on the market daily, sometimes even by the hour. The Bank of England's money market management until 1997 has been a notable example of this (King 1994). In the United States outright open-market operations are used, above all, for supplying the banks with the central bank money that they can be expected to need as their basic requirement. Usually only a few transactions are carried out every year. Short-term liquidity fluctuations are almost always smoothed out by means of securities repos. The argument in favour of interest-rate targeting using outright open-market operations is not particularly easy to understand for countries in which this instrument is not used. The analogy with funding via a credit facility will therefore be explained with the help of an example.

Suppose that a bank has a portfolio of short-term government paper made up of equal proportions of securities with a residual maturity period of one month, two months, and three months. For the purposes of the bank's liquidity planning, it is essential that it should at all events receive central bank money when these securities fall due, that is to say *without* a money market operation. By selling them outright to the central bank (or indeed to another bank), it can bring forward the date on which it receives this liquidity. If it does so, it will seek to ensure that the residual maturity period of the paper it sells coincides with the period for which it expects to need additional liquidity. It will therefore sell one-month paper if it anticipates increased liquidity needs for one month. Were it to use paper with a residual maturity period of three months, it will be faced with the problem, after the month has expired, of having to reinvest the funds at an interest rate that cannot be predicted today. The bank would thus incur an avoidable interest rate risk.

In terms of its economic logic, an open-market operation is identical to the following chain of transactions. The bank keeps the security, but raises a money market loan for the length of its residual maturity period from another bank. This interbank loan is then repaid using the redemption proceeds from the government security, which become payable on the same date. From the practical point of view, therefore, the sale of open-market paper with a residual maturity period of one month is equivalent to raising a one-month loan on the interbank market. In accordance with the logic of arbitrage, the yield on this short-term paper must always correspond to the comparable money market rate. From the bank's point of view, the costs of funding via true open-market operations consist of the interest loss that it incurs by exchanging an interest-bearing security for non-interest-bearing central bank money.

When a central bank pursues a policy of interest-rate targeting using outright open-market operations, it must first of all be clear which actual money market rate it wishes to manage as the operating target. If we assume that it is the interest rate for one month, this means that the central bank must seek to ensure, by buying and selling paper with a one-month residual maturity, that the yield on such paper corresponds to its targeted money market rate. Therefore, management of the money market rate, which in accordance with the above-mentioned arbitrage logic always coincides with the yield on such paper, will take place (unlike under a system of central bank borrowing facilities) not via the direct borrowing costs, but via the opportunity costs of acquiring central bank money.

Here too, as in the case of funding via a credit facility, the problem arises that a central bank cannot control all the money market maturity ranges at the same time. For example, when a central bank is targeting the rate for one-month money, the situation can arise whereby the banks require additional liquidity in the short term (e.g. for one day). But they will not necessarily be willing to sell paper with a residual maturity period of one month. This can mean that efforts to smooth out liquidity movements on the market for overnight money are only partially effective, with the result that the rate for overnight money shows very much sharper fluctuations than the rate for one-month money. Table 10.3 compares outright open-market operations with funding via a credit facility and securities repos in the context of interest rate targeting.

Table 10.3. *Interest rate targeting using various instruments*

	Outright open–market operations	Repos	Refinancing facility
Maturity of the refinancing operation	Residual maturity of the paper sold/purchased	Difference between the date of selling and the date of repurchase	Maturity of the facility
Costs of refinancing	Yield of the paper that has been sold	Repo rate	Refinancing rate

Regardless of whether they are used in interest rate or monetary base targeting, outright open-market operations have two major disadvantages compared with securities repos.

1. Whenever securities are purchased or sold outright by the central bank, such transactions always influence the market prices of the securities in question. Usually, however, the influence of open-market operations on securities prices is very small; this is particularly true of the United States, where there is a very large amount of short-term government paper (Treasury bills) in circulation. This is only true, however, in the absence of exceptional disturbances. For example, in the wake of the ERM crises of 1992 and 1993, the Bundesbank had to take up to DM92 billion of central bank money out of the market within the space of a week. If central bank money had been made available by way of outright open-market operations, this would have created substantial short-term supply-side pressure, which would have inevitably affected market prices. In major economies, therefore, a large volume of outright open-market operations is acceptable only if the central bank is not obliged to engage in significant foreign exchange market intervention.

2. Outright open-market operations have the serious disadvantage that they can always be used as a way of circumventing the ban on central bank financing of public-sector deficits. Such a prohibition, which is found in many central banking acts (see Section 7.2.4), can only prevent direct lending to the State: it is always open to a central bank to purchase government securities from the banks on the secondary market. Thus, a compliant central bank may supply unlimited finance to the State via true open-market operations. In the interests of monetary policy independence, therefore, it would be preferable if the central bank in principle also refrained from the indirect purchase of government securities.

Moreover, since, in their method of functioning, securities repos hardly differ from true open-market operations, there is no reason, even in the case of monetary base targeting, for making central bank money available in the form of an outright purchase of securities. Similarly, in the context of interest rate targeting, central bank borrowing facilities are superior to true open-market operations, since not only are they technically much simpler to organize, but they also have no side-effects on securities prices, nor do they imply lending to the public sector.

10.3.2. *Securities repos*

Defined in very general terms, repurchase operations ('repos') are operations in which a person sells an object to another person, the contracting parties agreeing at the same time that the object shall be repurchased at a later date. From a legal point of view, securities repos are similarly open-market operations. However, in terms of their economic significance, securities repos have much more in common with central bank borrowing facilities than with true open-market operations.[7] This is principally because in the case of securities repos the central bank is not a buyer or seller on the bond market, but rather the depository for the banks of a given amount of securities. On the occasion of each transaction, securities from this securities deposit are transferred to the central bank. They are transferred back to the banks on expiry of the transaction. Basically, the securities in this case are only serving as *collateral* for a direct loan from the central bank to the banks.

In the euro area, the level of the banks' securities holdings, at about €1,400 billion, is much higher than the average amount of outstanding securities repos with the Eurosystem of some €200 billion. Thus, the banks usually do not need to purchase securities in order to take part in a securities repo. These transactions should not normally, therefore, have any effect on securities prices.

When considered in these terms, the difference between securities repos and a central bank borrowing facility is extremely small, especially since securities are also required as collateral when such facilities are activated (Laurens 1994). However, a particular feature of securities repos is the way in which the interest rate is determined.

- In a *variable rate tender* the central bank auctions a given amount of credit, which goes to those banks that bid the highest interest rate. This procedure may take place either in the form of a *Dutch auction*, in which all bids are satisfied at the equilibrium interest rate level, or in the form of a *US auction*, where each bidder must pay the interest rate tendered. The problem with a Dutch auction is that smaller bidders bid unrealistically high rates, in order to be sure of being included in the allotment. From the central bank's point of view, a US auction has the advantage that it can absorb the whole of the banks' consumer surplus (perfect price discrimination).
- In a *fixed rate tender* the borrowing rate is fixed *ex ante*. If the banks bid for a larger volume than that which the central bank wishes to allot, the individual bids are scaled down and are satisfied for only a given percentage.

It is clear that variable rate tenders are very suitable for monetary base targeting. They enable the central bank to control the monetary base accurately,

---

[7] See Bank of England (2000a: 2): 'In effect, gilt repo is a cash loan with the gilts used as security.'

the money market interest rate being endogenously determined by the banks' demand. The length of time separating the individual operations must correspond to the period during which the central bank wishes to keep the monetary base at a constant level. Fixed rate tenders, on the other hand, are not easily compatible with monetary base targeting, because it is virtually impossible for a central bank to fix the allotment rate *ex ante* so that it corresponds to the equilibrium rate on the money market.

From the point of view of interest rate targeting, the comparative advantages of the two instruments are diametrically opposite. Whereas a variable rate tender can lead to undesirable fluctuations in interest rates, a fixed rate tender fits in very well with interest rate targeting. The maturity period of the operations must be the same as that relating to the money market rate that the central bank wishes to control. However, since the initiative for a securities repo must always come from the central bank, interest rate targeting that is conducted exclusively via a fixed rate tender requires active money market management. This is the main disadvantage of this instrument compared with a standing facility.

10.3.3. *Minimum reserves*

Minimum reserves are one of the traditional monetary policy instruments, although their role in monetary policy worldwide has diminished over the last few years. Pressure of competition among the major international financial centres has forced all central banks significantly to ease the burden imposed on their banks by compulsory reserves.

The minimum reserve requirements usually comprise the following:[8]

1. *Rules for calculating the required reserve.* These state which of the banks' balance sheet positions are to serve as the basis for calculating the minimum reserve. They might comprise *asset* positions, e.g. bank lending, or as *liability* positions, i.e. certain categories of deposit. In practice, *liability-based reserves* are the preferred solution. In their choice of which deposits to include in the reserve requirement, central banks tend to focus on the monetary aggregates M1–M3. That is to say, the minimum reserve requirement is based mainly on the deposits that form part of those aggregates. The required reserve is then obtained by multiplying the liabilities subject to the requirement by the respective reserve ratio.

2. *Rules for calculating the actual reserve.* Once the reserve requirement has been calculated, it is necessary to determine how a bank is meant to meet that requirement. First, the timing has to be decided; in other words, it is necessary to decide how the period for holding the required reserve

---

[8] For details, see Hardy (1993) and Blenck (2000).

relates to the period on which the calculation is based. We can have either a 'contemporaneous reserve requirement', where the two periods coincide, or a 'lagged reserve requirement', where the period for which the reserve is held is later than the calculation period. In the latter case, the banks know in advance how much they are required to hold. The rules must also stipulate the period over which the banks must meet the requirement, e.g. whether the reserve is to be held on a daily basis or simply as an average over the reserve period, which will usually be one month.

A survey of the key elements of reserve requirements in the euro area, in Japan, and in the United States is presented in Table 10.4.

The functions of the minimum reserves are many and varied. When the instrument was first introduced early in the twentieth century, its main purpose was to maintain the solvency of the banks.[9] Nowadays, however, there are specific banking supervisory regulations aimed at ensuring solvency, and so in the monetary policy context the main interest in the minimum reserves stems from

1. the fact that their implementation makes the banking system dependent on the central bank;
2. their use in the management of bank liquidity and thus in the management of short-term interest rates;
3. their use as a means of ensuring a stable money creation multiplier.

10.3.3.1. *Making the banking system dependent on the central bank*

The minimum reserve requirement is an important determinant of the banks' demand for central bank money. The European Central Bank (1998: 52) regards this as an important justification for the use of this instrument:

The ESCB's minimum reserve system contributes to creating or enlarging a structural liquidity shortage. This may be helpful in order to improve the ability of the ESCB to operate efficiently as a supplier of liquidity.

As is explained in Chapter 3, the existence of a demand for central bank money on the part of the banks is an essential precondition for the central bank to be able to exert any influence over the economic process. On the other hand, the minimum reserves are required to perform this specific function only if there is a significant decline in the demand for cash in the economy. Despite the considerable technological advances made in payment systems generally, there is no sign of this happening yet in any country (Seitz 1995). In the euro area at the present time, the minimum reserve

---

[9] See Menkhoff (1995: 46). He points out that they were also seen as a source of revenue for the State and that this consideration was a factor in their introduction.

Table 10.4. *Key elements of reserve requirements*

	Bank of Japan	European Central Bank	Federal Reserve
Covered institutions	Depository institutions (city banks, regional banks, etc.)	All credit institutions	Depository institutions (banks, thrifts, etc.)
Covered liabilities having a non-zero requirement ratio and some other liabilities	Time deposits, other deposits, bank debentures, money in trusts and foreign currency deposits	Overnight deposits, deposits and debt securities with a maturity of up to 2 years, and money market paper	Transactions deposits
Key requirement ratios	Ratios range from 0.05% to 1.20%	2% on all the above liabilities	10% top marginal requirement ratio applies to most deposits
Maintenance period structure	1 month, starting on the 16th day of each month and ending on the 15th day of the following month	1 month, starting on the 24th calendar day of each month and ending on the 23rd day of the following month	Two-week periods, beginning on every other Thursday
Required reserve computation period	Partly lagged; based on average deposits over the entire calendar month in which the maintenance period begins	Fully lagged; based on balance sheet data from the end of nearest calendar month preceding the start of the maintenance period	Fully lagged; based on average deposits in the 2-week period beginning 30 days before the start of the corresponding maintenance period
Eligible assets for satisfying requirements	Central bank balances only	Central bank balances only	Central bank deposits held during the maintenance period, plus vault cash (up to the level of requirements)

Table 10.4. *(Continued)*

	Bank of Japan	European Central Bank	Federal Reserve
Remuneration on assets held to satisfy requirements	None	Average rate of the main refinancing operations over the maintenance period	None
Carry-over provisions	None	None	Up to 4 per cent of requirements of one maintenance period may be met with balances held in the following period
Penalty structure for failing to meet reserve requirements	3.75 percentage points plus the official discount rate	2.5 percentage points plus the marginal lending rate	2 percentage points plus the discount rate is levied against reserve deficiencies beyond the carry-forward amount

Source: Blenck (2000).

requirement works out at around €110 billion against a note and coin circulation of some €370 billion.

Another question that needs to be considered is whether, even without the compulsion of a minimum reserve requirement, the banks can be expected to hold *voluntary reserves* ('working balances') at the central bank. In fact, this will depend essentially on the central bank's management of the money market. In the United Kingdom, where the minimum reserve is not used as a monetary policy instrument, it appears that working balances tend towards zero when the central bank pursues a policy of interest rate targeting on the money market.

This can be relatively easily deduced from the Baumol–Tobin model (Section 2.2.2). We need to make the assumption that the banks' demand for central bank money is primarily the result of a demand for transaction balances. Like private individuals in the Baumol–Tobin model, the banks have to choose whether they are to hold non-interest-bearing but liquid central bank balances or interest-bearing claims on other banks or non-banks, which they will not be able to use directly for cash payments or for the settlement of balances in the clearing. If the structure of this model is transferred to a demand for central bank money, the following determinants for working balances can be derived:

1. the transaction costs of acquiring central bank money;
2. the opportunity costs of holding central bank money;
3. the expected balances between in-payments and out-payments (in the Baumol–Tobin model these are derived from income due once a month and current consumer expenditure).

In the present model it is relatively easy to show that working balances will tend towards zero, since for the banks the fixed transaction costs (c) of procuring central bank money are extremely small. Normally central banks deduct no charges for in-payments or out-payments. Even in interbank money market dealings there are no significant transaction costs. Thus, the numerator in Baumol and Tobin's square root formula (equation (2.24)) is zero.

A positive figure for working balances can be derived only if we assume certain frictions in payments between the banks or in payments between a bank and the central bank. For example, a situation could arise in which, in order for a bank to meet a payment liability in the clearing with other banks, it needs central bank balances which it can acquire only from the central bank or on the money market with a certain time lag. The demand for working balances would then have the character of a precautionary balance and would be determined primarily by the time stipulated for meeting unforeseeable payment liabilities in the clearing. In practice, however, the rules on payment liabilities in the clearing are framed in such a way as to ensure that a bank can always acquire the necessary central bank balances from the central bank or other banks in good time. For this reason, no significant demand for working balances can be derived by way of the 'precautionary balance', either.

10.3.3.2. *Managing bank liquidity and expanding the sterilization potential*

In the 1960s and 1970s the minimum reserve requirement was mainly used in order to manage the liquidity of the banking system. An increase (reduction) in the reserve ratio leads to an increase (reduction) in the banks' demand for central bank money. Used in this way, the minimum reserve was regarded e.g. by the Bundesbank as one of the 'classic liquidity policy instruments' (Deutsche Bundesbank 1995: 98). It is an appropriate instrument for interest rate targeting on the money market if,

- faced with substantial *liquidity inflows*, the central bank is unable to quickly reduce its funding facilities and/or has no adequate means of mopping up the surplus liquidity, or if,
- in the event of substantial *liquidity outflows*, the central bank is unable to increase its lending to the banking system rapidly enough.

As an instrument of liquidity absorption, above all in situations with strong foreign exchange market interventions to prevent an appreciation of the domestic currency, the minimum reserve requirement has become dispensable to the extent that the central banks have moved away from rediscount credit, which was relatively difficult to reduce in the short term, in favour of the very flexible repo facilities. In addition, this function of the minimum reserve can also be replaced by an absorption facility.

The minimum reserve is also no longer an ideal instrument for supplying liquidity to the banking system. For the purposes of interest rate targeting on the money market, it would not be advisable for a central bank simply to release a given amount of monetary base by reducing the minimum reserve ratio in order to trigger an expansionary impulse. The interest rate effect of such a measure would be very much harder to predict than in the case of an interest rate reduction on a central bank refinancing facility or in a fixed rate tender. In this context the minimum reserve would be needed only if the banks no longer had a sufficient quantity of the debt instruments that needed to be lodged at the central bank in order to qualify for additional central bank money. However, such a situation is unlikely to arise.

10.3.3.3. *Ensuring a stable money multiplier*

Another function of the minimum reserve is to help stabilize the money multiplier. As the description of the money supply process in Chapter 3 shows, this multiplier is determined by the cash holding ratio and the reserve ratio. As has been explained above, in a system without minimum reserves, banks hold extremely few working balances. The money multiplier would thus be determined almost entirely by the cash holding ratio. Given the instability of the latter, this could result in a considerable degree of instability in the relationship between the monetary base and the money supply. A minimum reserve requirement, on the other hand, ensures a more stable multiplier process at all times.

However, this function of the minimum reserve cannot be viewed in isolation from the particular operating procedure that a central bank pursues. As demonstrated in Chapter 3, multiplier shocks are to be regarded as a problem only when a central bank uses the monetary base as an operating target: in this case, an unstable multiplier means an unstable money supply. However, all central banks that use the instrument of the minimum reserve (in particular, the Federal Reserve and the European Central Bank) pursue a policy of interest rate targeting on the money market.

10.3.3.4. *Costs of the minimum reserve*

When minimum reserves are non-interest-bearing, they represent a tax on all credit chains in the banking system. Given the very low transaction costs on the financial markets, it is not surprising that the burden imposed by the minimum reserve requirement can lead to massive switches by the banks to those countries that have no such requirement.

In the past, minimum reserve requirements in Germany have led to a strong transfer, especially of time deposits, to countries without this instrument, above all the United Kingdom and Luxembourg. As a consequence, the ECB has decided to pay market-related interest rates on the banks' minimum reserves. In the United States and Japan minimum reserves are still not interest-bearing, but the reserve ratios are now very low (see Table 10.4).

10.3.4. **The individual instruments needed in both targeting options**

Generally speaking, it can be seen that the advantages of individual monetary policy instruments can never be viewed in isolation. The answer to the question of whether they are suitable and necessary in a given situation depends solely on which particular targeting policy the central bank is pursuing (Table 10.5).

Table 10.5. *Suitable instruments for monetary base targeting and interest rate targeting*

Instrument	Monetary base targeting	Interest rate targeting
Refinancing facilities	Incompatible	Suitable
Outright open-market transactions	Suitable, but negative side-effects on bond prices and risk of implicit government financing	Possible, but high transaction costs, negative side-effects on bond prices, and a risk of implicit government financing
Repurchase agreements	Variable rate tender: suitable Fixed rate tender: incompatible	Variable rate tender: incompatible Fixed rate tender: suitable
Minimum reserve requirements	Useful for stabilizing the multiplier	Not required
Absorption facility	Incompatible	Suitable for situations with strong foreign exchange market interventions

In this context it is important to note that the practice of distinguishing between 'market-conforming' and 'non-market-conforming' instruments, although common, is not particularly helpful.[10] Apart from instruments that manifestly distort the allocation process on the financial markets (interest rate ceilings or minimum reserves), all other central bank funding instruments discussed in this section are equally compatible with effective competition among the banks. As the description of money market management has shown, instruments cannot be described as 'non-market-conforming' simply because they involve the central bank setting a fixed interest rate. Because of the monopoly position of the central bank—as sole supplier of central bank money—it makes no categorical difference whether it is the price or the quantity of the monetary base supplied by the central bank that is set.

10.4. MONEY MARKET MANAGEMENT BY THE EUROPEAN CENTRAL BANK

A comprehensive survey of the ECB's money market operations and a detailed description of its instruments is provided by the European Central Bank (2000). In this section we will focus on the most important issues of its money market management.

---

[10] See e.g. Deutsche Bundesbank (1994: 67): 'The Bundesbank as a rule prefers the interest rate tender [i.e. variable rate tender] as a "market-conforming" instrument which allows room for competition among the banks.' Similarly, Laurens (1994: 6) speaks of 'market-oriented operations'.

10.4.1. *Policy rate and operating targets*

In its meetings, which take place every two weeks, the ECB's governing council decides on the rates for its main refinancing operations and for its standing facilities. In addition to these policy rates, the ECB has no official operating targets. Blenck states:

The European Central Bank (ECB) does not have an official operating target for interbank rates. Generally speaking, the regular operations are used to satisfy demands for central bank balances in a smooth fashion over the course of each maintenance period. (Blenck 2000: 2)

At the same time the European Central Bank has made clear that it intends to steer short-term money rates:

Among the open market operations, the 'main refinancing operation', i.e. a weekly tender with a two-week maturity, plays a pivotal role in the Eurosystem's monetary policy framework. Indeed, it is mainly through this operation that the Eurosystem steers movements in short-term market interest rates and refinances the banking system. (ECB 1999*a*: 18)

The movements in the rates for overnight money, one-month money and three-month money (Table 10.6) provide clear evidence of the role of short-term money markets rate as the ECB's operating target.

- The rate for *overnight money* fluctuates within an interest rate band of two percentage points. Its upper limit is set by the rate for the marginal lending facility. The lower limit is determined by the rate for deposit facility. An additional stabilizing influence is exerted by particular characteristics of the ECB's minimum reserve system. All these instruments are described in more detail below. The average absolute daily fluctuation is 2.73% (January 1999–April 2000).
- The rates for *one-month money* and *three-month money* show relatively small daily fluctuations over the month. The average daily fluctuation is 0.47% for the one-month rate and 0.34% for the three-month rate. The determining factor here is the allotment rate for securities repos and the

Table 10.6. *Variability of money market rates (average magnitude of daily change in %)*

	Overnight rate	One-month rate	Three-month rate
Euro area	2.73	0.47	0.34
United Kingdom	3.60	0.77	0.77
United States	2.37	–	0.73

Source: Authors' calculations for the period January 1999–April 2000; data provided by Deutsche Bundesbank.

policy of interest rate smoothing. The mechanisms at work here will also be described in more detail below.

Thus, the ECB's money market management can be clearly defined as interest rate targeting, in which the rate for one-month or three-month money apparently plays a dominant role. In the following we will consider how the ECB seeks to control these rates through the range of instruments at its disposal.

10.4.2. *Instruments available to the European Central Bank*

The use of an interest rate band that is used primarily for controlling the rate for overnight money in conjunction with fine-tuning of the rate for one-month and three-month money represents a specific combination of the monetary policy instruments described in Section 10.3.

10.4.2.1. *Upper limit set by the rate for the marginal lending facility*

The upper limit on the rate for overnight money is set by the rate for the marginal lending facility. This lending always constitutes the most expensive form of funding, which in principle is not subject to any quantitative limit. The ECB defines the character of this facility as follows:

The facility is intended to satisfy counterparties' temporary liquidity needs. (ECB 2000: 22)

The maturity of the facility is overnight. Thus, its rate acts as a ceiling for the rate for overnight money because no bank will borrow overnight from another bank if it is asked to pay a higher rate of interest than the rate at which it can borrow unlimited amounts at call from the ECB.

As collateral for the marginal lending facility, the ECB requires specific types of asset that have to meet its creditworthiness criteria.

- *Tier 1 assets* must be debt instruments and must meet high credit standards.[11] They must be located in the euro area (so that realization is subject to the law of a member state of the euro area), transferable in book-entry form, and deposited with a national central bank or with a central securities depository which fulfils the minimum standards established by the ECB. They must be denominated in euros and must be issued (or guaranteed) by entities established in the European Economic Area. They must, at least, be listed or quoted on a regulated market

---

[11] In the assessment of the credit standard of debt instruments, the ECB takes into account, *inter alia*, available ratings by market agencies as well as certain institutional criteria that would ensure particularly high protection of the holders.

as defined according to the Investment Services Directive, or listed, quoted, or traded on certain non-regulated markets as specified by the ECB.

- *Tier 2 assets* must be debt obligations against, or equities of (or be guaranteed by), entities that are deemed to be financially sound by the national central bank that has included the assets in its tier 2 list; furthermore, they must be easily accessible to the national central bank that has included the assets in its tier 2 list. They must be located in the euro area (so that realization is subject to the law of a member state of the euro area); they must be denominated in euros; and they must be issued (or guaranteed) by entities established in the euro area.

These assets are required as collateral for all refinancing transactions of the ECB. A differentiation between tier 1 and tier 2 assets is relevant only for ECB's outright open-market operations, for which only tier 1 assets can be used.

Seen in quantitative terms, marginal lending has been of very limited importance. The weekly consolidated financial statements of the Eurosystem show that the funding via this instrument seldom exceeds a level of €400 million, which represents around 2 per 1,000 of the ECB total refinancing.

10.4.2.2. *Lower limit set by the rate for the deposit facility*

As became clear in the case of the minimalist approach described above, in order to manage the rate for overnight money, an *absorption instrument* is always needed when the banks obtain a major portion of their funding via instruments that run for longer than one day. The ECB is the only major central bank in the world that makes use of such an instrument. The technical features of these instruments have already been described.

Compared with open-market transactions, the main advantage of a standing facility for the absorption of liquidity is that it is principle *unlimited*. Thus, if such an instrument is used for the sterilization of the liquidity effects of intervention, there is no limit to the 'sterilization potential' of the ECB.

With some exceptions, the amount of funds deposited with this facility has been very low. Again, on most dates for which the ECB publishes its financial statement, it has remained below a threshold of €400 million. At same dates (e.g. 28 April 2000), the financial statement shows that banks have simultaneously made use of the deposit and the marginal lending facility, which indicates that the euro money market is not yet perfectly integrated.

10.4.2.3. *Stabilization of the rate for overnight money by the minimum reserve*

The minimum reserve also plays an important role in interest rate targeting. For this reason, the European Central Bank has decided to adopt this instrument:

The averaging provision of the ESCB's minimum reserve system aims to contribute to the stabilisation of money market interest rates by giving institutions an incentive to smooth the effects of temporary liquidity fluctuations. (ECB 2000e: 52)

In the euro area all credit institutions are subject to the minimum reserve requirement in respect of the following liabilities:

- *deposits* (overnight, up to two years' agreed maturity and notice period);
- *debt securities* (up to two years' agreed maturity) and money market paper.

For these assets a 2% reserve coefficient is applied. In principle, the ECB also regards deposits over two years' agreed maturity and notice period, debt securities over two years' agreed maturity, and repos as a part of the reserve base of credit institutions, but it applies a 0% reserve coefficient to them.

It should be noted that a bank's liabilities towards another domestic credit institution are not subject to reserves. In contrast to the practice of the Bundesbank, the ECB's minimum reserve requirements make no distinction between domestic and foreign deposits.

The reserve requirements that must be held for one month are calculated by applying to the amount of eligible liabilities (which are based on balance sheet data from the end of the month) the reserve ratios for the corresponding categories of liabilities.

As the balance sheet data for the end of one month are normally available about three weeks later, the *reserve maintenance period* starts on the 24th calendar day of each month. It lasts one month and ends on the 23rd calendar day of the following month. Thus, the ECB has established a fully lagged reserve requirement. This calculation procedure means that in the short term the banks' demand for reserves is completely interest-rate-inelastic, since the only factor determining it—apart from non-banks' demand for cash, which is not very amenable to control—is the exogenously decided reserve requirement. Thus, in the short run the ECB has, so to speak, to follow in the wake of the banks (Bockelmann 1978: 45). If the ECB fails to cover the banks' demand for central bank balances created in this way (monetary base targeting), this will lead to massive interest rate increases on the money market at the end of the maintenance period.

The individual banks will seek to cover their liquidity shortfall via the money market. This interest rate movement will, however, be ineffective, since the global difference between the liquidity needs of the banking system and the liquidity made available by the ECB will not be eliminated in this way; and so at the end of the maintenance period some banks will not be able to meet their minimum reserve requirement.[12]

The assets that are eligible to satisfy reserve requirements are central bank balances held during the maintenance period. As already mentioned, a bank has to fulfil its reserve holdings as an average so that its daily central bank balances can be higher or lower than the daily average of its monthly reserve requirement. Thus, if a bank is confronted with a temporary excess or a shortage of liquidity, there is no immediate need to borrow to or to lend from the money market. This effect is especially important in the earlier parts of the maintenance period. During the end of this period, a bank is under a stronger compulsion to fine-tune its reserve holdings in order to meet the reserve requirement.

In the daily data on the overnight rates of the euro area, the impact of the minimum reserve requirement can be clearly detected. Overnight rates are relatively stable from the beginning of the maintenance period until about the 20th calendar day of the following month. The last two or three days of the maintenance period are normally characterized by a higher volatility of the overnight rate.

- If it falls below the repo rate, the ECB has provided too much liquidity via its main refinancing instrument.
- If it exceeds the repo rate, the overall provision of liquidity has been too low.

Since January 1999 both cases could be observed. But, especially in 1999, the ECB had a preference for a rather generous provision of liquidity towards the end of the reserve period.

A specific feature of the ECB's reserve system is the *remuneration* of reserve holdings. Holdings of required reserves are remunerated at the average rate for the ECB's main financing operation rations. This average is calculated as a weighted average according to the number of calendar days. Reserve holdings exceeding the required reserves are not remunerated. As already mentioned, the remuneration of minimum reserves avoids the allocative distortions of this instrument. It has no effect on the management of money market rates.

---

[12] In this event, a special rate of interest (2.5 percentage points above the marginal lending rate) would be payable for a period of thirty days on the difference between the reserve requirement and the actual reserves held.

The importance of the minimum reserve requirement for the ECB's management of the money market rate is due to the following:

1. Since the ECB knows precisely at the beginning of the maintenance period how much central bank money the banking system will need for its reserve holdings, it is relatively well positioned in this period to supply the banks' liquidity needs in such a way as to avoid major fluctuations in the money market rate.

2. In the *first half* of the maintenance period it is particularly important that the actual reserve holdings are calculated as a monthly average. If the ECB supplies too much (too little) liquidity in this phase, the banks will react to this situation by maintaining higher (lower) central bank balances than they would be expected to do in order to meet the reserve requirement. Thus, a liquidity surplus in the banking system does not necessarily lead to pressure on the money market in the first half of the maintenance period.

3. In the *second half* the maintenance period money market management becomes more difficult. As excess reserves are not remunerated, the banks are now trying to keep their reserve holdings very close to their reserve requirements. Thus, an aggregate liquidity surplus (deficit) will lead to overnight rates that are lower (higher) than the repo rate. If the ECB wants to avoid such effects, it has to forecast the aggregate liquidity needs of the banking system very precisely. Volatile overnight rates at the end of the reserve period can therefore be regarded as an indication of forecast errors.

The ECB's minimum reserve system, therefore, helps to curb the fluctuations in the overnight money market rate. However, the macroeconomic importance of this effect should not be overrated. As we will see in the next section, perfectly stable overnight rates are not necessary for a control over the one-month and three-month interest rates, which are closer to the rates that are relevant for firms and households.

10.4.2.4. *Targeting the rate for one-month and three-month money*
Table 10.6 shows that, compared with the fluctuation margin of the overnight rate, the rates for one-month and three-month money are surprisingly stable. The main factors at work here are the ECB's main refinancing instrument and the policy of interest rate smoothing.

10.4.2.4.1. *Securities repos as the chief instrument of money market management* From the mid-1980s, securities repos have become the most important instrument in the toolbox of almost all central banks in the world. The ECB provides about 99% of its refinancing in the form of repurchase agreements. It uses securities repos in the form of both fixed rate and variable rate tenders.

The main refinancing operations are executed on a weekly basis. Tuesday is the usual trading day and the operations usually have a maturity of two weeks. For a policy of interest rate targeting, *fixed rate tenders* are the most suitable instrument: in the first eighteen months of its existence, the ECB used only this variant for its main refinancing operations. *Variable rate tenders* are by their very nature not compatible with interest rate targeting on the money market. In the past the Bundesbank resolved this problem by considerably modifying the form in which these operations are conducted. Whereas in the classic form of a variable rate tender a central bank sets the amount to be allotted *ex ante* and then determines the rate at which the funds are allotted via an auction, the Bundesbank chose not to announce the amount of monetary base it intended to offer on a given allotment date. In fact, it decided on the amount only when all the bids by the banks were known. Thus, it was in possession of what might be described as a concrete demand function, which enabled it to determine the targeted combination of interest rate and volume. In this form a variable rate tender can thus be used as an instrument for managing the money market rate. From an economic point of view, it can be regarded as fixed rate tender in disguise. The ECB started with variable tenders on 28 June 2000 because it was confronted with the problem that the sum of the individual banks' bids in the fixed rate tender by far exceeded the amount of liquidity needed by the banking system. On 7 June 2000 the sum of individual bids was €8,491,195 million while the allotment that corresponds with the aggregate liquidity needs was only €75,000 million (see Box 10.1).

With its main refinancing operations, the ECB is able to control the money market rate fairly satisfactorily within the two-week maturity period range. The individual bank has to decide whether to borrow for two weeks on the interbank market or whether to bid in a securities repo. The rate for borrowing from another bank must not be higher than the expected allotment rate. On the other hand, it cannot be significantly below this rate, since banks that have surplus liquidity for this period will not lend their central bank balances to another bank, but instead will reduce the amount for which they bid in the securities repo. As there is no money market rate for two weeks, the main impact of the repos is on the one-month rate.

10.4.2.4.2. *Interest rate smoothing*   As we have seen, the three-month rate is even more stable than the one-month rate. In order to control this

Box 10.1. *Reasons for overbidding in the ECB's fixed rate tenders*

From the very beginning, the fixed rate tenders of the ECB were confronted with the problem that the sum of individual bids by far exceeded the aggregate liquidity needs of the banking system. This problem increased over time, so that on 7 June 2000 the allotment rate was only 0.9%.

The reason for such an overbidding is relatively simple. The decision process of an individual bank can be described as follows. It can either decide to participate at a fixed rate tender, or it can borrow the liquidity it needs on the money market after the allotment is made. If it takes part in the tender, and if it bids for an amount that exceeds its liquidity needs, it can lend the excess liquidity on the money market. Thus, the decisive interest rates are the repo rate for the tender and the money market rate after the allotment.

If all banks are systematically overbidding, this is a clear indication that they expect a money market rate that exceeds the repo rate. In other words, the expectations value of difference between both rates must be positive.

The difference between these two rates depends above all on the allotment by the ECB and the actual liquidity needs of the banking system. If the ECB's allotment is identical with the liquidity needs, there is no reason for a bias of the money market rate over the repo rate. In other words, overbidding is an indication that the ECB has supplied systematically too little liquidity to the banking system.

A second reason for overbidding is the expectation of a rising repo rate. Since repos are offered weekly, there is a risk that the rate for the following tender is higher than for the actual tender, at least if the ECB governing council meets between these two dates.

While both reasons might play a role, the second argument would explain an overbidding only when an interest rate increase is imminent. However, the data show that overbidding was excessive even immediately after interest rate decisions of the ECB and also at dates when no council meeting took place before the next tender operation.

Thus, the main reason is a systematically too low supply of liquidity via the fixed rate tenders. This is confirmed by the fact that, 'on average in 1999, the EONIA [euro overnight index average of interbank overnight rates] was $2\frac{1}{2}$ basis points higher than the rate on the MROs [main refinancing operations]' (ECB 2000c: 50).

maturity with an instrument that has a maturity of only two weeks, the ECB has to practice the strategy of interest rate smoothing (Goodhart 1996).

1. By avoiding changing the signs when changing the allotment rates, care is taken from the outset to ensure that the deviations in the rate for three-month money can go in only one direction. Thus, in periods of falling interest rates three-month rates can only realistically be expected to be below the repo rate, since a bank will hardly want to obtain liquidity for three months at a rate that is above the expected rates for two-week securities repos. Accordingly, in periods of rising interest rates, deviations in the three-month rate can only be in an upward direction.

2. A second element of interest rate smoothing is that changes in repo rates are usually changed in small steps, i.e. scarcely more than one-half

a percentage point each month. According to the expectations theory of the yield curve (see Appendix 8.1), the three-month rate is the average of the expected allotment rates for two-week securities repos over the coming three-month period. On a three-month perspective, therefore, even assuming that there is a half percentage point rise in each of the two months, the three-month rate can deviate in an upward direction only by 0.5 percentage point from the current repo rate.[13] The policy of 'small steps' that is followed by the ECB and most other central banks is thus a *sine qua non* for a control over the rate for three-month money.[14]

In addition to its main refinancing operations, the ECB executes regular refinancing operations with a *three-month maturity*. These longer-term refinancing operations are traded monthly at the first Wednesday of each minimum reserve maintenance period. They are offered in the form of a genuine variable rate tender where the amount to be allotted is set *ex ante*. Thus, the marginal interest rate for which an allotment is possible can be used as an indication of the markets' forecast of the central bank interest rate policy. Currently the ECB allocates about one-third of its total refinancing in the form of longer-term repos. As already mentioned, a variable rate tender is incompatible with a strategy of interest rate targeting. But, since the ECB's longer-term repos are used mainly for a base refinancing of the banking system, they have no impact on the money market rates in the euro area.

10.4.3. *General conclusion*

Overall, it appears that the ECB has an inherently well balanced arsenal of instruments at its disposal, whereby it can at all times manage its operating targets as it considers necessary in order to achieve the ultimate goal of price stability. However, when compared with the minimalist approach to interest rate targeting described earlier (see Section 10.2.3), the manner in which the ECB uses its instruments does have some drawbacks:

1. The overall approach is not very transparent. Above all, the ECB's armoury includes far too many instruments. In addition to the main instruments that have been described above, the ECB disposes of instruments for so-called fine-tuning and structural operations (foreign exchange swaps, collection of fixed-term deposits, outright sales and purchases, issuance of debt certificates).[15] Most of these instruments

---

[13] It is assumed here that the interest rate increases take place on the first day of the second and third months.

[14] Marvin Goodfriend (1991) was the first to draw attention to this fact in the context of the Fed.

[15] A detailed description can be found in ECB (2000*d*).

were devised at a time when securities repos had not developed into the important and sophisticated instrument that they are today and when the instrument of the deposit facility was not available.

2. The instrument of minimum reserves is not necessary for a control over the one-month and three-month money market rate. It would be sufficient to keep the overnight rate within the 2% band set by the marginal refinancing and the deposit rate. As the example of the Bank of England shows (see Section 10.6 and Table 10.6), short-term fluctuations of the overnight rate are not incompatible with a rather stable one-month or three-month money market rate.

10.5. MONEY MARKET MANAGEMENT BY THE FEDERAL RESERVE SYSTEM

10.5.1. *Federal funds rate as the operating target*

The US Federal Reserve System[16] also uses the money market interest rate as an operating target in its conduct of monetary policy. It specifically targets the federal funds rate, i.e. the rate at which central bank balances, or *federal funds*, are lent for one day. It is therefore equivalent to the rate for overnight money. This rate serves simultaneously as the policy rate (i.e. the rate that is decided by the Federal Open Market Committee) and the official operating target. Table 10.6 shows that the fluctuations in this short-term money market rate are smaller in the United States than in other major countries, with the sole exception of Japan.

In the United States interest rate decisions are taken by the Federal Open Market Committee (FOMC) which meets eight times a year, normally on a Tuesday. It expresses its operating target as a specified level of the *federal funds rate*–the interest rate on interbank loans of balances held on deposit at the Federal Reserve. After each of its policy meetings, the FOMC issues a written directive to the Trading Desk, instructing it to foster conditions in reserve markets consistent with maintaining the federal funds rate at an average of around the target rate.

The main difference between the Fed's and the ECB's operating procedures is the *de facto* lack of standing facilities in the United States. In particular, there is no facility whereby the authorities can set an upper limit on the money market rate. Thus, all refinancing is provided by repurchase agreements and outright open market operations. As a consequence, the control over the overnight rate requires the Federal Reserve to act in the

---

[16] For institutional details of the US central banking system, see Board of Governors (1994).

markets daily, while the ECB usually conducts open-market operations only once a week.

10.5.2. *Interest rate targeting with open-market operations*

As was observed in Section 10.3, open-market operations are not an ideal instrument for interest rate targeting on the money market. Unlike lending facilities, they require the central bank to be continually intervening on the money market. This is particularly the case if the minimum reserve requirements have been significantly reduced, as they have been over the past few years in the United States, among other countries.

In the open-market operations of the Fed, a distinction has to be made between its outright open-market operations and its repo operations. The Fed uses outright operations for the base refinancing of the banking system. Thus, its portfolio of securities increases over time, mainly to keep up with the growth of currency. For the management of money market rates, these operations play no role. For that purpose the Fed uses securities repos (temporary open-market operations). These are always arranged as variable rate tenders. Most operations are usually conducted in the morning between 9.25 and 9.50 am to take advantage of the greater market liquidity at that time (Blenck 2000). The repos can be used for the provision of funds (system repurchase agreements) or for the absorption of liquidity (matched sale–purchase transactions). The maturity period of the securities repos can range from several days to ninety days (fixed-term repurchase agreements), but one-day transactions are also common (overnight system repurchase agreements). Repos with longer maturities may include a provision for early termination on the part of the banks (withdrawable term system repurchase agreements) but this provision was curtailed and was not offered at all in 1999.[17]

10.5.3. *Discount credit*[18]

Discount credit plays a relatively unimportant role in the US system. Although the discount rate is usually below the money market rate, the amount of central bank balances made available in this way (known as *borrowed reserves*) as a proportion of total central bank funding has been negligible in the last few years. Currently less than one per thousand of the total monetary base is provided via discount credit. The reason for the lack

[17] For details, see Federal Reserve Bank of New York (2000).
[18] For a more detailed analysis, see Schnadt (1994).

of demand for this form of central bank funding is that the Federal Reserve grants this facility only in exceptional cases. It is in principle a discretionary form of Fed financing. Moreover, since the early 1990s market participants have tended to regard a bank's recourse to discount credit as a sign of an unsound financial situation (Borio 2000: 10).

In the United States there are three different types of discount credit. For short-term liquidity shortages there is *adjustment credit*, which the big banks are required to repay after one day. *Seasonal credit* is granted for longer periods and is made available to smaller banks that experience marked seasonal fluctuations in their deposits or lending. *Extended credit* is provided for banks that experience serious solvency difficulties.

As far as the Fed's interest-rate targeting is concerned, discount credit has no significant role to play. Because of the banks' reluctance to use this facility, it can serve as neither a lower nor an upper limit for the federal funds rate.

10.5.4. *Minimum reserve policy*

In the United States, as in Germany, the minimum reserve requirement has been significantly reduced in the last fifteen years. A minimum reserve requirement exists only in respect of transactions deposits, to which a reserve ratio of 10% has applied since 20 December 1994.[19] The minimum reserve requirement is based on two-week periods that begin every other Tuesday. The system is fully lagged: the reserve requirement is calculated from average deposits in the two-week period beginning thirty days before the start of the corresponding maintenance period. The actual minimum reserve held is calculated as an average over the two-week period.

Because of the averaging possibility, banks in the United States are able to smooth out short-term liquidity surpluses or deficits simply by allowing their central bank balances to fluctuate in response to such conditions. But this stabilizing effect of the minimum reserve instrument is less pronounced than in the euro area because of (1) the much shorter maintenance period, and (2) the fact that the vault cash can be used as an eligible asset for satisfying the reserve requirement. Currently a reserve requirement of $40 billion is fulfilled by vault cash of $36 billion. Thus, a bank with a temporary excess balance at the Fed has little leeway for using it in the form of a reserve requirement. This effect is only very partially reduced by the possibility of carrying forward 4% of any surplus or deficit in reserves held into the next two-week period.

---

[19] In the case of banks with transaction balances of less than $54 million, a reserve ratio of 3% is required.

10.5.5. *Summary*

The example of US monetary policy shows that a policy of interest rate targeting can be conducted almost exclusively without central bank credit facilities. It is not a very efficient way of proceeding, since it requires very active intervention by the central bank on the money market. The banks' demand for central bank balances is difficult to forecast, particularly if the minimum reserve ratios have already been significantly reduced. If it were to create a facility similar to the marginal lending facility in the euro area, the Fed could still pursue its policy of interest rate targeting, but it would need to intervene very much less on the money market.

10.6. MONEY MARKET MANAGEMENT BY THE BANK OF ENGLAND

10.6.1. *Policy rate and operating targets*

In its monthly meetings, the Monetary Policy Committee, the Bank of England's decision-making body, decides on the level of the repo rate, which is the rate applied in the Bank's open-market operations with a maturity of two weeks. In addition to this policy rate the Bank has no official operating target.

The general observation that the methods of managing the money market are far from transparent is particularly true in the case of the United Kingdom. Although the system was changed considerably in 1997, some of the main criticisms mentioned by Mervyn King[20] are still valid:

- the system is complicated;
- the frequency of intervention is greater than needed for purposes of monetary policy;
- overnight rates are more volatile than elsewhere. (King 1994: 65)

This complexity due mainly to the fact that the Bank of England conducts its interest rate targeting exclusively via open-market operations and makes no use of minimum reserves. The overall design of the system becomes obvious when we look at Table 10.6, which shows that overnight rates are indeed more volatile than in the United States and in the euro area. At the same time, one-month and three-month rates are fairly stable. Thus, the operating target is either the one-month or the three-month rate. This view is confirmed by King (1994: 67), who speaks of the 'all-important

---

[20] King (1994: 65) takes the view that 'many, if not all, of these criticisms are based on a misunderstanding of the market for liquidity in the UK'.

one-month to three-month maturity range–the range affecting banks'
base rates'.

10.6.2. *Money market management without the minimum reserves*

As minimum reserves are not used as an instrument of monetary policy,[21]
the banks are not prepared to hold a significant amount of voluntary
central bank balances (working balances). In fact, in the UK they are
equivalent to only 0.1% of total bank liabilities.

For interest rate targeting on the money market, doing without minimum reserves is not without its problems, especially if the central bank
does not make any standing facilities available. For then the banks, in their
daily liquidity management, have to ensure that their central bank account
is at all times in surplus, even though they will also try to keep the balance
as low as possible. Unlike in the case of a minimum reserve system as practised in Germany or the USA, the daily fluctuations in a bank's liquidity
position will always have to be offset by recourse to the money market.
This also applies to the banking system as a whole, which is similarly
unable to smooth out liquidity fluctuations within the reserve-holding
period.

Since banks' demand for monetary base, which is now determined solely
by the demand for cash in the economy, is very rigid in the short term, the
central bank must supply the necessary central bank balances to the banks
on a daily basis. Otherwise, individual banks could end up being unable to
meet their daily liabilities. The rate for overnight money would then no
longer be able to deliver market equilibrium.

10.6.3. *Open-market operations*

As a result of the specific institutional arrangements, the Bank of England
is much more active in the money market than the ECB and the Federal
Reserve. It usually conducts open-market operations three times a day: at
9.45 am (if large liquidity shortages of the banking system are expected), at
noon, and at 2.30 pm. It is also prepared to offer a late repo facility between
3.50 and 3.55 pm at a rate $\frac{1}{4}$ percentage point above the repo rate applied
in the bank's open-market operations.

---

[21] In order to provide the central bank with income, the banks are required to hold minimum reserves
equal to 0.15% of their average outstanding liabilities with maturities of up to two years (Bank of
England 2000*a*).

In each of these rounds the Bank adopts the following procedure (Bank of England 2000*a*):

- It publishes a forecast of the market's liquidity shortage or surplus for the day.
- If the market's position is one of liquidity shortage, as is typically the case, and if the shortage is large enough, the Bank will invite a round of open-market operations.
- Open-market operations will generally be conducted on a fixed rate, but variable rate tenders are also possible. The maturity of the funds that are provided is on average around two weeks.
- For these operations banks have a choice of acquiring the funds through repo or through outright sales. Normally both forms are treated on the same basis. If banks offer bills, the residual maturity can be up to the longest dated repo invited. The Bank will not buy outright bank bills within seven days of the date of their acceptance.
- If the bids exceed the forecast of the remaining shortage, the Bank will pro-rate bids.
- On days when the market is forecast to be in surplus, the Bank will 'mop' up the surplus by offering outright sales of short-dated Treasury bills.

Counterparties of these transactions are banks, building societies, and securities firms that are subject to appropriate prudential supervision.

The relatively high volatility of the overnight rate can be explained mainly by the fact that all refinancing operations of the Bank of England normally have a maturity of two weeks. As the system lacks an instrument with a one-day maturity, it is not astonishing that the overnight rate fluctuates considerably. Thus, when an individual bank has a liquidity shortage for one day, it will not always be willing to increase its liquidity for two weeks, which will entail an interest rate risk. Depending on the concrete situation, it may require major changes in the overnight rate until the banks are induced to bid for additional funds.

10.6.4. *Overall assessment*

In spite of their complexity, the Bank of England's money market operating procedures are certainly no impediment to an efficient transmission of monetary policy impulses. In the words of Mervyn King,

But, from a macroeconomic perspective, the real issue is whether the short rate volatility disrupts monetary policy signalling. That is, whether noise at the short end of the yield curve infects points further up that curve—points where expectations of future policy actions are crucial and where savings and investment decisions are made. (King 1994: 65)

Table 10.6 shows that such an infection does not take place, although one cannot deny that the longer-term rates are less controllable in the United Kingdom than in the euro area. In addition, it seems questionable whether the Bank of England maintains procedures that are labour-intensive for itself as well as for financial institutions.

10.7. MONEY MARKET MANAGEMENT BY THE BANK OF JAPAN

10.7.1. *Policy rate and operating target*

The Bank of Japan's operating procedures are relatively similar to those of the Federal Reserve System. Its policy rate is the uncollateralized overnight call rate (an overnight rate among banks) which is also the market rate that serves as operating target.

In the last few years, the monetary policy operations of the Bank of Japan (BoJ) differ from those of other central banks in that all short-term interest rates are close to 0%. The so-called *zero interest rate policy* was adopted on 12 February 1999 when a policy guideline was decided which stated that 'the Bank of Japan will flexibly provide ample funds and encourage the uncollateralized overnight rate to move as low as possible'. This led to an overnight rate in a range between 0.02% and 0.03%. Although the zero interest rate policy was ended on 11 August 2000 with a target rate of 0.25% for the overnight rate, it still makes no sense to analyse the short-term fluctuations of the rates for different maturities as we did for the three other central banks in Table 10.6.

The BoJ toolbox includes minimum reserves and open-market operations. The Bank also disposes of a discount instrument, but such credit is extended at its discretion rather than automatically on bank's request (Blenck 2000: 10). Thus, standing facilities play no role in the Japanese monetary policy framework. The main elements of the Bank of Japan's minimum reserve system are summarized in Table 10.4. Although the reserve requirements are higher than in the United States, the system is not able by itself to stabilize money market rates. Borio (2000: 14) explains this as the 'high volatility of autonomous factors' affecting the money market, i.e. changes in banknotes, government deposits, and the 'float' of the banking system (changes in liquidity that are due to the length of settlement).

10.7.2. *Open-market operations*[22]

Because of its policy rate and operating target, the stabilization of the overnight rate requires that the Bank of Japan conducts money market operations at least daily, so that it is almost as active as the Bank of England. The regular daily schedule is as follows (Miyanoya 2000):

- 9.20 am (for same-day settlement): purchases/sales of Treasury bills (TBs) and financing bills (FBs) under repurchase agreements, outright purchases of bills, and outright sales of bills drawn by the Bank;
- 9.30 am (for future-day settlement): borrowing of Japanese government bonds (JGBs) against cash collateral;
- 10.10 am (for future-day settlement): purchases/sales of TBs and FBs, outright purchases of TBs and FBs, sales of commercial paper under repurchase agreements, and outright purchases of JGBs;
- 12.10 pm (for same-day settlement): outright sales of bills issued by the Bank of Japan;
- 12.10 pm (for future-day settlement): outright purchases of bills, outright purchases of bills backed by corporate debt obligations, and outright sales of bills issued by the Bank of Japan.

Thus, the Bank of Japan's open-market instruments include outright purchases and repurchase agreements. The most frequently used instrument for providing liquidity are purchases of short-term government bills under repurchase agreements. The maturity of these operations ranges from one week to three months in most cases. In the same way as the Federal Reserve, the Bank of Japan uses outright purchases (twice a month) mainly for the permanent provision of funds that are required for the increase in currency. In the last few years the amount of funds provided on a temporary basis has increased markedly and now it exceeds the amount of funds provided on a permanent basis. For absorbing funds, sales of short-term government bills under repurchase agreements are used, along with outright sales of bills issued by the Bank of Japan. All open-market transactions are conducted in the form of variable rate tenders.

10.8. THE NEW POLITICAL ECONOMY AND MONETARY POLICY INSTRUMENTS

The above discussion of the money market management of four major central banks demonstrates the complexity and lack of transparency of the

---

[22] This section draws on Blenck (2000: 7).

procedures (for a survey see Table 10.7). Although some improvements have been made in the last few years, in general, what Schnadt said some years ago, in a study about EU central banks, is still true:

At present, the operating procedures of all central banks within the Community are typically neither transparent nor simple, and are not well understood in the larger financial community, the financial press and amongst monetary economists. (Schnadt 1994: 31)

A comparison with the minimalist approach to interest rate targeting described earlier prompts one to ask why the central banks prefer to act in such a non-transparent manner. To a large degree, this could reflect the fact that central banks are operating within structures that have been historically determined. But, while this undoubtedly helps to explain the preference for certain individual instruments, it cannot be the only reason why the various countries' monetary policy instruments are, generally speaking, so complex. We may therefore need to consider this question not only in purely economic terms, but also in the light of the New Political Economy. The latter would regard central banks as bureaucracies whose main priority is to preserve, and possibly strengthen, their political power. This argument implies that, in their use of monetary policy instruments, central banks can be expected to

1. choose particularly labour-intensive instruments, and
2. adopt a targeting method characterized by a general lack of transparency.

The use of labour-intensive instruments enables central banking bureaucracies to maintain large numbers of staff, which in turn strengthens the power of the bureaucracy *vis-à-vis* other institutions and the politicians. Such instruments include minimum reserves, as well as the daily open-market operations practised in Japan, the United Kingdom, and the United States.

If the instruments used are not transparent, it is difficult for politicians and the public at large to assess how effective the central bank is in its individual operations. This is one way in which the central banking bureaucracy can reduce the exercise of political influence on monetary policy (which, even with formally independent central banks, will always be present). Of particular significance in this connection are all the instruments that create the impression that money market rates are determined not by the central bank, but by the market. These include the kind of securities repos in the form of variable rate tenders that are conducted by the Federal Reserve and the Bank of Japan and are included in the toolbox of the ECB.

Table 10.7. *Monetary policy instruments of the four main central banks*

Central bank	Policy rate	Operating target	Standing facilities	Minimum reserves	Open–market operations frequency	Open–market operations main maturity
Bank of England	Repo rate (2 weeks)	Unofficial: 1 month/3 months	Not available	Not used for monetary policy purposes	Several times per day	2 weeks
Bank of Japan	Overnight rate	Overnight	Not available	Applied	Several times per day	1 week–3 months
ECB	Repo rate (2 weeks)	Unofficial: 1 month/3 months	Deposit and marginal refinancing facility	Applied	Weekly	2 weeks
Federal Reserve	Federal Funds Rate	Overnight	Discount window, but of no importance for monetary policy	Applied, but no important role	Daily	Overnight

Deciding on the amount of the allotment after the bids are known effectively turns these into disguised volume tenders.

Even Borio (2000: 9) fails to recognize this character of the variable rate
tenders when he states: 'variable tenders are used to allow market forces to
play a greater role in determining the corresponding rate'.

Obviously, many authors find it difficult to appreciate that the central
bank as the monopolistic supplier of central bank money inevitably determines autonomously a particular combination of money market interest
rate and monetary base. Given the preference for interest rate targeting on
the money market shown by all central banks nowadays, there is simply no
room for 'market-determined' money market rates.

11

Seigniorage and Inflation Tax

What this chapter is about

In Chapter 4 we have already seen that in the past many countries repeatedly suffered from strong inflationary processes which were due primarily to excessive government expenditure financed by recourse to 'the banknote printing press'. This chapter focuses mainly on seigniorage, which describes the government revenue that can be obtained from having a central bank. More specifically, it will discuss
- the relationship between increases in the monetary base and government revenue;
- how much seigniorage a government can obtain without threatening macroeconomic stability (maximum seigniorage);
- how the attempt of governments to raise more than a maximum seigniorage will lead to a process of very high inflation.

11.1. INTRODUCTION

The concept of seigniorage plays an important role in monetary theory and policy. Although there are different definitions of seigniorage, they all try to capture the revenue that accrues to a government from the fact that it owns a national central bank.[1]

The expression *seigniorage* dates from the time of the gold standard, when every citizen was entitled to have gold bars minted in the form of gold coin. A duty was payable on this service, which was known in English as 'seigniorage', since it was due to the ruler (*seigneur*) who enjoyed the prerogative of money issue. In the twentieth century, and especially after the Second World War, throughout the world there have been only paper currencies (*fiat money*), involving no promise to redeem them in gold. Therefore seigniorage has had to be defined differently. In its most simple definition, seigniorage can be defined as the difference between the face value of the money issued by the State (banknotes, coins, and central bank balances) and their relatively low production costs.

---

[1] The revenue effects from seigniorage constitute a main advantage of the arrangement of a currency board (see Ch. 6) compared with the outright introduction of a foreign currency.

The political significance of this form of revenue was first systematically discussed by Keynes (1923). His definition of seigniorage was developed against the background of the hyperinflation being experienced in Germany and other countries at that time:[2]

A government can live for a long time, even the German government or the Russian government, by printing paper money. That is to say, it can by this means secure the command over real resources, resources just as real as those obtained by taxation. The method is condemned, but its efficacy, up to a point, must be admitted. A government can live by this means when it can live by no other. (Keynes 1923: 37)

11.2. MONETARY SEIGNIORAGE AND FISCAL SEIGNIORAGE

The most simple definition of seigniorage assumes that any increase in the monetary base is identical to a revenue of government. In Chapter 3 we have seen that the monetary base is created by all credit transactions between the central bank and the government, domestic banks and foreign institutions. In first differences, equation (3.1) can be written as:

$$\Delta B = \Delta NP_{CB/F} + \Delta NP_{CB/G} + \Delta Cr_{CB/B} - \Delta BAL_{CB/OAL}. \tag{3.1'}$$

In the context of this chapter, it is important to use a gross definition of central bank credits to the government instead of the net concept $\Delta NP_{CB/G}$. Thus,

$$\Delta NP_{CB/G} = \Delta Cr_{CB/G} - \Delta D_{CB/G}. \tag{11.1}$$

Changes in the net position of the central bank *vis-à-vis* the government are defined as the differences between the increase in central bank credits ($\Delta Cr_{CB/G}$) and the increase in government deposits with the central bank ($\Delta D_{CB/G}$).

The quote from Keynes also makes clear that the main issue regarding seigniorage is how far it gives the State command over *real* resources. For this reason, seigniorage is normally defined as a real magnitude. This leads to the definition of the so-called *monetary seigniorage* (SE^M):

$$SE^M \equiv \frac{B_t - B_{t-1}}{P_{t-1}} = \frac{\Delta B_t}{P_{t-1}}. \tag{11.2}$$

---

[2] According to the widely accepted terminology of Cagan (1956: 25), hyperinflation refers to a situation where the monthly inflation rate is higher than 50%. This is equivalent to an annual inflation rate of 12,875%.

If (11.2) is extended by B_{t-1}, seigniorage is obtained as the product of growth rate in the monetary base and the real monetary base:

$$SE^M \equiv \frac{B_t - B_{t-1}}{B_{t-1}} \frac{B_{t-1}}{P_{t-1}}. \tag{11.3}$$

This definition shows that seigniorage is always determined by two factors:

1. the growth rate of a monetary aggregate;
2. a real money stock.

This definition rests on the assumption that any increase in the monetary base is identical to a revenue of the government. However, this is not generally true. While it provides a good description of situations in which the government has an unlimited access to the central bank's printing press, it is not very useful today, where most central bank laws explicitly exclude any central bank financing of government deficits (see Section 7.2.4). Under such conditions, the so-called *fiscal seigniorage* is a more suitable concept. This focuses on

1. the central bank's profit that is transferred to the government;
2. the amount of government bonds that were bought by the central bank in open-market operations.

The profit of the central bank is obtained as

$$\Pi_{CB} = NP_{CB/F}i^*S + iCr_{CB/B} + iCr_{CB/G} - iR - V - O. \tag{11.4}$$

The earnings components comprise the central bank's interest income on (net) external assets ($i^*NP_{CB/F}$) multiplied by the exchange rate (S), lending to the State ($iCr_{CB/G}$), and to the banks ($iCr_{CB/B}$). Assuming that no direct central bank credit to government is allowed, $Cr_{CB/B}$ can only consist of government bonds that the central bank bought in outright open-market operations. Expenditure comprises interest rates on central bank reserves (iR) if reserves are interest-bearing (see Section 10.3.3), day-to-day operating costs (O), and valuation losses (gains) in the event of an appreciation (depreciation) in the domestic currency (V). We assume that interest rates for credits to banks and the government and for bank reserves are identical, as are the interest rates for foreign assets and liabilities of the central bank.

Additionally, a government can obtain financial resources from the central bank if the central bank buys government bonds in outright open-market operations ($\Delta Cr_{CB/G}$). At the same time, the government must make interest payments for the bonds that are held by the central bank. Thus, the overall cash flow (F) that the government can obtain in countries where direct central bank financing of the government is prohibited is

$$F = \Pi_{CB} + \Delta Cr_{CB/G} - iCr_{CB/G}. \tag{11.5}$$

The concept of fiscal seigniorage is based on this definition of government revenue from the central bank which is deflated by the price index:

$$SE^F = \frac{F}{P} = \frac{\Pi_{CB} + \Delta Cr_{CB/G} - iCr_{CB/G}}{P}. \tag{11.6}$$

If we compare (11.3) with (11.6), we can see that the two definitions of seigniorage can lead to very different results. This especially so in regions like the euro area, where most of the increase of the monetary base results from credits of the central bank to commercial banks. In 1999 the monetary base increased by €64 billion and credits to the banking system increased by almost the same amount (€65 billion). In the same period the Eurosystem's holdings of government bonds decreased by €1 billion.

In other words, the concept of monetary seigniorage constitutes an extreme simplification, which is useful only in situations where most of the increase in the monetary base is financed by credits to the government and where this increase is relatively large compared with the central bank's profits. Thus, monetary seigniorage can be regarded as a rule of thumb mainly for periods with high inflation resulting from excessive government lending from the central bank. Fiscal seigniorage provides a good description of the revenues that a government obtains from owning a central bank. It is almost identical with the central bank profit in those countries (currency areas) where outright open-market operations do not play a major role.

11.3. MACROECONOMIC STABILITY AND SEIGNIORAGE FINANCING

As most macroeconomic analyses focus on the impact of seigniorage on inflation, it is understandable that they are based mainly on the concept of monetary seigniorage. Normally an additional simplification is made. Instead of defining monetary seigniorage for the monetary base, it is defined for the money stock M1. This simplification is again advisable only for situations with very high and strongly growing central bank credits to the government: as the government uses such credits for spending and the private sector holds the receipts in form of M1, increases in the money stock are not very different from increases in the monetary base.

The definition of monetary seigniorage is then as follows:

$$SE^M = \frac{\Delta M_t}{P_{t-1}}, \tag{11.7}$$

or, in continuous time,

$$SE^M = \frac{dM}{P}. \tag{11.8}$$

Multiplying the right-hand side of (11.8) by M/M gives us

$$SE^M = \frac{dM}{M}\frac{M}{P} = \mu\,\frac{M}{P}. \tag{11.9}$$

Thus, monetary seigniorage can be represented as the product of the growth rate in the money supply (μ) and the real money supply (M/P). But the growth rate in the nominal money supply is the sum of the rate of change in the real money supply (g) and the inflation rate (π), and so we can write

$$SE^M = g\,\frac{M}{P} + \pi\,\frac{M}{P}. \tag{11.10}$$

The first term on the right-hand side of (11.10) is the *growth component* (Issing 1998: 247). Since, in a growing economy with rising per capita income, the real money supply demanded also rises (Chapter 2), the central bank can, on an ongoing basis, appropriate real resources from private individuals to the amount of the increase in the real money supply. If the central bank increases the nominal money supply beyond the amount of private individuals' additional demand caused by the rise in incomes, then prices and hence the price level in the economy will rise until money supply equals money demand (Chapter 4). As a result, inflation will erode the value of private individuals' real money holdings. This erosion of the value of real money holdings is known as *inflation tax* and is expressed by the second term of (11.10). Thus, the inflation tax (IT) is defined as[3]

$$IT = \pi\,\frac{M}{P}. \tag{11.11}$$

If we assume a long-term equilibrium ('golden age equilibrium'), the growth rate in the real money supply (g) is equal to the real rate of interest (r).

---

[3] As $d(M/P) = (dM\,P - dP\,M)/P^2$, $d(M/P)|_{dM=0} = -\,(dP/P)(M/P)$ indicates the reduction (erosion in value) in real money holdings resulting from an increase in the price level.

Using the simplified Fisher relationship ($i = r + \pi$), we obtain from (11.10) another concept of seigniorage:

$$SE^M = r\frac{M}{P} + \pi\frac{M}{P} = i\frac{M}{P} \qquad (11.12)$$

This measure for seigniorage is known as *opportunity cost seigniorage*,[4] because it reflects lost interest income which private individuals must forgo by holding non-interest-bearing money instead of interest-bearing investments. The advantage of such a definition of seigniorage is that it shows the value that private individuals attach to the holding of money. Opportunity cost seigniorage can therefore be interpreted as the saving of resources in a society that results from the fact that an economy uses a wholly paper currency and not a gold currency. The opportunity cost concept will correctly give the income accruing to the State from the money issue only if one chooses as the nominal rate of interest the effective rate of interest on government securities, since only then can equation (11.12) be interpreted as the real interest saving that the State makes by issuing money instead of interest-bearing securities (Gros 1989: 27).

In practice, the difference between the two concepts of seigniorage defined by (11.9) and (11.12) depends on the difference between i and μ (or π). For high inflation rates, the real interest rate component in the nominal interest rate becomes negligible. Empirical studies show that, although the absolute amounts of the revenue from seigniorage determined in this way differ, the hierarchy of the various countries in a comprehensive country analysis is largely independent of which concept is chosen (De Haan *et al.* 1993: 313).

As was demonstrated with equation (11.7), seigniorage represents revenue for the State. It is of interest from the analytical point of view then to ask how the State or the central bank can maximize this revenue. For that purpose, it is helpful to regard seigniorage—by analogy with taxation theory—as the product of the tax base and the tax rate, where the tax rate is the State's action parameter. In the case of seigniorage, the growth rate in the nominal money supply μ represents the tax rate and the real money supply (M/P) represents the tax base, as expressed in (11.9).

11.3.1. *Seigniorage maximization in a steady-state equilibrium*

As with other taxes, the State cannot increase the revenue from seigniorage at will. Although a faster growth rate in the money supply tends to

---

[4] The concept of opportunity cost seigniorage is found in the works of, e.g., Bailey (1956), Johnson (1969), Auernheimer (1974), Phelps (1973), Barro (1982), and Gros (1989, 1996).

increase the seigniorage (this would correspond to a higher tax rate), it reduces the real money supply held in an economy (this would correspond to a narrower tax basis), since the faster money supply growth and the resulting increase in nominal interest rates lead to an increase in the opportunity costs of holding money.

We will discuss the influence of these two contrary effects in a very simple model, which represents a stationary economy in steady-state equilibrium. This implies constancy in the real money supply and hence identity between the growth rate in the nominal money supply and the inflation rate in each steady-state equilibrium ($\mu = \pi$). If such an economy is confronted with a permanent change in the growth rate of the money supply, this leads in equilibrium to a corresponding increase in the inflation rate. If one assumes a real money demand function that depends negatively on the nominal rate of interest and positively on real income (see Chapter 2), this nominal interest rate increase will in turn imply a decline in the real money supply. Thus, in steady-state conditions a particular real money supply will correspond to each rate of money supply growth (= inflation rate). How this relationship will work out in practice will depend on the specific form of the money demand function. In Figure 11.1, for the sake of simplicity, a linear real money demand function has been assumed, where

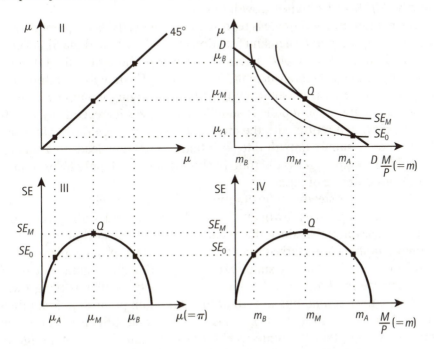

Figure 11.1. *Maximum seigniorage with linear money demand*

the real money stock demanded will depend only on the expected inflation rate (line *DD*). It must also be assumed that the actual inflation rate is always perfectly anticipated ($\pi^e = \pi$).

Analytically, the State's problem of how to obtain optimum seigniorage can be treated in the same way as the situation of a monopolist on a commodity market. The money demand function is to be regarded as the inverse demand function for the central bank. Since with the concept of monetary seigniorage the costs of 'money production' are regarded as negligible, the seigniorage obtained corresponds not only to an enterprise's earnings, but also to its profit, so that the optimum seigniorage is identical to the maximum seigniorage.

We will examine this in more detail using Figure 11.1. In accordance with equation (11.9) and the assumptions made above ($\pi^e = \pi = \mu$), seigniorage is obtained as the product of the growth rate in the nominal money supply (μ) and the real money supply (M/P). In diagram I of Figure 11.1 the hyperbola SE_0 thus reflects all the combinations of growth rate in the nominal money supply and real money supply that would produce a given volume of seigniorage SE_0. Thus, with a given real money demand, SE_0 can be achieved both as a combination of a higher real money supply $(M/P)_A$ and a lower growth rate μ_A, and as a combination of a lower real money supply $(M/P)_B$ and a higher growth rate μ_B.

The maximum seigniorage is represented graphically as the point of tangency of the real money demand function *DD* and the hyperbola SE_M. There the nominal money supply increases at a rate μ_M, at which the inflation elasticity of the real money demand is equal to 1. The rate μ_M therefore corresponds to the Cournot solution (Q) of the underlying monopoly case, in which the State as monopolistic supplier maximizes its revenue by equating the marginal return with the marginal cost of 0. Each further increase in the money supply growth rate (= inflation rate) now leads to a smaller amount of seigniorage, as diagram III shows; diagram II only helps to mirror the growth rate of money.

Thus, in each steady-state situation an amount of seigniorage is precisely assigned to each growth rate. When the growth rate is rising, seigniorage increases initially, since the negative effect of the decline in the real money supply is less marked than the positive effect of the higher growth rate in the nominal money supply. However, with a linear money demand this increase in seigniorage becomes progressively smaller as the growth rate rises, until it amounts to zero at the maximum point SE_M. From then on, a rising growth rate ($\mu > \mu_M$) has such a strong influence on the real money demand that the State receives less revenue from seigniorage in real terms than with a weaker growth in the money supply.

For the revenue from seigniorage to behave in the way described here, the assumption that only steady-state situations are being considered is crucial. This not only implies perfect controllability of the inflation rate; it also ensures—because of the assumption of constant growth rates—that private individuals can perfectly anticipate the actual inflation rate.

The assumption of a linear real money demand does, however, represent a considerable simplification. For this reason, economists frequently operate with an exponential money demand function which assumes a constant semi-elasticity (α) of real money demand in relation to inflation expectations (π^e). The money demand of the Cagan type has been discussed in Chapter 2:

$$\frac{M}{P} = L(\pi^e) = e^{-\alpha\pi^e}. \tag{11.13}$$

As already mentioned, the omission of real GDP growth rate and the real rate of interest is justifiable on the grounds that when inflation rates are high these real magnitudes are no longer of central importance for money demand.

The revenue from seigniorage in steady-state equilibrium ($\pi^e = \pi = \mu$) amounts to

$$SE = \mu\frac{M}{P} = \mu e^{-\alpha\mu}. \tag{11.14}$$

The maximum seigniorage (SE_{max}) is obtained by deriving with respect to μ and setting equation (11.14) at zero:

$$\frac{dSE}{d\mu} = e^{-\alpha\mu} + (-\alpha\mu)e^{-\alpha\mu} = (1 - \alpha\mu)e^{-\alpha\mu} = 0. \tag{11.15}$$

It is then achieved when the growth rate in the money supply is equal to the reciprocal value of the semi-elasticity of the money demand:

$$\mu^* = \frac{1}{\alpha}. \tag{11.16}$$

Assuming steady-state conditions and an exponential money demand function, as used here, a similar relationship is obtained between the growth rate of money supply (= inflation rate) and seigniorage to that already represented in Figure 11.1, with the only difference that the seigniorage cannot be zero (Figure 11.2).

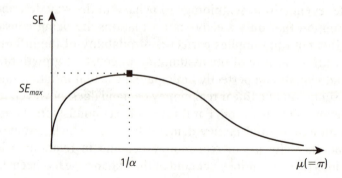

Figure 11.2. *Maximum seigniorage with semi-logarithmic money demand*

Neumann (1992) shows for the USA that such a *Laffer curve*[5] for financing from seigniorage is also obtained from empirical values. Instead of the above exponential function, he uses a quadratic estimator. He determines the maximum value of monetary seigniorage with an annual inflation rate of 7.9%. Moreover, it is not only monetary seigniorage that can be mapped in this way. Fiscal seigniorage shows a very similar curve. The maximum here occurs with an annual inflation rate of 7.2%.

The shape of the seigniorage curve suggests that each state seeking to maximize its revenue determines, and also achieves, the money supply expansion rate (or inflation rate) that is optimal for it. In the case of financing via seigniorage, one would then expect a positive, but *constant*, inflation rate. There would therefore be no threat to macroeconomic stability. However, the inflation rates observed in practice have neither maximized the seigniorage, nor have they been constant.

Research by Cagan (1956) shows that in many cases of hyperinflation the values of μ—and therefore, on the assumptions made, the values of π also—lie significantly above $1/\alpha$. Similarly, constant inflation rates are rarely to be found for countries with massive seigniorage financing. In fact, such financing frequently involves the risk of hyperinflation (Bruno and Fischer 1990). Steadily rising inflation rates are due above all to the fact that the conditions of steady-state equilibrium assumed here are not present in practice.

11.3.2. *Seigniorage in a non-steady-state world*

Contrary to what has been assumed here, in reality private individuals are not always able to perfectly anticipate the actual inflation rate. The expected

---

[5] This name comes from the American economist Arthur B. Laffer, who sought to justify the tax-cutting policy pursued by the Reagan government at the beginning of the 1980s by arguing that the lower tax rates would lead to an increase in the tax base, with the result that total tax revenue would rise. He was wrong.

inflation rate underlying their money demand may be higher or lower than the actual inflation rate. This has two possible consequences, either of which can lead to hyperinflation:

1. It can lead to an inherent instability in the demand for money.
2. The expectation errors give the State the opportunity to increase the seigniorage beyond SE_{max}.

An inherent instability in the demand for money can arise if accelerating inflation, once begun, is not halted, because the rise in the actual inflation rate and the resulting increase in the expected inflation rate have a cumulative effect on each other. An increase in the actual inflation rate will result in rising inflation expectations. Private individuals will seek to reduce their real cash holdings, which will result in higher prices being paid for the existing production of goods, which in turn will lead to an increase in inflation. This will again influence the expected inflation rate, and so on. Whether the inflation rate will stabilize will depend crucially on the stability characteristics of the demand for money (Marty and Thornton 1995: 28–30). Cagan (1956: 64–73) shows that the important factor here is the formation of private individuals' expectations.

If one assumes, following Cagan (1956: 37), adaptive expectations, then the following applies:

$$\frac{d\pi^e}{dt} = \beta(\pi - \pi^e) \quad \text{with } \beta > 0. \tag{11.17}$$

The change in the inflation expectation thus depends positively on the expectation error. If one again assumes a real money demand with constant semi-elasticity (equation (11.13)) and derives this with respect to time, one obtains the following:[6]

$$\mu - \pi = -\alpha \frac{d\pi^e}{dt}. \tag{11.18}$$

Equation (11.18) and the logarithmic version of (11.13) inserted in (11.17) give

$$\frac{1}{\alpha}(\mu - \pi) = \beta \left[\pi + \frac{1}{\alpha}(\ln M - \ln P) \right], \tag{11.19}$$

or

$$\beta(\ln P - \ln M) = \mu - (1 - \alpha\beta)\pi. \tag{11.19'}$$

---

[6] The results derived here for macroeconomic stability apply not only when a Cagan money demand function is used: they also apply to functions that take account of real income and the real interest rate.

For the change in inflation depending on price level changes, i.e.

$$\frac{\partial \pi}{\partial P} = \frac{-\beta}{1-\alpha\beta} \frac{1}{P},$$ (11.20)

this means that the actual inflation rate converges only with a denominator greater than 0, i.e., it does not increase without limit as a result of a one-off disturbance. It is thus of determining importance for stability that $\alpha\beta < 1$.[7] Otherwise, the smallest increase in the price level immediately means that the inflation rate increases without limit and thus money holdings are completely abandoned; i.e., steady-state conditions are not stable.

Superficially, the stability observations can be used as an argument for a positive inflation rate (Marty and Thornton 1995: 28), since, if it is assumed that the interest rate elasticity of the demand for money (ε_i) is constant in times of relative price level stability, the semi-elasticity α used in (11.13) declines with a higher nominal rate of interest and hence with a higher steady-state inflation rate. A higher inflation rate thus tends to contribute to stability in the economy. However, such a conclusion requires that the velocity of adjustment β remains constant. But this cannot be assumed with rising inflation rates, and so the increased stability as a result of the higher inflation rate is by no means necessarily guaranteed. The faster private individuals adjust their inflation expectations, the greater is the danger of instability in the demand for money.

It can be seen from Figure 11.1 that, with the exception of the maximum seigniorage, each amount of seigniorage can occur with both a low and a high inflation rate. Bruno and Fischer (1990: 356) show that the above-mentioned stability condition is also the condition for ensuring that a given volume of revenue will be achieved with the low inflation rate.

Even when this stability condition exists, however, hyperinflation can also be generated by the government's desire to increase the revenue from seigniorage beyond SE_{max}. This case is presented in Figure 11.3. The starting point here is again diagram II, which represents the real money demand of private individuals. If the State wants to achieve SE_M, and if private individuals have correct expectations, the nominal money supply must be increased by the rate μ_M, as a result of which private individuals hold the volume of real money m_M that corresponds to their real money demand.[8]

If the State aims not at revenue SE_M but at the higher revenue SE_Z, it can achieve the latter only if it is able to mislead private individuals by a policy

---

[7] Convergence towards a final inflation rate occurs when the rise in the price level (the inflation rate) increases at a less than proportionate rate with rising P, i.e. when $-\beta/(1 - \alpha\beta)$ is less than zero. Since $\alpha, \beta > 0$, this is equivalent to the condition $\alpha\beta < 1$.

[8] In the following analysis it will always be assumed that the inflation rate is equal to the growth rate in the nominal money supply.

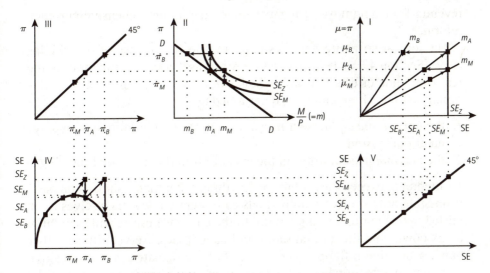

Figure 11.3. *Surprise inflation and seigniorage*

of *surprise inflation*. It can be seen from diagram I that, with a real money supply (m_M) that is constant in the short term, the State must achieve the growth rate μ_A. However, as soon as private individuals realize that they now hold too large a volume of real money in relation to the now higher inflation rate $(\pi_A = \mu_A)$, they will reduce their holdings accordingly (m_A), so that seigniorage falls to SE_A (diagrams II–IV). As a result, the attempt to increase seigniorage beyond SE_M leads to a decline in seigniorage.

If the State wishes to maintain its excessive seigniorage SE_Z, its only option is to bring about an even higher rate of money supply expansion than in the previous period (μ_B), in order to mislead private individuals once again. But this too will result in private individuals adjusting their real money holdings (m_B), which will lead to a very much more marked decline in seigniorage (SE_B). In the end, such a policy of continuing surprise inflation will result in astronomically high inflation rates and a situation in which the national currency will eventually no longer be used as a means of payment at all. It will be rejected by the population and replaced by foreign currencies to the extent that trade is not conducted on a purely barter basis. At the end of the hyperinflation phase seigniorage falls towards zero.[9] At that point, if the State is to recover even a modicum of

[9] Just how fast seigniorage falls to 0 will depend on the real money demand function. In Fig. 11.3 the system 'explodes' after private individuals have been misled only twice. In other words, the money supply expansion rate that is necessary after μ_B in order to achieve S_Z already results in the volume of real money holdings falling to 0 and hence in seigniorage also amounting to 0. This is different from what happens with money demand of the Cagan type, where seigniorage can never be 0 (Fig. 11.2).

revenue from seigniorage, it must undertake a comprehensive currency reform.

The logical structure here is similar to that in the case of the Phillips curve (Section 4.5.6). In both cases there are, as it were, natural limits to the real economic effects that politicians can achieve by pursuing an inflationary policy. These limits are determined by

1. the *natural unemployment rate* in the event of an inflationary employment policy, and
2. the *maximum seigniorage* in the event of inflationary state financing.

To attempt to exceed these limits on anything other than a short-term basis is possible only if private individuals consistently allow themselves to be misled to an ever increasing extent. In the end this process will inevitably break down, and the natural limits will have to be observed. On the other hand, a positive inflation rate, if it is fully anticipated, has no positive employment effects, whereas on these assumptions positive revenue can be obtained from seigniorage.

11.4. OPTIMAL SEIGNIORAGE

The quotation from Keynes (1923) at the beginning of this chapter shows that it is possible to answer the question of whether financing by means of seigniorage justifies the risks to macroeconomic stability only if the macroeconomic costs of such a form of financing (or its efficiency) are known and are compared with the costs of other types of financing. For a given volume of state expenditures, tax, credit, and seigniorage financing are all possible alternatives, and so the question arises as to which method of financing is preferable. In this context the desirable level of seigniorage financing is regarded as *optimal seigniorage.*[10]

The basic issue therefore concerns not so much the growth rate in the nominal money supply (inflation rate), which maximizes seigniorage only, but the combination of tax rates (including the inflation rate), where the negative welfare effects of taxation are minimized:

Both explicit and implicit taxes are distortionary. The distortion of the inflation tax [i.e. seigniorage] is the diversion of resources or loss of utility associated with the scarcity of money, already mentioned. But there are also distortions in explicit taxes; lump-sum taxes are not available. The problem is to optimize the choice

---

[10] The question of the optimal level of seigniorage and the advantages that seigniorage may have over other forms of taxation was first raised by Bailey (1956). The point was pursued in numerous other studies by, e.g., Phelps (1973), Calvo (1978), Goff and Thoma (1993), Calvo and Guidotti (1993), and Easterly *et al.* (1995).

of taxes, given the necessity of government expenditure. This formulation correctly connects the money-supply process to the government budget. (Tobin 1986: 11)

The negative welfare effects of seigniorage financing are always equated in economic literature with the welfare costs of inflation (Chapter 5). We have seen that these costs arise because of a sub-optimal level of money holdings. Thus, it would be advisable to avoid this form of financing entirely if it were possible to obtain tax revenue without negative welfare effects. But this is the case only with the poll tax: only when the State is able to raise revenue via this tax ('first-best' world) is there no sound reason for financing via seigniorage.[11]

If, however, one shares Tobin's view (1986) that there is no such thing as a tax that is free from distortion, or at least one that can be implemented politically, the inflation tax can be theoretically defended as a component of an optimal tax system in such a 'second-best' world (*optimal tax theorem*).[12] Here the State must ensure that the marginal social costs of seigniorage financing are in line with those of other forms of financing, in particular financing by taxation (Dornbusch and Fischer 1993: 4). Marginal social costs refer to the net welfare loss caused to society (both private individuals and the State) by one unit of money additionally raised by the State by way of seigniorage or tax financing.

[11] This is the conclusion arrived at by Friedman, who considers only the welfare costs of inflation using partial analysis (Friedman 1969).

[12] This second-best approach was originated by Phelps (1973). He, however, assumes that the marginal costs of the various forms of financing rise the more they are used.

PART III

MONETARY POLICY IN AN OPEN ECONOMY

Parts I and II discussed monetary policy mainly from the perspective of a closed economy. While this approach can be justified for didactical reasons, and to some extent for a large currency area like the United States or the euro area, a comprehensive analysis of monetary policy requires a systematic treatment of (1) the theoretical building blocks of open-economy macroeconomics, and (2) the monetary policy options and rules that are available in such a context.

Part III concentrates on the presentation of the theoretical building blocks to issues that are policy-relevant so that the book cannot be regarded as a substitute for a text on open-economy macroeconomics.

12

Important Building Blocks of Open-Economy Macroeconomics

What this chapter is about

- It examines the most important theoretical building blocks that are needed for a discussion of monetary policy in an open economy.
- At the level of the operating targets of monetary policy, it is important to regard the consistency requirements between the operating target of short-term interest rates and the operating target of the exchange rate.
- The uncovered interest parity theory (UIP) describes the interrelationship between the domestic and the foreign interest rate and the expected change in the exchange rate. It is mainly suitable as a theory for fixed exchange rate regimes.
- The purchasing power parity theory (PPP) analyses the interrelationship between the domestic and the foreign inflation rate and changes in the exchange rate. It provides the most important theoretical basis for flexible exchange rates.
- The Ricardo–Balassa–Samuelson model applies the PPP to emerging market economies with above-average productivity growth.

12.1. INTRODUCTION

The most obvious implication of the switch from a closed-economy to an open-economy perspective is the more complex structure of the monetary policy transmission process.

- At the level of *operating targets*, the central bank can target the exchange rate directly with foreign exchange market interventions. Thus, in addition to the monetary base and to money market interest rates, it has a third operating target at its disposal.
- At the level of *intermediate targets*, the central bank can target the exchange rate indirectly with the interest rate(s) that it uses as its operating target. This relationship is described by the covered and uncovered interest parity theory.
- At the level of *final targets*, in addition to the channels described in Chapter 4, the central bank can target the price level with a fixed or a 'crawling' exchange rate target *vis-à-vis* a stable key currency. This

relationship is described by the purchasing power parity theory. In addition, exchange rate targets can play an important role for the expectations channel of monetary policy.

12.2. THE EXCHANGE RATE AS AN OPERATING TARGET OF MONETARY POLICY

In Chapter 10 an operating target was characterized as a variable that can directly be controlled by a central bank's instruments. To some extent this is certainly true for the exchange rate. By buying or purchasing foreign assets on the foreign exchange market, a central bank can directly influence the exchange rate of its currency. Thus, foreign exchange market intervention can be regarded as an instrument comparable to outright open-market transactions which a central bank can use in order to target the short-term money market rate. As the role of the exchange rate as an operating target of monetary policy is not generally accepted, it will be explained in more detail using a simplified balance sheet of the central bank (Table 12.1). This allows us to see the scope and the limitations of this approach:

1. If a central bank tries to avoid a *depreciation* of its currency, a limit is set by the amount of its foreign exchange reserves (plus credit lines with other central banks or the International Monetary Fund).
2. If a central bank tries to avoid an *appreciation* of its currency, such a 'hard budget constraint' is absent. In other words, a central bank can always buy foreign exchange without limit, simply by selling deposits denominated in its own currency to the market.

Thus, if the exchange rate is used as an operating target of monetary policy, there is a fundamental difference between a central bank operating in the situation of a depreciation or in that of an appreciation of the domestic currency.

A central bank's interventions on the foreign exchange market have a direct impact on its domestic operating target. The central bank balance sheet equation (equation (3.4)) shows that

- purchases of foreign exchange are associated with an increase in the monetary base, and
- sales of foreign exchange are associated with a decrease in the monetary base.

However, a central bank can try to sever this link by conflicting variations of the monetary base. This approach, which is labelled *sterilization*, implies that in the case of an increase (decrease) in the monetary base induced by

Table 12.1. *Simplified central bank balance sheet*

Assets	Liabilities
Foreign exchange reserves	Monetary base
Domestic assets (credits to the banking system)	

interventions, the central bank reduces (increases) its credits to the domestic banking system (Argy and Kouri 1974). Given the two alternative domestic operating targets, sterilization can be defined as a policy that keeps either the monetary base or the money market interest rate constant. While the theoretical literature has some preference for the former definition, the latter will be used here, since it is compatible with the standard practice of central banks to use a certain money market rate as their operating target.

When, for instance, the ECB buys a major amount of US dollar assets, this increases the euro monetary base and reduces money market interest rates. The ECB can sterilize the additional liquidity by

1. buying short-term bonds from commercial banks (*outright open-market operations*) or
2. reducing the amount of liquidity supplied in the next main refinancing operation or completely suspending such an operation. With an amount of the weekly tender of €50 billion–€80 billion, the ECB could very rapidly sterilize a large amount of liquidity.

With the *deposit facility* (see Section 10.4.2.2) the ECB's toolbox includes an instrument that provides an automatic sterilization. When the liquidity of the banking system is too high compared with its liquidity needs, the money market rate drifts downwards; but as the banks can always invest excess liquidity in the deposit facility, the interest rate of this facility constitutes a floor for the money market rate.

In the opposite case—that of interventions supporting the euro *vis-à-vis* the dollar—the liquidity of the banking system would be reduced. Sterilization would require that the ECB increase the amount of liquidity supplied by the main refinancing operation. Otherwise the banks would have recourse to the marginal refinancing facility. This would lead to an increase in the money market rate relative to the marginal refinancing rate.

When sterilization is defined as a policy that leaves the money market rate unchanged, the ECB in both cases adjusts the interest rates for the respective facility to the level of the repo rate. Thus, in principle, it is not impossible for the central bank to target the exchange rate and the money market rate simultaneously. However, such a dual strategy is limited

1. to the case of interventions that support the home currency against a depreciation by the amount of foreign exchange reserves (and credit lines) (*intervention potential*);
2. to the case of interventions that try to limit an appreciation of the home currency by the amount of resources that can be supplied to the banking system in order to absorb excess liquidity (*sterilization potential*). If a central bank has a deposit facility at its disposal, there is, in principle, no limit to such a dual strategy.

In the second case, an additional limitation of sterilization can be caused by its costs.[1] When sterilization reaches large amounts, the simplified central bank balance sheet can be described as in Table 12.2. The costs of sterilization are related to the interest rate income that a central bank obtains from its foreign exchange reserves and to the interest rate payments it has to make for its deposit facility. As foreign exchange reserves are normally invested in short-term money market instruments, the relevant interest rate is the short-term rate abroad (i^*) . The deposit facility is remunerated with the domestic money market rate (i). Thus, the interest costs of sterilization per unit of domestic currency that is supplied (C^{is}) depend mainly on the differential between these two rates:

$$C^{is} = i - i^*. \tag{12.1}$$

When domestic rates are higher than foreign rates, a limitation on the dual strategy is set by the interest costs of sterilization.

For the total costs of sterilization (C^{TS}) the valuation gains or losses of the assets that are purchased have to be taken into account. Defined per unit of domestic currency, the valuation gain/loss C^{VS} is identical with the depreciation/appreciation of the domestic currency. Thus,

$$C^{TS} = C^{VS} + C^{is} = i - i^* - \Delta s. \tag{12.2}$$

Thus, if a central bank tries to target a *constant* nominal exchange rate ($\Delta s = 0$) in a situation where the domestic interest rate is higher than the foreign rate, it is not able to defend its currency against a strong appreciation pressure for long. A solution to this problem is an adjustable nominal exchange rate target: sterilization costs are zero if the domestic currency depreciates by a rate that is identical with the interest rate differential.

---

[1] A different definition of the costs of sterilized interventions is given by Eijffinger and Verhagen (1997:6): 'This cost can be explained by transaction costs and the fact that the central bank may incur a loss on its purchases (sales) of foreign exchange if these turn out to be unsuccessful in preventing the domestic currency from appreciating (depreciating).' As it neglects interest rates, this definition is incomplete.

Table 12.2. *Simplified central bank balance sheet after massive sterilized intervention*

Assets	Liabilities
Foreign exchange reserves	Monetary base
	Deposit facility

In this case, the interest rate losses that a central bank incurs because of its sterilization policy are compensated by valuation gains of its foreign assets.

The relationship between money market rates (or domestic operating targets of monetary policy in general) and exchange rate targets has been discussed intensively in the literature. The Mundell–Fleming model shows very clearly that a fixed exchange rate is incompatible with a domestically oriented interest rate policy. The same result is presented under the label of the 'inconsistency triangle' (or 'unholy trinity'), which maintains that fixed exchange rates, free capital mobility, and an autonomous monetary policy are inconsistent (see Padoa-Schioppa 1987).

However, these prominent approaches are incomplete, since they analyse neither the logic of sterilized interventions nor the option of a crawling peg or of managed floating. Thus, there is always a possibility of pursuing a domestically oriented interest policy and at the same time targeting a one-sided exchange rate path that is compatible with the interest rate differential. Of course, it is only possible to avoid an appreciation of the domestic currency from this path. With a sufficient sterilization potential (above all with an absorption facility), a central bank can turn the inconsistency triangle into a *consistency triangle* that includes:

1. free capital movements;
2. a domestically oriented interest rate policy;
3. a one-sided target path for the exchange rate determined by the interest rate differential.

The additional policy options that can be derived from this consistency triangle will be discussed in more detail in Chapter 13.

12.3. THE EXCHANGE RATE AS AN INTERMEDIATE TARGET OF MONETARY POLICY

12.3.1. *The logic of the interest rate parity conditions*

In most textbooks and theoretical papers the exchange rate is treated as an intermediate target of monetary policy. According to this view, a central bank targets the exchange rate indirectly with short-term money market rates. The theoretical basis for this approach is the interest parity theory of exchange rates.

If the international capital markets are free from capital controls, and if domestic and foreign financial instruments are perfect substitutes, then arbitrage should ensure that the corresponding rates of return on domestic and foreign paper are identical. The rates of return are derived, first, from direct interest income (i for domestic financial instruments and i^* for foreign financial instruments) and, second, from exchange rate changes. Any divergence in the rates of return will lead to capital movements that are designed to take advantage of the profit opportunities and will continue until a new equilibrium is reached.

This process can be illustrated by an example in which an economic agent must choose between investing an amount X at interest on her domestic market or abroad. In the former case she will receive over a given period (e.g. a year) a rate of return $E_D = (1 + i) X$ in the domestic currency unit:

$$E_D = (1 + i)X. \quad \textit{return on the domestic financial instrument} \quad (12.3)$$

If, on the other hand, the money is invested abroad, the amount X must first of all be converted into foreign currency units at the spot exchange rate (S). This gives X/S. Then a total amount in the foreign currency of $(1 + i^*)X/S$ will be earned, which must be converted back into domestic currency at the end of the investment period. Since at the time the investment decision is taken it is not known what the exchange rate will be at the end of the investment period, only expectations can be formed concerning the future exchange rate S^e. The alternative to this exchange rate risk is the forward sale of the foreign currency amount at the very beginning of the period at the forward rate (F); then the return on foreign financial instruments (E_F) will be either

$$E_F^e = (1 + i^*)\frac{X}{S}S^e \quad \begin{array}{l}\textit{return on the foreign financial}\\ \textit{instrument with exchange risk}\end{array} \quad (12.4a)$$

or

$$E_F = (1 + i^*)\frac{X}{S}F. \quad \begin{array}{l}\textit{return on the foreign financial}\\ \textit{instrument with hedging of exchange}\\ \textit{rate risk via a forward transaction}\end{array} \quad (12.4b)$$

An investment on the domestic market will be preferred for as long as the return obtained there exceeds the return on the foreign financial instrument. In that case, we get for (12.4a)

$$(1 + i)X > (1 + i^*)\frac{X}{S}S^e. \quad (12.5)$$

A few transformations of equation (12.5) give us

$$\frac{1+i}{1+i^*} > \frac{S^e}{S},$$

$$\frac{1+i}{1+i^*} - \frac{1+i^*}{1+i^*} > \frac{S^e}{S} - \frac{S}{S},$$

$$\frac{i-i^*}{1+i^*} > \frac{S^e - S}{S}.$$

For the sake of simplification for i^*, the term $(1 + i^*)$ is usually assumed to equal unity. However, the approximation error here is insignificant only for small values of i^*. This gives

$$i - i^* > \frac{S^e - S}{S}. \tag{12.6}$$

This makes it clear that capital will continue to flow into the country for as long as the interest rate difference exceeds the depreciation expectation regarding the domestic currency. This automatically leads to an international equalization of the rates of return. The capital inflow creates an additional supply of capital and causes a fall in domestic interest rates, whereas a tightening of the supply of capital abroad leads to a rise in foreign interest rates. There is also an increased demand on the foreign exchange market for the domestic currency, which appreciates (i.e. S falls), leading to increased depreciation expectations. All three mechanisms operate to bring about an equalization of the domestic and foreign rates of return:

$$i - i^* = \frac{S^e - S}{S}. \tag{12.7}$$

In this form equation (12.7) is referred to as 'uncovered interest parity'– 'uncovered' because the investment involves an exchange risk which could be eliminated by selling forward the foreign currency amount as soon as the funds are invested abroad. The latter case is an example of so-called *covered interest parity*. This equilibrium condition can be derived from (12.4b) in a similar way to (12.7):

$$i - i^* = \frac{F - S}{S}. \tag{12.8}$$

If domestic and foreign investors are risk-averse rather than risk-neutral, (12.7) has to be supplemented by a *risk premium* (α) so that the expected rate of appreciation or depreciation of the home currency can deviate from the interest rate differential:

$$i - i^* = \frac{S^e - S}{S} + \alpha.$$
(12.9)

12.3.2. *Empirical evidence*

For an empirical test, it is useful to formulate uncovered interest parity (UIP) (equation (12.7)) as follows:

$$E_t(\Delta s_{t+1}) = i_t - i_t^*,$$
(12.10)

where s_t denotes the logarithm of the spot exchange rate (defined as the price of the foreign currency in terms of the home currency) at time t; and i_t and i_t^* are nominal interest rates on comparable domestic and foreign assets.[2] In the literature, there is typically no explicit discussion for which time horizon(s) this condition is valid.

In the same way, the covered interest rate parity (CIP) condition (equation (12.8)) can be formulated as

$$f_t - s_t = i_t - i_t^*,$$
(12.11)

where f_t denotes the logarithm of the forward rate. Combining UIP (12.10) and CIP (12.11) leads to

$$E_t(\Delta s_{t+1}) = f_t - s_t.$$
(12.12)

Thus, under risk neutrality, the difference between the forward rate and the spot rate (*forward premium*) can be used as a predictor of the expected change in spot rate. The forward rate allows us to identify the market's rational expectation of the future spot rate:

$$E_t(s_{t+1}) = f_t.$$
(12.13)

These basic relationships are tested empirically in the following ways. Equation (12.13) implies

$$s_{t+1} = \alpha_1 + \beta_1 f_t + \varepsilon_{1,t+1}.$$
(12.14)

Subtracting s_t from both sides of (12.14) and assuming that β_1 equals 1 leads to

$$\Delta s_{t+1} = \alpha_2 + \beta_2(f_t - s_t) + \varepsilon_{2,t+1}.$$
(12.15)

---

[2] As already mentioned, this is only an approximation. The correct formulation is: $E_t(\Delta s_{t+1}) = \ln(1 + i_t) - \ln(1 + i_t^*)$. In addition, if i is the interest rate per annum, the equation holds only for a one-year time horizon.

Because of the CIP relation and the fact that the forward rate is quoted on the basis of interest rate differentials, empirical tests of (12.15) that test the efficiency of the foreign exchange market are identical with tests of UIP:

$$\Delta s_{t+1} = \alpha_2 + \beta_2(i_t - i_t^*) + \varepsilon_{2,t+1}. \tag{12.16}$$

UIP and market efficiency are given if $\alpha_2 = 0$ and $\beta_2 = 1$. In addition, if $\beta_1 = 1$, then β_2 and α_2 are identical to β_1 and α_1.

It is well known that the empirical evidence of (12.14) differs completely from that of (12.15).[3] This can be seen from Table 12.3, which presents the results for OLS estimations of the dollar exchange rate of five major currencies in the period February 1986–December 1998. The time horizon of the forward rate is one month. Equation (12.14) leads to extremely good results for all currencies: α is close to 0, β is close to 1 and highly significant, R^2 is very high. Moreover, it is clear that the data are non-stationary, so these estimates are very problematic. Thus, most researchers prefer (12.15), which yields rather bad results. For two currencies (dollar and yen) β has the wrong sign, and except for the French franc and the pound β is not significant at the 5% level. However, for all five currencies R^2 is almost 0; the best result is again obtained for the franc with an R^2 of 0.05. Thus, UIP is obviously not a good theory for forecasting exchange rate changes. The negative sign of β was especially pronounced in the period 1980–5 and is well documented in the literature. It is the basis of the often mentioned 'forward premium puzzle' (Froot and Thaler 1990).

These results, and above all the empirical anomalies for (12.15), can be explained if one considers the economics of UIP under fixed and flexible interest rates. The main difference between these two arrangements concerns the role of the interest rate differential. It will be shown that this differential is endogenous under fixed rates while it is exogenous and policy-determined under flexible rates.

12.3.3. *UIP under fixed exchange rates*

Although UIP has been tested mainly for flexible exchange rates, its economic rationale can be demonstrated much better for a regime of fixed exchange rates. Such an arrangement (e.g. the Bretton Woods or European Monetary System) is typically characterized by a 'large country' (United States and Germany, respectively) in which the domestic central bank sets the domestic short-term interest rate exogenously as the main operating target of its monetary policy. All other countries behave as 'small

---

[3] For an overview of the literature, see Froot and Thaler (1990).

Table 12.3. *OLS estimates for uncovered interest parity (equations (12.14) and (12.15)), February 1986–December 1998*

Exchange rates	Variables	Estimates (S.E.)		Statistics		
		Constant	Slope	R^2	S.E.	D.W.
DM/US$	s_t on f_{t-1}	0.0353 (0.0126)	0.929 (0.0235)	0.911	0.0316	1.77
DM/£	s_t on f_{t-1}	0.0178 (0.0164)	0.984 (0.0161)	0.961	0.0225	1.57
DM/yen	s_t on f_{t-1}	0.0130 (0.0071)	0.953 (0.0223)	0.923	0.030	1.52
DM/Ffr	s_t on f_{t-1}	0.2906 (0.0830)	0.914 (0.0243)	0.903	0.0061	1.89
DM/US$	$s_t - s_{t-1}$ on $f_{t-1} - s_{t-1}$	−0.0023 (0.0026)	−0.053 (0.937)	0.000	0.0323	1.81
DM/£	$s_t - s_{t-1}$ on $f_{t-1} - s_{t-1}$	0.0012 (0.0021)	0.740 (0.3296)	0.032	0.0225	1.59
DM/yen	$s_t - s_{t-1}$ on $f_{t-1} - s_{t-1}$	0.0016 (0.0032)	−0.363 (1.0626)	0.001	0.0298	1.59
DM/Ffr	$s_t - s_{t-1}$ on $f_{t-1} - s_{t-1}$	0.0007 (0.0007)	0.844 (0.2901)	0.052	0.0063	1.92
DM/US$	s_t on s_{t-1}	0.0379 (0.0124)	0.923 (0.0231)	0.913	0.0313	1.80
DM/£	s_t on s_{t-1}	0.0291 (0.0163)	0.970 (0.0159)	0.960	0.0226	1.60
DM/yen	s_t on s_{t-1}	0.0131 (0.0071)	0.959 (0.0224)	0.923	0.0295	1.55
DM/Ffr	s_t on s_{t-1}	0.3983 (0.0782)	0.882 (0.0231)	0.905	0.006	1.99

Source: Own calculations with data from Deutsche Bundesbank. s_t denotes the logarithm of spot and f_t the logarithm of 1-month forward rates at the end of each month.

countries', which means that their central banks have to adjust their domestic short-term rates passively in order to keep the balance of payments in equilibrium. In this setting the interest rate differential is completely endogenous.[4]

In addition, under a system of fixed rates the spot rate is at least temporarily held relatively constant—in the Bretton Woods system the margins most of the time were only ±0.75%, and in the EMS until July 1993 the 'normal margins' were ±2.25%. What is also important is the fact that in these regimes the sign of possible exchange rate adjustments was very often clear to all market participants (a 'one-way bet').

Thus, for a satellite central bank the UIP relationship sets highly stringent limits on its domestic interest rate policy. If it wants to keep the exchange rate stable, it has to follow an interest rate policy that keeps the interest rate differential in line with the market's expectation of parity realignments. Under the EMS, for instance, a country like France or Italy could not afford to reduce its short-term rates under the German level. On the contrary, in periods of speculative attacks domestic rates had to be raised considerably over the German rates. Two attempts by the Banque de France to lower its rate to less than the German level (in early 1981 and June 1993) immediately led to a strong speculative attack. The same happened (but the other way round) to the Bundesbank under the Bretton Woods system. Several attempts by the Bundesbank to increase its rates to above the US level (above all in 1960 and in the period 1971–March 1973) led to huge capital inflows which required either a reduction of the German rates, an appreciation of the Deutschmark, or the imposition of very comprehensive capital import controls—or combinations of these measures (Emminger 1986).

These relationships are well known and can be found in any textbook that discusses the Mundell–Fleming model. Empirically, however, one can also see some problems with equation (12.15). Table 12.3 shows that for the French franc β has the right sign and is not very far from 1. However, R^2 is also very low.

In sum, for fixed rate systems UIP seems to be a very important relationship since it clearly shows the constraints under which the 'satellite central banks' are operating. Above all, we can see that for the franc/Deutschmark the problem of a negative β did not exist.

---

[4] As shown in Section 12.2, the hard-budget constraint of foreign exchange reserves prevents a small country from keeping its interest rates below the level that is required by financial markets. This would lead to capital outflows that are unsustainable. This constraint is absent if the small country maintains interest rates that are higher than the level required by the expected change in the exchange rate and the risk premium. However, with a constant nominal exchange rate the policy leads to high sterilization costs, so that this approach too is not sustainable. Thus, an additional degree of freedom is available only if the depreciation of the domestic currency is targeted; see Section 13.3.

12.3.4. *UIP under flexible exchange rates*

Under flexible exchange rates the rationale of UIP becomes completely different. The main difference concerns the behaviour of central banks. Instead of a clear leader–follower relationship, flexible rate regimes are often characterized by central banks setting short-term interest rates–the operating targets of their monetary policy–autonomously. This is especially pronounced in the case of large currency areas like the United States, Japan, the euro area, and the United Kingdom. Typically, regressions for UIP or foreign exchange market efficiency are run for the currencies of these countries.

Thus, the interest rate differential can be regarded as an exogenous, policy-determined variable. Of course even 'large' central banks take exchange rate developments into consideration when they set their domestic rates, but the good fit of the purely domestically oriented Taylor rule (see Chapter 9) and the large fluctuations of flexible exchange rates show that this influence can be very slight.[5] The hypothesis of an exogenously determined interest differential is at first sight difficult to reconcile with the standard interpretation of UIP. In the words of Froot and Thaler (1990: 181), 'Thus, uncovered interest parity implies that the interest rate differential is an estimate of the future exchange rate change.'

While the standard view implies that expected exchange rate changes drive an endogenous interest rate differential, the approach presented here assumes that under flexible rates the interest rate differential becomes endogenous. This can be explained as follows. Assume an equilibrium situation where

$$E_t(\Delta s_{t+1}) = f_t - s_t = i_t - i_t^*. \tag{12.17}$$

Now suppose that some 'good' news for the domestic currency comes into the market and leads to a downward revision of $E_t s_{t+1}$ such that the following disequilibrium results:

$$E_t(\Delta s_{t+1}) < f_t - s_t = i_t - i_t^*. \tag{12.18}$$

If the home and foreign central bank are not willing to change their short-term rates, such a disequilibrium can be dissolved only by an immediate adjustment of the spot rate. Thus, changes in expectations about the future spot rate lead to parallel movements of the forward and the spot rate.

Two conclusions can be drawn from this. First, the sign of β depends on the 'quality' of the news; i.e., good news coincides with a negative β and

---

[5] McCallum (1994) attaches great importance to these effects. However, in his paper he presents no evidence for the concrete reaction function of the four central banks; instead, he uses completely arbitrary and not very plausible parameter values.

vice versa. The negative coefficient in the case of the Deutschmark–dollar rate (see Table 12.3) thus indicates that bad (good) news concerning the Deutschmark (dollar) has dominated.

In sum, the hypothesis that UIP (or market efficiency) requires a positive β is adequate only under the regime of fixed rates where the spot rate is constant and where news has a direct effect on the interest rate differential. Under flexible rates, a constant (positive or negative) interest rate differential is compatible with an appreciation or depreciation of the currency depending on positive or negative 'news'.

In addition, one should expect a parallel movement of the spot and the forward rate, whenever the future spot rate changes as a result of 'news'. Empirically, it can be shown that the link between the contemporaneous spot and the forward rate—as well as between the first differences of these rates—is indeed very strong (Figure 12.1).

Thus, the main difference of UIP between fixed and flexible rates is due to the flexibility of the spot rate. Under fixed rates any new information affects the forward rate and the interest differential, whereas under flexible rates the impact is on the forward rate and the spot rate. This allows a policy-determined interest rate differential to be maintained even under strongly changing expectations among the foreign exchange market participants. These differences between flexible and fixed rates are presented in Table 12.4.

12.3.5. *A solution to the forward discount puzzle*

In the literature an intensive analysis of the UIP under flexible exchange rates has led to the conclusion that the negative sign of β reflects an 'anomaly' (Froot and Thaler 1990) for which, so far, no convincing solution has been

Table 12.4. *Uncovered interest parity under flexible and fixed exchange rates*

	Fixed rates	Flexible rates
Spot rate	Exogenous (relatively stable from day to day)	Endogenous (with strong daily variations)
Home interest rate	Small country: endogenous	Large country: exogenous
Foreign interest rate	Large country: exogenous	Large country: exogenous
Interest differential	Endogenous	Exogenous
Forward rate	Endogenous	Endogenous
Sign of expected spot rate changes	Almost certain ('one-way bets')	Unclear
Changes in market expectations	Reflected in changes in the forward rate and changes in the interest differential	Reflected in parallel changes in the forward and the spot rate

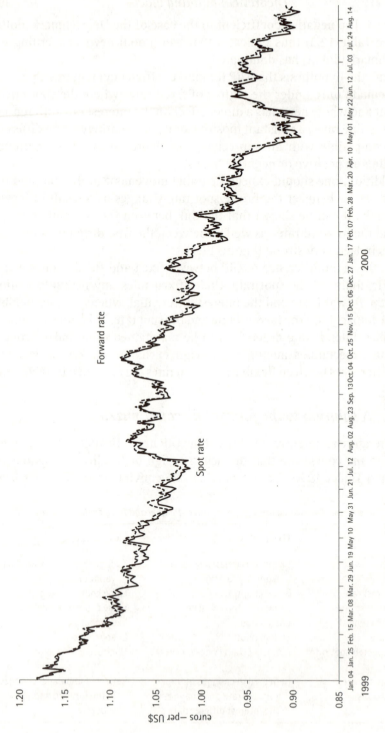

Figure 12.1. *Euro–US$ spot rates and three-month forward rates, January 1999–August 2000*

Source: Deutsche Bundesbank.

found. In the words of Isard, who provides a good survey of the main explanations for this 'forward rate bias',

Although the prevailing opinion today is that none of the five interpretations [of the
anomaly] by itself provides a sufficiently convincing explanation, in combination
several of them deserve further attention. (Isard 1995: 88)

A solution to this puzzle requires an explanation of how it can be possible
that, in the period from 1978 to the spring of 1985 (and again in the period
after January 1999), the interest rate for dollar investments was higher than
the interest rate for Deutschmark investments (euro instruments), while at the
same time the dollar was constantly appreciating *vis-à-vis* the Deutschmark
(the euro). The UIP implies that, given the positive interest rate differential
for the dollar, market participants were constantly expecting a depreciation
of the dollar while at the same time the dollar was always appreciating.

For a simple explanation of this seeming inefficiency, it is important to
have a closer look at the time horizon under which the actors on foreign
exchange markets operate. Almost all empirical studies assume implicitly
that the relevant period is one or three months, i.e. the periods for which
data on forward rates are available. However, from interviews with practitioners, it becomes obvious that their investment decisions are typically
made for much shorter periods.

Most foreign exchange trading is done intra-day; i.e., traders buy or sell
foreign exchange which they then sell or resell before the end of the day.
Open positions are held only during the day, but not overnight. In this case,
the interest rate differential is no longer a part of the investment decision,
as interest payments are made for overnight positions only. Thus, from
(12.1) and (12.13) we get

$$E_t(s_{t+1}) = s_t. \tag{12.19}$$

The time subscript now means different hours of the same day. The regression
of s_{t+1} on s_t becomes a simple random walk process.

Of course, there are some investors who do hold open positions overnight. But this does not mean that the situation is qualitatively different
from a random walk. For a time horizon of one day, the interest rate differential in (12.19) is still negligible. In the period 1978–85, and also after
January 1999, the difference between dollar and Deutschmark (euro) interest rates has normally been between 2 and 4 percentage points per annum.
On a daily basis this means an interest premium of 0.005% and 0.001%.
Thus, the expected exchange rate that is calculated on the basis of (12.19)
is not distinguishable from an expected exchange rate that is generated
from a random walk process.

In sum, assuming a very short time horizon of foreign exchange market participants, the period for which the 'forward bias' can be identified can also be interpreted as a period where most investors were following a random-walk process. This finding is supported above all by the very low predictive power of all regressions for (12.15). It has already been mentioned that the correlation coefficient is normally lower than 0.05. On the other hand the random-walk structure would explain the good fit of (12.14), which can be formulated as

$$s_{t+1} = \alpha_1 + \beta_1 s_t + \beta_1(i_t - i_t^*). \tag{12.20}$$

Figure 12.2 shows that, even for monthly data, the value of the interest differential is very low compared with the actual fluctuations of the spot rate. In other words, in this regression the spot rate is explained mainly by its own lagged values.

12.3.6. *Reconciling the bankers' view and the academics' view*

Whenever bankers and academics are talking about the forward rate, a pronounced difference of opinion can be predicted. Bankers usually maintain that the forward rate is calculated by adding a given interest rate differential to the spot rate: therefore, they say, the forward rate—and also the forward premium—has nothing to do with expectations. For instance,

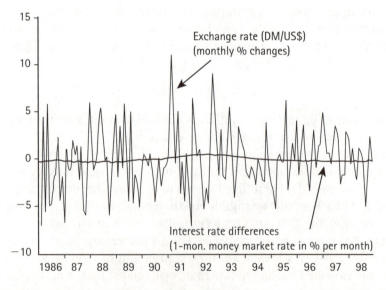

Figure 12.2. *Interest rate differentials and monthly exchange rate change in %, 1986–1998*
Source: Own calculations based on data from Deutsche Bundesbank.

Reuters (1999: 53) writes: 'The forward rate is not a prediction of what the future spot rate will be.' For many academics, on the other hand, there is no doubt that expectations determine interest rate differentials.

As this analysis shows, both sides are right, depending on the underlying institutional framework. The academics' view gives a perfect description of the situation in a system of fixed exchange rates. In this regime, the 'satellite central banks' try to maintain an interest differential that keeps the balance of payments in equilibrium. This avoids having to stabilize the exchange rate by foreign exchange market interventions. Thus, the bankers' general observation is formally correct, but they overlook the fact that the interest rate differential is set so as to compensate existing exchange rate expectations.

On the other hand, in a world of floating rates, the academics are wrong. While the underlying logic of UIP is still valid, the academics miss the point that the interest rate differential is now exogenous. In addition, they misinterpret the one-month and three-month interest rate differentials as the 'relevant expectation' of the market. In a world of flexible exchange rates, the time horizon of the relevant actor is extremely short, so that the interest rate differential is irrelevant for most transactions. Thus, contrary to UIP, there is no link between expectations and interest rate differentials.

Finally, academics and bankers also have a different view of the forward market. Contrary to many textbooks, speculation is almost never carried out via the forward market. The main reason for this is that a broad market exists for standard maturities (one month, three months) only. Thus, if a speculator enters a forward transaction, just one day later he already has a non-standard maturity for which it is relatively difficult to find a new partner.

In sum, any theory about exchange rates should clearly define the time horizon for which it is set up. For the very short term (intra-day, one day, or several days), which seems to be the most relevant time horizon, interest rates do not play the role that is attributed to them in standard economic textbooks.

12.4. THE CONTROL OF THE PRICE LEVEL IN AN OPEN ECONOMY

In an open economy the exchange rate constitutes an important determinant of the price level. It affects the inflation rate in two ways:

- directly, via the purchasing power parity theory (PPP);
- indirectly, via the expectations channel.

12.4.1. *Purchasing power parity theory*[6]

Purchasing power parity (PPP) is a very old theory of exchange rate deter-mination.[7] It is based on the Law of One Price, which states that, apart from tariffs and transaction costs, international commodity arbitrage will equalize the prices for tradable goods in all locations when quoted in the same currency. Thus, for each good the domestic price p_i is identical with its foreign price p_i^* times the exchange rate:

$$p_i = Sp_i^*. \tag{12.21}$$

Let us assume that the domestic price index $P = f(p_1, \ldots, p_i, \ldots, p_n)$ and the foreign price index $P^* = g(p_1^*, \ldots, p_i^*, \ldots, p_n^*)$ are made up of the same goods with same weights, so that the homogeneous-of-degree-one $g(\cdot)$ and $f(\cdot)$ functions are the same. Under these conditions, the Law of One Price that applied to individual goods becomes a law of *price levels*, which is the absolute version of the PPP:

$$S = \frac{P}{P^*} = \frac{\textit{domestic price of the standard market basket of goods}}{\textit{foreign price of the same standard basket}}.$$

$$\tag{12.22}$$

In reality, the assumptions concerning the absolute version of the PPP are hardly met. Even for perfectly homogeneous commodities, there are trans-actions costs, tariffs, and indirect taxes. In addition, price indices differ from country to country and they include many goods and services that are not tradable. Thus, absolute PPP is modified as follows:

$$S = \theta \frac{P}{P^*}, \tag{12.23}$$

where θ is a constant reflecting transaction costs, tariffs, and taxes.

Focusing on changes in the exchange rate over time leads to the *relative version* of the PPP:

$$\Delta s = \pi - \pi^*. \tag{12.24}$$

In monetary policy the relative version of the PPP plays an important role. Many proponents of a system of flexible exchange rates believed that

---

[6] The following section draws heavily on Dornbusch (1987).

[7] An early version was developed by the Salamanca School in sixteenth-century Spain and in the writings of Gerard de Malynes at the beginning of the seventeenth-century in England. For a compre-hensive presentation of the history of the PPP, see Einzig (1970).

countries could choose their national inflation rates according to their specific preferences, and that the flexible exchange rate would passively compensate for the inflation differential:

Flexible exchange rates would allow each country to pursue the mixture of unemployment and price trend objectives it prefers, consistent with internal equilibrium, equilibrium being secured by appreciation of the currencies of 'price-stability' countries relative to currencies of 'full-employment' countries. (Johnson 1972: 210)

Alternatively, many countries have adopted a fixed exchange rate target *vis-à-vis* the currency of a country with low inflation in order to import that price stability.

The experience shows that both applications of relative PPP can be quite problematic. Currencies with flexible exchange rates have experienced large deviations from relative PPP in the short term (*volatility*) and medium term (*misalignments*). Such deviations are measured by the real exchange rate (*q*). For the absolute version of PPP, the real exchange rate is

$$Q = S \frac{P^*}{P}. \tag{12.25}$$

When absolute PPP holds, the real exchange rate is always 1. Again, normally the relative version is used. Changes in the real exchange rate (Δq) are defined as follows:

$$\Delta q = \pi^* + \Delta s - \pi. \tag{12.26}$$

When relative PPP holds, the real exchange rate remains constant. Figure 9.6 shows that the real exchange rates of the dollar, the Deutschmark, and, above all, the yen have fluctuated considerably since 1973. Such strong deviations from relative PPP are due to three main factors:

1. CPI indices include services and non-tradable goods, for which the law of one price does not hold.
2. Instead of passively accommodating inflation differentials, exchange rates have become an autonomous source for PPP deviations.
3. Transaction costs and other barriers to trade (tariffs and non-tariff restrictions) are still high. Thus, it can often be observed that companies react to autonomous exchange rate changes by not adjusting their local prices. In the case of an appreciation of the domestic currency, such a 'pricing-to-market' (Krugman 1987) allows market shares to be maintained at the price of reduced profit margins. As this leads to nationally differentiated prices, it is possible only if there are some frictions for arbitrage transactions.

For the same reasons, under systems with fixed exchange rates, inflation rates can differ considerably over time.

12.4.2. *The Ricardo–Balassa–Samuelson effect*

A related explanation for deviations from the relative PPP is described as the Ricardo–Balassa–Samuelson effect. It refers to changes in the *trend in productivity* of different countries, and can explain why under fixed exchange rates fast-growing emerging market economies often have higher inflation rates than developed countries. This effect was first described by Ricardo and later by Balassa (1964) and Samuelson (1964). It applies equation (12.23) to price indices for tradable goods (P_T):[8]

$$P_T = \theta S P_T^*.$$

(12.27)

It then assumes that the overall domestic price index (P) is the weighted average of the price indices for tradable and non-tradable goods (P_N):

$$P = \alpha P_T + (1 - \alpha)P_N,$$

(12.28)

where α is the weighting factor. The equilibrium relative price between the tradable and non-tradable goods sector is represented by the factor β:

$$\beta = \frac{P_N}{P_T}.$$

(12.29)

If (12.29) is restated in the terms of P_N and the result is incorporated in (12.28), then the overall domestic price level is

$$P = \underbrace{[\alpha + (1 - \alpha)\beta]}_{\gamma} P_T$$

(12.30)

and the domestic price level for tradable goods is

$$P_T = \frac{P}{\gamma}.$$

(12.31)

The same applies to the foreign price levels:

$$P^* = \underbrace{[\alpha^* + (1 - \alpha^*)\beta^*]}_{\gamma^*} P_T^*$$

(12.32)

and

$$P_T^* = \frac{P^*}{\gamma^*}.$$

(12.33)

---

[8] For the following transformations, see also Willms (1995: 112-14).

If the two definitions of the price indexes for tradable goods at home and abroad (equations (12.31) and (12.33)) are incorporated in the PPP equation (12.27), the nominal exchange rate is obtained as

$$S = \frac{1}{\theta} \frac{P}{P^*} \frac{\gamma^*}{\gamma}, \tag{12.34}$$

or formulated as growth rates:

$$\Delta s = (\pi - \pi^*) + (\hat{\gamma} - \hat{\gamma}^*), \tag{12.35}$$

where it is assumed that factor θ remains constant over time. The rates of change $\hat{\gamma}$ and $\hat{\gamma}^*$ express the real economic effect on exchange rate movements and on the inflation rate, where the exchange rate is not available as an adjustment mechanism because it is fixed by the central bank. In practice, they depend on factors α and β (shifts in the weighting of the tradable goods in the currency basket of the country in question; changes in the relative price between the two sectors and countries). Changes $\hat{\gamma}$ and $\hat{\gamma}^*$ can thus be triggered by shifts in demand, changes in factor endowments and, as we shall see below, differences in productivity trends. In order to incorporate this into the analysis, it will be assumed that labour is perfectly mobile between the sectors of a country, i.e. that nominal wages (W) are the same in both sectors. However, it is also assumed that labour does not move between the two countries. It is paid on the basis of its marginal productivity (m_T and m_N):

$$\frac{W}{P_T} = m_T \tag{12.36}$$

and

$$\frac{W}{P_N} = m_N. \tag{12.37}$$

If (12.36) is solved in terms of W and incorporated in (12.37), we obtain

$$P_N = \frac{m_T}{m_N} P_T. \tag{12.38}$$

If in (12.28) the price index for non-tradable goods is replaced by the term from (12.38), then, following a few transformations, the price index for tradable goods is obtained as

$$P_T = \frac{P}{\alpha + (1 - \alpha)(m_T/m_N)}, \tag{12.39}$$

or, for prices abroad,

$$P_T^* = \frac{P^*}{\alpha^* + (1 - \alpha^*)(m_T^*/m_N^*)}. \tag{12.40}$$

Inserting (12.39) and (12.40) into the PPP equation (12.27), we obtain

$$S = \frac{1}{\theta} \frac{P_T}{P_T^*} = \frac{1}{\theta} \frac{P[\alpha^* + (1 - \alpha^*)(m_T^*/m_N^*)]}{P^*[\alpha + (1 - \alpha)(m_T/m_N)]}. \tag{12.41}$$

Equation (12.41) can now, like equation (12.35), be converted into growth rates. For this purpose we take as a simplifying assumption that the share of tradable goods in both countries is at the same level and constant ($\alpha = \alpha^* = $ constant) and the marginal productivities of the sectors of a country coincide in initial equilibrium ($m_T = m_N$ and $m_T^* = m_N^*$). We also assume that $\theta = 0$. Without this simplifying assumption, the relationship becomes very complex and virtually impossible to interpret economically. This gives us

$$\Delta s = (\pi - \pi^*) - (1 - \alpha)[(\hat{m}_T - \hat{m}_T^*) - (\hat{m}_N - \hat{m}_N^*)]. \tag{12.42}$$

If the exchange rate is fixed by monetary policy, i.e. if its rate of change is equal to 0 ($\Delta s = 0$), the domestic inflation rate will be determined as follows:

$$\pi = \pi^* + (1 - \alpha)[(\hat{m}_T - \hat{m}_T^*) - (\hat{m}_N - \hat{m}_N^*)]. \tag{12.43}$$

The domestic inflation rate is thus determined by the inflation in the anchor country and by the differences in productivity trends. Thus, for example, the domestic inflation rate will be higher than the rate abroad if the domestic economy has achieved a greater productivity growth in the tradable goods sector.

This can best be illustrated by an example using hypothetical figures (Table 12.5). Here factor $\alpha = 0.5$ is assumed, together with the assumptions made above (remuneration of marginal productivity, setting of nominal wages on the basis of the productivity growth in the tradable goods sector, international immobility of the factor labour).

In our example, when inflation abroad is only 0.5% ($\pi^* = 0.5 \times 0\% + 0.5 \times 1\% = 0.5\%$), the domestic economy will have an inflation rate of

Table 12.5. *Numerical example of the Ricardo–Balassa effect (%)*

	$\hat{m}_T$	$\hat{m}_N$	Δw	π_T	π_N	π
Domestic	6	1	6	0	5	2.5
Foreign	2	1	2	0	1	0.5

2.5% ($\pi = 0.5\% + 0.5\,[(6\% - 2\%) - (1\% - 1\%)]$). The reason for this is the very much greater rise in productivity in the domestic economy's tradable goods sector.

12.4.3. *The expectations channel in an open economy*

In Chapter 4 we saw that the expectations channel plays a decisive role in the determination of inflation rates. It relies on the fact that prices for contracts in the future have to be set on the basis of expectations of future price developments. Because of purchasing power parity, the exchange rate is an important determinant of inflation in an open economy. Thus, it can be rational for private agents to base their inflation expectations on their expectations of the future exchange rate.

In the past, many countries have tried to influence inflation expectations with announcements of exchange rate targets (see Chapter 13). When such an announcement is regarded as a 'credible commitment', it can serve as a focal point for wage-setters, above all in an environment with decentralized wage setting. In this case the direct effects of the exchange rate target on domestic inflation is enhanced by the indirect effects via wages and costs. In the 1980s, many economists thought that a central bank could use a fixed exchange rate as a commitment technology, so that private inflation expectations (and unemployment) would be lower than under pure discretion (Giavazzi and Pagano 1988). In fact, in many macroeconomic stabilization programmes in the 1980s and 1990s an exchange rate anchor was used in order to stabilize inflation expectations (Bofinger 1996).

This mechanism also reveals a possible weakness of an exchange rate target. If the negotiating parties feel the exchange rate target to be not very credible, the result will fairly soon be a real appreciation in the domestic currency and a loss of international competitiveness. The greater the probability that sooner or later the central bank will give in and seek to remedy the situation by devaluation, the less the unions will be prepared to allow corrections to the wage level. The external economic situation will deteriorate to such an extent that eventually a devaluation will appear inevitable.

Especially in developing countries, there are many examples of the breakdown of exchange rate pegs because of an unsustainable real appreciation. A prominent example in Europe is the temporary exit of the Italian lira from the Exchange Rate Mechanism of the European Monetary System in September 1992 after a strong real overvaluation of the Italian currency.

13

Monetary Policy Strategies in an Open Economy

What this chapter is about

- It shows that the central banks of large currency areas are able to combine a domestically oriented interest rate policy with an exchange rate policy that avoids an unwarranted real appreciation of their currency.
- For smaller economies, it discusses the rule of a fixed nominal exchange rate which looks attractive because of its simplicity. However, this rule is applicable only under very specific conditions.
- The dual requirement of a UIP equilibrium and adequate domestic monetary conditions can often be achieved only if countries adopt a strategy whereby they target a path for their exchange rate together with a domestic real interest rate. The limits of this approach are set by strong speculative capital outflows. Purely flexible exchange rates are not a practicable solution for smaller countries and therefore are not applied very often.

13.1. INTRODUCTION

In Part II monetary policy was presented from the perspective of a closed economy. This final part of the book will show that in general it is useful for large currency areas (e.g. the United States, the euro area, Japan) to adopt such a closed-economy perspective for their overall monetary policy strategy. This implies above all that the short-term interest rate is determined only by domestic considerations, e.g. according to a Taylor rule. However, as the example of Japan has shown (Section 9.5), even for such large currency areas it is neither necessary nor advisable to adopt a policy of 'benign neglect' *vis-à-vis* the exchange rate.

For small and relatively open economies, the conduct of monetary policy is more complicated. As already mentioned, most economists agree today[1]

---

[1] See Eichengreen (2000) and Mundell (2000). A very similar view can be found as early as Friedman (1953).

that for those countries only two corner solutions are advisable:

- adopt freely floating exchange rates and a monetary policy determined by domestic considerations based on rules that discussed in Part II, or
- use an absolutely fixed exchange rate, preferably in the form of currency board (Section 6.2). In this setting the exchange rate commitment serves as an explicit policy rule. An implicit rule for short-term interest rates can be derived from the need to keep the nominal exchange rate stable. We will show that such an externally determined monetary policy is advisable only under very specific conditions.

This latter view is represented by the so-called *inconsistency triangle*, which shows that a combination of fixed exchange rates, an autonomous monetary policy, and free capital mobility is not compatible (see Chapter 12). As already mentioned, I will argue that for small open economies it can be also useful to adopt a third way, based on two pillars for macroeconomic stabilization: the real interest rate and the real exchange rate. Although this approach is conceptually more difficult than a constant nominal exchange rate rule, it avoids serious problems and comes close to the practice of many central banks.

13.2. LARGE-CURRENCY AREAS

For large-currency areas it would make little sense to use the exchange rate as a 'rule' for monetary policy. This applies to both interpretations of the term 'rule' that were presented in Chapters 6 and 8:

1. the exchange rate cannot be used as a device to constrain the discretion of policy-makers;
2. the exchange rate cannot provide a 'simple rule' to facilitate the decision-making process of policy-makers in a very complex environment.

Thus, interest rates have to be set according to the rules that were discussed in Chapter 8. Nevertheless, there is no reason to disregard exchange rate movements in the conduct of monetary policy. As already discussed in Section 9.5, the experience of Japan in the 1990s shows that it can be very dangerous to adopt a completely passive attitude *vis-à-vis* the exchange rate.

We have seen in Chapter 12 that a domestically oriented interest policy allows a central bank to defend a one-sided target path for the exchange rate. It requires the exchange rate path to be determined according to the prevailing interest rate differential. Figure 13.1 shows that in the case of Japan such an exchange rate path would have been more or less identical to a bilateral PPP path.

Thus, for large-currency areas there is an additional degree of freedom for monetary policy that has been overlooked so far by most economists. In fact,

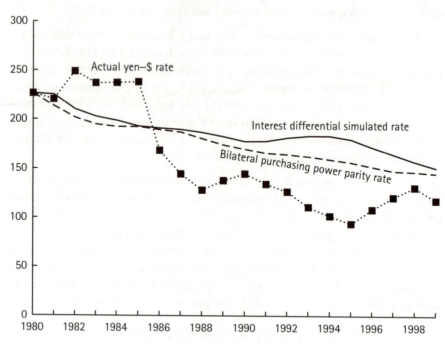

Figure 13.1. *Simulation of the Yen–US$ rate by the interest rate differential, 1980–1999*
Source: Own calculations based on data from OECD, *Economic Outlook.*

the Bank of Japan has bought large amounts of dollars, above all in 1999 and 2000, in order to prevent a further appreciation of the yen (Figure 13.2). With this policy it was possible to stabilize the yen above the 100 yen–dollar threshold in 2000. Of course, for the Japanese authorities there was no difficulty in combining these large interventions with the Zero Interest Rate Policy (Schwartz 2000). But it would have also been possible for the US authorities to stabilize the euro–dollar rate (i.e. to avoid a depreciation of the euro below a target path) in 1999/2000 without losing control over domestic interest rates. In this case, it would have been necessary to establish a deposit facility (see Section 10.4.2.2) and then to target a depreciation of the dollar *vis-à-vis* the euro that is identical to the prevailing differential of short-term interest rates.

13.3. SMALL OPEN ECONOMIES WITH TARGETED EXCHANGE RATES

For small open economies, the choice of a monetary policy strategy is more complex. On the one hand, their economies are influenced by closed-economy transmission processes that were described in Part II; on the other

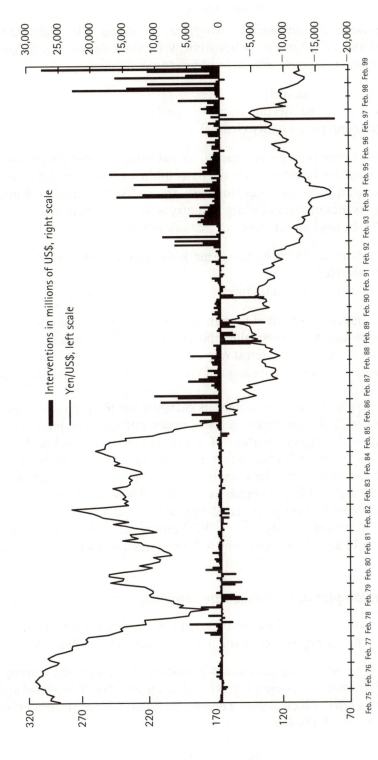

Figure 13.2. *Yen–US$ exchange rates and monthly interventions by the Bank of Japan, 1975–1999.*
Source: IMF, *International Financial Statistics.*

hand, the effects of exchange rate changes are too strong to be neglected in the formulation of a monetary policy strategy. For these reasons, the following transmission channels have to be observed simultaneously:

- the expectations channel;
- the interest rate channel (aggregate demand channel);
- the purchasing power parity channel.

As far as monetary rules are concerned, the exchange rate can now be used as an intermediate target rule. On the basis of the exchange rate, a simple explicit rule can be formulated as follows. Target a fixed nominal exchange rate *vis-à-vis* the currency of a large country with stable prices (an 'anchor currency'). The implicit rule requires that one either

- intervenes on the foreign exchange market when the market rate deviates from the targeted rate, or
- adjusts domestic short-term interest rates.

Given the budget constraint of foreign exchange reserves, the implicit rule can be formulated as follows: when the level of foreign exchange reserves declines, raise short-term interest rates. If there is an increase in reserves, interest rates should be reduced, but there is no constraint to pursue such a policy.

If a country wants neither to float its currency nor to keep the nominal exchange rate stable, a more complicated policy rule has to be formulated. This requires that a combination of a real interest rate level and real exchange rate changes is chosen that is compatible with a given inflation target. At the same time, the combination of the two operating targets (interest rate and exchange rate) has to be compatible with the requirements of the uncovered interest parity condition. In the literature, this approach has been discussed mainly under the heading of the 'crawling peg' (Williamson 1996) or 'open-economy inflation targeting' (Svensson 2000*a*).

13.3.1. *Examples of exchange rate targeting*

There are many examples for countries that have targeted either a constant nominal exchange rate or a crawling peg. The latter can be subdivided into

- an 'active crawl', which aims at a depreciation of the domestic currency *vis-à-vis* the anchor currency that is less than the inflation differential, and
- a 'passive crawl', which aims at a depreciation that fully compensates for the inflation differential.

Prominent examples of an exchange rate policy that aims at a constant nominal exchange rate include the following.

- In the period of the Bretton Woods system (1946–73) most market economies maintained a fixed nominal exchange rate *vis-à-vis* the US dollar. Parity adjustments were not very frequent under this scheme.
- In the Exchange Rate Mechanism of the European Monetary System (March 1979–December 1998) many European countries targeted their exchange rates *vis-à-vis* the Deutschmark.[2] From January 1987 to September 1992, nominal parities of all participating currencies *vis-à-vis* the Deutschmark were held stable. After the crises of September 1992 and July 1993, a group of core countries (Belgium, Denmark, France, Netherlands, Luxembourg) continued to target a fixed nominal exchange rate *vis-à-vis* the Deutschmark. Denmark, which did not join EMU, now targets a constant nominal exchange rate *vis-à-vis* the euro in the framework of the EMS II.
- Outside the EMS, Austria followed a policy of a completely stable nominal exchange rate *vis-à-vis* the Deutschmark from 1979 until the start of EMU (the so-called 'Hartwährungspolitik').[3] A similar approach was adopted by Estonia in 1992 with its currency board based on an exchange rate of 8 crowns to 1 Deutschmark. A stable nominal exchange rate *vis-à-vis* a currency basket was targeted by the Czech National Bank until the crisis of May 1997 (Kopits 1999).
- In the 1990s, many Asian countries (Hong Kong, China, Korea, Malaysia, Thailand) targeted a stable nominal exchange rate *vis-à-vis* the US dollar. With the exception of China and Hong Kong, all these pegs had to be abandoned in the Asian crisis of 1997.[4]

Important examples for crawling pegs include the following.

- In the period from March 1979 to January 1987, the parities in the EMS were changed quite frequently. In most cases an active crawl *vis-à-vis* the Deutschmark was followed. Of course, the parity adjustments were not announced *ex ante* (discrete devaluations).
- In Central and Eastern Europe, Poland and Hungary followed an active crawl *vis-à-vis* a currency basket during the 1990s (Kopits 1999). In April 2000 Poland switched to independently floating rates.
- In Asia, Indonesia targeted a passive crawl *vis-à-vis* the dollar in the 1990s. Because of strong contagion effects of the Asian crisis, it had to abandon this policy in 1997.

[2] For a survey see Collignon *et al.* (1994), Gros and Thygesen (1998), and Bofinger (2000*b*).
[3] See Hochreiter and Winckler (1995).
[4] See Mishkin (1999) and Radelet and Sachs (1998).

- In Latin America active and passive crawls could be found in several countries in the 1990s (Chile, Colombia, Brazil). In all cases they were abandoned by the end of the decade.[5]

13.3.2. *The mechanics of exchange rate targeting*[6]

For all forms of open-economy monetary policy, it is important to note that a central bank can use two operating targets simultaneously (see Chapter 12): the short-term interest rate, and the nominal exchange rate. Because of short-term price rigidities, the two operating targets can also be expressed as the real short-term interest rate and the real exchange change. The combined effects of these two levers on the aggregate demand are usually measured with a monetary conditions index (MCI). This index is based on the assumption that positive or negative effects on aggregate demand are caused by deviations of the short-term real interest rate from a neutral level ($\bar{r}$) and also of the log real exchange rate from a neutral level ($\bar{q}$) (see Deutsche Bundesbank 1999a, and Mayes and Virén 2000). The MCI allows us to add up the demand effects of both operating targets to arrive at a single figure:

$$MCI_t = r_t - \bar{r} - \delta(q_t - \bar{q}). \tag{13.1}$$

A crucial parameter is the weighting factor δ, which measures the relative demand impact of these two levers of monetary policy. In practice, δ has to be estimated from a macroeconomic model. An important assumption that underlies the construction of MCIs is the perfect substitutability of both levers as far as their demand-side effects are concerned.

On the basis of the MCI, the task of monetary policy in an open economy can be described as follows. As a first step, a central bank has to evaluate the relative demand impact of real interest rate and real exchange rate changes. As a second step, it has to determine a target inflation rate and a loss function. As a third step, it has to set the MCI in a way that the loss function is minimized, given expected shocks on the demand and the supply side. An explicit analysis of this procedure can be found in Gerlach and Smets (2000). For the following, it is assumed that a central bank has determined an optimum MCI (MCI^{opt}). This allows us to focus on the question of which concrete combination of the real interest rate and the real exchange rate will be chosen to achieve such an MCI value. The solution is given by

---

[5] See Williamson (1996). Since 1991 Israel has also followed a crawling peg with an increasing band width.

[6] This section is the result of a joint research project with Timo Wollmershäuser.

the constraint of the uncovered interest rate parity (UIP). This constraint has to be considered if a country wants to avoid speculative inflows or outflows of short-term funds that sooner or later would lead to a currency crisis. In other words, the task of a central bank in an open economy can be described by the dual task of maintaining internal and external equilibrium. Internal equilibrium is achieved by an optimum MCI value, external equilibrium by observing the UIP constraint.

In formal terms this can be described as follows. First, for the purpose of exchange rate policy, the MCI is rearranged as follows. The log real exchange rate in t can be expressed as

$$q_t = \Delta q + q_{t-1}. \tag{13.2}$$

This leads to

$$MCI = r_t - \bar{r} - \delta(\Delta q + q_{t-1} - \bar{q}). \tag{13.3}$$

As a matter of simplification, some of the terms are added up to get

$$\kappa_t = \bar{r} - \delta(q_{t-1} - \bar{q}). \tag{13.4}$$

Omitting the time subscripts leads to

$$MCI = r - \delta(\Delta q) + \kappa. \tag{13.5}$$

The change in the real exchange rate can be expressed as

$$\Delta q = \Delta s + \pi^* - \pi, \tag{13.6}$$

and with the Fisher equation the real interest rate is

$$r = i - \pi. \tag{13.7}$$

Thus, we come to the following definition of the MCI, which shows that it depends on the setting of the two operating targets, the nominal exchange rate and the nominal interest rate:

$$MCI = i - \pi - \delta(\Delta s + \pi^* - \pi) + \kappa. \tag{13.8}$$

As already mentioned, it is assumed that the optimum value of the MCI has been determined with a macroeconomic model using a loss function and a given target value for the inflation rate. Thus, s and i have to be set in order to generate MCI^{opt}:

$$MCI^{opt} = i - \pi - \delta(\Delta s + \pi^* - \pi) + \kappa. \tag{13.9}$$

One can see that a given value of an MCI can be reached with different combinations of i and Δs. However, a policy-maker also has to observe the uncovered interest parity condition in order to avoid destabilizing inflows or outflows of short-term capital:

$$\Delta s + \alpha = i - i^*. \tag{13.10}$$

The targeted depreciation of the logarithm of the domestic currency Δs plus a risk premium α on the expected depreciation has to equal the difference between the home interest rate i and the interest rate of the anchor country i^*. If a central bank follows a monetary policy that is compatible with UIP, this also has the advantage that the costs of sterilization are rather low, which is an important requirement for a policy of exchange rate targeting. It was already mentioned (equation (12.2)) that the total costs of sterilization are

$$C^{TS} = i - i^* - \Delta s. \tag{12.2}$$

Thus, if UIP is maintained, the costs are equal to the risk premium α. As the example of the Czech Republic in 1996 has shown, the costs can become very high if a country tries to maintain a positive interest differential under a fixed exchange rate policy.

With these two equations, it becomes possible to derive optimum values for the two operating targets. One can assume that the following variables are exogenous for this purpose. The domestic and the foreign inflation are exogenous in the short run because of price rigidities. The optimum MCI has been determined at the level of the monetary policy strategy. The foreign interest rate is exogenous since we assume that it is the interest rate of a large country. The risk premium is exogenous for the policy-maker since it is determined by international financial markets. The term κ includes only exogenous or predetermined variables. Thus, there are two equations and the endogenous policy variables. This allows us to solve the simple model for the values i and Δs that have to be targeted by the central bank:

$$\Delta s = \pi - \pi^* + \frac{1}{1 - \delta}(MCI^{opt} - r^* - \alpha - \kappa); \tag{13.11}$$

$$i = \pi + \frac{1}{1 - \delta}(MCI^{opt} - \delta r^* - \delta\alpha - \kappa). \tag{13.12}$$

Thus, for any given situation there is always only one combination of Δs and i that satisfies at the same time the requirements of external and internal equilibrium. In other words, any exchange rate strategy that relies on a constant exchange rate or an active or passive crawl can be regarded as a second-best solution only since it determines an MCI that is not necessarily identical with MCI^{opt}. The MCIs generated by these three strategies are always determined by variables that are exogenous for the domestic central bank. A policy of fixed exchange rates ($\Delta s = 0$) leads to

$$MCI^{fix} = r^* + \alpha + (1 - \delta)(\pi - \pi^*) + \kappa. \tag{13.13}$$

For an active crawl ($\Delta s = \pi^T - \pi^*$), the MCI is

$$MCI^{act} = r^* + \alpha + (1 - \delta)(\pi^T - \pi^*) + \kappa. \tag{13.14}$$

With a passive crawl ($\Delta s = \pi - \pi^*$), the MCI becomes

$$MCI^{pas} = r^* + \alpha + \kappa. \tag{13.15}$$

These three equations show that the foreign real exchange rate is an important determinant of the domestic MCI under all traditional exchange rate strategies. If it is very low, it becomes difficult for the anchoring country to maintain a restrictive MCI. In fact, periods with low real interest rates in the United States (the years 1971–3 and the period 1992–4) often coincided with frictions in its anchoring countries. On the other hand, a very high real interest rate in the anchor country creates a restrictive monetary policy stance in its satellite countries. A good example for tensions that arise out of such a situation are the crises in the EMS in the years 1992–3, which were characterized by high real interest rates in Germany (Bofinger 2000*b*). In other words, if a country wants to choose its MCI autonomously, it cannot rely on such traditional strategies. Instead, it has to choose its optimum exchange rate change in each period according to equation (13.11).

13.3.3. *A constant nominal exchange rate target as a simple rule*

As already mentioned, many central banks have conducted their monetary policy under the simple rule of a constant nominal exchange rate. For this strategy the MCI is given by (13.13). Thus, with a constant nominal exchange rate, the domestic MCI is a completely exogenous variable which is determined by

1. the real interest rate in the anchor country,
2. the risk premium,
3. the differential between the foreign and the domestic inflation rate, where the MCI declines with an increase of the domestic inflation rate as far as $\delta < 1$.

This leads to the well-known result of the Mundell–Fleming model that, under fixed exchange rates, no autonomous monetary policy is possible. But compared with this model, the approach presented here shows explicitly by which concrete parameters the domestic monetary policy is determined under such a regime and it allows us to circumscribe the following conditions under which the simple rule of a constant nominal exchange rate leads to satisfactory results.

1. The central bank in the anchor currency follows an interest rate policy that is compatible with its domestic macroeconomic situation.
2. The business cycles of the home economy and the anchor economy are relatively strongly synchronized so that changes in r^* are compatible with the domestic macroeconomic situation.
3. Inflation differentials and risk premia are relatively low.

Such conditions could be observed in the period 1952–65, where the Bretton Woods system was in operation. While there were some business cycles in this postwar period, they remained relatively moderate; inflation was very low in all countries, and the Federal Reserve followed a stability-oriented monetary policy. This approach also allows us to explain the exchange rate stability between Germany, the Netherlands, and Austria in the 1980s and 1990s. All three countries had very similar inflation rates and their economic cycles were rather similar. This is in line with the general observation that most countries that were able to maintain a fixed nominal exchange for longer periods of time are typically very small countries (Mussa *et al.* 2000: 23). The requirement of low inflation differentials under a fixed exchange rate regime is also shown by the EMS experience in the period 1979–92. After the first few years, with frequent realignments some countries were able to maintain a fixed nominal exchange rate *vis-à-vis* the Deutschmark (Table 13.1), while

Table 13.1. *Critical inflation differentials for a fixed nominal peg: the ERM I experience*

	Date of realignment (entry)	Inflation differential to Germany[a]	Last realignment?
Netherlands	21.03.83	−0.49	Yes
Denmark	12.01.87	3.79	Yes
Belgium	12.01.87	1.48	Yes
France	12.01.87	3.15	Yes
Italy	12.01.87	4.25	No
	25.11.96	1.50	Yes
Spain	19.06.89 (entry)	3.86	No
	06.03.95	2.56	Yes
Portugal	06.04.92 (entry)	4.25	No
	06.03.95	2.17	Yes
Greece	16.03.98 (entry)	3.60	Yes
Sweden	17.05.91 (peg)[b]	8.10	No
Finland	14.10.96 (entry)	−0.84	Yes
UK	08.10.90 (entry)	7.43	No
Austria	12.81 (peg)	0.12	Yes

[a] Averages of monthly CPI rates (6 months before and 6 months after realignment).
[b] Sweden pegged its currency to the ECU from 17 May 1991 to 19 November 1992.
Source: Own calculations based on data from IMF, *International Financial Statistics.*

others were forced to abandon this nominal peg in 1992. The EMS experience indicates that the critical inflation differential seems to lie in the range of 3.75 percentage points. A similarly dismal experience was made by the Czech Republic and Mexico, which tried to maintain constant nominal exchange rates at a time when they still had pronounced inflation differentials against their anchor countries (more than ten percentage points in the Czech Republic in 1993 and about nine percentage points in Mexico in November 1991).

Thus, with high inflation differentials, a constant nominal exchange rate target cannot be maintained for long. While it can be a useful policy tool in the early stages of a macroeconomic stabilization strategy (Bofinger 1996), with a low credibility of policy-makers and a high risk premium, an exit strategy is needed (Eichengreen and Masson 1998) as soon as the risk premium declines.

The experience of the Asian countries can also be interpreted within this framework. On the one hand, the long periods of a stable dollar rate in Malaysia and Thailand fit the observation that a fixed rate can be sustainable if the inflation differentials are very low. In the second half of the 1980s both countries had lower inflation rates than the United States. In this area the crises were initiated by the very low real short-term dollar rates in the period 1992–6 combined with a substantial dollar depreciation *vis-à-vis* the yen. Thus, the UIP condition required low nominal interest rates in Asian countries with a fixed dollar peg. Table 13.2 shows that from 1992 to 1996 the nominal interest rate in Thailand was lower than a Taylor rate, which can be regarded as cause for domestic overheating. However, when the Thai central bank switched to a somewhat more restrictive interest rate policy in 1995, huge amounts of foreign short-term capital flooded into the country. Thus, in 1995 the country was confronted with a dual disequilibrium: its domestic

Table 13.2. *The dual disequilibrium of Thailand, 1990–1998*[a]

	1990	1991	1992	1993	1994	1995	1996	1997	1998
Net short-term inflows (US$ m)	6,785	9,922	7,489	8,929	11,294	20,727	18,081	−20,243	−21,155
Money market rate minus Taylor rate	1.6	0.4	−1.3	−1.0	−3.4	−1.8	−3.1	5.7	13.0
Memorandum item: short-term US dollar rate	8.2	5.9	3.8	3.2	4.7	6.0	5.4	5.7	5.5

[a] Net short-term inflows are calculated from the financial account (line 78*bjd* of IMF, *International Financial Statistics*) minus net direct investment (lines 78*bdd* and 78*bed*). The Taylor rate is calculated on the basis of an average real interest rate of 3% and an inflation target of 2%. The output gap is calculated with a Hodrick–Prescott filter. The output gap and the inflation term are both given a weight of 50%.

monetary conditions were still not restrictive enough, but nominal interest rates were too high to provide a UIP equilibrium. In 1996 the central bank obviously decided to give priority to the international equilibrium and lowered nominal interest rates. As a result, domestic macroeconomic conditions were even more expansionary. In retrospect, it is not surprising that this policy dilemma ended in a disaster.

13.3.4. *Monetary policy with an adjustable nominal exchange rate target ('managed floating')*

For countries that are not able to meet at least the criteria for a constant nominal exchange rate, this simple rule should not be adopted. Today for most economists the only alternative is flexible exchange rates. However, the experience shows that this alternative is rather problematic. The main flaw of this approach is that flexible exchange rates have behaved completely differently from what most textbooks and theoretical studies assume. Over the last twenty-five years countless econometric studies on the determinants of flexible exchange rates have been published. Almost all of them have come to the clear result that 'fundamentals', however defined, have no systematic impact on the exchange rate under a floating system—at least, not over time horizons of up to four or five years. Isard summarizes the evidence as follows:

In short, neither the behavioural relationships suggested by theory, nor the information obtained through autoregression, provided a model that could forecast significantly better than a random walk. And furthermore, while the random walk model performed at least as well as other models, it predicted very poorly. (Isard 1995: 138)[7]

Thus, for a small open economy (with a high δ), a completely unpredictable flexible exchange rate makes it very difficult to achieve a domestic equilibrium. If a central bank is determined to achieve an optimum MCI, a strongly fluctuating nominal exchange rate would require a permanent adjustment of the nominal interest rate, which would lead to instability of the domestic financial sector. In addition, this approach would lead to permanent allocative shifts between the domestic and the international sectors of the economy. If a central bank disregards the MCI and sets interest rates independently of the exchange rate, domestic monetary conditions can become overly expansionary or restrictive. In addition, in emerging market economies foreign exchange markets are relatively thin, so that the risk of unstable exchanges

---

[7] See also Lyons (2000:1): 'Exchange rate economics is in a crisis. It is in a crisis in the sense that current macroeconomic approaches to exchange rates are empirical failures.'

rates is especially high. Thus, Eichengreen and Masson have come to the following conclusion:

For developing and transition countries, as with the smaller industrial countries, there are good reasons why the right exchange rate regime (except perhaps in cases of continuing high inflation) is not something close to an unfettered float. (Eichengreen and Masson 1998: 3)

It is not, therefore, surprising that there are only very few developing and emerging market countries that have been willing to accept a completely market-determined exchange rate. Several studies have shown that this also applies to those countries that, in the classification by the IMF's *International Financial Statistics*, are labelled as 'independently floating' (Calvo and Reinhart 2000*a*; Yeyati and Sturzenegger 1999; Reinhard 2000).

A compromise between a rigid nominal exchange rate and a completely flexible exchange rate is an exchange rate policy that targets a nominal exchange rate path ('exchange rate targeting'). Such a strategy is conceptually more difficult than the two corner solutions, since it requires a skilful combination of the interest rate and the exchange rate levers of monetary policy which are used simultaneously as operating targets. The mechanisms of this approach were laid down in Section 13.3.2. In the past, there are several examples of countries that successfully targeted the exchange rate and the interest rate simultaneously.

The French monetary and exchange rate policy in the first eight years of the EMS shows how this approach can be implemented (Bofinger 2000*b*). In the period 1979–87 realignments took place very often and at irregular intervals; in addition, there was a ± 2.25% fluctuation band. From Figure 13.3 one can see that from 1981 onwards French monetary policy relied mainly on high real interest rates, while the exchange rate policy was characterized by a real depreciation *vis-à-vis* the Deutschmark. As Figure 13.4 shows, the intervention activity of the Banque de France was relatively high.[8] This policy was successful in three respects. It allowed the French government to

1. reduce the French inflation rate to German levels;
2. maintain a stable depreciation path of the franc–Deutschmark rate, which was changed into a stable nominal exchange rate target in January 1997 (Figure 13.3);
3. avoid strong short-term capital inflows, although there was a major interest rate differential in favour of the franc.

---

[8] The total Deutschmark interventions in the ERM are shown in Table 13.1.

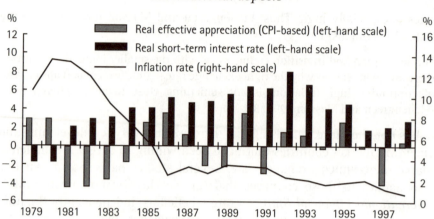

Figure 13.3. *Real interest rates and real exchange rates in France, 1979–1998*
Source: Own calculations based on data from IMF, *International Financial Statistics.*

Other successful examples of exchange rate targeting can be found in Central and Eastern Europe. In the 1990s Poland, Hungary, and Slovenia relied on an exchange rate policy that targeted a controlled depreciation of their currencies *vis-à-vis* the Deutschmark and to some extent *vis-à-vis* the US dollar (Corker *et al.* 2000). The exchange rate targeting of Slovenia is especially interesting. The country never announced any target for the exchange rate; nevertheless, it kept its Deutschmark rate within a very narrow band (Figure 13.5). The marked increase of its foreign exchange reserves from 1992 until 1998 indicates that this country was always intervening in order to avoid an appreciation or a depreciation that was less pronounced than targeted. In retrospect, one can see that all three transition countries with targeted exchange rate paths were able to achieve higher and more stable growth rates of real GDP than the Czech Republic and Estonia, which both relied on a fixed nominal exchange rate strategy. In addition, while the Czech Republic was confronted with a currency crisis in 1997, the three 'exchange rate targeters' were able to avoid such problems.

The limitations to a policy with adjustable exchange rate targets are set by strong capital outflows. The best policy against outflows is a monetary policy strategy that is in line with UIP and thus avoids strong short-term inflows. Some protection can also be provided if a central bank had been able to built up a buffer stock of exchange reserves in periods of an appreciation pressure. But there will always be situations where a prolonged defence against a speculative attack is impossible, so that a central bank has to give up its exchange rate target and accept a stronger depreciation than targeted. If a certain setting of its monetary condition index is to be maintained, a central bank has to increase short-term real interest rates.

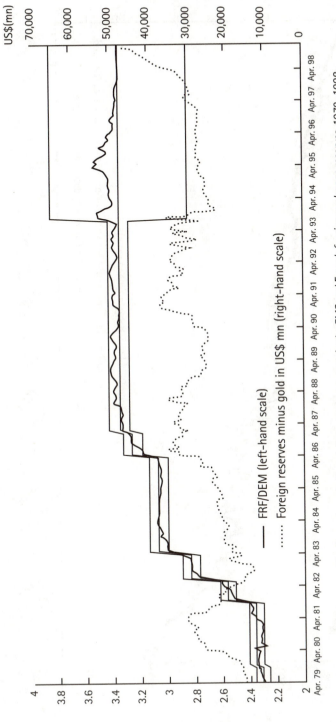

Figure 13.4. *The Deutschmark–French franc exchange rate in the EMS and French foreign exchange reserves, 1979–1998*

Source: Data from Deutsche Bundesbank and IMF, *International Financial Statistics.*

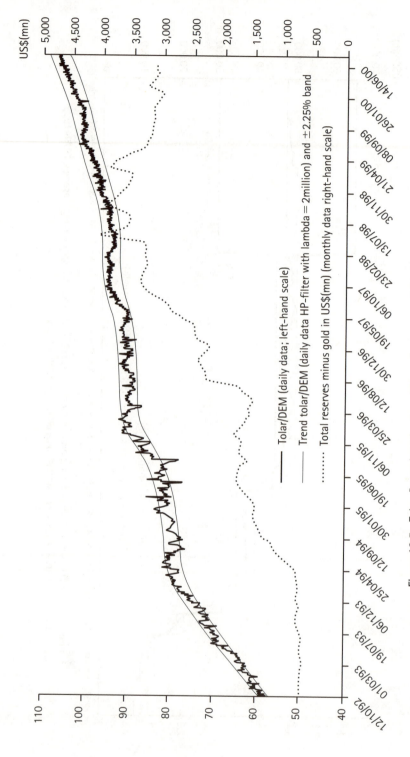

Figure 13.5. *Tolar–Deutschmark rate and Slovenian reserves, 1992–2000*

Source: Own calculations based on data from IMF, *International Financial Statistics* and Datastream.

As a result, monetary policy puts a higher pressure on the domestic sector of the economy, while the international sector experiences a mixture of expansionary impulses via devaluation and restrictive impulses via the higher real rate. Such allocative distortions are the price that has to be paid for an international monetary order in which each country is obliged to defend its own currency unilaterally.

Table 13.3. *Deutschmark interventions in the Exchange Rate Mechanism of the EMS, 1979–1994 (DM bn)*

Period		Obligatory	Intra-marginal	Total
A: By calendar years				
1979	Purchases	–	2.7	2.7
	Sales	3.6	8.1	11.7
	Balance	−3.6	−5.4	−9.0
1980	Purchases	5.9	5.9	11.8
	Sales	–	1.0	1.0
	Balance	+5.9	+4.9	+10.8
1981	Purchases	2.3	8.1	10.4
	Sales	17.3	12.8	30.1
	Balance	−15.0	−4.7	−19.7
1982	Purchases	–	9.4	9.4
	Sales	3.0	12.8	15.8
	Balance	−3.0	−3.4	−6.4
1983	Purchases	16.7	19.1	35.8
	Sales	8.3	12.9	21.2
	Balance	+8.4	+6.2	+14.5
1984	Purchases	–	28.9	28.9
	Sales	4.7	7.6	12.3
	Balance	−4.7	+21.4	+16.6
1985	Purchases	–	29.1	29.1
	Sales	0.4	30.8	31.1
	Balance	−0.4	−1.6	−2.0
1986	Purchases	19.0	33.6	52.6
	Sales	4.1	74.0	78.1
	Balance	+14.8	−40.4	−25.5
1987	Purchases	–	47.8	47.8
	Sales	15.0	61.7	76.8
	Balance	−15.0	−13.9	−28.9
1988	Purchases	–	26.8	26.8
	Sales	–	16.3	16.3
	Balance	–	+10.5	+10.5
1989	Purchases	–	20.4	20.4
	Sales	5.0	8.6	13.6
	Balance	−5.0	+11.8	+6.8

Table 13.3. *(Continued)*

Period	Obligatory	Intra-marginal	Total
1990 Purchases	1.5	32.5	34.1
Sales	–	12.3	12.3
Balance	+1.5	+20.2	+21.8
1991 Purchases	–	6.4	6.4
Sales	–	21.9	21.9
Balance	–	−15.5	−15.5
1992 Purchases	–	75.1	75.1
Sales	63.7	199.7	263.4
Balance	−63.7	−124.6	−188.3
1993 Purchases	–	92.0	92.0
Sales	25.1	166.0	191.1
Balance	−25.1	−74.0	−99.1
1994 Purchases	–	52.6	52.6
Sales	–	5.5	5.5
Balance	–	47.1	47.1
B: *By selected periods, net*			
21 March 1983–8 July 1985: from the first trading day after the realignment of 21 March 1983 to the end of major Deutschmark Purchases by partner countries	−11.8	−49.8	−61.6
8 July 1986–9 January 1987: from the end of major Deutschmark Purchases by partner countries to the last trading day before the realignment of 12 January 1987	+18.9	+44.1	+63.0
3 June 1992–25 September 1992: Deutschmark in ERM appreciated; devaluation of partner currencies and exit of pound and lira	−63.7	−120.4	−184.2
26 September 1992–17 November 1992: return of foreign exchange movements in the ERM	−0.0	47.7	47.7
8 July 1993–1 August 1993: the ever-increasing strength of the Deutschmark in the ERM is followed by a widening of the band	−24.7	−82.4	−107.0
6 December 1993–5 December 1994: calm in the ERM		52.3	52.3

+ Deutschmark sales or expansionary impact on liquidity in Germany.
− Deutschmark purchases or contractionary impact on liquidity in Germany.

Source: Deutsche Bundesbank, annual reports.

References

Akerlof, G., Dickens, W., and Perry, G. (1996), 'The Macroeconomics of Low Inflation', *Brooking Papers on Economic Activity*, 1–59.

Alesina, A. (1988), 'Macroeconomics and Politics', in S. Fischer (ed.), *NBER Macroeconomics Annual*, Cambridge, Mass.: MIT Press: 13–52.

—— (1989), 'Politics and Business Cycles in Industrial Democracies', *Economic Policy*, 8: 58–98.

—— and Summers, L. H. (1993), 'Central Bank Independence and Macroeconomic Performance: Some Comparative Evidence', *Journal of Money, Credit, and Banking*, 25 (2): 150–162.

Argy, V., and Kouri, P. J. K. (1974), 'Sterilization Policies and the Volatility in International Reserves', in R. Z. Aliber (ed.), *National Monetary Policies and the International Financial System*, Chicago and London: University of Chicago Press.

—— Brennan, A., and Stevens, G. (1990), 'Monetary Targeting. The International Experience', *The Economic Record* (Economic Society of Australia), 66: 37–62.

Auernheimer, L. (1974), 'The Honest Government's Guide to the Revenue from the Creation of Money', *Journal of Political Economy*, 82 (3): 598–606.

Axelrod, R. (1984), *The Evolution of Cooperation*, New York: Basic Books.

Backus, D., and Driffill, J. (1985), 'Inflation and Reputation', *American Economic Review*, 75 (3): 530–538.

Bade, R., and Parkin, M. (1988), 'Central Bank Laws and Monetary Policy', unpublished paper, Department of Economics, University of Western Ontario.

Bailey, M. J. (1956), 'The Welfare Cost of Inflationary Finance', *Journal of Political Economy*, 64 (2): 93–110.

Balassa, B. (1964), 'The Purchasing Power Doctrine: A Reappraisal', *Journal of Political Economy*, 72 (6): 584–596.

Ball, L. (1998), 'Another Look at Long-run Money Demand', NBER Working Paper no. 6597, Cambridge, Mass.

Baltensperger, E. (1980), 'Alternative Approaches to the Theory of the Banking Firm', *Journal of Monetary Economics*, 6, S. 1–37.

Bank for International Settlements (BIS) (1999*a*), *Annual Report*, Basle; internet: www.bis.org.

—— (1999*b*), 'Monetary Policy Operating Procedures in Emerging Market Economies', BIS Policy Papers no. 5; internet: www.bis.org.

Bank of England (1999), 'Economic Models at the Bank of England', London: Bank of England.

—— (2000*a*), 'Monetary Policy in the United Kingdom', fact sheet; internet: www.bankofengland.co.uk.

—— (2000*b*), *Inflation Report*, August 2000; internet: www.bankofengland.co.uk.

Barnett, W. (1978), 'The User Costs of Money', *Economic Letters*, 1: 145–149.

—— (1980), 'Economic Monetary Aggregates', *Journal of Econometrics*, 14:11–48.

—— (1982), 'Divisia Indices', in N. Johnson and S. Kotz (eds.), *Encyclopaedia of Statistical Sciences*, Vol. 2, New York: John Wiley: 412–415.

—— Fisher, D., and Serletis A. (1992), 'Consumer Theory and the Demand for Money', *Journal of Economic Literature*, 30: 2086–2119.

Barro, R. J. (1982), 'Measuring the Fed's Revenue from Money Creation', *Journal of Political Economy*, 82 (3): 598–606.

— (1991), 'Economic Growth in a Cross Section of Countries', *Quarterly Journal of Economics*, 106: 407–433.

— (1995), 'Inflation and Economic Growth', *Bank of England Quarterly Bulletin*, 35 (2): 166–176.

— (1997), *Determinants of Economic Growth*. Cambridge, Mass.: MIT Press.

— and Gordon, D. B. (1983a), 'A Positive Theory of Monetary Policy in a Natural Rate Model', *Journal of Political Economy*, 91 (4): 589–610.

— and — (1983b), 'Rules, Discretion, and Reputation in a Model of Monetary Policy', *Journal of Monetary Economics*, 17 (1): 101–122.

Baumol, W. J. (1952), 'The Transaction Demand for Cash: An Inventory Theoretic Approach', *Quarterly Journal of Economics*, 66: 545–556.

Bean, C. (1983), 'Targeting Nominal Income: An Appraisal', *Economic Journal*, 93: 806–819.

Berk, J. M., and van Bergeijk, P. (2000), 'Is the Yield Curve a Useful Information Variable for the Eurosystem?' ECB Working Paper no. 11, Frankfurt.

Bernanke, B. S., and Gertler, M. (1995), 'Inside the Black Box: The Credit Channel of Monetary Policy Transmission', *Journal of Economic Perspectives*, 9 (4): 27–48.

— and Mihov, I. (1998), 'Measuring Monetary Policy', *Quarterly Journal of Economics*, 113: 869–902.

— and Mishkin, F. S. (1992), 'Central Bank Behavior and the Strategy of Monetary Policy: Observations from Six Industrialized Countries', NBER Working Paper no. 4082, Cambridge, Mass.

— and Woodford, M. (1997), 'Inflation Forecasts and Monetary Policy', *Journal of Money, Credit and Banking*, 29: 653–684.

— Gertler M., and Gilchrist, S. (1994), 'The Financial Accelerator and the Flight to Quality', NBER Working Paper no. 4789, Cambridge, Mass.

— Laubach, T., Mishkin, F., and Posen, A. (1999), *Inflation Targeting: Lessons from the International Experience*, Princeton: Princeton University Press.

Bernholz, P. (1986), 'The Implementation and Maintenance of a Monetary Constitution', *Cato Journal*, 6 (2): 477–511.

Blackburn, K., and Christensen, M. (1989), 'Monetary Policy and Policy Credibility: Theories and Evidence', *Journal of Economic Literature*, 27 (1): 1–45.

Blanchard, O., and Fischer, S. (1989), *Lectures on Macroeconomics*, Cambridge, Mass.: MIT Press.

Blenck, D. (2000), 'Main Features of the Monetary Policy Frameworks of the Bank of Japan, the Federal Reserve System and the Eurosystem', paper presented at an ECB Conference on 5/6 May 2000; internet: www.ecb.int.

Blinder, A. (1987), 'The Rules-versus-Discretion Debate in the Light of Recent Experience', *Weltwirtschaftliches Archiv*, 123 (3): 399–414.

— (1994), 'On Sticky Prices: Academic Theories Meet the Real World', in G. Mankiw (ed.), *Monetary Theory*, Chicago and London: University of Chicago Press: 117–154.

— (1997), 'What Central Bankers Could Learn from Academics—and Vice Versa', *Journal of Economic Perspectives*, 11: 3–19.

— (1998), *Central Banking in Theory and Practice*, Cambridge, Mass.: MIT Press.

Bloomfield, A. (1963), 'Short-term Capital Movements under the pre-1914 Gold Standard', *Princeton Studies in International Finance*, no. 21.

Board of Governors (1994), *The Federal Reserve System, Purposes and Functions*, Washington, DC: Federal Reserve Board.

Bockelmann, H. (1978), 'Streitfragen zur Kontrolle der Geldschöpfung durch die Notenbank', in W. Ehrlicher and A. Oberhauser (eds.), *Probleme der Geldmengensteuerung*, Schriften des Vereins für Socialpolitik, N.F. Bd. 99, Berlin: Dunker and Humblot: 39–48.

Bofinger, P. (1991), *Festkurssysteme and geldpolitische Koordination*, Baden-Baden: Nomos Verlagsgesellschaft.

—— (1992), 'The Experience with Monetary Policy in an Environment with Strong Microeconomic Distortions', *Economic Systems*, 16 (2): 247–268.

—— (1996), 'The Economics of Orthodox Money-based Stabilisations (OMBS): The Recent Experience of Kazakstan, Russia and the Ukraine', *European Economic Review*, 40: 663–671.

—— (2000*a*), 'The Non-cash Economy in the CIS', *Economic Systems*, 24 (1): 71–76.

—— (2000*b*), 'The European Monetary System (1979–1988): Achievements, Flaws and Applicability to Other Regions of the World', background paper for Special Session IV on Global Financial Issues, UN/ECE conference 'Financing for Development', December 2000; internet: www.unece.org/press/specialevent/00rcmfd_documents/bofinger.pdf.

Bordo, M. D., and Eichengreen, B. J. (eds.) (1993), *A Retrospective on the Bretton Woods System: Lessons for International Monetary Reform*, National Bureau of Economic Research Project Report, Chicago: University of Chicago Press.

—— and Schwartz, A. (eds.) (1984), *A Retrospective on the Classical Gold Standard, 1821–1931*, Chicago: University of Chicago Press.

Borio, C. (1997), 'The Implementation of Monetary Policy in Industrial Countries: A Survey', BIS Economic Papers, no. 47, Basle.

—— (2000), 'Monetary Policy Operating Procedures in the United States, Japan and EMU: A Comparative Assessment', paper prepared for the EBC Conference, Frankfurt, 5–6 May 2000; internet: www.ecb.int.

Boskin, M. J., Dulberger, E. R., Gordon, R. J., Griliches, Z., and Jorgenson, D. W. (1996), 'Toward a More Accurate Measure of the Cost of Living', Final Report to the Senate Finance Committee, 4 December.

Bradley, M. D., and Jansen, D. W. (1989), 'Understanding Nominal GNP Targeting', *Federal Reserve Bank of St Louis Review*, 71 (6): 31–40.

Briault, C., Haldane, A., and King, M. (1996), 'Central Bank Independence and Accountability: Theory and Evidence', *Bank of England Quarterly Bulletin*, 36 (1): 63–68.

Brunner, K. (1968), 'The Role of Money and Monetary Policy', *Federal Reserve Bank of St Louis Review*, 50: 8–24.

—— (1981), 'The Art of Central Banking', Center for Research in Government Policy and Business, Working Paper no. GPB 81-6.

—— (1984), 'Monetary Policy and Monetary Order', *Außenwirtschaft*, 39 (3): 187–206.

—— and Meltzer, A. (1964), 'Some Further Investigations of Demand and Supply Functions for Money', *Journal of Finance*, 19: 240–283.

—— and —— (1966), 'A Credit Market Theory of the Money Supply and an Explanation of Two Puzzles in US Monetary Policy', *Rivista Internazionale di Scienze Economiche e Commerciali*, 13: 405–432.

—— and —— (1971), 'The Uses of Money: Money in the Theory of an Exchange Economy', *American Economic Review*, 61: 784–805.

Bruno, M. (1993), *Crisis, Stabilization, and Economic Reform: Therapy by Consensus*, Oxford: Clarendon Press.

—— and Fischer, S. (1990), 'Seigniorage, Operating Rules, and the High Inflation Trap', *Quarterly Journal of Economics*, 105 (2): 353–374.

432 *References*

Buch, C., Koop, M. J., Schweickert, R., and Wolf, H. (1995), *Währungsreformen im Vergleich*, Tübingen: J.C.B. Mohr (Paul Siebeck).

Buiter, W. H. (1999), 'Alice in Euroland', CEPR Policy Paper no. 1, London.

Cagan, P. (1956), 'The Monetary Dynamics of Hyperinflation', in M. Friedman (ed.), *Studies in the Quantity Theory of Money*, Chicago: University of Chicago Press: 25–117.

Calvo, G. A. (1978), 'On the Time Consistency of Optimal Policy in a Monetary Economy', *Econometrica*, 46 (6): 1411–1428.

— and Guidotti, P. (1993), 'On the Flexibility of Monetary Policy: The Case of the Optimal Inflation Tax', *Review of Economic Studies*, 60 (3): 667–687.

— and Reinhart, C. M. (2000), 'Fixing for Your Life', paper prepared for the Brookings Trade Forum 2000, mimeo.

Campell, J. (1995), 'Some Lessons from the Yield Curve', *Journal of Economic Perspectives*, 9 (3): 129–152.

Canzoneri, M. B. (1985), 'Monetary Policy Games and the Role of Private Information', *American Economic Review*, 75 (5): 1056–1070.

Capie, F., Goodhard, C., and Schnadt, N. (1994), 'The Development of Central Banking', in Bank of England, *The Future of Central Banking: The Tercentenary Symposium of the Bank of England*, Cambridge: Cambridge University Press: 1–231.

Caplin, A. (1992), 'Menu Costs', in J. Eatwell, M. Milgate, and P. Newman (eds.), *The New Palgrave: A Dictionary of Money and Finance*, Vol. 2, London: Macmillan: 694–697.

Cecchetti, S. G. (1995), 'Distinguishing Theories of the Monetary Transmission Mechanism', *Federal Reserve Bank of St Louis Review*, 77 (3): 83–97.

Cecchetti, S. (2000), 'Legal Structure, Financial Structure and the Monetary Policy Transmission Mechanism', in Deutsche Bundesbank (ed.), *The Monetary Transmission Process*, Houndsmills, Basingstoke: Palgrave: 170–194.

Christiano, L. J. (1989), 'P*: Not the Inflation Forecaster's Holy Grail', *Quarterly Review*, Federal Reserve Bank of Minneapolis, Fall: 3–18.

Clarida, R., and Gertler, M. (1996), 'How the Bandesbank Conducts Monetary Policy', NBER Working Paper no. 5581, Cambridge, Mass.

— Gali, J., and Gertler, M. (1999), 'The Science of Monetary Policy: A New Keynesian Perspective', *Journal of Economic Literature*, 37: 1661–1707.

— — and — (2000), 'Monetary Policy Rules and Macroeconomic Stability: Evidence and Some Theory', *Quarterly Journal of Economics*, 115: 147–180.

Coenen, G., and Vega, J.-L. (1999), 'The Demand for Money in the Euro Area', ECB Working Paper, no. 6, Frankfurt.

Cohen, D., Hassett K., and Hubbard, G. (1999), 'Inflation and the User Cost of Capital: Does Inflation Still Matter?' in M. Feldstein (ed.), *The Costs and Benefits of Price Stability*, Chicago and London: University of Chicago Press: 199–230.

Collignon, S., Bofinger, P., Johnson, C., and de Maigret, B. (1994), *Europe's Monetary Future*, London: Pinter.

Cooley, T. F., and Hansen, G. D. (1991), 'The Welfare Costs of Moderate Inflation', *Journal of Money, Credit, and Banking*, 23 (3): 483–503.

Corker, R., Beaumont, C., van Elkan, R., and D. Iakova, Dora (2000), 'Exchange Rate Regimes in Selected Advanced Transition Economies: Coping with Transition, Capital Inflows, and EU Accession', IMF Policy Discussion Paper, No. 00/3, Washington, DC.

Cornwall, J. (1987), 'Inflation and Growth', in J. Eatwell, M. Milgate, and P. Newman (eds.), *The New Palgrave Dictionary of Economics*, Vol. 2, London: Macmillan: 839–841.

Croushore, D., and Stark, T. (1995), 'Evaluating McCallum's Rule for Monetary Policy', *Federal Reserve Bank of Philadelphia Business Review*, January/February: 3–14.

Cukierman, A. (1986), 'Central Bank Behavior and Credibility: Some Recent Theoretical Developments', *Federal Reserve Bank of St Louis Review*, 68 (5): 5–17.

— (1992), *Central Bank Strategy, Credibility, and Independence*, Cambridge, Mass.: MIT Press.

— Webb, Steven B., and Bilin, N. (1992), 'Measuring the Independence of Central Banks and its Effect on Policy Outcomes', *World Bank Economic Review*, 6 (3): 353–398.

— Kalaitzidakis, P., Summers, L. H., and Webb, S. B. (1993), 'Central Bank Independence, Growth, Investment, and Real Rates', *Carnegie–Rochester Conference Series on Public Policy*, 39: 95–140.

Culbertson, J. M. (1957), 'The Term Structure of Interest Rates', *Quarterly Journal of Economics*, 71 (4): 485–517.

Dale S., and Haldane, A. (1993), 'A Simple Model of Money, Credit and Aggregate Demand', Bank of England Working Paper Series, no. 7, London.

Davis, R. G. (1990), 'Intermediate Targets and Indicators for Monetary Policy: An Introduction to the Issues', *Federal Reserve Bank of New York Quarterly Review*, Summer: 71–82.

De Grauwe, P. (2000), *The Economics of Monetary Integration*, 4th edn, Oxford: Oxford University Press.

De Gregorio, J. (1993), 'Inflation, Taxation, and Long-run Growth', *Journal of Monetary Economics*, 31: 271–298.

De Haan, J., and Sturm, J. E. (1992), 'The Case for Central Bank Independence', *Banca Nazionale del Lavoro Quarterly Review*, 182: 305–327.

— Knot, K., and Sturm, J. E. (1993), 'On the Reduction of Disinflation Costs: Fixed Exchange Rates or Central Bank Independence?' *Banca Nazionale del Lavoro Quarterly Review*, 187: 429–444.

De Long, J. B., and Summers, L. H. (1992), 'Macroeconomic Policy and Long-Run Growth', *Federal Reserve Bank of Kansas City Economic Review*, 77 (4): 5–30.

Debelle, G. (1999), 'Inflation Targeting and Output Stabilisation', Research Discussion Paper no. 1999-08, Reserve Bank of Australia, Sydney, June.

— and Fischer, S. (1995), 'How Independent Should a Central Bank Be?' in J. C. Fuhrer (ed.), *Goals, Guidelines, and Constraints facing Monetary Policymakers*, Boston: Federal Reserve Bank of Boston conference volume, 195–221.

Deutsche Bundesbank (1992), 'The Exchange Rate Realignment in the European Monetary System and the Interest Rate Decisions of the Bundesbank', *Monthly Report*, 45 (10): 14–19.

— (1993), The Recent Monetary Policy Decisions and Developments in the European Monetary System', *Monthly Report*, 46 (8): 19–27.

— (1994), *Macroeconometric Model of the German Economy*, Frankfurt am Main.

— (1995), *The Monetary Policy of the Bundesbank*, Frankfurt am Main.

— (1999*a*), 'Taylor Interest Rate and Monetary Conditions Index', *Monthly Report*, 51 (4) : 47–63.

— (1999*b*), Financial Accounts 1990 to 1998; internet: www.bundesbank.de.

— (1999*c*), 'Corporate Finance in Germany and France: A Comparative Analysis', *Monthly Report*, 51 (10): 29–46.

— (2000*a*), 'Monetary Policy Transparency', *Monthly Report*, 52 (3): 15–29.

— (2000*b*), *Annual Report 1999*; internet: www.bundesbank.de.

— (2001), 'The Information Content of Survey Data on Expected Price Developments for Monetary Policy', *Monthly Report*, 53 (1): 35–49.

Dickey, D., and Fuller, W. (1981), 'Likelihood Ratio Statistics for Autoregressive Time Series with a Unit Root', *Journal of the American Statistical Association*, 74: 427–431.

Diewert, W. (1992), 'Index Numbers', in P. Newmann, M. Murray, and J. Eatwell (eds.), *The New Palgrave Dictionary of Money and Finance*, Vol. 2, London: Macmillan: 364–379.

Döpke, J. and Langfeld, E. (1995), 'Zur Qualität von Konjunkturprognosen für Westdeutschland 1976–1994', Kieler Diskussionspapiere No. 247, Kiel.

Dornbusch, R. (1987), 'Purchasing Power Parity', in J. Eatwell, M. Milgate, and P. Newmann (eds.), *The New Palgrave: A Dictionary of Economics*, Vol. 3, London: Macmillan: 1073–1085.

— and S. Fischer (1993), 'Moderate Inflation', *World Bank Economic Review*, 7 (1): 1–44.

Driffill, J., Mizon, G. E., and Ulph, A. (1990), 'Costs of Inflation', in B. M. Friedman and F. Hahn (eds.), *Handbook of Monetary Economics*, Vol. II, Amsterdam: North-Holland: 1011–1066.

Dueker, M. (1993), 'Can Nominal GDP Targeting Rules Stabilize the Economy?' *Federal Reserve Bank of St Louis Review*, 83 (3): 15–29.

Duisenberg, W. (1999a), 'The Eurosystem's Strategy for the Euro', speech at a conference organised by 'the Economist', Rome, 12 March; internet: www.ecb.int.

— (1999b), 'The Euro: The New European Currency', speech at the Council of Foreign Relations, Chicago, 1 February; internet: www.ecb.int.

— (1999c), 'Monetary Policy in the Euro Area', speech at the New Year's Reception organized by Deutsche Börse, 25 January; internet: www.ecb.int.

— (2000), 'Introductory statement', ECB press conference, Frankfurt am Main, 6 July; internet: www.ecb.int.

Easterly, W., Mauro, P., and Schmidt-Hebel, K. (1995), 'Money Demand and Seigniorage Maximizing Inflation', *Journal of Money, Credit, and Banking*, 27 (2): 583–603.

Edey, M. (1994), 'Costs and Benefits of Moving from Low Inflation to Price Stability', *OECD Economic Studies*, 23: 109–130.

Eichengreen, B. (2000), 'Solving the Currency Conundrum'; internet: http://emlab.berkeley.edu/users/eichengr/POLICY.HTM, 2000.

— and Masson, P. (1998), 'Exit Strategies, Policy Options for Countries Seeking Greater Exchange Rate Flexibility', International Monetary Fund Occasional Paper no. 168, Washington.

Eijffinger, S., and Schaling, E. (1993), 'Central Bank Independence in Twelve Industrial Countries', *Banca Nazionale del Lavoro Quarterly Review*, 184: 49–90.

— and Schaling, E. (1995), 'Central Bank Independence: Criteria and Indices', in H. Francke and E. Ketzel (eds.), *Konzepte and Erfahrungen der Geldpolitik*, Beihefte zu Kredit and Kapital, 13, Berlin: Duncker & Humblot: 185–218.

— and Verhagen, W. (1997), 'The Advantage of Hiding Both Hands: Foreign Exchange Intervention, Ambiguity and Private Information', Discussion Paper No. 9730, Center for Economic Research, Tilburg University.

Einzig, P. (1970), *The History of Foreign Exchange*, London and Basingstoke: Macmillan/St Martin's Press.

Emminger, O. (1986), *D-Mark, Dollar, Währungskrisen, Erinnerungen eines ehemaligen Bandesbankpräsidenten*, Stuttgart: Deutsche Verlags-Anstalt.

Engle, R. F., and Granger, C. W. J. (1987), 'Co-integration and Error Correction: Representation, Estimation and Testing', *Econometrica*, 55 (2): 251–276.

Ericsson, N. R. (1999), 'Empirical Modelling of Money Demand', in H. Lütkepohl and J. Wolters (eds.), *Money Demand in Europe*, Heidelberg: Physika Verlag: 29–50.

Estrella, A., and Mishkin, F. (1995), 'The Term Structure of Interest Rates and its Role in Monetary Policy for the European Central Bank', NBER Working Paper No. 5279, Cambridge, Mass.

Eucken, W. (1952), *Grundsätze der Wirtschaftspolitik*, 6th edn 1990, Tübingen: Mohr Siebeck.

European Central Bank (ECB) (1998), 'The Single Monetary Policy in Stage Three', September; internet: www.ecb.int.

— (1999a), 'The Stability Oriented Monetary Policy of the Eurosystem', *Monthly Bulletin*, January: 39–50; internet: www.ecb.int.

— (1999b), 'Key Issues for the Analysis of Real Interest Rates in the Euro Area', *Monthly Bulletin*, March: 16–18; internet: www.ecb.int.

— (1999c), 'Editorial', *Monthly Bulletin*, December 1999: 5–7; internet: www.ecb.int.

— (2000a), 'Measures of Expected Future Price Development in the Euro Area', *Monthly Bulletin*, March: 27–29.

— (2000b), 'Monetary Policy Transmission in the Euro Area', *Monthly Bulletin*, July: 43–58.

— (2000c), *Annual Report 1999*.

— (2000d), 'Economic Developments in the Euro Area', *Monthly Bulletin*, December: 9–62.

European Commission (1990), 'One Market, One Money', *European Economy*, No. 44.

Fase, M. (1998), 'Review of Peter Bofinger *et al.*: *Geldpolitik, Ziele, Institutionen, Strategien und Instrumente*, *De Economist: Quarterly Review of the Royal Netherlands Economic Association*, 146: 515–516.

— and Winder, C. (1999), 'Wealth and the Money Demand in the European Union', in H. Lütkepohl and J. Wolters (eds.), *Money Demand in Europe*, Heidelberg: Physica-Verlag: 239–258.

Federal Reserve Bank of New York (2000), Domestic Open Market Operations during 1999; internet: www.ny.frb.org/pihome/annual.html.

Feldstein, M. (1999), 'Capital Income Taxes and the Benefits of Price Stability', in M. Feldstein (ed.), *The Costs and Benefits of Price Stability*, Chicago and London: University of Chicago Press: 9–40.

— and Stock, J. H. (1994), 'The Use of a Monetary Aggregate to Target Nominal GDP', in N. Mankiw (ed.), *Monetary Policy*, Chicago and London: University of Chicago Press: 7–62.

Fischer, S. (1981), 'Towards an Understanding of the Costs of Inflation', *Carnegie–Rochester Conference Series on Public Policy*, 15: 5–41.

— (1990), 'Rules versus Discretion in Monetary Policy', in B. Friedman and F. Hahn (eds.), *Handbook of Monetary Economics*, Vol. II, Amsterdam: North-Holland: 1155–1184.

— (1993), 'The Role of Macroeconomic Factors in Growth', *Journal of Monetary Economics*, 32: 485–512.

— (1995), 'Central Bank Independence Revisited', *American Economic Review*, 85 (2): 201–206.

— and Modigliani, F. (1978), 'Towards an Understanding of the Real Effects and Costs of Inflation', *Weltwirtschaftliches Archiv*, 114: 810–833.

Fisher, I. (1896), *Appreciation and Interest*, AEA Publications 3 (11), August: 331–442; reprinted by August M. Kelley, New York, 1961.

— (1911), *The Purchasing Power of Money*, 2nd edn, 1926; reprinted by Augustus Kelley, New York, 1963.

— (1920), *The Purchasing Power of Money: Its Determination and Relation to Credit, Interest and Crises*, New York: Macmillan.

— (1930), *The Theory of Interest*; reprinted by Augustus M. Kelley, Fairfield, NJ, 1986.

Fratianni, M., and Huang, H. (1992), 'Central Bank Independence and Optimal Conservativeness', Indiana University of Graduate School Business Working Papers in Economics, no. 92-032, Bloomington, Ind.

Fratianni, M., von Hagen, J., and Waller, C. J. (1997), 'Central Banking as a Political Principal–Agent Problem', *Economic Inquiry*, 35 (2): 378–393.

Freixas, X., and Rochet, J.-C. (1997), *Microeconomics of Banking*, Cambridge, Mass.: MIT Press.

Friedman, M. (1953), *Essays in Positive Economics*, Chicago, University of Chicago Press.

— (1956), 'The Quantity Theory of Money: A Restatement', in *Studies in the Quantity Theory of Money*, Chicago: University of Chicago Press.

— (1959), *A Program for Monetary Stability*, New York: Fordham Press.

— (1966), 'Comments', in G. Shultz and R. Aliber (eds.), *Guidelines, Informal Controls and the Market Place*, Chicago: University of Chicago Press: 55–61.

— (1968), 'The Role of Monetary Policy', *American Economic Review*, 58 (1): 1–17.

— (1969), *The Optimum Quantity of Money and Other Essays*, Chicago: Aldine.

— (1971), 'A Theoretical Framework for Monetary Analysis', NBER Occasional Paper no. 112, Cambridge, Mass.

— (1987), 'Quantity Theory of Money', in J. Eatwell, M. Milgate, and P. Newmann (eds.), *The New Palgrave: A Dictionary of Economics*, Vol. 4, London: Macmillan, 3–20.

— and Schwartz, A. J. (1963), *A Monetary History of the United States, 1867–1960*, Princeton: Princeton University Press.

— and — (1970), *Monetary Statistics of the United States*, New York: Columbia Press for the NBER.

Froot, K., and Thaler, R. (1990), 'Anomalies; Foreign Exchange', *Journal of Economic Perspectives*, 4 (3): 179–192.

Fuhrer, J. C. (1997), 'The (Un)Importance of Forward-Looking Behavior in Price Specifications', *Journal of Money, Credit and Banking*, 29 (3): 338–350.

— and Moore, G. (1995), 'Inflation Persistence', *Quarterly Journal of Economics*, 110 (1): 127–159.

Furubotn, E., and Richter, R. (1997), *Institutions and Economic Theory: The Contribution of the New Institutional Economics*, Ann Arbor, Mich.: University of Michigan Press.

Gali, J., and Gertler, M. (1999), 'Inflation Dynamics: A Structural Econometric Analysis', *Journal of Monetary Economics*, 44: 195–222.

— — and Lòpez-Salido, D. (2000), 'European Inflation Dynamics', mimeo, New York University Department of Economics.

Geraats, P. M. (1999), 'Transparency and Reputation: Should the ECB Publish its Inflation Forecasts?' Paper presented at the conference on 'Monetary Policy-Making under Uncertainty', ECB/CFS, Frankfurt am Main, 3–4 December; internet: www.ecb.int.

Gerlach, S. (1995), 'Testing the Quantity Theory using Long-Run Averaged Cross-Country Data', BIS Working Paper no. 31, Basle.

— and Schnabel, G. (1999), 'The Taylor Rule and Interest Rates in the EMU Area: a Note', BIS Working Papers no. 73, Basle.

— and Smets, F. (2000), 'MCIs and Monetary Policy', *European Economic Review*, 44 (9): 1677–1700.

— and Svensson, L. E. O. (1999), 'Money and Inflation in the Euro Area: A Case for Monetary Indicators?' Internet: www.iies.su.se/leosven.

Gertler, M., and Gilchrist, S. (1993), 'The Role of Credit Market Imperfections in the Monetary Transmission Mechanism: Arguments and Evidence', *Scandinavian Journal of Economics*, 95: 43–46.

Giannini, C. (1994), 'Confidence Costs and the Institutional Genesis of Central Banks', Temi di discussione, No. 226, Banca d'Italia, Rome.

Giavazzi, F. and Pagano, M. (1988), 'The Advantage of Tying One's Hands', *European Economic Review*, 32 (5): 1055–1077.

Gigerenzer, G., Todd, P. M., and the ABC Research Group (1999), *Simple Heuristics that Make Us Smart*, Oxford: Oxford University Press.

— (2000), 'Precis of Simple Heuristics that Make Us Smart'; internet: www-abc.mpib-berlin.mpg.de/users/ptodd/SimpleHeuristics.BBS.

Goff, B., and Toma, M. (1993), 'Optimal Seigniorage, the Gold Standard and Central Bank Financing', *Journal of Money, Credit and Banking*, 25 (1): 79–95.

Goodfriend, M. (1991), 'Interest Rates and the Conduct of Monetary Policy', *Carnegie-Rochester Series on Public Policy*, 34: 7–30.

— (1995), 'Acquiring and Maintaining Credibility for Low Inflation: The US Experience', in L. Leiderman and L. Svensson (eds.), *Inflation Targets*, London: CEPR: 122–141.

Goodhart, C. A. E (1994), 'What Should Central Banks Do? What Should Be Their Macro-economic Objectives and Operations?' *Economic Journal*, 104: 1424–1436.

— (1996), 'Why Do the Authorities Smooth Interest Rates?' LSE Financial Markets Group Paper Series no. 81, London.

— (1999), 'Myths about the Lender of Last Resort', Special Paper No. 120, Financial Markets Group, London School of Economics.

Gordon, R. J. (1985), 'The Conduct of Domestic Monetary Policy', in A. Ando *et al.* (eds.), *Monetary Policy in Our Times*, Cambridge, Mass.: MIT Press: 45–81.

— (1990), 'The Phillips Curve Now and Then', NBER Working Paper no. 3393, Cambridge, Mass.

Greenspan, A. (1997), Remarks at the 15th Anniversary Conference of the Center for Economic Policy Research at Stanford University, 5 September.

Grier, K. B., and Tullock, G. (1989), 'An Empirical Analysis of Cross-National Economic Growth, 1951–80', *Journal of Monetary Economics*, 24: 259–276.

Grilli, V., Masciandaro, D., and Tabellini, G. (1991), 'Political and Monetary Institutions and Public Financial Policies in the Industrial Countries', *Economic Policy*, 13: 341–392.

Grimes, A. (1991), 'The Effects of Inflation on Growth: Some International Evidence', *Weltwirtschaftliches Archiv*, 127: 631–644.

Gros, D. (1989), 'Seigniorage in the EC: The Implications of the EMS and Financial Market Integration', IMF Working Paper No. 89/71, Washington, DC.

— (1996), 'Seigniorage and EMU: The Fiscal Implications of Price Stability and Financial Market Integration', in P. Bofinger and K. H. Ketterer (eds.), *Neuere Entwicklungen in Geldtheorie und Geldpolitik*, Tübingen: J.C.B. Mohr (Paul Siebeck).

— and Thygesen, N. (1998), *European Monetary Integration*, 2nd edn, Harlow, Essex: Longman.

Gujarati, D. (1995), *Basic Econometrics*, New York: McGraw-Hill.

Gylfason, T. (1991), 'Inflation, Growth, and External Debt: A View of the Landscape', *The World Economy*, 14 (3): 279–298.

Haldane, A. (1995), 'Inflation Targets', *Bank of England Quarterly Bulletin*, 35 (3): 250–259.

— (1997), 'Some Issues in Inflation Targeting'; internet: www.bankofengland.co.uk.

Hall, R. E. (1983), 'Macroeconomic Policy under Structural Change', in Federal Reserve Bank of Kansas City (ed.), *Industrial Change and Public Policy*, Kansas City: Federal Reserve System: 85–111.

— and Mankiw, N. G. (1994), 'Nominal Income Targeting', in N. Mankiw (ed.), *Monetary Policy*, Chicago: University of Chicago Press: 71–93.

Hall, T. E. (1990), 'McCallum's Base Growth Rule: Results for the United States, West Germany, Japan and Canada', *Weltwirtschaftliches Archiv*, 126 (4): 630–642.

Hallman, J. J., Porter, R. D., and Small, D. H. (1989), 'M2 per Unit of Potential GNP as an Anchor for the Price Level', Board of Governors of the Federal Reserve System Staff Study no. 157.

—— and — (1991), 'Is the Price Level Tied to the M2 Monetary Aggregate in the Long Run?' *American Economic Review*, 81 (4): 841–858.

Hardy, D. (1993), 'Reserve Requirements and Monetary Management: An Introduction', IMF Working Paper no. 93/35, Washington.

Hicks, J. R. (1946), *Value and Capital*, 2nd edn, Oxford: Clarendon Press.

— (1967), *Critical Essays in Monetary Theory*, Oxford: Clarendon Press.

Hochreiter, E., and Winkler, G. (1995), 'The Advantage of Tying Austria's Hands: The Success of the Hard Currency Strategy', *European Journal of Political Economy*, 11: 83–111.

Hoffmaister, A. W., and Schinasi, G. S. (1994), 'Asset Prices, Financial Liberalization, and the Process of Inflation in Japan', IMF Working Paper no. 94/153, Washington.

Hoover, K. (1995), 'Commentary', *Federal Reserve Bank of St Louis Review*, 77 (3): 26–32.

Isard, P. (1995), *Exchange Rate Economics*, Cambridge: Cambridge University Press.

Issing, O. (1993*a*), 'Die Geldpolitik der Bundesbank in nationaler und internationaler Verantwortung', speech given on 23 June 1993; reprinted in: Deutsche Bundesbank, *Auszüge aus Presseartikeln*, no. 15: 1–11.

— (1993*b*), 'Central Bank Independence and Monetary Stability', IEA Occasional Paper no. 89, London.

— (1994), 'Zinsstruktur oder Geldmenge? Die Suche nach dem optimalen Indikator der Geldpolitik', in Deutsche Bundesbank, *Auszüge aus Presseartikeln*, no. 46: 3–6.

— (1998), *Einführung in die Geldtheorie*, 11th edn, Munich: Vahlen.

— (1999*a*), 'The Euro: Four Weeks after the Start', speech delivered to the European–Atlantic Group, House of Commons, London, 28 January; internet: www.ecb.int.

— (1999*b*), 'The Eurosystem: Transparent and Accountable or "Willem in Euroland"', *Journal of Common Market Studies*, 37 (3): 503–519.

— (1999*c*), 'The Monetary Policy of the ECB: Stability, Transparency, Accountability', speech given at the Royal Institute of International Affairs, London, 25 October; internet: www.ecb.int.

— (1999*d*), 'The Monetary Policy of the ECB in a World of Uncertainty', speech given at the conference on 'Monetary Policy-making under Uncertainty', Frankfurt, 3 December; internet: www.ecb.int.

Jarchow, H.-J. (1998), *Theorie und Politik des Geldes 1*, 10th edn, Göttingen: Vandenhoeck & Ruprecht (UTB).

Jevons, W. S. (1882), *Money and the Mechanism of Exchange*, London: C. Kegan Paul.

Johnson, H. (1972), 'The Case for Flexible Exchange Rates 1969', in H. Johnson (ed.), *Further Essays in Monetary Economics*, London: George Allen & Unwin: 198–228.

Jonsson, G. (1999), 'The Relative Merits and Implications of Inflation Targeting for South Africa', IMF Working Paper no. 99/116, Washington.

Judd, J. P., and Motley, B. (1993), 'Using a Nominal GDP Rule to Guide Discretionary Monetary Policy', *Federal Reserve Bank of San Francisco Economic Review*, 3: 1–11.

Kahn, G. A. (1988), 'Nominal GNP: An Anchor for Monetary Policy', *Federal Reserve Bank of Kansas City Economic Review*, 73 (9): 18–35.

Kashyap, A. (1997), 'The Lending Channel and European Monetary Union', in S. Collignon (ed.), *European Monetary Policy*, London: Pinter: 42–71.

— and Stein, J. (2000), 'What Do a Million Observations on Banks Say About the Transmission of Monetary Policy?', *American Economic Review*, 90 (3): 407–428.

Keynes, J. M. (1923), *A Tract on Monetary Reform*, in *The Collected Writings of John Maynard Keynes*, Vol. IV; reprinted by Macmillan, London and Basingstoke, 1971.

— (1930), *A Treatise on Money: The Pure Theory of Money*, in *The Collected Writings of John Maynard Keynes*, Vol. V; reprinted by Macmillan, London and Basingstoke, 1971.

— (1936), *The General Theory of Employment, Interest and Money*, in *The Collected Writings of John Maynard Keynes*, Vol. VII, reprinted by Macmillan, London and Basingstoke, 1973.

King, M. (1994), 'Monetary Policy Instruments: The UK Experience', in *Monetary Policy Instruments: National Experiences and European Perspectives*, Bankhistorisches Archiv, Beiheft 27, Frankfurt am Main: Fritz Knapp Verlag: 59–72.

— (1998), 'Monetary Policy and the Labour Market', speech given at the Employment Policy Institute's Fourth Annual Lecture, 1 December; internet: www.bankofengland.co.uk.

— (1999), 'Challenges for Monetary Policy: Old and New', paper prepared for the symposium on 'New Challenges for Monetary Policy' sponsored by the Federal Reserve Bank of Kansas City at Jackson Hole, Wyoming, 27 August; internet: www.bankofengland.co.uk.

— (2000), 'Monetary Policy: Theory in Practice', address to the Joint Luncheon of the American Economic Association and the American Finance Association, Boston, 7 January; internet: www.bankofengland.co.uk.

Klein, M. A. (1971), 'A Theory of the Banking Firm', *Journal of Money, Credit and Banking*, 3, S. 205–218.

Klitgaard, T. (1999), 'Exchange Rates and Profit Margins: The Case of Japanese Exporters', *Economic Policy Review*, 5: 41–54.

Kopits, G. (1999), 'Implications of EMU for Exchange Rate Policy in Central and Eastern Europe, IMF Working Paper no. 99/9, Washington.

Koren, S. (1989), *Steuerreformen im internationalen Vergleich*, Berlin: Duncker und Humblot.

Kormendi, R. C., and Meguire, P. G. (1985), 'Macroeconomic Determinants of Growth', *Journal of Monetary Economics*, 16: 141–163.

Kozicki, S. (1999), 'How Useful Are Taylor Rules for Monetary Policy?' *Federal Reserve Bank of Kansas City Economic Review*, 84: 5–25.

Kreps, D. M. (1990), *A Course in Microeconomic Theory*, New York: Harvester Wheatsheaf.

Krugman, P. (1987), 'Pricing to Market When the Exchange Rate Changes', in S. W. Arndt and J. Richardson (eds.), *Real-Financial Linkages among Open Economies*, Cambridge and London: MIT Press: 49–70.

Kydland, F. E., and Prescott, E. C. (1977), 'Rules Rather than Discretion: The Inconsistency of Optimal Plans', *Journal of Political Economy*, 85 (3): 473–491.

Laidler, D. (1992), 'Deflation', in J. Eatwell, M. Milgate, and P. Newman (eds.), *The New Palgrave Dictionary of Money and Finance*, Vol. 1, London: Macmillan: 606–608.

— and Parkin, M. (1975), 'Inflation: A Survey', *Economic Journal*, 85: 741–809.

Lane, T., and van den Heuvel, S. (1998), 'The United Kingdom's Experience with Inflation Targeting', IMF Working Paper no. 98/87, Washington.

Lange, C. (1995), *Seigniorage*, Berlin: Duncker & Humblot.

Laurens, B. (1994), 'Refinance Instruments: Lessons from their Use in Some Industrial Countries', IMF Working Paper no. 94/51, Washington.

Leeson, R. (1994), 'A. W. H. Phillips M.B.E. (Military Division)', *Economic Journal*, 104: 605–618.

Leiderman, L., and Svensson, L. E .O. (eds.) (1995), *Inflation Targeting*, London: CEPR.

Levin, A., Wieland, V., and Williamson, J. (1999), 'The Performance of Forecast-based Monetary Policy Rules under Model Uncertainty'; internet: www.ecb.int.

Levine, R., and Renelt, D. (1992), 'A Sensitity Analysis of Cross-Country Growth Regressions', *American Economic Review*, 82 (4): 942–963.

Lipsey, R. G. (1960), 'The Relation between Unemployment and the Rate of Change of Money Wages in the United Kingdom, 1886–1957: A Further Analysis', *Economica*, 105: 1–37.

Loef, H.-E. (1989), 'The Case for Rules in the Conduct of Monetary Policy: A Critique on a Paper by B. T. McCallum', *Weltwirtschaftliches Archiv*, 125: 168–178.

Lohmann, S. (1992), 'Optimal Commitment in Monetary Policy: Credibility versus Flexibility', *American Economic Review*, 82: 273–286.

Lucas, R. E. (1972), 'Expectations and the Neutrality of Money', *Journal of Economic Theory*, 4 (2): 103–124.

— (1973), 'Some International Evidence on Output–Inflation Tradeoffs', *American Economic Review*, 63 (3): 326–334.

— (1976), 'Econometric Policy Evaluation: A Critique', in *The Phillips Curve and Labor Markets*, Carnegie–Rochester Conference Series on Public Policy, Vol. 1: 19–46.

— (1994), 'On the Welfare Cost of Inflation', CEPR Discussion Paper no. 394, London.

Lutz, F. A. (1941), 'The Structure of Interest Rates', *Quarterly Journal of Economics*, 55: 36–63.

Lyons, R. (2000), *The Microstructure Approach to Exchange Rates*, Cambridge and London: MIT Press; internet: www.haas.berkeley.edu/~lyons.

Maddala, G. S. (1992), *Introduction to Econometrics*, 2nd edn, New York: Macmillan.

Marshall, A. (1923), *Money, Credit and Commerce*, London: Macmillan.

Marston, R. D. (1990), 'Pricing to Market in Japanese Manufacturing', *Journal of International Economics*, 29: 217–236.

Marty, A., and Thornton, D. (1995), 'Is There a Case for "Moderate" Inflation?' *Federal Reserve Bank of St Louis Review* , 77 (4): 27–37.

Masciandaro, D., and Spinelli, F. (1994), 'Central Banks' Independence: Institutional Determinants, Rankings, and Central Bankers' Views', *Scottish Journal of Political Economy*, 41 (4): 434–443.

Mayer, T., and Fels, J. (1995), 'Time for a Multi-Year M3 Target', Goldman Sachs German Economic Commentary, 3 November.

Mayes, D. G., and Virén, M. (2000), 'The Exchange Rate and Monetary Conditions in the Euro Area'. *Weltwirtschaftliches Archiv*, 136 (2): 199–231.

McCallum, B. T. (1984), 'Monetarist Rules in the Light of Recent Experience', *American Economic Review*, 74 (2): 388–391.

— (1987), 'The Case for Rules in the Conduct of Monetary Policy: A Concrete Example', *Weltwirtschaftliches Archiv*, 123 (3): 415–429.

— (1988), 'Robust Properties of a Rule for Monetary Policy', Carnegie Rochester Conference Series on Public Policy, no. 29: 173–204.

— (1989), *Monetary Economics*, New York: Macmillan.

— (1999), 'Recent Developments in the Analysis of Monetary Policy Rules', *Federal Reserve Bank of St Louis Review*, 81 (6): 3–12.

— (1994), 'A Reconsideration of the Uncovered Interest Parity Relationship', *Journal of Monetary Economics*, 33: 105–132.

— and Goodfriend, M. (1987), 'Demand for Money: Theoretical Studies', in J. Eatwell, M. Milgate, and P. Newman (eds.), *The New Palgrave Dictionary of Economics*, Vol. 1, London: Macmillan: 775–781.

McKinnon, R., and Ohno, K. (2000), 'The Foreign Exchange Origins of Japan's Economic Slump and Low Interest Liquidity Trap', Stanford Working Papers in Economics no. 00–010.

Meade, J. (1978), 'The Meaning of International Balance', *Economic Journal*, 88: 423–435.

Meltzer, A. H. (1995), 'Information, Sticky Prices and Macroeconomic Foundations', *Federal Reserve Bank of St Louis Review*, 77 (3): 101–118.

Menkhoff, L. (1995), *Geldpolitsche Instrumente der Europäischen Zentralbank*, Stuttgart: Deutscher Sparkassenverlag.

Mieno, Y. (1993), 'Current Monetary and Economic Conditions in Japan', Bank of Japan Special Paper no. 231, Tokyo.

Mill, J. S. (1844), Review of Books by Thomas Tooke and R. Torrens, *Westminster Review*, 41.

—— (1848), *Principles of Political Economy*, 2 vols., London: John. W. Parker.

Minford, P. (1992), 'The United Kingdom', in M. Fratianni and D. Salvatore (eds.), *Monetary Policy in Developed Economies*. Handbook of Comparative Economic Policies, Vol. 3, Westport, Conn.: Greenwood Press: 405–431.

Mishkin, F. (1995), *The Economics of Money, Banking, and Financial Markets*, 4th edn, New York: HarperCollins.

—— (1999), 'Lessons from the Asian Crises', NBER Working Paper Series no. 7102, Cambridge, Mass.

Miyanoya, A. (2000), 'A Guide to the Bank of Japan's Market Operations', Financial Markets Department Working Paper Series; Bank of Japan, April.

Modigliani, F., and Sutch, R. (1966), 'Innovations in Interest Rate Policy', *American Economic Review*, Papers and Proceedings, 56: 178–197.

Molitor (2000), 'Currency Boards', *Deutsche Financial Times*, 14 July.

Monissen, H. G. (1982), *Makroökonomische Theorie, Bd. 1, Sozialprodukt, Preisniveau and Zinsrate*, Stuttgart: Kohlhammer.

Mori, N., Shigenori S., and Taguchi, H. (2000), 'Policy Responses to the Post-bubble Adjustments in Japan: A Tentative Review', Bank of Japan, IMES Discussion Paper no. 2000-E-13, Tokyo.

Motley, B. (1993), 'Growth and Inflation: A Cross-Country Study', Federal Reserve Bank of San Francisco Working Papers in Applied Economic Theory no. 93-11.

Moulton, B. R. (1996), 'Bias in the Consumer Price Index: What is the Evidence?' *Journal of Economic Perspectives*, 10 (4): 159–77.

Mundell, R. (2000), 'Currency Areas, Volatility and Intervention', *Journal of Policy Modeling*, 22 (3): 281–299.

Mussa, M., Masson, P., Swoboda, A., Jadresic, E., Mauro, P., and Berg, A. (2000), 'Exchange Rate Regimes in an Increasingly Integrated World Economy', IMF Occasional Paper No. 193, Washington, DC.

Muth, J. (1961), 'Rational Expectations and the Theory of Price Movements', *Econometrica*, 29: 315–335.

Neumann, M. J. M. (1974), 'Zwischenziele und Indikatoren der Geldpolitik', in K. Brunner, H. G. Monissen, and M. J. M. Neumann (eds.), *Geldtheorie*, Cologne: Kiepenheuer & Witsch: 360–377.

—— (1986), 'Preisstabilität durch mehrjährige Geldmengenziele sichern', *Wirtschaftsdienst*, 66: 591–596.

—— (1992), 'Central Bank Independence in Europe', in H. J. Vosgerau (ed.), *European Integration in the World Economy*, Berlin: Springer-Verlag: 17–25.

—— (1995), 'Comparative Study of Seigniorage: Japan and Germany', Sonderforschungsbereich 303, Rheinische Friedrich-Wilhelms-Universität Discussion Paper no. 304, Bonn.

—— (2000), 'Ist die direkte Inflationssteuerung einer Zwischenzielstrategie überlegen?' Mimeo, Universität Bonn.

Niehans J. (1988), *The Theory of Money*, Baltimore: Johns Hopkins University Press.

Nordhaus, W. D. (1975), 'The Political Business Cycle', *Review of Economic Studies*, 42 (2): 169–190.

OECD (1991), 'Economic Policy-Making since the mid-1960s', *OECD Economic Outlook*, 50: 1–11.

—— (1994), 'Inflation Objectives in the Medium and Longer Term', *OECD Economic Outlook*, 55: 31–36.

Okina, K., Shirakawa, H., and Shiratsuka, S. (2000), 'The Asset Price Bubble and Monetary Policy: Japan's Experience in the Late 1980s and the Lessons', Bank of Japan, IMES Discussion Paper, no. 2000-E-12, Tokyo.

Oliner, S., and Rudebusch, G. (1996*a*), 'Monetary Policy and Credit Conditions: Evidence from the Composition of External Finance: Comment', *American Economic Review*, 86: 300–309.

—— and —— (1996*b*), 'Is There a Broad Credit Channel for Monetary Policy?', *FRBSF Economic Review*: 3–13.

Olivera, J. (1967), 'Money, Prices, and Fiscal Lags: A Note on the Dynamics of Inflation', *Banca Nazionale del Lavoro Quarterly Review*, 20: 258–267.

Orphanides, A. (2000), 'The Quest for Prosperity without Inflation', EB Working Paper, no. 15, Frankfurt.

Orr, D., and Mellon, W. G. (1961), 'Stochastic Reserve Losses and Expansion of Bank Credit', *American Economic Review*, 51, S. 612–623.

Osborne, D. K. (1992), 'Defining Money', in J. Eatwell, M. Milgate, and P. Newman (eds.), *The New Palgrave Dictionary on Money and Finance*, Vol. 1, London: Macmillan: 602–606.

Padoa-Schioppa, T. (1987), *Efficiency, Stability, and Equity: A Strategy for the Evolution of the Economic System of the European Community*, Oxford: Oxford University Press.

Panico, C. (1987), 'Interest and Profit', in J. Eatwell, M. Milgate, and P. Newman (eds.), *The New Palgrave Dictionary of Economics*, Vol. 2, London: Macmillan: 877–879.

Parkin, M. (1987), 'Domestic Monetary Institutions and Deficits', in J. M. Buchanan, C. Rowley, and R. Tollison (eds.), *Deficits*, New York and Oxford: Basil Blackwell.

Persson, T., and Tabellini, G. (1990), *Macroeconomic Policy, Credibility and Politics, Fundamentals of Pure and Applied Economics*, Chur, Switzerland: Harwood Academic Publishers.

—— and —— (1993), 'Designing Institutions for Monetary Stability', *Carnegie–Rochester Conference Series on Public Policy*, 39: 53–84.

Phelps, E. S. (1967), 'Phillips Curves, Expectations of Inflation and Optimal Unemployment over Time', *Economica*, 34: 254–281.

—— (1973), 'Inflation in the Theory of Public Finance', *Swedish Journal of Economics*, 75: 867–882.

Phillips, A. W. (1958), 'The Relation between Unemployment and the Rate of Change of Money Wage Rates in the United Kingdom, 1861–1957', *Economica*, 25: 283–299.

Pigou, A. C. (1917), 'The Value of Money', *Quarterly Journal of Economics*, 37: 38–65.

Poole, W. (1970), 'Optimal Choice of Monetary Policy Instruments in a Simple Stochastic Macro Model', *Quarterly Journal of Economics*, 84 (1): 197–216.

Popper, K. (1959), *Logic of Scientific Discovery*, New York: Basic Books.

Radcliffe Report (1959), *Committee on the Working of the Monetary System*, London: Commercial Colour Press.

Radelet, S., and Sachs, J. (1998), 'The East Asian Financial Crises: Diagnosis, Remedies, Prospects', *Brookings Papers on Economic Activity*, 1: 1–74.

Rees, R. (1985), 'The Theory of Principal and Agents, Parts 1 and 2', *Bulletin of Economic Research*, 27: 3-26, 75-95.

Reinhart, C. (2000), 'The Mirage of Floating Rates', *American Economic Review* Papers and Proceedings, 90: 65-70.

Reischle, J. (2000), *Der Divisia-Geldmengenindex*, Frankfurt am Main: Peter Lang.

Reuters (1999), *An Introduction in Foreign Exchange and Money Markets*, Singapore: John Wiley.

Rogoff, K. (1985), 'The Optimal Degree of Commitment to an Intermediate Monetary Target', *Quarterly Journal of Economics*, 100 (4): 1169-1189.

— (1987), 'Reputational Constraints on Monetary Policy', *Carnegie-Rochester Conference Series on Public Policy*, 26: 141-182.

Romer, C. and Romer, D. (1990), 'New Evidence on the Monetary Transmission Process', *Brookings Papers on Economic Activity*, 149-213.

— and — (1993), 'Credit Channel or Credit Actions? An Interpretation of the Postwar Transmission Mechanism', NBER Working Paper Series no. 4485, Cambridge, Mass.

Romer, D. (2000), 'Keynesian Macroeconomics without the LM Curve', *Journal of Economic Perspectives*, 14: 149-169.

Roth, G. (1989), *Britische Geldpolitik 1971-1986: Analyse und kritische Bewertung*, Frankfurt am Main: Peter Lang Verlag.

Rudebusch, G. D. (2000), 'Assessing Nominal Income Rules for Monetary Policy with Model and Data Uncertainty', EB Working Paper no. 14, Frankfurt.

— and Svensson, L. E. O. (1998), 'Policy Rules for Inflation Targeting', in J. B. Taylor (ed.), *Monetary Policy Rules*, Chicago: University of Chicago Press: 203-253.

Sachs, J. D., and Larrain, F. (1993), *Macroeconomics in the Global Economy*, New York: Harvester Wheatsheaf.

Sachverständigenrat zur Begutachtung der gesamtwirtschaftlichen Entwicklung (1999), *Jahresgutachten 1999/2000*; internet: www.sachverstaendigenrat-wirtschaft.de.

Samuelson, P. A. (1964), 'Theoretical Notes on Trade Problems', *Review of Economics and Statistics*, 46: 145-154.

— and Solow, R. M. (1960), 'Problem of Achieving and Maintaining a Stable Price Level: Analytical Aspects of Anti-Inflation Policy', *American Economic Review*, 50 (2): 177-194.

Sargent, T. J., and Wallace, N. (1975), '"Rational" Expectations, the Optimal Monetary Instrument, and the Optimal Money Supply Rule', *Journal of Political Economy*, 83 (2): 241-254.

Saving, T. R. (1967), 'Monetary-Policy Targets and Indicators', *Journal of Political Economy*, 75 (4): 446-456.

Schächter, A. (1999), *Die geldpolitische Konzeption und das Steuerungsverfahren der Deutschen Bundesbank: Implikationen für die Europäische Zentralbank*, Tübingen: J.C.B. Mohr (Paul Siebeck).

Schlesinger, H., and Jahnke, W. (1987), 'Geldmenge, Preise und Sozialprodukt: Interdependenzzusammenhänge im Lichte ökonometrischer Forschungsergebnisse für die Bundesrepublik Deutschland', *Jahrbücher für Nationalökonomie und Statistik*, 203 (5/6): 576-590.

Schnadt, N. (1994), 'European Monetary Union and the Sterling Money Market', City Research Project, Subject Report VII, Paper II, London Business School.

Schumpeter, J. (1954), *History of Economic Analysis*, London: Oxford University Press.

Schwartz, A. (1987), *Money in Historical Perspective*, Chicago: University of Chicago Press:

— (2000), 'The Rise and Fall of Foreign Exchange Market Intervention', NBER Working Paper Series no. 7751, Cambridge, Mass.

444   *References*

Seitz, F. (1995), 'Der DM-Umlauf im Ausland', Volkswirtschaftliche Forschungsgruppe der Deutschen Bandesbank Diskussionspapier no. 1/95, Frankfurt.

Shapiro, M. D., and Wilcox, D. W. (1996), 'Mismeasurement in the Consumer Price Index: An Evaluation', in B. S. Bernanke and J. J. Rotemberg (eds.*), NBER Macroeconomics Annual*, Cambridge, Mass.: MIT Press: 93–154.

Shigehara, K. (1996) 'The Options Regarding the Concept of a Monetary Policy Strategy', in Deutsche Bundesbank (ed.), *Monetary Policy Strategies in Europe: A Symposium at the Deutsche Bundesbank*, Munich: Verlag Vahlen: 7–43.

Siklos, P. L. (1994), 'Varieties of Monetary Reforms', IMF Working Paper no. 94/57, Washington.

—— (1999), 'Inflation-Target Design: Changing Inflation Performance and Persistence in Industrial Countries', *Federal Reserve Bank of St Louis Review*, 81 (5): 47–58.

Simon, H. A. (1992), 'Bounded Rationality', in J. Eatwell, M. Milgate, and P. Newman (eds.), *The New Palgrave Dictionary of Money and Finance*, Vol. 1, London: Macmillan: 226–227.

Simons, H. (1936), 'Rules versus Authorities in Monetary Policy', *Journal of Political Economy*, 44 (1): 1–30.

Smets, F. (1995), 'Central Bank Macroeconometric Models and the Monetary Policy Transmission Mechanism', in Bank for International Settlements (BIS) (ed.), *Financial Structure and the Monetary Policy Transmission Mechanism*, Basle: BIS: 225–266.

Stiglitz, J. (1987), 'Principal and Agent', in J. Eatwell, M. Milgate, and P. Newmann (eds.), *The New Palgrave Dictionary of Economics*, Vol. 3, London: Macmillan: 966–971.

—— and Weiss, A. (1981), 'Credit Rationing in Markets with Imperfect Information', *American Economic Review*, 82: 393–410.

Stöß, E. (1996), 'Die Finanzierungsstruktur der Unternehmen und deren Reaktion auf monetäre Impulse: eine Analyse anhand der Unternehmensbilanzstatistik der Deutschen Bundesbank', Volkswirtschaftliche Forschungsgruppe der Deutschen Bundesbank, Diskussionspapier 96. 9, Frankfurt.

Strotz, R. (1956), 'Myopia and Inconsistency in Dynamic Utility Maximization, *Review of Economic Studies*, 23: 165–180.

Stützel, W. (1979), *Das Mark-gleich-Mark-Prinzip und unsere Wirtschaftsordnung*, Baden-Baden: Nomos Verlagsgesellschaft.

Summers, L. (1991), 'How Should Long-Term Monetary Policy Be Determined?' *Journal of Money, Credit and Banking*, 23 (3): 625–631.

Suzuki, Y. (ed.) (1987), *The Japanese Financial System*, Oxford: Clarendon.

Suzumura, K. (1987), 'Social Welfare Function', in J. Eatwell, M. Milgate, and P. Newman (eds.), *The New Palgrave Dictionary of Economics*, Vol. 4, London: Macmillan: 418–420.

Svensson, L. (1997), 'Inflation Forecast Targeting: Implementing and Monitoring Inflation Targets', *European Economic Review*, 41 (6): 1111–1146.

—— (1999a), 'Price Level Targeting vs. Inflation Targeting: A Free Lunch?' *Journal of Money, Credit and Banking*, 31: 277–295.

—— (1999b), 'Inflation Targeting as a Monetary Policy Rule', *Journal of Monetary Economics*, 43: 607–654.

—— (1999c), 'Price Stability as a Target for Monetary Policy: Defining and Maintaining Price Stability', paper presented at the Bundesbank conference on 'The Monetary Transmission Process', 26–27 March; http: www.iies.su.se/leosven.

—— (2000a), 'Open-Economy Inflation Targeting', *Journal of International Economics*, 50: 155–183.

— (2000*b*), 'The First Year of the Eurosystem: Inflation Targeting or Not?' *American Economic Review*: 90 (2): 95–99.

— and Woodford, M. (2000), 'Indicator Variables for Optimal Policy', ECB Working Paper Series no. 12, Frankfurt.

Swinburne, M., and Castello-Branco, W. (1991), 'Central Bank Independence: Issues and Experience', IMF Working Paper no. 91/58, Washington.

Tanzi, V. (1977), 'Inflation, Lags in Collection and the Real Value of Tax Revenue', *International Monetary Fund Staff Papers*, 24: 154–167.

Taylor, J. B. (1979), 'Staggered Wage Stetting in a Macro Model', *American Economic Review*, 69 (2): 108–113.

— (1980), 'Aggregate Dynamics and Staggered Contracts', *Journal of Political Economy*, 88 (1): 1–23.

— (1985), 'What Would Nominal GNP Targeting Do to the Business Cycle?' *Carnegie-Rochester Conference Series on Public Policy*, 22: 61–84.

— (1993), 'Discretion versus Policy Rules in Practice', *Carnegie-Rochester Conference Series on Public Policy*, 39: 195–214.

— (1995), 'The Monetary Transmission Process: An Empirical Framework', *Journal of Economic Perspectives*, 9 (4): 11–26.

— (1999), 'The Robustness and Efficiency of Monetary Policy Rules as Guidelines for Interest Rate Setting by the European Central Bank', *Journal of Monetary Economics,* 43: 655–679.

Tobin, J. (1956), 'The Interest Elasticity of Transactions Demand for Cash', *Review of Economics and Statistics*, 38: 241–247.

— (1958), 'Liquidity Preference as Behavior towards Risk', *Review of Economic Studies*, 25: 65–86.

— (1963), 'Commercial Banks as Creators of "Money"', in D. Carson (ed.), *Banking and Monetary Economics*, Homewood, Ill.: 408–419.

— (1965), 'Money and Economic Growth', *Econometrica*, 33 (4): 671–684.

— (1969), 'A General Equilibrium Approach to Monetary Theory', *Journal of Money, Credit and Banking*, 1 (1): 15–29.

— (1980), 'Redefining the Aggregates: Comments on the Exercise', in *Measuring the Money Aggregates: Compendium of Views prepared by the Subcommittee on Domestic Monetary Policy of the House Committee on Banking, Finance and Urban Affairs, 96th Congress, 2nd Session*, Washington DC: US Government Printing Office.

— (1983), 'Monetary Policy: Rules, Targets and Shocks', *Journal of Money, Credit, and Banking*, 15 (4): 506–518.

— (1986), 'On the Welfare Macroeconomics of Government Fiscal Policy', *Scandinavian Journal of Economics*, 88 (1): 9–24.

— (1995), 'Panel Discussion', in J. C. Fuhrer (ed.), *Goals, Guidelines, and Constraints facing Monetary Policymakers*, Boston: Federal Reserve Bank of Boston Conference volume: 232–236.

Tootell, G. M. (1994), 'Restructuring, the NAIRU, and the Phillips Curve', *New England Economic Review of the Federal Reserve Bank of Boston:* 26: 31–44.

Vickers, J. (1998), 'Inflation Targeting in Practice: the UK Experience', *Bank of England Quarterly Bulletin*, 38: 368–375.

von Hagen, J. (1999), 'Money Growth Targeting by the Bundesbank', *Journal of Monetary Economics*, 43: 681–701.

von Weizsäcker, C. C. (1978), 'Das Problem der Vollbeschäftigung heute', *Zeitschrift für Wirtschafts- and Sozialwissenschaften*: 33–51.

Wagner, H. (1992), *Stabilitätspolitik*, 2nd edn, Munich: Oldenbourg Verlag.

Waller, C. J. (1995), 'Performance Contracts for Central Bankers', *Federal Reserve Bank of St Louis Review*, 77 (5): 3–14.

Walsh, C. E. (1995a), 'Optimal Contracts for Central Bankers', *American Economic Review*, 85 (1): 150–167.

—— (1995b), 'Is New Zealand's Reserve Act of 1989 an Optimal Central Bank Contract?' *Journal of Money, Credit, and Banking*, 27 (4): 1179–1191.

—— (1998), *Monetary Theory and Policy*, Cambridge, Mass.: MIT Press.

Walters, A. A., and Hanke, S. (1987), 'Currency Boards', in J. Eatwell, M. Milgate, and P. Newman (eds.), *The New Palgrave Dictionary of Money and Finance*, Vol. 1, London: Macmillan: 558–561.

Whitehead, A. N. (1978), *Process and Reality*, corr. edn, New York: Free Press.

Wicksell, K. (1898), *Geldzins und Güterpreise*, Jena: G. Fischer; trans. R. F. Kahn as *Interest and Prices: A Study of the Causes Regarding the Value of Money*, London: Macmillan, 1936.

—— (1922), *Vorlesungen über Nationalökonomie*, Zweiter Band, Jena; reprinted by Scientia Verlag, Aalen, 1969.

Williamson, J. (1996), *The Crawling Band as an Exchange Rate Regime: Lessons from Chile, Colombia, and Israel*, Washington, DC: Institute for International Economics.

Willms, M. (1995), *Internationale Währungspolitik*, 2nd edn, Munich: Vahlen.

Winkler, B. (2000), 'Which Kind of Transparency: On the Need for Clarity in Monetary Policy-Making', ECB Working Paper no. 26, Frankfurt.

Woodford, M. (1990), 'The Optimum Quantity of Money', in B. M. Friedman and F. H. Hahn (eds.), *Handbook of Monetary Economics*, Vol. II, Amsterdam: North-Holland: 1067–1152.

Worms, A. (1998), *Bankkredite an Unternehmen und ihre Rolle in der geldpolitischen Transmission in Deutschland*, Frankfurt am Main: Lang.

Wynne, M. A. (1999), 'Core Inflation: A Review of Some Conceptual Issues', ECB Working Paper no. 5, Frankfurt.

Yeyati, E., and Sturzenegger, F. (1999), 'Classifying Exchange Rate Regimes: Deeds vs. Words, mimeo, International Monetary Fund, Washington, DC.

Yoshida, T., and Rasche, R. H. (1990), 'The M2 Demand in Japan: Shifted and Unstable?' *Bank of Japan, Monetary and Economic Studies*, 8 (2): 9–30.

Index of Names

Index of Subjects